THE
CRITICAL
READER

THE CRITICAL READER

RESPONDING THROUGH WRITING

William Lutz
Rutgers University—Camden

Harry Brent
Baruch College, The City University of New York

1817

Harper & Row, Publishers, New York
Grand Rapids, Philadelphia, St. Louis, San Francisco,
London, Singapore, Sydney, Tokyo

Sponsoring Editor: Lucy Rosendahl
Project Editor: Bonnie Biller
Art Direction: Lucy Krikorian
Text and Cover Design: Edward Smith Design, Inc.
Cover Coordinator: Mary Archondes
Cover Illustration: Picasso, "Femme Lisant" (Woman Reading), 1935. Copyright
  ARS N.Y./SPADEM, 1989.
Production: Paula Roppolo

THE CRITICAL READER: Responding Through Writing

Library of Congress Cataloging-in-Publication Data

The Critical reader : responding through writing   /   [edited by] William
   Lutz, Harry Brent.
      p.   cm.
   Includes index.
   ISBN 0-06-044111-9 (student ed.).—ISBN 0-06-044114-3 (teacher's
ed.)
   1. College readers.   2. English language—Rhetoric.   I. Lutz,
William.   II. Brent, Harry.
PE1417.C724   1990
808'.0427—dc20   89-35628
                                                                       CIP

For permission to use copyrighted material, grateful acknowledgment is made to the
copyright holders listed on pp. 519–521, which are hereby made part of this
copyright page.

89   90   91   92   9   8   7   6   5   4   3   2   1

ANNOTATED CONTENTS

Part II: Description   61

Part III: Process Analysis   129

THEMATIC CONTENTS

RELATIONSHIPS

CULTURAL CONTEXTS

THE SOCIAL FABRIC

CULTURAL LITERACY

PREFACE

This book of readings, chiefly expository essays, with selected short stories and poems, is meant to serve as a basis for active written and oral response by students. Given that its focus is on critical reading, collaborative learning, and the writing process, we could have arranged the readings in a variety of formats. We have chosen the traditional format of rhetorical modes for a variety of reasons—the principal one being that many instructors feel comfortable with this format, and that it naturally lends itself to an organized and progressive plan for a writing class. No matter how experienced the teacher, there is always the tendency in a writing class to get bogged down in the personal, self-reflective narrative writing with which many courses begin. The format we have chosen encourages a progression from narrative writing through various other forms, ultimately to argument, which for many students is the most useful kind of writing for other courses and for the practical realities of professional life. This narrative-to-argument framework easily translates into the creation of a coherent syllabus, thereby providing students with some indication of where the writing course is likely to take them. In courses taught without a syllabus, this framework gives implicit unity and direction to the progression of the term's work.

Our main aim in editing this reader and in writing the questions that follow each selection is to provoke critical thought and active written response. In our questions we encourage students to read closely, to engage in collaborative critical discussion, and to respond critically in writing. To this end we have arranged questions in two groups: "Reading Critically" and "Responding Through Writing." The questions in the first group are designed to elicit critical reader response within the dimensions of collaborative learning. The questions in the second group invite students to engage actively in the writing process.

When we ask students to write, we do not necessarily expect complete essays, much less fully developed essays according to specific rhetorical patterns. The "Responding Through Writing" questions often ask for a few informal paragraphs that might later be revised in such a way as to become part of a more formal piece of writing. All of the questions incorporate aspects of the writing process. Sometimes students are asked to make lists that can later help to structure an essay. Sometimes they are asked to write spontaneous reactions, which may be used for further development and revision as part of an assignment. Sometimes their reactions may take the form of private statements in their journals.

None of the questions necessarily calls for *completed* writing assignments or for specific imitations of the rhetorical pattern of the sample essay, although suggestions along both of these lines appear in the accompanying instructor's manual. In the textbook itself, our aim is to get students involved in critical reading and collaborative reaction, as well as in the initial steps of the writing process. All of this activity may or may not lead to a "formal" writing assignment, depending on the instructor's plans for the course. The instructor using this text, therefore, has a wide variety of options within the writing process, and students will have a great deal of flexibility, and we hope fun, in responding critically through their writing. Both types of questions also stress the importance of audience and purpose in the writing process.

Features

In each section we have included an introduction to the general principles underlying one particular kind of writing. Students should recognize, however, that almost all good writing is a composite of many different techniques and strategies. Rarely is a good piece of writing created by someone who picks a pattern and fills it in. There are many occasions, however, where familiarity with various patterns, at least at the back of the mind, can bring order and clarity to a student's writing, especially in essay exams and short papers in a variety of courses. And there are many expressive needs that can be easily and efficiently met if one is aware of some of the strategies that go into creating particular forms of writing. For example, if one needs to choose a college, it may help to know some techniques for classification. If one is asked to compare two styles of dance or two plans for public transport, it helps to know techniques about comparison and contrast.

Using patterns for writing is not necessarily contrary or alien to what we naturally go through in following the writing process of incubation, development, arrangement, revision, and editing. It is only when rhetorical patterns are set up as objects of memorization or as formulas to be filled in that they undermine the nature of that process. Used as guideposts, they can provide purpose and clarity in writing. They can also offer the student who has wandered a bit along the road of the writing process a shaping force at the moment when he or she must put ideas down on paper and hand in that paper.

Versatility is then the hallmark of this book. It will ennable students to develop and strengthen critical reading and writing skills and can be used to emphasize any of several steps in the writing process, from collaborative critical response, through journal and notebook work, to the formulation of the successive drafts of a student essay.

In the course of developing this book, we incurred many debts which we now gratefully acknowledge. We thank Lucy Rosendahl, English Editor at Harper & Row, for her encouragement and support throughout the time it took to complete the project. We are grateful also to Denise Gess for suggesting some of the fiction and poetry selections and to Louise Klusek whose bedside reading provided fertile ground in our search for women authors. Thanks also go to Nancy Underwood for her research and work in preparing the manuscript.

Finally, we are grateful to the following individuals for completing a reader questionnaire in the early stages of book development: Louise Ackley, Boise State University; Michael W. Bartos, William Rainey Harper College; Sue Belles, California State University at Long Beach; Alice Brand, SUNY–Brockport; James Burleson, Arkansas State University; Marvin Diogenes, San Diego State University; Gerald Duchovnay, Jacksonville University; Sterling K. Eisiminger, Clemson University; Larry Fink, Abilene Christian University; M. Marie Foster, Florida A&M University; James M. Haule, Pan American University; Sue Ellen Holbrook, Fordham University; Rich Ives, Everett Community College; James Kastely, University of Hawaii at Manoa; Thomas M. Kitts, St. John's University; Elizabeth Larsen, West Chester University; John Lucarelli, Community College of Allegheny County–Allegheny Campus; Fred Moramarco, San Diego State University; Linda Palmer, California State University at Sacramento; T.F. Richards, Clackamas Community College; Janet Seim, Mt. San Antonio College; Malinda Snow, Georgia State University; Harry M. Solomon, Auburn University; Sandra W. Stephan, Youngstown State University; Barbara Stout, Montgomery College; Vivian Tortorici, Hudson Valley Community College, and to the composition directors and instructors at other institutions who reviewed the manuscript and offered invaluable suggestions for its improvement. These include: Michael W. Bartos, William Rainey Harper College; Sue Belles, California State University at Long Beach; Alice Brand, SUNY–Brockport; Gerry Brookes, University of Nebraska–Lincoln; Marvin Diogenes, San Diego State University; Betty Dixon, Rancho Santiago Community College; Sterling K. Eisiminger, Clemson University; M. Marie Foster, Broward Community College; Jennifer Ginn, North Carolina State University; Michael Keene, University of Tennessee at Knoxville; E.J. Keller, Iowa Central Community College; Anne Matthews, Princeton University; Randall Popken, Tarleton State University; Sandra W. Stephan, Youngstown State University; Linda Yakle, Daytona Beach Community College.

As in previous collaborative works we have undertaken, the Blonde Bear and the Wet Dog invoke the spirit of Bomar. As the old saw goes, the mistakes are ours.

William Lutz
Harry Brent

PART I

NARRATION

Whenever you tell a story or anecdote, you are using narration. In the broadest definition, narration includes any writing that relates an event or a series of events. In this sense of the word, we most often associate narration with short stories and novels, a branch of literature. This kind of narration deals with fiction, or imaginary events. Another kind of narration is nonfictional narration, or narration dealing with real events.

A narrative essay is more than just a story: It is a story that makes a point. It gives the reader a detailed, vivid account of some personal experience—a young man's introduction to war, a woman's introduction to the bureaucracy of welfare, a child's view of growing up in a quiet neighborhood. Storytellers weave narratives that capture an audience. Through their stories they tell their audience more than a story; the narrative becomes not an end in itself but a means to an end. It is a device, a framework, that the writer uses to present an idea or make a point. This is the kind of narrative we are concerned with in this book.

As a writer you must be careful when you use the narrative mode of writing. Although it appears easy to use, narration is a demanding rhetorical form that requires careful control and planning. It may seem easy just to "tell a story," but a story that is effectively told is efficiently told, and efficiency requires that you have a clear view of your audience, maintain a consistent point of view, select details, and organize those details into a coherent framework. Moreover, you must keep in mind the purpose of your narrative and make sure that the narrative is consistent with that purpose.

Expressing Your Purpose

Since it will affect everything else in your story (point of view, details, and organization and structure), you must give careful thought to the purpose of your story. Purpose in narration simply means the writer's reason for writing the story, what the writer is trying to achieve. So you must ask yourself what you want to achieve in telling your story. Your story can have just about any purpose you want to express. The stories in this section have a variety of purposes, from showing the reality of colonialism on the personal level to revealing that those caught in the welfare bureaucracy are not lazy people looking for a free ride but lost human beings who need help or that war involves the killing of boys who are full of life and have not yet become men. Whatever your purpose, you must have it clearly in mind, not just before you begin to write but before you even plan your story.

You need to remember also that although your narrative must have a purpose, that purpose should probably not be directly expressed. If you have written your story effectively, your reader should be able to infer your purpose from the story itself. As children we all read stories that ended something like this: "And the moral of this story is that people who live in glass houses shouldn't throw stones." This expression of the moral of the story helps children understand something of what the story is about, but a moral is not the same as the purpose of the story. A moral is only one lesson that can be drawn from a particular kind of story, whereas the purpose of a story encompasses the full meaning of the story. The moral of a story may well be that people who live in glass houses shouldn't throw stones, but the purpose of the story might well be that no people should throw stones, whether they live in glass houses or not.

As children we probably needed an explanation of what a story meant. As adults we not only don't need an explanation, but also feel a little insulted if one is offered. A good story doesn't need a moral or any kind of explanation tacked on at the end. The story should speak for itself; it should *be* its meaning, its purpose. David Ross doesn't need to explain what his story is really about, nor does

George Orwell, Denise Gess, or any of the other writers in this section. A well-written story speaks for itself and needs no one to explain it. When you write a narrative, your story, too, should speak for itself and should not need you or anyone else to explain it.

Remember Your Audience

Good storytellers always look to their audiences. That is, they know who their audience is and what their audience knows and doesn't know. They are careful not to tell their audience what it already knows, just as they are careful to give their audience all the information it needs in order to understand the story. Although James Baldwin assumes his audience knows something about the geography of New York, he is careful to explain what the Hotel Braddock is, since few of his readers would know anything about it.

You must put yourself in your readers' place and look at your story from their point of view. What do your readers already know? What do they need to know in order to understand your story? Note the details that George Orwell must provide his audience, since he cannot assume that it is familiar with everyday life in colonial Burma. To a great extent your audience will control what information you put in your story and what you leave out, so the better you understand your audience, the easier it will be to shape your story, and the more effective your narration will be.

Selecting a Point of View

Selecting and maintaining a consistent point of view means that you must decide who the narrator is, that is, who is telling the story. The most common point of view in narration is the first person, telling the story from the view of a participant in the events, as in George Orwell's "A Hanging" and Denise Gess's "Catalina Court." On the other hand, you may choose the third-person point of view, one that gives a sense of objectivity and distance from the events. Whatever point of view you choose, remember that it will affect how you tell your story. It will also affect the way you communicate the purpose of your narrative. After reading Orwell's "A Hanging," ask yourself what would be lost if the story were told by a third-person narrator, one who had not participated in the hanging.

Point of view, then, affects your purpose, and it also affects your relationship with your audience. If you write your story in the first person, you are speaking directly, personally to your audience. This approach establishes a close relationship between writer and audience. You are asking your audience to experience through and with you an event or series of events. On the other hand, if you use the third-person point of view, you put a certain distance between you and your story and between you and your audience. Remember that selecting your point of view is very important because it affects how you tell your story, your relationship with your audience, and how effectively you achieve your purpose.

Selecting Details

You will often find that the point of view you have chosen will determine what details you can select and use in your story. Telling your story from the first-person point of view, for example, means that you can include only those details known to the first-person narrator. This is a limited point of view and may exclude some details you need to include in your narration. If that is the case, you should consider changing your point of view. You will discover that selecting your point of view and selecting the details for your narrative are not separate decisions but continuing, interactive decisions, with each affecting the other.

A good story depends on the effective use of clear, vivid,

appropriate detail. You should be careful, however, to avoid the extremes of too little and too much. You need to include enough detail so your reader knows what is happening, but you should avoid using so much detail that your reader is overwhelmed and thus cannot follow the story. You must select details that not only tell the story but also achieve your narrative purpose. Note, for example, how David Ross carefully selected his details in his short narrative essay. He certainly does not overwhelm his reader with details; he has carefully selected those needed to tell his story forcefully—thus, to achieve his purpose. Note also Georgeanne Keller's use of detail in her story, especially the details she uses to describe other people.

Organizing Your Narrative

Once you have selected details, you need to organize the events in your narrative. Since every chain of events has a beginning, a middle, and an end, the simplest method of organizing a narrative is chronologically, according to the sequence of events in time. However, the challenge is to organize your narrative in two ways: First, put the events into a proper (not necessarily chronological) sequence; second, select and organize the details that relate to the events and help you achieve the purpose of your narrative. The second part of organization is what gives most writers trouble. Telling what happened isn't a big problem; selecting the details that tell not only what happened but also what the larger meaning of the events might be is a bit more difficult.

The details you select and the way you organize them help the reader understand your intent in telling this story. Again, note how David Ross, Denise Gess, and Georgeanne Keller have arranged their details. Ask yourself what details these writers might have left out of their narratives and why those details are omitted. Remember that when you write a narrative, you select details for a purpose, not just to fill up space. Details are the building blocks of your narrative, and how you organize them determines to a great extent whether your narrative succeeds or fails.

Combining Rhetorical Types

Like the other rhetorical forms, narration is often combined with other types of writing, such as description, argument, or definition. A description of people or of a setting is frequently important to a story; thus, narration may contain description. Argument and definition often play a role in narration. A writer might tell a story in order to argue that war is horrible or to define *love*. This mixing of different rhetorical types is common. Pure narration—the simple recounting of events—is rare. What you will find in reading narratives, and in writing your own, is that one rhetorical type will dominate the writing, and it is this dominant type that classifies the essay. Good writers mix freely, using whatever is necessary to achieve their purpose.

Analyzing Narratives

We have said that when you write a narrative essay you should determine your purpose in writing the story, select and maintain a consistent point of view, select vivid and appropriate details, organize those details and the events of your narrative, and direct all these elements to the purpose of your narrative. Just as you should do all this in writing an effective narrative, so you should look for all these elements in reading a narrative. That is, you should read a narrative *as a writer*. When you read a narrative, determine the point of view, look for the details, analyze the organization of the narrative, and then determine the purpose of the story. If these elements are important to you as a writer, they are equally important to you as a reader.

When you read David Ross's short narrative, for example, determine, first, the point of view. Who is telling the story? What is the relation of the narrator to the people and events in the story? Is the narrator involved in the story or just an observer? Next, look for the details in the story. What details are you given? What details are left out of the story? What do the details contribute to the story? Then look at how the story is organized. Is the story told chronologically, or is there another principle of organization? You should now have enough information and enough of an understanding of the story to determine its purpose.

As you read the stories in this section, analyze them as you would your own writing. Look for the elements of good narrative that have been discussed here. Evaluate the effectiveness of these stories in terms of their point of view, use of detail, organization, and purpose.

SALVATION

LANGSTON HUGHES

(James) Langston Hughes (1902–1967) attended Columbia University from 1921 to 1922 and received a B.A. from Lincoln University in 1929. In 1937 he served as a correspondent covering the Spanish Civil War for the Baltimore Sun. *In addition to several volumes of poetry, Hughes wrote two novels,* Not Without Laughter *(1930) and* Tambourines to Glory *(1958). He also wrote several autobiographical pieces and short stories. His most famous collection of stories is perhaps* The Ways of White Folks *(1934). A central figure of the Harlem Renaissance of the 1920s, Hughes did not always find favor with contemporary black critics, who sometimes saw him as casting blacks in a bad light. Current critics of all races, however, praise his writing. The following is an excerpt from Hughes's autobiography,* The Big Sea *(1940).*

1   I was saved from sin when I was going on thirteen. But not really saved. It happened like this. There was a big revival at my Auntie Reed's church. Every night for weeks there had been much preaching, singing, praying, and shouting, and some very hardened sinners had been brought to Christ, and the membership of the church had grown by leaps and bounds. Then just before the revival ended, they held a special meeting for children, "to bring the young lambs to the fold." My aunt spoke of it for days ahead. That night I was escorted to the front row and placed on the mourners' bench

with all the other young sinners, who had not yet been brought to Jesus.

My aunt told me that when you were saved you saw a light, and something happened to you inside! And Jesus came into your life! And God was with you from then on! She said you could see and hear and feel Jesus in your soul. I believed her. I had heard a great many old people say the same thing and it seemed to me they ought to know. So I sat there calmly in the hot, crowded church, waiting for Jesus to come to me. 2

The preacher preached a wonderful rhythmical sermon, all moans and shouts and lonely cries and dire pictures of hell, and then he sang a song about the ninety and nine safe in the fold, but one little lamb was left out in the cold. Then he said: "Won't you come? Won't you come to Jesus? Young lambs, won't you come?" And he held out his arms to all us young sinners there on the mourners' bench. And the little girls cried. And some of them jumped up and went to Jesus right away. But most of us just sat there. 3

A great many old people came and knelt around us and prayed, old women with jet-black faces and braided hair, old men with work-gnarled hands. And the church sang a song about the lower lights are burning, some poor sinners to be saved. And the whole building rocked with prayer and song. 4

Still I keep waiting to *see* Jesus. 5

Finally all the young people had gone to the altar and were saved, but one boy and me. He was a rounder's son named Westley. Westley and I were surrounded by sisters and deacons praying. It was very hot in the church, and getting late now. Finally Westley said to me in a whisper: "God damn! I'm tired o' sitting here. Let's get up and be saved." So he got up and was saved. 6

Then I was left all alone on the mourners' bench. My aunt came and knelt at my knees and cried, while prayers and songs swirled all around me in the little church. The whole congregation prayed for me alone, in a mighty wail of moans and voices. And I kept waiting serenely for Jesus, waiting, waiting—but he didn't come. I wanted to see him, but nothing happened to me. Nothing! I wanted something to happen to me, but nothing happened. 7

I heard the songs and the minister saying: "Why don't you come? My dear child, why don't you come to Jesus? Jesus is waiting for you. He wants you. Why don't you come? Sister Reed, what is this child's name?" 8

"Langston," my aunt sobbed. 9

"Langston, why don't you come? Why don't you come and be saved? Oh, Lamb of God! Why don't you come?" 10

Now it was really getting late. I began to be ashamed of 11

myself, holding everything up so long. I began to wonder what God thought about Westley, who certainly hadn't seen Jesus either, but who was now sitting proudly on the platform, swinging his knickerbockered legs and grinning down at me, surrounded by deacons and old women on their knees praying. God had not struck Westley dead for taking his name in vain or for lying in the temple. So I decided that maybe to save further trouble, I'd better lie, too, and say that Jesus had come, and get up and be saved.

12   So I got up.

13   Suddenly the whole room broke into a sea of shouting, as they saw me rise. Waves of rejoicing swept the place. Women leaped in the air. My aunt threw her arms around me. The minister took me by the hand and led me to the platform.

14   When things quieted down, in a hushed silence, punctuated by a few ecstatic "Amens," all the new young lambs were blessed in the name of God. Then joyous singing filled the room.

15   That night, for the last time in my life but one—for I was a big boy twelve years old—I cried, I cried, in bed alone, and couldn't stop. I buried my head under the quilts, but my aunt heard me. She woke up and told my uncle I was crying because the Holy Ghost had come into my life, and because I had seen Jesus. But I was really crying because I couldn't bear to tell her that I had lied, that I had deceived everybody in the church, and I hadn't seen Jesus, and that now I didn't believe there was a Jesus any more, since he didn't come to help me.

Reading Critically

1. Do you identify with Hughes or with the more pragmatic Westley, who decides to get saved because "it's getting late"? Which of the two will have the easier time in life? Discuss with your classmates, citing specific points in the narrative to support your view.

2. In paragraph 2, Hughes's aunt tells him that people who are "saved" see a light. Does Hughes believe this literally? Did you, as

a child, take such metaphors literally? Discuss with your classmates, citing at least one specific example from your experience.

3. Why does Hughes's aunt (paragraph 10) refer to Hughes as a "Lamb of God"? What biblical image is Hughes relying upon? In what specific ways does the use of this reference enrich the narrative?

4. To what extent does shame operate as a motivation throughout the narrative? How does the meaning of shame change at the narrative's end? Discuss with your classmates.

Responding Through Writing

1. The story begins with the word "I" and ends with the word "me." What advantages does Hughes gain by keeping this an extremely personal narrative? Pick a section of the narrative and rewrite it from an impersonal, third-person perspective. In what ways is the result different from Hughes's original?

2. Is Hughes's aunt, as portrayed here, a believable character? What encounters have you had with characters, either real or fictional, that confirm your answer? Write a few paragraphs in your journal or notebook telling the story of one such encounter.

3. In what sense is this narrative about the topic of conformity versus individuality? Rewrite the end of the narrative so that individuality triumphs.

4. In the last paragraph of the essay, Hughes tells us why he cries. Can you expand upon those reasons? What does his belief or nonbelief in Jesus tell us about his growing up, about the transition between childhood and adolescence? Write on this topic for five or ten minutes in your journal or notebook. If you prefer, write for five or ten minutes on an experience of your own similar to the one narrated by Hughes.

AN ENORMOUS MAZE WITH NO READY EXIT

GEORGEANNE KELLER

Georgeanne Keller lives in Cherry Hill, New Jersey. When she was a college student, an unexpected long-term illness forced her to seek public assistance: ". . . I wanted to scream," she writes. "I knew how it felt to beg and be refused." Her essay recounting her experiences with the welfare system was originally published in the New York Times *in 1981.*

1   The first Wednesday of the month comes too soon, I thought as I climbed the stairs of the Municipal Building. I always felt sick when it was my day to report to the local Welfare Office.

2   I shivered, remembering when the social worker told me, "Welfare doesn't pay for college." What would she say if she knew that my doctor had agreed to let me return to school, provided I took only two classes?

3   After a six-month illness, this was a big step for me. As a student worker at my college, my part-time job had been enough to sustain me; however, when I became ill, I wasn't entitled to disability. Welfare was the only way to meet my living expenses and weekly medical bills.

I hated keeping this information from the social worker, but 4 I was sure what would happen if I didn't. Although it took considerable courage for me to accept public assistance, I was not yet able to accept the loss of my checks.

The waiting room was dark, stuffy and uninviting. The Welfare Office, a small, adjoining room, was alive with the sounds of a jangling telephone and the fast clicking of typewriter keys. 5

A tall, middle-aged black woman strode into the room, her 6 silver cane tapping lightly on the floor. Plopping a huge handbag down on the table, she opened it and rearranged something inside. Everything in order, she straightened, frowning angrily.

"You'd think they could do somethin' for somebody around 7 here," she said. "Well, they gonna do somethin' for me!"

The woman grabbed her handbag and headed toward the 8 Welfare Office, where she planted herself firmly in the doorway.

"Mrs. Reeves, why are you back here?" a voice asked sharply. 9

"You gonna help me," the woman snapped. 10

"I've told you that I couldn't help you until you found a place 11 to stay."

The social worker sounded disinterested. 12

"You gotta do somethin' 'cause they gonna throw me out of 13 my apartment!"

"Mrs. Reeves," the social worker said coldly, "if you persist, 14 I'll call the police. I can't handle a disturbance."

"I ain't leavin'!" 15

Within seconds, two police officers charged into the room. 16 The woman turned to them, her tear-filled eyes pleading for understanding.

"I have nowhere to go, and she says she can't help me." 17

"I told her," the social worker explained quickly, "that I can't 18 help her until she finds somewhere to live."

"I won't live in no housing project!" Mrs. Reeves shouted as 19 the officers grabbed her arms, shoving her firmly toward the door.

Feeling the sting of sudden fears, I recalled the articles on the 20 county housing projects, especially the poor and unsanitary conditions in which the tenants lived.

There's got to be better help available, I wanted to scream. I 21 knew how it felt to beg and be refused.

I was shocked that I was eligible for only $68 a month; because 22 I lived with my mother, I could not receive more. Once, after I had had bronchitis, the social worker informed me that welfare would have paid for my medicine, yet there was no mention of prescription payments when I called to tell her that I was too ill to keep my appointment.

23   Learning that it did no good to complain, I reported faithfully each month, feeling very resentful.

24   Mrs. Reeves was back within 10 minutes, asking to use the phone. The social worker, a short, plump woman, bustled out of the office, a thick black ledger under her arm.

25   I heard snatches of conversation from the room. Before long, the woman emerged, grinning. Thank God, I sighed with relief, now she won't need to worry.

26   Another two hours passed before I saw the social worker. She looked up from the stack of forms she was filling out as I entered the office.

27   "I know you've had a rough day," I told her, "but I felt badly for that woman."

28   She looked at me tiredly.

29   "It's really a shame," she said in her usually clipped tone. "She was recently released from the state hospital. I wish I could have helped her."

30   "I don't understand," I faltered. "She found a place, didn't she?"

31   The social worker nodded slowly.

32   "Yes, she found a room for the night, but welfare won't subsidize anyone to live in a motel."

33   My anger was still there when I reached the car. I thought about Mrs. Reeves facing one of the biggest adjustments for which the hospital might not have prepared her.

34   I also understood the social worker's position. A counselor to welfare recipients, she could only offer help within the existing system—a system, she explained, that still needs much improvement.

35   In a few months, I would return to work and a full schedule of classes. But for now, the three of us were victims of that sadly inadequate system: Three small mice running through an enormous maze that has no ready exit.

Reading Critically

1. Do you think that Keller acts immorally in accepting welfare payments to which she is not legally entitled (paragraphs 3 and 4)? On a scale of one to ten, how serious is her deception? Do you think that she should be tried and punished? Have you or any of your classmates ever carried out a similar deception?

2. Does it strike you as odd that Keller (paragraph 33) apparently owns a car? What does this say about the nature of poverty in America, as opposed to poverty in other areas of the world? Do members of your class think that welfare recipients ought to be made to give up their cars and other "luxuries"? Why?

3. Keller has to wait two hours to see her social worker. Have you or your classmates experienced similar enforced delays in other contexts (college registration, for example)? How does enforced waiting affect one's sense of self-esteem?

4. Do your classmates respond to Keller in terms of their own socioeconomic status? Who is more likely to be critical of Keller's lies, poor people or middle-class people? Why?

Responding Through Writing

1. As a prewriting activity, sketch the draft of a short essay on the current state of welfare and other public assistance programs in your area of the country. In your opinion do these programs help people, or do they perpetuate cycles of poverty? In preparing your draft, draw at least in part from articles appearing in newspapers and magazines.

2. Extend for a page or two in your notebook the dialogue between the homeless woman and the welfare worker in paragraphs 9 through 19. Note how the speech of the homeless woman differs from that of the welfare worker, whom Keller describes as having a "clipped" tone. Emphasize these two different tones as you extend the dialogue.

3. Write a page or two extending the metaphor of the mice and the maze that Keller draws in the final paragraph. In your sketch, try to show whether this metaphor accurately reflects the plight of welfare recipients. Write to an audience of middle-class people.

4. Why are the paragraphs in this essay so short? Is it because the essay is largely dialogue? Pick a paragraph that makes a major point and try to extend and develop that point for at least a page in your notebook.

WELCOME TO
THE WAR, BOYS

DAVID ROSS

A veteran of the Vietnam War, David Ross spent seven years organizing for the Vietnam Veterans Against the War. He has also worked actively in organizations dealing with veterans' affairs, holding a seat on the board of directors of the Project to Advance Veterans' Employment, as well as participating in readjustment counseling for vets. In Vietnam Ross learned that "things get beyond words." The following story first appeared in Everything We Had *(1981), edited by Al Santoli.*

A couple of us were just kind of hanging loose out in front 1
of the main hospital building, which was a big corrugated-tin
prefab. About forty new guys were lined up there to have their shot
records checked before being sent to their units.

The guys were all new, their first couple of days in–country, 2
and they were all wondering what it was going to be like. Joking,
smoking cigarettes, playing grab-ass in the line—it was pretty loose.
I mean, nobody was saying, "Straighten up. Stand in formation,"
none of that. People were just kind of leaning up against the
building.

All of a sudden, four choppers came in and they didn't even 3 touch down. They just dumped bags. One of the bags broke open and what came out was hardly recognizable as a human being. For those of us that were just sort of standing there looking in the direction of the new guys . . . it's not the kind of thing you laugh at. Irony or satire . . . things get beyond words. All the guys stopped laughing. Nobody was saying anything. And some people were shaking and some people were throwing up, and one guy got down and started to pray.

4   I said to myself, "Welcome to the war, boys."

Reading Critically

1. Do you and your classmates find this essay revolting? If so, what particular images make it so? Why do you think Ross shows the young soldiers playing "grab-ass" in the line? What impulses does this game act out? What is Ross indirectly saying about those impulses? Why does Ross end the essay with the word *boys?*

2. Discuss with your classmates how the Vietnam War differed from other wars fought in American history, specifically the Korean War and World War II. Would you have fought in or supported all of those wars? Would you have been actively opposed to any or all of them? Why?

3. Do you and your classmates tend to see the Vietnam War through the filters of the books, movies, and TV series that grew out of it? Which of these most (and least) accurately portrays the reality of that particular war? Why?

4. Discuss with your classmates whether this essay is a powerful indictment of war and its horrors or just a skillfully written piece of propaganda designed to diminish our patriotism? Are there any unstated assumptions about patriotism in this piece? What audience is Ross writing for?

Responding Through Writing

1. After reading Ross's essay, assemble a notebook of three or four items on the topic of the Vietnam War. Include historical articles, book reviews, interviews, and any other materials directly or indirectly pertinent to the war. Share your notebook with your classmates, and read and discuss theirs in preparation for writing a short essay on some aspect of the war.

2. If you know any Vietnam veterans, ask them whether they would be willing to be interviewed about their reactions to this essay. Write up the interviews in your notebook.

3. If your college has a film library, make an appointment to screen the movie *M*A*S*H* or a few episodes of the TV series of the same title. After the screening, write a short essay about the indirect statements that *M*A*S*H* makes about war.

4. Follow the same initial directions as in question 3, but this time choose two films, one that glorifies war and another that emphasizes war's horrors. Instead of writing an essay, just list some of the specific techniques that each film uses to achieve its purpose. Discuss those techniques in class.

CATALINA COURT

DENISE GESS

Denise Gess's first novel, Good Deeds *(1984), deals with a Jewish–Irish family living in south Philadelphia, the legendary Italian section of that city and the place where Gess was born in 1952 and spent her early childhood. After graduating from LaSalle University with a degree in psychology, Gess taught profoundly retarded children for three years. She then attended Our Lady of Lourdes School of Nursing in Camden, New Jersey, but left without completing her nursing degree in order to complete an M.A. degree in English at Rutgers University in Camden. Her second novel,* Red Whiskey Blues, *was published in 1989. Gess lives in Philadelphia and teaches creative writing at Temple University and Rutgers University. The following essay, part of a collection of essays by writers describing their neighborhoods, was first published in* Philadelphia Magazine *in December 1985.*

1   Transfers might plop a city boy smack in the middle of an Iowa cornfield, but no one offers a kid an astonishing increase in allowance if she'll just pack up her toy chest and dolls and move from the city to the suburbs. No one consulted me or my brother in 1955, the year our parents were seduced by the Lionel Construction Company; no one sat us down and asked what we thought of

the canary-yellow rancher sketched in the brochure that featured the homes of Catalina Hills in Somerdale, New Jersey.

"We are moving to the country!" my parents announced with   2
pioneer enthusiasm and particular emphasis on the "country." And so, in 1956, during the cold and snowy week between Christmas and New Year's, my brother and I said goodbye to the lopsided apartment over the butcher shop on the corner of 9th and McKean in South Philadelphia. We would return to the city many times—we'd left all of our relatives behind—but we'd return as The Jersey Kids.

I was assured that I would love this new place. There would   3
be *space,* they said, as if they'd bought into their own planet. I could have my own swing set. No more cement parks for this kid.

We'll have a car, they said: We'd have a driveway so we'd be   4
needing something to drive onto it. We'll have grass, they told me. Well, that was fine too—at last, a reason to own a shovel. You're going to be very, very happy here, they told me. Even at an early age it was my natural inclination to balk when any adult told me that I could be happier. I was a midget rebel without a cause, a resister to the new and the unknown. I liked the city. I enjoyed the routine; Passyunk Avenue on the weekends, treks to 7th Street on Friday nights, Longo's dry cleaners, Longo's grocery store. I loved to play in the alleys. I loved it that if I just walked around the corner to Hoffman Street I would find my grandparents, my Aunt Aggie, Aunt Norma and Uncle Bruni, my cousins Louis, Maryann and Joan and my Aunt Eileen. I loved the clean, cold marble steps and the awnings over the front doors of those narrow row houses. I was already happy.

You'll be even more happy, they said. And they were right.   5

We moved to the center of the world—600 Catalina Court,   6
a little like 77 Sunset Strip. Alliteration alone made the cul-de-sac in New Jersey seem special. Although my mother has often told me that it was the dream of having a single home that made her want to leave the city, I've always suspected that she also liked the sound of Catalina Court, for very personal reasons. All she needed to do was replace the "i" and the final "a" with the letters "a" and "o," and she'd have Catalano—her maiden name. Catalina Court rolled off the tongue, was as easy to spell as Main Street, and as exotic and appealing as Catalina Island. It seemed like a place made for an Italian-American family. The Piccolis of Catalina Court in the development of Catalina Hills.

Not for many more years would I know what it was like to   7
live on a real street, where houses lined up, facing each other, where

traffic passed by daily. In Catalina Court we had life-in-the-round, a development built with a sense of the theatrical. Unlike older streets of neighboring towns like Haddonfield and Collingswood, here there were no prior rules, no unwritten codes of behavior for residents to follow. The soul of the court would create itself out of its need for history. The goings-on of the Court would unfold like segments of a miniseries, because all of us in the six houses that comprised the Court were as new to suburban life as the ranchers and split-levels we inhabited.

8   My house, a three-bedroom rancher with a basement and a garage, was the central house, the one you gravitated toward as you made the right or left off of Warwick Road, the main traffic artery through the town. It sat far back from the curve, the driveway on an incline toward the garage. The lot upon which it was built seemed expansive to me as a child, and no less expansive to me as an adult. The front yard triggered my mother's lust for flowers and my father's desire for shrubbery. My mother worked diligently to create a circular garden on the front lawn in addition to planting rows of azaleas, red and pink, under the large picture window. My father, who loved the driveway, was quick to plant two fat evergreens at its edge. The desire to *landscape* at the slightest provocation must have been a carry-over from my grandmother's habit of scrubbing her marble steps and hosing down her section of the sidewalk in the city.

9   "We're the center house," my mother explained as I knelt beside her, pulling weeds. "We've got to make it look pretty."

10   Gardening caught on quickly. Soon everyone had azaleas, roses, lilacs and shrubs. The flowers were the pride of the women, and the shrubs the pride of the men. Not long after came serious gardening, the cultivation of edibles. In the far left corner of my back yard—a pie-shaped yard that could easily accommodate a built-in swimming pool and a tennis court—my mother started her vegetable garden. As her planting produced produce, the Cobbs, our neighbors on the right, began their garden, as did the Donahues on our left, and the Bodleys on *their* left. With just a little bit of coordination between houses and gardens, we could have been in lettuce and tomatoes up to our ears in a season. Also, the gardens turned out to be the best excuse to travel back and forth to each other's houses.

11   "Bring some of these carrots over to Mrs. Bodley," my mother would tell me. And I went, eagerly, because the Bodleys, who lived in the white rancher with the salmon-colored trim, were the most mysterious couple, and I looked for reasons to knock on their door

and be invited into their home. Instead of children they had cats—two gorgeous Siamese that kept watch over the house. Mrs. Bodley was a nurse, never out of uniform, with small, intelligent, dark eyes and a nervous, pinched but still oddly authoritative voice. Her uniform both frightened and intrigued me. She could be called upon for medical advice if we were sick; she could never be called upon to look relaxed. A lady with a mission as she slipped into her green sedan each morning; I imagined all sorts of things—needles, cotton balls, tongue depressors—filling up her slim black purse. No one will ever die here, I thought, with the dedicated Mrs. Bodley ever-present. Harry Bodley always looked relaxed. A balding man with glasses and eyes even more intelligent than his wife's, he strolled around the yard in chinos and a pale blue shirt, one hand in his pocket. He was a lab technician, so if there was something Mrs. Bodley didn't know, Harry probably did. The Bodleys arrived in Somerdale from College Park, Pennsylvania, and were, to the rest of the Court, arbiters of intelligence and education. We were more inclined to be articulate around them.

As the gardens multiplied, so did the families.   12

In 1959 my sister Mary was born, while next door, the Irish-   13
Catholic Donahue family continued to grow. I thought of Alice Donahue as the young woman who lived in the shoe, with a final count of eight children to her and husband Pat's credit. With a built-in crew of players, the center of the Court belonged to the children and our games of basketball, volleyball, kickball and bicycle riding, and—in times of moodiness and simple brattiness—The Pebble Wars.

For quite some time, instead of asphalt the Court was paved   14
in small black-gray pebbles, which came in handy in times of stress. Everyone was permitted time to gather a supply of weaponry into his or her wagon. After shoring up supplies, we positioned our wagons on opposing sides of the Court, created bunkers with cardboard boxes, and let the pebbles fly. My mother was usually the last to know of these battles. Her kitchen window faced the back yard, so she could only monitor the occasional war that took place on the green. Alice Donahue's kitchen window faced the Court, though, and minutes after we'd begin waging war, she'd emerge from the house to stop us. My mother and Alice would argue then, over whose children started these battles, but hours later they'd sit in each other's kitchens over coffee and the cakes they'd baked as peace offerings. They often struck me as the suburban Lucy and Ethel. My mother as Lucy, primed for adventure; and Alice, a tall, blond

woman, striking in her youth, the more realistic of the two. With eight children, it was hard not to be grounded in reality.

15   For counseling on the proper rearing of children, my mother, Alice and Anna Viteese sought advice from the Grande Dame of the Court, Mrs. McGuigan, the plump mother of two grown boys, the lady in the floral-print shirtwaists and black oxford shoes. Spring, summer and fall, Mrs. McGuigan could be found sitting in a lawn chair on her patio, a convenient lookout point that provided a birds-eye view of all Court activities. The front of her house faced Warwick Road, while the side door and porch faced our house head-on. It was a ritual on summer nights to amble across the Court and sit with Mrs. McGuigan. Around 6:30 or 7, Anna Viteese could be seen strolling over, carrying a folding chair, followed by Mrs. Bodley in her uniform, sometimes Harry, and my mother and Alice. My father, a compositor for the *Philadelphia Inquirer,* worked nights and missed out on these colloquia. There they all sat, sipping iced tea, while we were allowed to continue playing until the only street lamp in the Court lit up, at 9.

16   As we grew into teenagers, Mrs. McGuigan became a more ominous presence. Like the eyes of Dr. Eckleburg in *The Great Gatsby,* she would see and could report any unsavory behavior, such as boys in the house when our parents were out, making out in cars, and young lovers' arguments, of which there were many in our dating years.

17   We learned to instruct our various boyfriends to wave to Mrs. McGuigan as they drove out of the Court. Even now, she still sits out on the patio, and I wave to her as if nothing has changed. She waves back. She's witnessed my high school courtship with the man I married, my visits home with and without him, our visits home with our new baby, and my visits now that I'm divorced. And she waves. My daughter waves, too. Thirty years later, Catalina Court has history where there was none.

18   We lived at the center of the world. Looking back, I see that the sentiment was not the mere narcissistic projection of a 4-year-old, because everything and everyone came to us, to the Court. It had the insular quality of a castle and its wall-enclosed grounds. Before the Shop Rite was built on Warwick Road, necessities were brought to us: Ted the milkman brought in the supply of Abbotts milk, eggs, and butter; Charles Chips, a weird business, delivered potato chips, pretzels, cakes and cookies; the Wonder Bread truck came, too. Rarely did we venture across Warwick Road to play in the development of Catalina Hills proper, a place with street names like Beverly Drive and Wilshire Place. The children there crossed

over to our side, to play in the private playground where nothing could be disturbed by passing cars. My mother learned to ride a bike in that Court without embarrassment. Around and around she went, gathering momentum and confidence with only the people she knew well there to see her fall. On weekends the bus stopped across the street on Warwick Road. From the picture window I would see my grandparents, my grandmother carrying a Hanscom's shopping bag, enter the Court and walk right down the center, to our drive. Even the railroad chugged through our lives, the Reading Pennsylvania Seashore Line passing our back yard three times a day. As children, it was enough cause for us to rush to the window to see it in the winters or to gather together in one of the back yards to watch it in the summers. There we all stood, eight Donahues, three Piccolis, counting the cars going by.

While to some it is a contradiction in terms to be rhapsodic 19 about any suburban town in South Jersey, some feature of the life we were living there must have been infectious. My cousin Maryann from Hoffman Street and her husband visited often and finally bought a rancher of their own in Trivoli Gardens, an offshoot of Catalina Hills. When my grandmother, who was dying of cancer, was too sick to care for herself, she came there to live with us. It was Mrs. Bodley, of course, who came without fail to our house each day to administer my grandmother's B-12 shot. Whenever we visited Philadelphia on Sundays and holidays, the city streets seemed tight and small to me. My cousins seemed to have outgrown the childhood that was still feeding my imagination. They were tougher than we were, street smart, but they were also a bit jaded. I still needed the space, the insulation, the gardens and the barbecues, the Pebble Wars. I needed the freedom that sparseness brings so I could begin creating worlds in my mind. Life in the Court forced me to imagine other lives. What was it like where the train stopped? What were the names of the cows at Abbotts dairy farm? What did Charles Chips' family look like? What happened to make the Donahues separate?

My parents still live there. The house is now white, with 20 Wedgwood-blue trim. They've added a patio to the back, a large porch with a Colonial bench to the front. The garage is now a family room with an extra bath, a fireplace and a bay window with flower boxes outside. My mother is still planting flowers. My father grew tired of trimming the evergreens at the foot of the driveway and cut them down. The maple tree at the curb, which was 6 feet tall when we moved in, now towers over and shades the front yard.

The Cobbs are gone; now the Wells live in the house next door, integrating our Italian-Irish Court. Mr. Bodley has been dead many years and Mrs. Bodley has moved away, no doubt still in uniform. The Donahue children have children. Their house is still green and white, just as it was 30 years ago. Anna Viteese died before her husband Tony, but I remember most clearly how comfortable he was in allowing us to watch him dying. We all knew he was very sick, and he knew that we knew. Nightly, in the summer, he walked and walked around that Court where my mother learned to ride her bike. He wore black baggy pants and a sleeveless undershirt. Breathing heavily, he walked, knowing that he was among friends.

Reading Critically

1. Describe exactly what you mean by "neighborhood." What kind of a neighborhood would you like to live in when you graduate from college? When you retire? Why might people want to live in different neighborhoods at different times in their lives?

2. If you have ever moved from one town to another, or from one state to another, describe how the move affected you and how you reacted. Did you react the way Gess reacted to her move? How were your reactions similar to hers? How were they different? How is going to a new school (such as college) the same as moving from one town or state to another? How is it different?

3. Of all the people Gess describes, which one is the most memorable for you? Why is that person memorable? Which of the people she describes would you like to meet? What would you say to this character? Discuss with your classmates your choice and the reasons for your choice.

4. How much do you need to know of the geography of Philadelphia and southern New Jersey in order to understand Gess's

essay? Look on a map and locate Philadelphia; then locate southern New Jersey. Did Gess move very far from Philadelphia? Why does she refer to her brother and herself as "The Jersey Kids"? What does this phrase suggest?

Responding Through Writing

1. If you are keeping a journal or notebook in this class, write in it for five to ten minutes describing your neighborhood. You can describe the physical aspects of your neighborhood or the people who live there, or both. Write as quickly as you can, putting down your impressions as they come to you.

2. Choose one of the neighbors Gess describes and write a summary of her description of that person. Now choose someone you know—a neighbor, friend, or fellow student—and write a similar description. What did you have to concentrate on when you wrote your description—the physical appearance or some other characteristics of the person? What does your method of description reveal about the person being described?

3. Replace the five paragraphs Gess uses to introduce her essay with a one-paragraph introduction you have written. What is lost and what is gained by replacing the five paragraphs?

4. Write a list of the differences between living in Philadelphia and living in New Jersey that Gess gives in paragraphs 4 and 7. In a sentence or two, state which place you would prefer to live in, and why. If you prefer, pick two other geographical locations.

MY FATHER'S FUNERAL

JAMES BALDWIN

When American author James Baldwin (1924–1987) moved to France in the 1940s, many said it was to escape the bigotry that blanketed the United States. Baldwin, however, would say that he moved overseas more in search of his own identity than trying to lose it. This deep quest for self-knowledge marks all of Baldwin's works. Although he came to be known as a great spokesman for the civil rights movement, Baldwin always insisted that his mission as a writer was to discover the inner truths common to all men and women. In 1986 the French government presented Baldwin with the Commander of the Legion of Honor, one of the highest tributes in France. Baldwin's most famous novels include Go Tell It on the Mountain *(1953),* Notes of a Native Son *(1955), and* If Beale Street Could Talk *(1974). Baldwin also wrote numerous plays, many of which mix profound pain and anger with the lightness of comedy. His nonfiction works have been compiled in one volume,* The Price of the Ticket *(1985). The following essay was first published in* Harper's *magazine in November of 1955.*

1   For my father's funeral I had nothing black to wear and this posed a nagging problem all day long. It was one of those problems,

simple, or impossible of solution, to which the mind insanely clings in order to avoid the mind's real trouble. I spent most of that day at the downtown apartment of a girl I knew, celebrating my birthday with whiskey and wondering what to wear that night. When planning a birthday celebration one naturally does not expect that it will be up against competition from a funeral and this girl had anticipated taking me out that night, for a big dinner and a night club afterwards. Sometime during the course of that long day we decided that we would go out anyway, when my father's funeral service was over. I imagine *I* decided it, since, as the funeral hour approached, it became clearer and clearer to me that I would not know what to do with myself when it was over. The girl, stifling her very lively concern as to the possible effects of the whiskey on one of my father's chief mourners, concentrated on being conciliatory and practically helpful. She found a black shirt for me somewhere and ironed it and, dressed in the darkest pants and jacket I owned, and slightly drunk, I made my way to my father's funeral.

The chapel was full, but not packed, and very quiet. There   2
were, mainly, my father's relatives, and his children, and here and there I saw faces I had not seen since childhood, the faces of my father's one-time friends. They were very dark and solemn now, seeming somehow to suggest that they had known all along that something like this would happen. Chief among the mourners was my aunt, who had quarreled with my father all his life; by which I do not mean to suggest that her mourning was insincere or that she had not loved him. I suppose that she was one of the few people in the world who had, and their incessant quarreling proved precisely the strength of the tie that bound them. The only other person in the world, as far as I knew, whose relationship to my father rivaled my aunt's in depth was my mother, who was not there.

It seemed to me, of course, that it was a very long funeral. But   3
it was, if anything, a rather shorter funeral than most, nor, since there were no overwhelming, uncontrollable expressions of grief, could it be called—if I dare to use the word—successful. The minister who preached my father's funeral sermon was one of the few my father had still been seeing as he neared his end. He presented to us in his sermon a man whom none of us had ever seen—a man thoughtful, patient, and forbearing, a Christian inspiration to all who knew him, and a model for his children. And no doubt the children, in their disturbed and guilty state, were almost ready to believe this; he had been remote enough to be anything and, anyway, the shock of the incontrovertible, that it was really our father lying up there in that casket, prepared the mind for anything. His sister moaned and this grief-stricken moaning was taken as corrobo-

ration. The other faces held a dark, non-committal thoughtfulness. This was not the man they had known, but they had scarcely expected to be confronted with *him;* this was, in a sense deeper than questions of fact, the man they had not known, and the man they had not known may have been the real one. The real man, whoever he had been, had suffered and now he was dead: this was all that was sure and all that mattered now. Every man in the chapel hoped that when his hour came he, too, would be eulogized, which is to say forgiven, and that all of his lapses, greeds, errors, and strayings from the truth would be invested with coherence and looked upon with charity. This was perhaps the last thing human beings could give each other and it was what they demanded, after all, of the Lord. Only the Lord saw the midnight tears, only He was present when one of His children, moaning and wringing hands, paced up and down the room. When one slapped one's child in anger the recoil in the heart reverberated through heaven and became part of the pain of the universe. And when the children were hungry and sullen and distrustful and one watched them, daily, growing wilder, and further away, and running headlong into danger, it was the Lord who knew what the charged heart endured as the strap was laid to the backside; the Lord alone who knew what one *would* have said if one had had, like the Lord, the gift of the living word. It was the Lord who knew of the impossibility every parent in that room faced: how to prepare the child for the day when the child would be despised and how to *create* in the child—by what means?—a stronger antidote to this poison than one had found for oneself. The avenues, side streets, bars, billiard halls, hospitals, police stations, and even the playgrounds of Harlem—not to mention the houses of correction, the jails, and the morgue—testified to the potency of the poison while remaining silent as to the efficacy of whatever antidote, irresistibly raising the question of whether or not such an antidote existed; raising, which was worse, the question of whether or not an antidote was desirable; perhaps poison should be fought with poison. With these several schisms in the mind and with more terrors in the heart than could be named, it was better not to judge the man who had gone down under an impossible burden. It was better to remember: *Thou knowest this man's fall; but thou knowest not his wrassling.*

4   While the preacher talked and I watched the children—years of changing their diapers, scrubbing them, slapping them, taking them to school, and scolding them had had the perhaps inevitable result of making me love them, though I am not sure I knew this then—my mind was busily breaking out with a rash of disconnected

impressions. Snatches of popular songs, indecent jokes, bits of books I had read, movie sequences, faces, voices, political issues—I thought I was going mad; all these impressions suspended, as it were, in the solution of the faint nausea produced in me by the heat and liquor. For a moment I had the impression that my alcoholic breath, inefficiently disguised with chewing gum, filled the entire chapel. Then someone began singing one of my father's favorite songs and, abruptly, I was with him, sitting on his knee, in the hot, enormous, crowded church which was the first church we attended. It was the Abyssinia Baptist Church on 138th Street. We had not gone there long. With this image, a host of others came. I had forgotten in the rage of my growing up, how proud my father had been of me when I was little. Apparently, I had had a voice and my father had liked to show me off before the members of the church. I had forgotten what he had looked like when he was pleased but now I remembered that he had always been grinning with pleasure when my solos ended. I even remembered certain expressions on his face when he teased my mother—had he loved her? I would never know. And when had it all begun to change? For now it seemed that he had not always been cruel. I remembered being taken for a haircut and scraping my knee on the footrest of the barber's chair and I remembered my father's face as he soothed my crying and applied the stinging iodine. Then I remembered our fights, fights which had been of the worst possible kind because my technique had been silence.

I remembered the one time in all our life together when we had really spoken to each other.   5

It was on a Sunday and it must have been shortly before I left home. We were walking, just the two of us, in our usual silence, to or from church. I was in high school and had been doing a lot of writing and I was, at about this time, the editor of the high school magazine. But I had also been a Young Minister and had been preaching from the pulpit. Lately, I had been taking fewer engagements and preached as rarely as possible. It was said in the church, quite truthfully, that I was "cooling off."   6

My father asked me abruptly, "You'd rather write than preach, wouldn't you?"   7

I was astonished at his question—because it was a real question. I answered, "Yes."   8

That was all we said. It was awful to remember that that was all we had *ever* said.   9

The casket now was opened and the mourners were being led up the aisle to look for the last time on the deceased. The assumption   10 was that the family was too overcome with grief to be allowed to make this journey alone and I watched while my aunt was led to the casket and, muffled in black, and shaking, led back to her seat. I disapproved of forcing the children to look on their dead father, considering that the shock of his death, or, more truthfully, the shock of death as a reality, was already a little more than a child could bear, but my judgment in this matter had been overruled and there they were, bewildered and frightened and very small, being led, one by one, to the casket. But there is also something very gallant about children at such moments. It has something to do with their silence and gravity and with the fact that one cannot help them. Their legs, somehow, seem *exposed,* so that it is at once incredible and terribly clear that their legs are all they have to hold them up.

11   I had not wanted to go to the casket myself and I certainly had not wished to be led there, but there was no way of avoiding either of these forms. One of the deacons led me up and I looked on my father's face. I cannot say that it looked like him at all. His blackness had been equivocated by powder and there was no suggestion in that casket of what his power had or could have been. He was simply an old man dead, and it was hard to believe that he had ever given anyone either joy or pain. Yet, his life filled that room. Further up the avenue his wife was holding his newborn child. Life and death so close together, and love and hatred, and right and wrong, said something to me which I did not want to hear concerning man, concerning the life of man.

12   After the funeral, while I was downtown desperately celebrating my birthday, a Negro soldier, in the lobby of the Hotel Braddock, got into a fight with a white policeman over a Negro girl. Negro girls, white policemen, in or out of uniform, and Negro males—in or out of uniform—were part of the furniture of the lobby of the Hotel Braddock and this was certainly not the first time such an incident had occurred. It was destined, however, to receive an unprecedented publicity, for the fight between the policeman and the soldier ended with the shooting of the soldier. Rumor, flowing immediately to the streets outside, stated that the soldier had been shot in the back, an instantaneous and revealing invention, and that the soldier had died protecting a Negro woman. The facts were somewhat different—for example, the soldier had not been shot in the back, and was not dead, and the girl seems to have been as dubious a symbol of womanhood as her white counterpart in Georgia usually is, but no one was interested in the facts. They preferred the invention because this invention expressed and corroborated their hates and fears so perfectly. It is just as well to

remember that people are always doing this. Perhaps many of those legends, including Christianity, to which the world clings began their conquest of the world with just some such concerted surrender to distortion. The effect, in Harlem, of this particular legend was like the effect of a lit match in a tin of gasoline. The mob gathered before the doors of the Hotel Braddock simply began to swell and to spread in every direction, and Harlem exploded.

The mob did not cross the ghetto lines. It would have been easy, for example, to have gone over Morningside Park on the west side or to have crossed the Grand Central railroad tracks at 125th Street on the east side, to wreak havoc in white neighborhoods. The mob seems to have been mainly interested in something more potent and real than the white face, that is, in white power, and the principal damage done during the riot of the summer of 1943 was to white business establishments in Harlem. It might have been a far bloodier story, of course, if, at the hour the riot began, these establishments had still been open. From the Hotel Braddock the mob fanned out, east and west along 125th Street, and for the entire length of Lenox, Seventh, and Eighth avenues. Along each of these avenues, and along each major side street—116th, 125th, and 135th, and so on—bars, stores, pawnshops, restaurants, even little luncheonettes had been smashed open and entered and looted—looted, it might be added, with more haste than efficiency. The shelves really looked as though a bomb had struck them. Cans of beans and soup and dog food, along with toilet paper, corn flakes, sardines and milk tumbled every which way, and abandoned cash registers and cases of beer leaned crazily out of the splintered windows and were strewn along the avenues. Sheets, blankets, and clothing of every description formed a kind of path, as though people had dropped them while running. I truly had not realized that Harlem *had* so many stores until I saw them all smashed open; the first time the word *wealth* ever entered my mind in relation to Harlem was when I saw it scattered in the streets. But one's first, incongruous impression of plenty was countered immediately by an impression of waste. None of this was doing anybody any good. It would have been better to have left the plate glass as it had been and the goods lying in the stores.

It would have been better, but it would also have been intolerable, for Harlem had needed something to smash. To smash something is the ghetto's chronic need. Most of the time it is the members of the ghetto who smash each other, and themselves. But as long as the ghetto walls are standing there will always come a moment when these outlets do not work. That summer, for example, it was not enough to get into a fight on Lenox Avenue, or curse out one's cronies in the barber shops. If ever, indeed, the violence which fills Harlem's churches, pool halls, and bars erupts outward in a more direct fashion, Harlem and its citizens are likely to vanish in an apocalyptic flood. That this is not likely to happen is due to a great many reasons, most hidden and powerful among them the Negro's real relation to the white American. This relation prohibits, simply, anything as uncomplicated and satisfactory as pure hatred. In order really to hate white people, one has to blot so much out of the mind—and the heart—that this hatred itself becomes an exhausting and self-destructive pose. But this does not mean, on the other hand, that love comes easily: the white world is too powerful, too complacent, too ready with gratuitous humiliation, and, above all, too ignorant and too innocent for that. One is absolutely forced to make perpetual qualifications and one's own reactions are always canceling each other out. It is this, really, which has driven so many people mad, both white and black. One is always in the position of having to decide between amputation and gangrene. Amputation is swift but time may prove that the amputation was not necessary—or one may delay the amputation too long. Gangrene is slow, but it is impossible to be sure that one is reading one's symptoms right. The idea of going through life as a cripple is more than one can bear, and equally unbearable is the risk of swelling up slowly, in agony, with poison. And the trouble, finally, is that the risks are real even if the choices do not exist.

15   "But as for me and my house," my father had said, "we will serve the Lord." I wondered, as we drove him to his resting place, what this line had meant for him. I had heard him preach it many times. I had preached it once myself, proudly giving it an interpretation different from my father's. Now the whole thing came back to me, as though my father and I were on our way to Sunday school and I were memorizing the golden text: *And if it seem evil unto you to serve the Lord, choose you this day whom you will serve; whether the gods which your fathers served that were on the other side of the flood, or the gods of the Amorites, in whose land ye dwell: but as for me and my house, we will serve the Lord.* I suspected in these familiar lines a meaning which had never been there for me before. All of my father's texts and songs, which I had decided were meaningless, were arranged before me at his death like empty bottles, waiting to hold the meaning which life would give them for me. This was his legacy: nothing is ever escaped. That bleakly memorable morning I hated the unbelievable streets and the Negroes and whites who had, equally, made them that way. But I knew that it was folly, as my

father would have said, this bitterness was folly. It was necessary to hold on to the things that mattered. The dead man mattered, the new life mattered; blackness and whiteness did not matter; to believe that they did was to acquiesce in one's own destruction. Hatred, which could destroy so much, never failed to destroy the man who hated and this was an immutable law.

It began to seem that one would have to hold in the mind   16 forever two ideas which seemed to be in opposition. The first idea was acceptance, the acceptance, totally without rancor, of life as it is, and men as they are: in the light of this idea, it goes without saying that injustice is a commonplace. But this did not mean that one could be complacent, for the second idea was of equal power: that one must never, in one's own life, accept these injustices as commonplace but must fight them with all one's strength. This fight begins, however, in the heart and it now had been laid to my charge to keep my own heart free of hatred and despair. This intimation made my heart heavy and, now that my father was irrecoverable, I wished that he had been beside me so that I could have searched his face for the answers which only the future would give me now.

Reading Critically

1. Look up "Harlem" in an encyclopedia or a similar reference source and prepare a short report for your classmates. Be sure to include such information as where Harlem is located, its history, and what is distinctive about it.

2. Baldwin writes in paragraph 1 that he spent most of the day of his father's funeral "at the downtown apartment of a girl I knew, celebrating my birthday with whiskey and wondering what to wear that night." In what way are you not surprised by Baldwin's behavior? Where in his essay does Baldwin express his grief over the death of his father?

3. What does the riot have to do with the death of Baldwin's father? What is the "invention" that causes the riot Baldwin de-

scribes in paragraphs 12 and 13? What does Baldwin mean when he writes in paragraph 12 that people were not interested in the facts; they "preferred the invention because this invention expressed and corroborated their hates and fears so directly"? Give at least one instance when you ignored facts that contradicted what you wanted to believe, and discuss with your classmates why you did this.

4. In paragraph 16 Baldwin writes that "It began to seem that one would have to hold in the mind forever two ideas which seemed to be in opposition." What are the two opposing ideas that Baldwin says you have to hold in your mind forever? Why does Baldwin believe you have to do this? How is it possible to hold two opposing ideas in your mind? With your classmates, discuss at least two instances where we as a country hold two opposing ideas in our minds. You might think of such examples as our believing in the aggressive nature of the human race while at the same time working to eliminate war, or our believing in the capitalistic economic system, which holds that some people will be rich and others poor, while at the same time working to eliminate poverty.

Responding Through Writing

1. Write a paragraph in which you summarize Baldwin's relationship with his father. Before you write your paragraph, review the direct and indirect evidence Baldwin gives you about that relationship. Note that Baldwin says in paragraph 5 that there was only one time in his life when he had really spoken to his father. What did they say to each other? Why does Baldwin say in paragraph 9, "It was awful to remember that that was all we had *ever* said"?

2. You might expect that Baldwin would begin his essay with a tone of mourning, yet he doesn't. What is the tone of the first paragraph of the essay? Where does the tone change in the essay, and to what kind of tone does it change? Choose one of the first three paragraphs and rewrite it so that it has a tone of mourning.

3. In paragraph 4 Baldwin uses memories of his childhood and his father to express his feelings about his father and his life. Imitating the structure of Baldwin's paragraph, write a paragraph in which you use memories to express your feelings about a person.

4. Although Baldwin began his essay with a specific incident and concrete detail, he ends it with an abstract discussion. In what way does Baldwin's conclusion in paragraph 16 develop the theme he introduces in the first paragraph? Write a concluding paragraph for the essay that is similar to the opening paragraph, that is, a conclusion using an incident and specific details. Alternatively, write an introductory paragraph that is similar to the concluding paragraph, that is, an introduction that is an abstract discussion.

A HANGING

GEORGE ORWELL

George Orwell, the pen name of Eric Blair (1903–1950), is best known for his novels Nineteen Eighty-Four *(1949) and* Animal Farm *(1945) and for his essays on language and politics, which appeared in publications including the* London Observer *and the* London Times. *Orwell was born in Bengal, India, and educated at Eton. A great traveler throughout his life, he worked as a dishwasher, private tutor, teacher, and part-time bookstore assistant, among other jobs during his travels, and fought for the Loyalist forces in the Spanish Civil War. He spent the years 1922 to 1927 serving in the British colonial police in Burma, during which time the incident he describes here took place. Among Orwell's novels are* Down and Out in Paris and London *(1933),* Burmese Days *(1934), and* Keep the Aspidistra Flying *(1936); his nonfiction works include* The Road to Wigan Pier *(1937) and* Homage to Catalonia *(1938). Orwell once wrote that "when I sit down to write a book, I do not say to myself, 'I am going to produce a work of art.' I write it because there is some lie that I want to expose." Orwell died of tuberculosis at the age of 46 after living in seclusion on the island of Jura off the coast of Scotland. Two other selections by Orwell, "Shooting an Elephant" and "Politics and the English Language," are also included in this book. The following selection was originally published in* Adelphi *magazine in August 1931.*

It was in Burma, a sodden morning of the rains. A sickly light,   1
like yellow tinfoil, was slanting over the high walls into the jail
yard. We were waiting outside the condemned cells, a row of sheds
fronted with double bars, like small animal cages. Each cell measured about ten feet by ten and was quite bare within except for a
plank bed and a pot of drinking water. In some of them brown silent
men were squatting at the inner bars, with their blankets draped
round them. These were the condemned men, due to be hanged
within the next week or two.

One prisoner had been brought out of his cell. He was a   2
Hindu, a puny wisp of a man, with a shaven head and vague liquid
eyes. He had a thick, sprouting moustache, absurdly too big for his
body, rather like the moustache of a comic man in the films. Six
tall Indian warders were guarding him and getting him ready for
the gallows. Two of them stood by with rifles with fixed bayonets,
while the others handcuffed him, passed a chain through his handcuffs and fixed it to their belts, and lashed his arms tight to his sides.
They crowded very close about him, with their hands always on
him in a careful, caressing grip, as though all the while feeling him
to make sure he was there. It was like men handling a fish which
is still alive and may jump back into the water. But he stood quite
unresisting, yielding his arms limply to the ropes, as though he
hardly noticed what was happening.

Eight o'clock struck and a bugle call, desolately thin in the wet   3
air, floated from the distant barracks. The superintendent of the jail,
who was standing apart from the rest of us, moodily prodding the
gravel with his stick, raised his head at the sound. He was an army
doctor, with a grey toothbrush moustache and a gruff voice. "For
God's sake hurry up, Francis," he said irritably. "The man ought to
have been dead by this time. Aren't you ready yet?"

Francis, the head jailer, a fat Dravidian in a white drill suit and   4
gold spectacles, waved his black hand. "Yes sir, yes sir," he bubbled.
"All iss satisfactorily prepared. The hangman iss waiting. We shall
proceed."

"Well, quick march, then. The prisoners can't get their break-   5
fast till this job's over."

We set out for the gallows. Two warders marched on either   6
side of the prisoner, with their files at the slope; two others marched

close against him, gripping him by arm and shoulder, as though at once pushing and supporting him. The rest of us, magistrates and the like, followed behind. Suddenly, when we had gone ten yards, the procession stopped short without any order or warning. A dreadful thing had happened—a dog, come goodness knows whence, had appeared in the yard. It came bounding among us with a loud volley of barks, and leapt round us wagging its whole body, wild with glee at finding so many human beings together. It was a large woolly dog, half Airedale, half pariah. For a moment it pranced round us, and then, before anyone could stop it, it had made a dash for the prisoner, and jumping up tried to lick his face. Everyone stood aghast, too taken aback even to grab at the dog.

7   "Who let that bloody brute in here?" said the superintendent angrily. "Catch it, someone!"

8   A warder, detached from the escort, charged clumsily after the dog, but it danced and gambolled just out of his reach, taking everything as part of the game. A young Eurasian jailer picked up a handful of gravel and tried to stone the dog away, but it dodged the stones and came after us again. Its yaps echoed from the jail walls. The prisoner, in the grasp of the two warders, looked on incuriously, as though this was another formality of the hanging. It was several minutes before someone managed to catch the dog. Then we put my handkerchief through its collar and moved off once more, with the dog still straining and whimpering.

9   It was about forty yards to the gallows. I watched the bare brown back of the prisoner marching in front of me. He walked clumsily with his bound arms, but quite steadily, with that bobbing gait of the Indian who never straightens his knees. At each step his muscles slid neatly into place, the lock of hair on his scalp danced up and down, his feet printed themselves on the wet gravel. And once, in spite of the men who gripped him by each shoulder, he stepped slightly aside to avoid a puddle on the path.

10   It is curious, but till that moment I had never realised what it means to destroy a healthy, conscious man. When I saw the prisoner step aside to avoid the puddle, I saw the mystery, the unspeakable wrongness, of cutting a life short when it is in full tide. This man was not dying, he was alive just as we were alive. All the organs of his body were working—bowels digesting food, skin renewing itself, nails growing, tissues forming—all toiling away in solemn foolery. His nails would still be growing when he stood on the drop, when he was falling through the air with a tenth of a second to live. His eyes saw the yellow gravel and the grey walls, and his brain still remembered, foresaw, reasoned—reasoned even about puddles. He and we were a party of men walking together,

seeing, hearing, feeling, understanding the same world; and in two minutes, with a sudden snap, one of us would be gone—one mind less, one world less.

The gallows stood in a small yard, separate from the main grounds of the prison, and overgrown with tall prickly weeds. It was a brick erection like three sides of a shed, with planking on top, and above that two beams and a crossbar with the rope dangling. The hangman, a grey-haired convict in the white uniform of the prison, was waiting beside his machine. He greeted us with a servile crouch as we entered. At a word from Francis the two warders, gripping the prisoner more closely than ever, half led, half pushed him to the gallows and helped him clumsily up the ladder. Then the hangman climbed up and fixed the rope round the prisoner's neck.   11

We stood waiting, five yards away. The warders had formed in a rough circle round the gallows. And then, when the noose was fixed, the prisoner began crying out on his god. It was a high, reiterated cry of "Ram! Ram! Ram! Ram!", not urgent and fearful like a prayer or a cry for help, but steady, rhythmical, almost like the tolling of a bell. The dog answered the sound with a whine. The hangman, still standing on the gallows, produced a small cotton bag like a flour bag and drew it down over the prisoner's face. But the sound, muffled by the cloth, still persisted, over and over again: "Ram! Ram! Ram! Ram! Ram!"   12

The hangman climbed down and stood ready, holding the lever. Minutes seemed to pass. The steady, muffled crying from the prisoner went on and on, "Ram! Ram! Ram!" never faltering for an instant. The superintendent, his head on his chest, was slowly poking the ground with his stick; perhaps he was counting the cries, allowing the prisoner a fixed number—fifty, perhaps, or a hundred. Everyone had changed colour. The Indians had gone grey like bad coffee, and one or two of the bayonets were wavering. We looked at the lashed, hooded man on the drop, and listened to his cries— each cry another second of life; the same thought was in all our minds: oh, kill him quickly, get it over, stop that abominable noise!   13

Suddenly the superintendent made up his mind. Throwing up his head he made a swift motion with his stick. "Chalo!" he shouted almost fiercely.   14

There was a clanking noise, and then dead silence. The prisoner had vanished, and the rope was twisting on itself. I let go of the dog, and it galloped immediately to the back of the gallows; but when it got there it stopped short, barked, and then retreated into a corner of the yard, where it stood among the weeds, looking timorously out at us. We went round the gallows to inspect the prisoner's body.   15

He was dangling with his toes pointed straight downwards, very slowly revolving, as dead as a stone.

16   The superintendent reached out with his stick and poked the bare body; it oscillated, slightly. "*He's* all right," said the superintendent. He backed out from under the gallows, and blew out a deep breath. The moody look had gone out of his face quite suddenly. He glanced at his wristwatch. "Eight minutes past eight. Well, that's all for this morning, thank God."

17   The warders unfixed bayonets and marched away. The dog, sobered and conscious of having misbehaved itself, slipped after them. We walked out of the gallows yard, past the condemned cells with their waiting prisoners, into the big central yard of the prison. The convicts, under the command of warders armed with lathis, were already receiving their breakfast. They squatted in long rows, each man holding a tin pannikin, while two warders with buckets marched round ladling out rice; it seemed quite a homely, jolly scene, after the hanging. An enormous relief had come upon us now that the job was done. One felt an impulse to sing, to break into a run, to snigger. All at once everyone began chattering gaily.

18   The Eurasian boy walking beside me nodded towards the way we had come, with a knowing smile: "Do you know, sir, our friend (he meant the dead man), when he heard his appeal had been dismissed, he pissed on the floor of his cell. From fright.—Kindly take one of my cigarettes, sir. Do you not admire my new silver case, sir? From the boxwallah, two rupees eight annas. Classy European style."

19   Several people laughed—at what, nobody seemed certain.

20   Francis was walking by the superintendent, talking garrulously: "Well, sir, all hass passed off with the utmost satisfactoriness. It wass all finished—flick! like that. It iss not always so—oah, no! I have known cases where the doctor wass obliged to go beneath the gallows and pull the prisoner's legs to ensure decease. Most disagreeable!"

21   "Wriggling about, eh? That's bad," said the superintendent.

22   "Ach, sir, it iss worse when they become refractory! One man, I recall, clung to the bars of hiss cage when we went to take him out. You will scarcely credit, sir, that it took six warders to dislodge him, three pulling at each leg. We reasoned with him. 'My dear fellow,' we said, 'think of all the pain and trouble you are causing to us!' But no, he would not listen! Ach, he wass very troublesome!"

23   I found that I was laughing quite loudly. Everyone was laughing. Even the superintendent grinned in a tolerant way. "You'd

better all come out and have a drink," he said quite genially. "I've got a bottle of whisky in the car. We could do with it."

We went through the big double gates of the prison, into the road. "Pulling at his legs!" exclaimed a Burmese magistrate suddenly, and burst into a loud chuckling. We all began laughing again. At that moment Francis's anecdote seemed extraordinarily funny. We all had a drink together, native and European alike, quite amicably. The dead man was a hundred yards away. 24

Reading Critically

1. On the surface, "A Hanging" is a narrative, but beneath the surface it is a powerful argument, not only against capital punishment, but about the readiness of human beings to be cruel to one another. List the details in the story that speak most vividly of that cruelty and compare your list with those of your classmates. Which specific details stand out?

2. Would you call the characters in the story "good" people? What of the hangman in paragraph 13? What of the superintendent in paragraph 16? What of the warders? Is the behavior of these people inhuman? If so, can you still call them "good" people? Discuss with your classmates the meaning of the phrase "good people."

3. What purpose does the dog (paragraph 6) serve? Why does Orwell introduce the dog at the moment when the condemned man is being marched to the gallows? What contrast is Orwell setting up?

4. This is not a very pleasant essay for most readers. Discuss with your classmates your reaction not only to this essay, but to stories about capital punishment you read in the newspapers. Do you think that some readers of Orwell's essay could find sympathy for

the condemned man yet remain abstractly in favor of capital punishment?

Responding Through Writing

1. Would you be willing to witness an execution? Would you *want* to witness one? What do you think your answer says about your sense of justice and your values? In your notebook or journal, write a draft of a short essay in which you relate your attitude toward capital punishment to your general sense of justice.

ᐧ 2. What crime has the condemned man committed? Orwell doesn't tell us. Do you think Orwell has simply forgotten about his audience, or does he have a specific purpose in focusing on the man's punishment rather than his crime? How would the essay have to be rewritten if Orwell had mentioned a specific crime? Rewrite at least the introduction to the new essay.

3. This narrative is set far away and long ago, among a different people living under a colonial administration. Does this make the story less effective than it would be were it set in contemporary America? Pick a specific part of the narrative that appeals to you and rewrite it for a contemporary audience.

4. Reread the final portion of the essay, beginning with paragraph 18. What purpose do the stories of the warders serve? Pick a portion of the narrative and rewrite it from the point of view of one of the warders. Begin by jotting in your notebook or journal some of what you think the warder's random perceptions might be.

ONE ORDINARY DAY, WITH PEANUTS

SHIRLEY JACKSON

The most famous short fiction by Shirley Jackson (1919–1965), "The Lottery," reveals only one facet of her work. Jackson's short stories, which have been anthologized in The Magic of Shirley Jackson *(1966), range from the tragic to the comic. Two collections of family sketches,* Life Among the Savages *(1953) and* Raising Demons *(1957), provide often hilarious glimpses into the strange and confused Jackson household. One of her novels,* The Birds Nest *(1954), is an account of a young girl with four personalities. Jackson's other works include* We Have Always Lived in the Castle *(1962) and* The Haunting of Hill House *(1959), which was made into a movie entitled* The Haunting *(1963). The following short story first appeared in* Fantasy and Science Fiction *in 1954.*

Mr. John Philip Johnson shut his front door behind him and came down his front steps into the bright morning with a feeling that all was well with the world on this best of all days, and wasn't the sun warm and good, and didn't his shoes feel comfortable after the resoling, and he knew that he had undoubtedly chosen the precise very tie which belonged with the day and the sun and his comfortable feet, and, after all, wasn't the world just a wonderful place? In spite of the fact that he was a small man, and the tie was perhaps a shade vivid, Mr. Johnson irradiated this feeling of well-being as he came down the steps and onto the dirty sidewalk, and he smiled at people who passed him, and some of them even smiled back. He stopped at the newsstand on the corner and bought his paper, saying *"Good* morning" with real conviction to the man who sold him the paper and the two or three other people who were lucky enough to be buying papers when Mr. Johnson skipped up. He remembered to fill his pockets with candy and peanuts, and then he set out to get himself uptown. He stopped in a flower shop and bought a carnation for his buttonhole, and stopped almost immediately afterward to give the carnation to a small child in a carriage, who looked at him dumbly, and then smiled, and Mr. Johnson smiled, and the child's mother looked at Mr. Johnson for a minute and then smiled too.

2　　When he had gone several blocks uptown, Mr. Johnson cut across the avenue and went along a side street, chosen at random; he did not follow the same route every morning, but preferred to pursue his eventful way in wide detours, more like a puppy than a man intent upon business. It happened this morning that halfway down the block a moving van was parked, and the furniture from an upstairs apartment stood half on the sidewalk, half on the steps, while an amused group of people loitered, examining the scratches on the tables and the worn spots on the chairs, and a harassed woman, trying to watch a young child and the movers and the furniture all at the same time, gave the clear impression of endeavoring to shelter her private life from the people staring at her belongings. Mr. Johnson stopped, and for a moment joined the crowd, and then he came forward and, touching his hat civilly, said, "Perhaps I can keep an eye on your little boy for you?"

3　　The woman turned and glared at him distrustfully, and Mr. Johnson added hastily, "We'll sit right here on the steps." He beckoned to the little boy, who hesitated and then responded agreeably to Mr. Johnson's genial smile. Mr. Johnson brought out a handful of peanuts from his pocket and sat on the steps with the boy, who at first refused the peanuts on the grounds that his mother did not allow him to accept food from strangers; Mr. Johnson said that probably his mother had not intended peanuts to be included, since elephants at the circus ate them, and the boy considered, and then agreed solemnly. They sat on the steps cracking peanuts in a comradely fashion, and Mr. Johnson said, "So you're moving?"

"Yep," said the boy. 4

"Where you going?" 5

"Vermont." 6

"Nice place. Plenty of snow there. Maple sugar, too; you like 7
maple sugar?"

"Sure." 8

"Plenty of maple sugar in Vermont. You going to live on a 9
farm?"

"Going to live with Grandpa." 10

"Grandpa like peanuts?" 11

"Sure." 12

"Ought to take him some," said Mr. Johnson, reaching into 13
his pocket. "Just you and Mommy going?"

"Yep." 14

"Tell you what," Mr. Johnson said. "You take some peanuts 15
to eat on the train."

The boy's mother, after glancing at them frequently, had 16
seemingly decided that Mr. Johnson was trustworthy, because she
had devoted herself wholeheartedly to seeing that the movers did
not—what movers rarely do, but every housewife believes they
will—crack a leg from her good table, or set a kitchen chair down
on a lamp. Most of the furniture was loaded by now, and she was
deep in that nervous stage when she knew there was something she
had forgotten to pack—hidden away in the back of a closet somewhere, or left at a neighbor's and forgotten, or on the clothesline—
and was trying to remember under stress what it was.

"This all, lady?" the chief mover said, completing her dismay. 17

Uncertainly, she nodded. 18

"Want to go on the truck with the furniture, sonny?" the 19
mover asked the boy, and laughed. The boy laughed too and said
to Mr. Johnson, "I guess I'll have a good time at Vermont."

"Fine time," said Mr. Johnson, and stood up. "Have one more 20
peanut before you go," he said to the boy.

The boy's mother said to Mr. Johnson, "Thank you so much; 21
it was a great help to me."

"Nothing at all," said Mr. Johnson gallantly. "Where in Ver- 22
mont are you going?"

The mother looked at the little boy accusingly, as though he 23
had given away a secret of some importance, and said unwillingly,
"Greenwich."

"Lovely town," said Mr. Johnson. He took out a card, and 24
wrote a name on the back. "Very good friend of mine lives in
Greenwich," he said. "Call on him for anything you need. His wife

makes the best doughnuts in town," he added soberly to the little boy.

25   "Swell," said the little boy.

26   "Goodbye," said Mr. Johnson.

27   He went on, stepping happily with his new-shod feet, feeling the warm sun on his back and on the top of his head. Halfway down the block he met a stray dog and fed him a peanut.

28   At the corner, where another wide avenue faced him, Mr. Johnson decided to go on uptown again. Moving with comparative laziness, he was passed on either side by people hurrying and frowning, and people brushed past him going the other way, clattering along to get somewhere quickly. Mr. Johnson stopped on every corner and waited patiently for the light to change, and he stepped out of the way of anyone who seemed to be in any particular hurry, but one young lady came too fast for him, and crashed wildly into him when he stooped to pat a kitten which had run out onto the sidewalk from an apartment house and was now unable to get back through the rushing feet.

29   "Excuse me," said the young lady, trying frantically to pick up Mr. Johnson and hurry on at the same time, "terribly sorry."

30   The kitten, regardless now of danger, raced back to its home. "Perfectly all right," said Mr. Johnson, adjusting himself carefully. "You seem to be in a hurry."

31   "Of course I'm in a hurry," said the young lady. "I'm late."

32   She was extremely cross and the frown between her eyes seemed well on its way to becoming permanent. She had obviously awakened late, because she had not spent any extra time in making herself look pretty, and her dress was plain and unadorned with collar or brooch, and her lipstick was noticeably crooked. She tried to brush past Mr. Johnson, but, risking her suspicious displeasure, he took her arm and said, "Please wait."

33   "Look," she said ominously. "I ran into you and your lawyer can see my lawyer and I will gladly pay all damages and all inconveniences suffered therefrom but please this minute let me go because *I am late.*"

34   "Late for what?" said Mr. Johnson; he tried his winning smile on her but it did no more than keep her, he suspected, from knocking him down again.

35   "Late for work," she said between her teeth. "Late for my employment. I have a job and if I am late I lose exactly so much an hour and I cannot really afford what your pleasant conversation is costing me, be it *ever* so pleasant."

36   "I'll pay for it," said Mr. Johnson. Now these were magic words, not necessarily because they were true, or because she seri-

ously expected Mr. Johnson to pay for anything, but because Mr. Johnson's flat statement, obviously innocent of irony, could not be, coming from Mr. Johnson, anything but the statement of a responsible and truthful and respectable man.

"What *do* you mean?" she asked. 37

"I said that since I am obviously responsible for your being late 38
I shall certainly pay for it."

"Don't be silly," she said, and for the first time the frown 39
disappeared. "*I* wouldn't expect you to pay for anything—a few
minutes ago I was offering to pay *you*. Anyway," she added, almost
smiling, "it *was* my fault."

"What happens if you don't go to work?" 40

She stared. "I don't get paid." 41

"Precisely," said Mr. Johnson. 42

"What do you mean, precisely? If I don't show up at the office 43
exactly twenty minutes ago I lose a dollar and twenty cents an hour,
or two cents a minute or . . ." She thought. ". . . Almost a dime
for the time I've spent talking to you."

Mr. Johnson laughed, and finally she laughed, too. "You're 44
late already," he pointed out. "Will you give me another four cents
worth?"

"I don't understand why." 45

"You'll see," Mr. Johnson promised. He led her over to the 46
side of the walk, next to the buildings, and said, "Stand here," and
went out into the rush of people going both ways. Selecting and
considering, as one who must make a choice involving perhaps
whole years of lives, he estimated the people going by. Once he
almost moved, and then at the last minute thought better of it and
drew back. Finally, from half a block away, he saw what he wanted,
and moved out into the center of the traffic to intercept a young
man, who was hurrying, and dressed as though he had awakened
late, and frowning.

"Oof," said the young man, because Mr. Johnson had thought 47
of no better way to intercept anyone than the one the young woman
had unwittingly used upon him. "Where do you think you're
going?" the young man demanded from the sidewalk.

"I want to speak to you," said Mr. Johnson ominously. 48

The young man got up nervously, dusting himself and eyeing 49
Mr. Johnson. "What for?" he said. "What'd *I* do?"

"That's what bothers me most about people nowadays," Mr. 50
Johnson complained broadly to the people passing. "No matter
whether they've done anything or not, they always figure someone's
after them. About what you're going to do," he told the young man.

"Listen," said the young man, trying to brush past him, "I'm 51 late, and I don't have any time to listen. Here's a dime, now get going."

52   "Thank you," said Mr. Johnson, pocketing the dime. "Look," he said, "what happens if you stop running?"

53   "I'm late," said the young man, still trying to get past Mr. Johnson, who was unexpectedly clinging.

54   "How much do you make an hour?" Mr. Johnson demanded.

55   "A communist, are you?" said the young man. "Now will you please let me—"

56   "No," said Mr. Johnson insistently, "*how* much?"

57   "Dollar fifty," said the young man. "And *now* will you—"

58   "You like adventure?"

59   The young man stared, and, staring, found himself caught and held by Mr. Johnson's genial smile; he almost smiled back and then repressed it and made an effort to tear away. "I got to *hurry,*" he said.

60   "Mystery? Like surprises? Unusual and exciting events?"

61   "You selling something?"

62   "Sure," said Mr. Johnson. "You want to take a chance?"

63   The young man hesitated, looked longingly up the avenue toward what might have been his destination and then, when Mr. Johnson said, "I'll pay for it," with his own peculiar and convincing emphasis, turned and said, "Well, okay. But I got to *see* it first, what I'm buying."

64   Mr. Johnson, breathing hard, led the young man over to the side where the girl was standing; she had been watching with interest Mr. Johnson's capture of the young man and now, smiling timidly, she looked at Mr. Johnson as though prepared to be surprised at nothing.

65   Mr. Johnson reached into his pocket and took out his wallet. "Here," he said, and handed a bill to the girl. "This about equals your day's pay."

66   "But no," she said, surprised in spite of herself. "I mean, I *couldn't.*"

67   "Please do not interrupt," Mr. Johnson told her. "And *here,*" he said to the young man, "this will take care of *you.*" The young man accepted the bill dazedly, but said, "Probably counterfeit" to the young woman out of the side of his mouth. "Now," Mr. Johnson went on, disregarding the young man, "what is your name, miss?"

68   "Kent," she said helplessly. "Mildred Kent."

69   "Fine," said Mr. Johnson. "And you, sir?"

70   "Arthur Adams," said the young man stiffly.

"Splendid," said Mr. Johnson. "Now, Miss Kent, I would like 71
you to meet Mr. Adams. Mr. Adams, Miss Kent."

Miss Kent stared, wet her lips nervously, made a gesture as 72
though she might run, and said, "How do you do?"

Mr. Adams straightened his shoulders, scowled at Mr. Johnson, 73
made a gesture as though he might run, and said, "How do you do?"

"Now *this,*" said Mr. Johnson, taking several bills from his 74
wallet, "should be enough for the day for both of you. I would
suggest, perhaps, Coney Island—although I personally am not fond
of the place—or perhaps a nice lunch somewhere, and dancing, or
a matinee, or even a movie, although take care to choose a really
good one; there are *so* many bad movies these days. You might,"
he said, struck with an inspiration, "visit the Bronx Zoo, or the
Planetarium. Anywhere, as a matter of fact," he concluded, "that
you would like to go. Have a nice time."

As he started to move away Arthur Adams, breaking from his 75
dumbfounded stare, said, "But see here, mister, you *can't* do this.
Why—how do you know—I mean, *we* don't even know—I mean,
how do you know we won't just take the money and not do what
you said?"

"You've taken the money," Mr. Johnson said. "You don't have 76
to follow any of my suggestions. You may know something you
prefer to do—perhaps a museum, or something."

"But suppose I just run away with it and leave her here?" 77

"I know you won't," said Mr. Johnson gently, "because you 78
remembered to ask *me* that. Goodbye," he added, and went on.

As he stepped up the street, conscious of the sun on his head 79
and his good shoes, he heard from somewhere behind him the young
man saying, "Look, you know you don't *have* to if you don't want
to," and the girl saying, "But unless *you* don't want to . . ." Mr.
Johnson smiled to himself and then thought that he had better hurry
along; when he wanted to he could move very quickly, and before
the young woman had gotten around to saying, "Well, *I* will if
you will," Mr. Johnson was several blocks away and had already
stopped twice, once to help a lady lift several large packages into
a taxi and once to hand a peanut to a seagull. By this time he was
in an area of large stores and many more people and he was buffeted
constantly from either side by people hurrying and cross and late
and sullen. Once he offered a peanut to a man who asked him for
a dime, and once he offered a peanut to a bus driver who had
stopped his bus at an intersection and had opened the window next
to his seat and put out his head as though longing for fresh air and
the comparative quiet of the traffic. The man wanting a dime took

the peanut because Mr. Johnson had wrapped a dollar bill around it, but the bus driver took the peanut and asked ironically, "You want a transfer, Jack?"

80   On a busy corner Mr. Johnson encountered two young people—for one minute he thought they might be Mildred Kent and Arthur Adams—who were eagerly scanning a newspaper, their backs pressed against a storefront to avoid the people passing, their heads bent together. Mr. Johnson, whose curiosity was insatiable, leaned onto the storefront next to them and peeked over the man's shoulder; they were scanning the "Apartments Vacant" columns.

81   Mr. Johnson remembered the street where the woman and her little boy were going to Vermont and he tapped the man on the shoulder and said amiably, "Try down on West Seventeen. About the middle of the block, people moved out this morning."

82   "Say, what do you—" said the man, and then, seeing Mr. Johnson clearly, "Well, thanks. Where did you say?"

83   "West Seventeen," said Mr. Johnson. "About the middle of the block." He smiled again and said, "Good luck."

84   "Thanks," said the man.

85   "Thanks," said the girl as they moved off.

86   "Goodbye," said Mr. Johnson.

87   He lunched alone in a pleasant restaurant, where the food was rich, and only Mr. Johnson's excellent digestion could encompass two of their whipped-cream-and-chocolate-and-rum-cake pastries for dessert. He had three cups of coffee, tipped the waiter largely, and went out into the street again into the wonderful sunlight, his shoes still comfortable and fresh on his feet. Outside he found a beggar staring into the windows of the restaurant he had left and, carefully looking through the money in his pocket, Mr. Johnson approached the beggar and pressed some coins and a couple of bills into his hand. "It's the price of the veal cutlet lunch plus tip," said Mr. Johnson. "Goodbye."

88   After his lunch he rested; he walked into the nearest park and fed peanuts to the pigeons. It was late afternoon by the time he was ready to start back downtown, and he had refereed two checker games and watched a small boy and girl whose mother had fallen asleep and awakened with surprise and fear which turned to amusement when she saw Mr. Johnson. He had given away almost all of his candy, and had fed all the rest of his peanuts to the pigeons, and it was time to go home. Although the late-afternoon sun was pleasant, and his shoes were still entirely comfortable, he decided to take a taxi downtown.

89   He had a difficult time catching a taxi, because he gave up the first three or four empty ones to people who seemed to need them

more; finally, however, he stood alone on the corner and—almost like netting a frisky fish—he hailed desperately until he succeeded in catching a cab which had been proceeding with haste uptown and seemed to draw in toward Mr. Johnson against its own will.

"Mister," the cab driver said as Mr. Johnson climbed in, "I figured you was an omen, like. I wasn't going to pick you up at all." 90

"Kind of you," said Mr. Johnson ambiguously. 91

"If I'd of let you go it would of cost me ten bucks," said the driver. 92

"Really?" said Mr. Johnson. 93

"Yeah," said the driver. "Guy just got out of the cab, he turned around and gave me ten bucks, said take this and bet it in a hurry on a horse named Vulcan, right away." 94

"Vulcan?" said Mr. Johnson, horrified. "A fire sign on a Wednesday?" 95

"What?" said the driver. "Anyway, I said to myself if I got no fare between here and there I'd bet the ten, but if anyone looked like they needed the cab I'd take it as a omen and I'd take the ten home to the wife." 96

"You were very right," said Mr. Johnson heartily. "This is Wednesday, you would have lost your money. Monday, yes, or even Saturday. But never never never a fire sign on a Wednesday. Sunday would have been good, now." 97

"Vulcan don't run on Sunday," said the driver. 98

"You wait till another day," said Mr. Johnson. "Down this street, please, driver. I'll get off on the next corner." 99

"He *told* me Vulcan, though," said the driver. 100

"I'll tell you," said Mr. Johnson, hesitating with the door of the cab half open. "You take that ten dollars and I'll give you another ten dollars to go with it, and you go right ahead and bet that money on any Thursday on any horse that has a name indicating . . . let me see, Thursday . . . well, grain. Or any growing food." 101

"Grain?" said the driver. "You mean a horse named, like Wheat or something?" 102

"Certainly," said Mr. Johnson. "Or, as a matter of fact, to make it even easier, any horse whose name includes the letters C, R, L. Perfectly simple." 103

"Tall Corn?" said the driver, a light in his eye. "You mean a horse named, like, Tall Corn?" 104

"Absolutely," said Mr. Johnson. "Here's your money." 105

"Tall Corn," said the driver. "Thank *you,* mister." 106

"Goodbye," said Mr. Johnson. 107

He was on his own corner and went straight up to his apart- 108 ment. He let himself in and called "Hello?" and Mrs. Johnson answered from the kitchen, "Hello, dear, aren't you early?"

109   "Took a taxi home," Mr. Johnson said. "I remembered the cheesecake, too. What's for dinner?"

110   Mrs. Johnson came out of the kitchen and kissed him; she was a comfortable woman, and smiling as Mr. Johnson smiled. "Hard day?" she asked.

111   "Not very," said Mr. Johnson, hanging his coat in the closet. "How about you?"

112   "So-so," she said. She stood in the kitchen doorway while he settled into his easy chair and took off his good shoes and took out the paper he had bought that morning. "Here and there," she said.

113   "I didn't do so badly," Mr. Johnson said. "Couple young people."

114   "Fine," she said. "I had a little nap this afternoon, took it easy most of the day. Went into a department store this morning and accused the woman next to me of shoplifting, and had the store detective pick her up. Sent three dogs to the pound—*you* know, the usual thing. Oh, and listen," she added, remembering.

115   "What?" asked Mr. Johnson.

116   "Well," she said, "I got onto a bus and asked the driver for a transfer, and when he helped someone else first I said that he was impertinent, and quarreled with him. And then I said why wasn't he in the army, and I said it loud enough for everyone to hear, and I took his number and I turned in a complaint. Probably got him fired."

117   "Fine," said Mr. Johnson. "But you do look tired. Want to change over tomorrow?"

118   "I *would* like to," she said. "I could do with a change."

119   "Right," said Mr. Johnson. "What's for dinner?"

120   "Veal cutlet."

121   "Had it for lunch," said Mr. Johnson.

Reading Critically

1. Would you like to live in a world where everyone behaved like Mr. Johnson, or a world in which some people behaved like Mr. Johnson and some like Mrs. Johnson? Discuss with your classmates your choice and the reasons for your choice.

2. Describe a time when you did something good (or a little bad) spontaneously, without thinking about your actions. How is Jackson's story about the seeming randomness of life? Discuss with your classmates whether Jackson is suggesting that good and bad things happen for no reason, and whether she is suggesting that people are good or bad for no reason.

3. Summarize all the information Jackson gives you in the first two paragraphs of the story. Why is it important to know that Mr. Johnson walked down streets chosen at random and that he "pursued his eventful way in wide detours, more like a puppy than a man intent upon business"? Discuss with your classmates how the information in these two paragraphs makes you feel toward Mr. Johnson. Why is it important to the story that you are made to feel this way toward Mr. Johnson?

4. What did Mrs. Johnson do all day? Why are you given such a short description in paragraphs 114 and 116 of what she did all day? What does Mr. Johnson mean in paragraph 117 when he asks Mrs. Johnson, "Want to change over tomorrow?" In what way do you think you live in a world where people behave like Mr. and Mrs. Johnson?

Responding Through Writing

1. Write a one-paragraph description of Mr. Johnson. How tall is he, how old, what kind of face does he have, how is he dressed? Point out what evidence there is in the story for your description. What does the information, or lack of information, about Mr. Johnson's appearance contribute to the story?

2. What is the significance of paragraph 117? Why does Jackson wait until the end of the story to give Mr. Johnson's motivation for his behavior? If you are keeping a journal or notebook in this course, write in it for five to ten minutes on your reaction to the ending of the story. Is the ending fair, or did Jackson give you information throughout the story to prepare you for the ending? Why do you like or dislike the ending?

3. Write the first draft of an essay in which you narrate a day of activity for you. Do not simply list a series of things you did, but try to present your day as organized, meaningful activity over which you exercised control. However, you should also mention things that happened over which you had no control. Discuss your draft with your classmates, then rewrite it, taking as the central point of your narrative that either you control your life or that events control you.

4. Read paragraph 117 again and then write one sentence in which you state the theme of this story. Compare your sentence with those written by your classmates. How much agreement and disagreement is there about the theme of the story? What is the source of the disagreement? What does this disagreement suggest about how each of you reads a story and about how your background and beliefs influence how you read any story?

RICHARD CORY

EDWIN ARLINGTON ROBINSON

Edwin Arlington Robinson (1869–1935) is often cited as a truly American poet. Born in Maine and living mostly in Boston and New York, Robinson infuses his poems with a particularly American air of life. Although he lived to accept three Pulitzer Prizes for his poetry (1922, Collected Poems; 1925, The Man Who Died Twice; *and 1928,* Tristram*), Robinson was never confident of his talents. While critics labeled him a pessimist, it is more accurate to say that his concerns rest with humankind's frustration, but not futility, in searching for truth. The following poem, one of Robinson's most famous, was first published in 1897 in a poetry collection entitled* Children of the Night.

Whenever Richard Cory went down town,
We people on the pavement looked at him:
He was a gentleman from sole to crown,
Clean favored, and imperially slim.   4

And he was always quietly arrayed,
And he was always human when he talked;
But still he fluttered pulses when he said,
"Good-morning," and he glittered when he walked.   8

And he was rich—yes, richer than a king—
And admirably schooled in every grace:
In fine, we thought that he was everything
12 To make us wish that we were in his place.

So on we worked, and waited for the light,
And went without the meat, and cursed the bread;
And Richard Cory, one calm summer night,
16 Went home and put a bullet through his head.

Reading Critically

1. Who was Richard Cory? Ignoring for the moment the last line of the poem, do you, like the townspeople, wish you were in his place? Discuss with your classmates what Richard Cory had that you would like to have, and what he didn't have.

2. Why are the people on the pavement when they see Cory? Where is Cory? What does this physical positioning of Cory and the people tell you about Cory, the people, and their social and economic positions in the town? Where does Cory live? (Read the first line of the poem again carefully to help you answer this question.)

3. What does it mean in line 13 that the townspeople "waited for the light"? What are its possible meanings here, and what do those meanings contribute to the poem?

4. What does line 14 ("and went without the meat, and cursed the bread") mean? What does this line tell you about the economic condition of the people in the town? What does this line tell you about their reason for envying Cory?

Responding Through Writing

1. Why would it be a mistake to summarize this poem as simply meaning "money isn't everything"? Write your own summary of this poem in one sentence, then compare your summary with those written by your classmates. How much agreement and disagreement among you is there? What is the source of your disagreement?

2. Who is narrating this poem? What do you know about the narrator? What is the narrator's relation to Cory? Why do you think the narrator is never identified? Write a paragraph in which you tell as much as you can about the narrator.

3. Examine the description of Richard Cory. What is distinctive about the description? What aspects of Cory are emphasized? What aspects are not mentioned? Why is what is not mentioned just as important as what is mentioned? Write a description of Cory that covers not just his physical appearance, but his personality as well. Why is it significant that the townspeople envy Cory but do not hate him?

4. Write the first draft of an essay in which you discuss what Cory had that the townspeople wanted and what the townspeople had that Cory didn't have. In your essay, discuss what you think the poem emphasizes as more important. After discussing your essay with your classmates, revise it and write a final version.

PART II

DESCRIPTION

Descriptive writing starts with a paradox. In some ways, it is the easiest kind of writing to do; in other ways, one of the hardest. To describe something, you simply have to tell your audience *about* it. You don't have to analyze or argue; you simply tell how your subject appears to the senses. And yet many experienced writers find description one of the most challenging expressive modes. Try to describe a stalk of celery or the face of a friend. The basic facts are easy enough to convey with words like *long, green, round, pretty,* and so on, but good writers know that long strings of adjectives diminish the impact of writing the longer they become, and eventually bore the reader. To write good description, you have to do more than string adjectives together. Compare the following descriptions of the interior of a mosque:

> **A.** The place had a real lot of big stuff in it. I mean really big things like pots and rugs and huge stands, gigantic stuff, really big! And they must do all kinds of different things with those big things. This place is really impressive, really awesome!
>
> **B.** There are two big pots near the entrance that are of Arabian origin, as are the two green rugs nearby. There is also a large lectern for religious services, as well as some small lecterns.

Which paragraph offers the better description? If you picked paragraph B, then you have good judgment about the nature of descriptive writing. Paragraph A is not good description because it relies on vague adjectives that might be applied as well to the pyramids of Egypt or to the freeways of Los Angeles: *big, gigantic, impressive, awesome.* Paragraph B is better because in place of vague adjectives it gives the reader some concrete details: It tells what the "awesome stuff" in the mosque actually is: big pots, green rugs, lecterns of various sizes. Still, paragraph B could be improved upon by adding further details, as in paragraph C:

> **C.** Near the entrance are two great alabaster urns each capable of holding 250 gallons of water, said to have been the gift of Sultan Murad in the sixteenth century. . . . Two green rugs on the wall nearby are of special sanctity, having come from Mecca. There is the high pulpit, the *mimbar* from which the Khatib preaches on Friday, and a subsidiary pulpit, the *dikke,* in the form of an oriental throne, used mainly by his assistants who repeat teachings for the benefit of those who are too far off to hear what is said from the *mimbar.* [1]

The information in paragraph C is much more specific. In place of the vague "big stuff" of paragraph A and the slightly less vague "big pots" of paragraph B, the writer of paragraph C gives us "two great alabaster urns each capable of holding 250 gallons of water, said to have been the gift of Sultan Murad in the sixteenth century." The rugs are not vaguely "nearby," but "on the wall" and we learn that they are not only of "Moslem origin" but that "they come from Mecca." In each instance the writer of paragraph C has made the description more specific, relying less on general adjectives and more on concrete details.

Paragraph C illustrates the first rule of descriptive writing: Be specific. When writing description, avoid vague words like *big, impressive, beautiful, overwhelming, bad, awesome.* Instead, use more precise words. If a person is "beautiful," give us details so that we too can see "her radiant blonde hair backlit by the winter sun."

If you find yourself using strings of vague adjectives, try to become more specific by "translating" the adjectives into the five senses:

1. sight
2. hearing
3. smell
4. touch
5. taste

---

1. A. Goodrich-Freer, *Things Seen in Constantinople* (London: Steely, Service, 1926), p. 33.

Try this with the adjective *impressive*. An "impressive sight" becomes "a drawn and weary, ashen-faced old man." An "impressive sound" becomes "the mellow strings of the Philadelphia Orchestra." An "impressive smell" becomes "the cranberry vapors of my mother's breakfast cake." An "impressive texture" becomes "the smooth, cold marble of the altar." An "impressive taste" becomes "the salt-edged bite of the sea."

The second rule of good descriptive writing is to *focus* on a particular aspect of what you are attempting to describe. In paragraph C, the focus is on the *Moslem* character of the place being described, the Church of Santa Sophia in Istanbul which is now a mosque. If you are describing a person, do not just randomly list his or her various characteristics. Pick *one* characteristic (good humor, weariness, awkwardness) and use specific details to develop that characteristic. This is what Gustave Flaubert does in the following passages from his novel *Madame Bovary:*

> The new boy, standing in the corner behind the door so that he could hardly be seen, was a country lad of about fifteen, and taller than any of us. His hair was cut square on his forehead like a village choir boy; he looked reliable, but very ill at ease. Although he was not broad-shouldered, his short jacket of green cloth with black buttons must have been tight about the armholes, and showed at the opening of the cuffs red wrists accustomed to being bare. His legs, in blue stockings, looked out from beneath yellowish trousers, drawn tight by suspenders. He wore stout, ill-cleaned, hob-nailed boots.[2]

In this descriptive passage, all the details point to the *awkwardness* of the young schoolboy. The square haircut, mismatched clothes, and clompy boots carry that notion.

In another passage, Flaubert again uses descriptive details to create a specific point of focus:

> At the upper end of the table, alone amongst all the women, bent over his full plate, and his napkin tied round his neck like a child, an old man sat eating, letting drops of gravy drip from his mouth. His eyes

---

2. Gustave Flaubert, *Madame Bovary,* Paul deMan, ed. and trans. (New York: Norton, 1965), pp. 1–2.

> were bloodshot, and he wore his hair in a little queue
> tied with a black ribbon. He was the Marquis's
> father-in-law . . . , and had been, it was said, the
> lover of Queen Marie Antoinette. . . . He had lived
> at court and slept in the bed of queens![3]

In this piece of description the focus is a little more complex. Flaubert's focus is on the ironic dissimilarity between the old man's past and present existence. We see him "bent" and senile "like a child." His eyes are red with the weariness of age and he can barely control his bodily functions—gravy runs down his chin. Yet we learn that he "had slept in the bed of queens." The contrast between these details is the focus of Flaubert's descriptive effort.

The third rule of descriptive writing, which is optional but very useful, is to compare the object being described to something vivid. If comparisons go on for too long, however, focus can easily be lost. Keep such comparisons short and pointed:

> The soldiers just stood there *like bowling pins.*
> The whaler's *rocklike* captain refused to abandon the
>   hunt.
> *Checkerboard* rice fields covered the valley.

There are, of course, other useful techniques for descriptive writing, many of which are illustrated in the essays that appear in this section. As you read these essays, note how experienced writers use comparison as an aid to description, how they bring a specific focus to bear, and above all how they use concrete, specific language.

Audience and Purpose

A final note: As with other kinds of writing, keep your audience in mind when writing description. The same crime scene, for example, might be described very differently by a newspaper reporter writing for the general public and a police investigator writing for colleagues. Your description of your house in a letter to a friend would be different from a tax assessor's in an audit. A sports columnist writing for a newspaper audience would describe

3. Ibid., pp. 34–35.

a jogging path much differently than a civil engineer writing for other engineers.

As with other kinds of writing, keep in mind your purpose when describing. No other kind of writing, except perhaps narrative, lends itself so easily to going off the track. It is very easy to get carried away describing the urban landscape when your main purpose is to argue a point in city planning; it is tempting to dwell too long on the physical mannerisms of a politician when your purpose is to analyze his or her ideas. Use description as a tool to meet your purpose as a writer, but do not let it obscure that purpose.

SISTER FLOWERS

MARGUERITA ("MAYA") ANGELOU

Marguerita Angelou was born in 1928 in St. Louis, Missouri. Prior to her career as a writer, she was a professional actress and singer. Her most famous book is an autobiography of her early years, entitled I Know Why the Caged Bird Sings *(1970), a work widely praised for its vivid depiction of the grim realities in the life of a young black girl in Arkansas and Missouri during the 1930s. Angelou continued her autobiography in four more books:* Gather Together in My Name *(1974),* Singin' and Swingin' and Gettin' Merry Like Christmas *(1977),* The Heart of a Woman *(1981), and* All God's Children Need Traveling Shoes *(1986). She has also written several plays and four volumes of poetry, among these,* Just Give Me a Cool Drink of Water 'fore I Diiie. *The following selection was first published in* I Know Why the Caged Bird Sings.

1   For nearly a year, I sopped around the house, the Store, the school and the church, like an old biscuit, dirty and inedible. Then I met, or rather got to know, the lady who threw me my first life line.

2   Mrs. Bertha Flowers was the aristocrat of Black Stamps. She had the grace of control to appear warm in the coldest weather, and on the Arkansas summer days it seemed she had a private breeze

which swirled around, cooling her. She was thin without the taut look of wiry people, and her printed voile dresses and flowered hats were as right for her as denim overalls for a farmer. She was our side's answer to the richest white woman in town.

Her skin was a rich black that would have peeled like a plum if snagged, but then no one would have thought of getting close enough to Mrs. Flowers to ruffle her dress, let alone snag her skin. She didn't encourage familiarity. She wore gloves too. 3

I don't think I ever saw Mrs. Flowers laugh, but she smiled often. A slow widening of her thin black lips to show even, small white teeth, then the slow effortless closing. When she chose to smile on me, I always wanted to thank her. The action was so graceful and inclusively benign. 4

She was one of the few gentlewomen I have ever known, and has remained throughout my life the measure of what a human being can be. 5

Momma had a strange relationship with her. Most often when she passed on the road in front of the Store, she spoke to Momma in that soft yet carrying voice, "Good day, Mrs. Henderson." Momma responded with "How you, Sister Flowers?" 6

Mrs. Flowers didn't belong to our church, nor was she Momma's familiar. Why on earth did she insist on calling her Sister Flowers? Shame made me want to hide my face. Mrs. Flowers deserved better than to be called Sister. Then, Momma left out the verb. Why not ask, "How *are* you, *Mrs.* Flowers?" With the unbalanced passion of the young, I hated her for showing her ignorance to Mrs. Flowers. It didn't occur to me for many years that they were as alike as sisters, separated only by formal education. 7

Although I was upset, neither of the women was in the least shaken by what I thought an unceremonious greeting. Mrs. Flowers would continue her easy gait up the hill to her little bungalow, and Momma kept on shelling peas or doing whatever had brought her to the front porch. 8

Occasionally, though, Mrs. Flowers would drift off the road and down to the Store and Momma would say to me, "Sister, you go on and play." As I left I would hear the beginning of an intimate conversation. Momma persistently using the wrong verb, or none at all. 9

"Brother and Sister Wilcox is sho'ly the meanest—" "Is," Momma? "Is"? Oh, please, not "is," Momma, for two or more. But they talked, and from the side of the building where I waited for the ground to open up and swallow me, I heard the soft-voiced Mrs. Flowers and the textured voice of my grandmother merging and melting. They were interrupted from time to time by giggles that 10 must have come from Mrs. Flowers (Momma never giggled in her life). Then she was gone.

11   She appealed to me because she was like people I had never met personally. Like women in English novels who walked the moors (whatever they were) with their loyal dogs racing at a respectful distance. Like the women who sat in front of roaring fireplaces, drinking tea incessantly from silver trays full of scones and crumpets. Women who walked over the "heath" and read morocco-bound books and had two last names divided by a hyphen. It would be safe to say that she made me proud to be Negro, just by being herself.

12   She acted just as refined as whitefolks in the movies and books and she was more beautiful, for none of them could have come near that warm color without looking gray by comparison.

13   I was fortunate that I never saw her in the company of po-whitefolks. For since they tend to think of their whiteness as an evenizer, I'm certain that I would have had to hear her spoken to commonly as Bertha, and my image of her would have been shattered like the unmendable Humpty-Dumpty.

14   One summer afternoon, sweet-milk fresh in my memory, she stopped at the Store to buy provisions. Another Negro woman of her health and age would have been expected to carry the paper sacks home in one hand, but Momma said, "Sister Flowers, I'll send Bailey up to your house with these things."

15   She smiled that slow dragging smile, "Thank you, Mrs. Henderson. I'd prefer Marguerite, though." My name was beautiful when she said it. "I've been meaning to talk to her, anyway." They gave each other age-group looks.

16   Momma said, "Well, that's all right then. Sister, go and change your dress. You going to Sister Flowers's."

17   The chifforobe was a maze. What on earth did one put on to go to Mrs. Flowers' house? I knew I shouldn't put on a Sunday dress. It might be sacrilegious. Certainly not a house dress, since I was already wearing a fresh one. I chose a school dress, naturally. It was formal without suggesting that going to Mrs. Flowers' house was equivalent to attending church.

18   I trusted myself back into the Store.

19   "Now, don't you look nice." I had chosen the right thing, for once. . . .

20   There was a little path beside the rocky road, and Mrs. Flowers walked in front swinging her arms and picking her way over the stones.

21   She said, without turning her head, to me, "I hear you're doing very good school work, Marguerite, but that it's all written. The

teachers report that they have trouble getting you to talk in class."
We passed the triangular farm on our left and the path widened to
allow us to walk together. I hung back in the separate unasked and
unanswerable questions.

"Come and walk along with me, Marguerite." I couldn't have   22
refused even if I wanted to. She pronounced my name so nicely. Or
more correctly, she spoke each word with such clarity that I was
certain a foreigner who didn't understand English could have understood her.

"Now no one is going to make you talk—possibly no one can.   23
But bear in mind, language is man's way of communicating with
his fellow man and it is language alone which separates him from
the lower animals." That was a totally new idea to me, and I would
need time to think about it.

"Your grandmother says you read a lot. Every chance you get.   24
That's good, but not good enough. Words mean more than what
is set down on paper. It takes the human voice to infuse them with
the shades of deeper meaning."

I memorized the part about the human voice infusing words.   25
It seemed so valid and poetic.

She said she was going to give me some books and that I not   26
only must read them, I must read them aloud. She suggested that
I try to make a sentence sound in as many different ways as possible.

"I'll accept no excuse if you return a book to me that has been   27
badly handled." My imagination boggled at the punishment I would
deserve if in fact I did abuse a book of Mrs. Flowers's. Death would
be too kind and brief.

The odors in the house surprised me. Somehow I had never   28
connected Mrs. Flowers with food or eating or any other common
experience of common people. There must have been an outhouse,
too, but my mind never recorded it.

The sweet scent of vanilla had met us as she opened the door.   29

"I made tea cookies this morning. You see, I had planned to   30
invite you for cookies and lemonade so we could have this little
chat. The lemonade is in the icebox."

It followed that Mrs. Flowers would have ice on an ordinary   31
day, when most families in our town bought ice late on Saturdays
only a few times during the summer to be used in the wooden
ice-cream freezers.

She took the bags from me and disappeared through the   32
kitchen door. I looked around the room that I had never in my
wildest fantasies imagined I would see. Browned photographs leered
or threatened from the walls and the white, freshly done curtains
pushed against themselves and against the wind. I wanted to gobble

up the room entire and take it to Bailey, who would help me analyze and enjoy it.

33 "Have a seat, Marguerite. Over there by the table." She carried a platter covered with a tea towel. Although she warned that she hadn't tried her hand at baking sweets for some time, I was certain that like everything else about her the cookies would be perfect.

34 They were flat round wafers, slightly browned on the edges and butter-yellow in the center. With the cold lemonade they were sufficient for childhood's lifelong diet. Remembering my manners, I took nice little lady-like bites off the edges. She said she had made them expressly for me and that she had a few in the kitchen that I could take home to my brother. So I jammed one whole cake in my mouth and the rough crumbs scratched the insides of my jaws, and if I hadn't had to swallow, it would have been a dream come true.

35 As I ate she began the first of what we later called "my lessons in living." She said that I must always be intolerant of ignorance but understanding of illiteracy. That some people, unable to go to school, were more educated and even more intelligent than college professors. She encouraged me to listen carefully to what country people called mother wit. That in those homely sayings was couched the collective wisdom of generations.

36 When I finished the cookies she brushed off the table and brought a thick, small book from the bookcase. I had read *A Tale of Two Cities* and found it up to my standards as a romantic novel. She opened the first page and I heard poetry for the first time in my life.

37 "It was the best of times and the worst of times . . ." Her voice slid in and curved down through and over the words. She was nearly singing. I wanted to look at the pages. Were they the same that I had read? Or were there notes, music, lined on the pages, as in a hymn book? Her sounds began cascading gently. I knew from listening to a thousand preachers that she was nearing the end of her reading, and I hadn't really heard, heard to understand, a single word.

38 "How do you like that?"

39 It occurred to me that she expected a response. The sweet vanilla flavor was still on my tongue and her reading was a wonder in my ears. I had to speak.

40 I said, "Yes, ma'am." It was the least I could do, but it was the most also.

41 "There's one more thing. Take this book of poems and memorize one for me. Next time you pay me a visit, I want you to recite."

I have tried often to search behind the sophistication of years 42
for the enchantment I so easily found in those gifts. The essence
escapes but its aura remains. To be allowed, no, invited, into the
private lives of strangers, and to share their joys and fears, was a
chance to exchange the Southern bitter wormwood for a cup of
mead with Beowulf or a hot cup of tea and milk with Oliver
Twist. When I said aloud, "It is a far, far better thing that I do,
than I have ever done . . ." tears of love filled my eyes at my
selflessness.

On that first day, I ran down the hill and into the road (few 43
cars ever came along it) and had the good sense to stop running
before I reached the Store.

I was liked, and what a difference it made. I was respected not 44
as Mrs. Henderson's grandchild or Bailey's sister but for just being
Marguerite Johnson.

Childhood's logic never asks to be proved (all conclusions are 45
absolute). I didn't question why Mrs. Flowers had singled me out
for attention, nor did it occur to me that Momma might have asked
her to give me a little talking to. All I cared about was that she had
made tea cookies for *me* and read to *me* from her favorite book.
It was enough to prove that she liked me.

Reading Critically

1. Sister Flowers tells Angelou (paragraph 35) that "some
people, unable to go to school, were more educated and even more
intelligent than college professors." What is the difference between
intelligence and education? Can you cite examples to confirm Sister
Flowers's statement? Do you know some "uneducated" people who
are "more intelligent than college professors"? Discuss with your
classmates.

2. Why does Angelou not want to see Sister Flowers together
with "powhitefolks" (paragraph 13)? Why does she use the phrase
"powhitefolks"? What are some of the uses of nonstandard English
in writing? Discuss with your classmates.

3. What are the "age-group looks" (paragraph 15) that Sister Flowers and Angelou's mother give each other? Do you and your classmates also communicate by "age-group looks"? Specify some of these and discuss them.

4. Discuss the parallel that Angelou makes between Sister Flowers and the female characters of nineteenth-century British novels (paragraph 11). What is the basis for Angelou's comparison? If anyone in the class is familiar with these novels, discuss in specific terms how the parallel works.

Responding Through Writing

1. Sister Flowers says (paragraph 24): "Words mean more than what is set down on paper. It takes the human voice to infuse them with the shades of deeper meaning." In your private notebook discuss the meaning of this statement in terms of both this essay and your own life.

2. Why does Angelou's mother leave out the verb or use the wrong verb form in speaking to Sister Flowers (paragraphs 6–10)? Why doesn't Angelou understand her mother's motive? Do you see any parallel situations in your own life having to do with similar use of language? Write two or three paragraphs in response to these questions.

3. Reread the essay with an eye for Angelou's use of detail. How do seemingly minor details, such as the gloves worn by Sister Flowers (paragraph 3), enrich the essay? List ten of the most important details and write short comments on them.

4. Do you find the final paragraph a bit confusing in terms of the selection's focus? Is the selection essentially a personal story or a larger comment about the nature of literacy? Write two or three paragraphs in response to these questions.

NEW YORK

GAY TALESE

Gay Talese's Thy Neighbor's Wife, *a study of sexual practices in America, has provoked controversy concerning what appear to be self-participatory research methods. Born in 1932, Talese has been a journalist since the 1950s. His impressions of life in the streets of New York for the* New York Times *and* Esquire *magazine are examples of the "new journalism," the application of fictional techniques to works of nonfiction. He has also contributed many articles and essays to periodicals, including the* Saturday Evening Post, Reader's Digest, *and* Life. *His books include* Honor Thy Father *(1972),* The Kingdom and the Power *(1970), and his latest,* Fame and Obscurity *(1984). "New York" was first published in* Esquire *in 1960.*

New York is a city of things unnoticed. It is a city with cats 1 sleeping under parked cars, two stone armadillos crawling up St. Patrick's Cathedral, and thousands of ants creeping on top of the Empire State Building. The ants probably were carried up there by wind or birds, but nobody is sure; nobody in New York knows any more about the ants than they do about the panhandler who takes taxis to the Bowery; or the dapper man who picks trash out of Sixth Avenue trash cans; or the medium in the West Seventies who claims, "I am clairvoyant, clairaudient and clairsensuous."

2   New York is a city for eccentrics and a center for odd bits of information. New Yorkers blink twenty-eight times a minute, but forty when tense. Most popcorn chewers at Yankee Stadium stop chewing momentarily just before the pitch. Gumchewers on Macy's escalators stop chewing momentarily just before they get off—to concentrate on the last step. Coins, paper clips, ballpoint pens, and little girls' pocketbooks are found by workmen when they clean the sea lion's pool at the Bronx Zoo.

3   A Park Avenue doorman has parts of three bullets in his head—there since World War I. Several young gypsy daughters, influenced by television and literacy, are running away from home because they don't want to grow up and become fortunetellers. Each month a hundred pounds of hair is delivered to Louis Feder at 545 Fifth Avenue, where blond hairpieces are made from German women's hair; brunette hairpieces from Italian women's hair; but no hairpieces from American women's hair which, says Mr. Feder, is weak from too frequent rinses and permanents.

4   Some of New York's best informed men are elevator operators, who rarely talk, but always listen—like doormen. Sardi's doormen listen to the comments made by Broadway's first-nighters walking by after the last act. They listen closely. They listen carefully. Within ten minutes they can tell you which shows will flop and which will be hits.

5   On Broadway each evening a big, dark, 1948 Rolls-Royce pulls into Forty-sixth Street—and out hop two little ladies armed with Bibles and signs reading, "The Damned Shall Perish." These ladies proceed to stand on the corner screaming at the multitudes of Broadway sinners, sometimes until three A.M., when their chauffeur in the Rolls picks them up and drives them back to Westchester.

6   By this time Fifth Avenue is deserted by all but a few strolling insomniacs, some cruising cabdrivers, and a group of sophisticated females who stand in store windows all night and day wearing cold, perfect smiles. Like sentries they line Fifth Avenue—these window mannequins who gaze onto the quiet street with tilted heads and pointed toes and long rubber fingers reaching for cigarettes that aren't there.

7   At five A.M. Manhattan is a town of tired trumpet players and homeward-bound bartenders. Pigeons control Park Avenue and strut unchallenged in the middle of the street. This is Manhattan's mellowest hour. Most *night* people are out of sight—but the day people have not yet appeared. Truck drivers and cabs are alert, yet they do not disturb the mood. They do not disturb the abandoned

Rockefeller Center, or the motionless night watchmen in the Fulton Fish Market, or the gas-station attendant sleeping next to Sloppy Louie's with the radio on.

At five A.M. the Broadway regulars either have gone home or to all-night coffee shops where, under the glaring light, you see their whiskers and wear. And on Fifty-first Street a radio press car is parked at the curb with a photographer who has nothing to do. So he just sits there for a few nights, looks through the windshield, and soon becomes a keen observer of life after midnight.

"At one A.M.," he says, "Broadway is filled with wise guys and with kids coming out of the Astor Hotel in white dinner jackets— kids who drive to dances in their fathers' cars. You also see cleaning ladies going home, always wearing kerchiefs. By two A.M. some of the drinkers are getting out of hand, and this is the hour for bar fights. At three A.M. the last show is over in the nightclubs, and most of the tourists and out-of-town buyers are back in hotels. And small-time comedians are criticizing big-time comedians in Hanson's Drugstore. At four A.M., after the bars close, you see the drunks come out—and also the pimps and prostitutes who take advantage of drunks. At five A.M., though, it is mostly quiet. New York is an entirely different city at five A.M."

At six A.M. the early workers begin to push up from the subways. The traffic begins to move down Broadway like a river. And Mrs. Mary Woody jumps out of bed, dashes to her office and phones dozens of sleepy New Yorkers to say in a cheerful voice, rarely appreciated: "Good morning. Time to get up." For twenty years, as an operator of Western Union's Wake-Up Service, Mrs. Woody has gotten millions out of bed.

By seven A.M. a floridly robust little man, looking very Parisian in a blue beret and turtleneck sweater, moves in a hurried step along Park Avenue visiting his wealthy lady friends—making certain that each is given a brisk, before-breakfast rubdown. The uniformed doormen greet him warmly and call him either "Biz" or "Mac" because he is Biz Mackey, a ladies' masseur *extraordinaire*. He never reveals the names of his customers, but most of them are middle-aged and rich. He visits each of them in their apartments, and has special keys to their bedrooms; he is often the first man they see in the morning, and they lie in bed waiting for him.

The doormen that Biz passes each morning are generally an obliging, endlessly articulate group of sidewalk diplomats who list among their friends some of Manhattan's most powerful men, most beautiful women and snootiest poodles. More often than not, the doormen are big, slightly Gothic in design, and the possessors of eyes sharp enough to spot big tippers a block away in the year's thickest fog. Some East Side doormen are as proud as grandees, and their uniforms, heavily festooned, seem to come from the same tailor who outfitted Marshal Tito.

13   Shortly after seven-thirty each morning hundreds of people are lined along Forty-second Street waiting for the eight A.M. opening of the ten movie houses that stand almost shoulder-to-shoulder between Times Square and Eighth Avenue. Who are these people who go to the movies at eight A.M.? They are the city's insomniacs, night watchmen, and people who can't go home, do not want to go home, or have no home. They are derelicts, homosexuals, cops, hacks, truck drivers, cleaning ladies and restaurant men who have worked all night. They are also alcoholics who are waiting at eight A.M. to pay forty cents for a soft seat and to sleep in the dark, smoky theatre. And yet, aside from being smoky, each of Times Square's theatres has a special quality, or lack of quality, about it. At the Victory Theatre one finds horror films, while at the Times Square Theatre they feature only cowboy films. There are first-run films for forty cents at the Lyric, while at the Selwyn there are always second-run films for thirty cents. But if you go to the Apollo Theatre you will see, in addition to foreign films, people in the lobby talking with their hands. These are deaf-and-dumb movie fans who patronize the Apollo because they read the subtitles. The Apollo probably has the biggest deaf-and-dumb movie audience in the world.

14   New York is a city of 38,000 cabdrivers, 10,000 bus drivers, but only one chauffeur who has a chauffeur. The wealthy chauffeur can be seen driving up Fifth Avenue each morning, and his name is Roosevelt Zanders. He earns $100,000 a year, is a gentleman of impeccable taste and, although he owns a $23,000 Rolls-Royce, does not scorn his friends who own Bentleys. For $150 a day, Mr. Zanders will drive anyone anywhere in his big, silver Rolls. Diplomats patronize him, models pose next to him, and each day he receives cables from around the world urging that he be waiting at Idlewild, on the docks, or outside the Plaza Hotel. Sometimes at night, however, he is too tired to drive anymore. So Bob Clarke, his chauffeur, takes over and Mr. Zanders relaxes in the back.

15   New York is a town of 3,000 bootblacks whose brushes and rhythmic rag-snaps can be heard up and down Manhattan from midmorning to midnight. They dodge cops, survive rainstorms, and thrive in the Empire State Building as well as on the Staten Island Ferry. They usually wear dirty shoes.

New York is a city of headless men who sit obscurely in   16
subway booths all day and night selling tokens to people in a hurry.
Each weekday more than 4,500,000 riders pass these money changers
who seem to have neither heads, faces, nor personalities—only
fingers. Except when giving directions, their vocabulary consists
largely of three words: "How many, please?"

In New York there are 200 chestnut vendors, and they average   17
$25 on a good day peddling soft, warm chestnuts. Like many
vendors, the chestnut men do not own their own rigs—they borrow
or rent them from pushcart makers such as David Amerman.

Mr. Amerman, with offices opposite a defunct public bath-   18
house on the Lower East Side, is New York's master builder of
pushcarts. His father and grandfather before him were pushcart
makers, and the family has long been a household word among the
city's most discriminating junkmen, fruit vendors and hot-dog ped-
dlers.

In New York there are 500 mediums, ranging from semi-   19
trance to trance to deep-trance types. Most of them live in New
York's West Seventies and Eighties, and on Sundays some of these
blocks are communicating with the dead, vibrating to trumpets, and
solving all problems.

The Manhattan Telephone Directory has 776,300 names, of   20
which 3,316 are Smith, 2,835 are Brown, 2,444 are Williams, 2,070
are Cohen—and one is Mike Krasilovsky. Anyone who doubts this
last fact has only to look at the top of page 876 where, in large black
letters, is this sign: "There is only one Mike Krasilovsky. Sterling
3–1990."

In New York the Fifth Avenue Lingerie shop is on Madison   21
Avenue; the Madison Pet Shop is on Lexington Avenue; the Park
Avenue Florist is on Madison Avenue; and the Lexington Hand
Laundry is on Third Avenue. New York is the home of 120 pawn-
brokers and it is where Bishop Sheen's brother, Dr. Sheen, shares an
office with one Dr. Bishop.

New York is a town of thirty tattooists where interest in   22
mankind is skin-deep, but whose impressions usually last a lifetime.
Each day the tattooists go pecking away over acres of anatomy. And
in downtown Manhattan, Stanley Moskowitz, a scion of a distinguished family of Bowery skin-peckers, does a grand business.

When it rains in Manhattan, automobile traffic is slow, dates   23
are broken and, in hotel lobbies, people slump behind newspapers
or walk aimlessly about with no place to sit, nobody to talk to,
nothing to do. Taxis are harder to get; department stores do between

fifteen and twenty-five percent less business, and the monkeys in the Bronx Zoo, having no audience, slouch grumpily in their cages looking more bored than the lobby-loungers.

24   While some New Yorkers become morose with rain, others prefer it, like to walk in it, and say that on rainy days the city's buildings seem somehow cleaner—washed in an opalescence, like a Monet painting. There are fewer suicides in New York when it rains. But when the sun is shining, and New Yorkers seem happy, the depressed person sinks deeper into depression, and Bellevue Hospital gets more suicide calls.

25   New York is a town of 8,485 telephone operators, 1,364 Western Union messenger boys, and 112 newspaper copyboys. An average baseball crowd at Yankee Stadium uses over ten gallons of liquid soap per game—an unofficial high mark for cleanliness in the major leagues; the stadium also has the league's top number of ushers (360), sweepers (72) and men's rooms (34).

26   New York is a town in which the brotherhood of Russian Bath Rubbers, the only union advocating sweatshops, appears to be heading for its last rubdown. The union has been going in New York City for years, but now most of the rubbers are pushing seventy and are deaf—from all the water and the hot temperatures.

27   Each afternoon in New York a rather seedy saxophone player, his cheeks blown out like a spinnaker, stands on the sidewalk playing *Danny Boy* in such a sad, sensitive way that he soon has half the neighborhood peeking out of windows tossing nickels, dimes and quarters at his feet. Some of the coins roll under parked cars, but most of them are caught in his outstretched hand. The saxophone player is a street musician named Joe Gabler; for the past thirty years he has serenaded every block in New York and has sometimes been tossed as much as $100 a day in coins. He is also hit with buckets of water, empty beer cans and eggs, and chased by wild dogs. He is believed to be the last of New York's ancient street musicians.

28   New York is a town of nineteen midget wrestlers. They all can squeeze into the Hotel Holland's elevator, six can sleep in one bed, eight can be comfortably transported to Madison Square Garden in the chauffeur-driven Cadillac reserved for the midget wrestlers.

29   In New York from dawn to dusk to dawn, day after day, you can hear the steady rumble of tires against the concrete span of George Washington Bridge. The bridge is never completely still. It trembles with traffic. It moves in the wind. Its great veins of steel swell when hot and contract when cold; its span often is ten feet

closer to the Hudson River in summer than in winter. It is an almost restless structure of graceful beauty which, like an irresistible seductress, withholds secrets from the romantics who gaze upon it, the escapists who jump off it, the chubby girl who lumbers across its 3,500-foot span trying to reduce, and the 100,000 motorists who each day cross it, smash into it, short-change it, get jammed up on it.

When street traffic dwindles and most people are sleeping in New York, some neighborhoods begin to crawl with cats. They move quickly through the shadows of buildings; night watchmen, policemen, garbage collectors and other nocturnal wanderers see them—but never for long.   30

There are 200,000 stray cats in New York. A majority of them hang around the fish market, or in Greenwich Village, and in the East and West Side neighborhoods where garbage cans abound. No part of the city is without its strays, however, and all-night garage attendants in such busy neighborhoods as Fifty-fourth Street have counted as many as twenty of them around the Ziegfeld Theatre early in the morning. Troops of cats patrol the waterfront piers at night searching for rats. Subway track-walkers have discovered cats living in the darkness. They seem never to get hit by trains, though some are occasionally liquidated by the third rail. About twenty-five cats live seventy-five feet below the west end of Grand Central Terminal, are fed by the underground workers, and never wander up into the daylight.   31

New York is a city in which large, cliff-dwelling hawks cling to skyscrapers and occasionally zoom to snatch a pigeon over Central Park, or Wall Street, or the Hudson River. Bird watchers have seen these peregrine falcons circling lazily over the city. They have seen them perched atop tall buildings, even around Times Square. About twelve of these hawks patrol the city, sometimes with a wingspan of thirty-five inches. They have buzzed women on the roof of the St. Regis Hotel, have attacked repairmen on smokestacks, and, in August, 1947, two hawks jumped women residents in the recreation yard of the Home of the New York Guild for the Jewish Blind. Maintenance men at the Riverside Church have seen hawks dining on pigeons in the bell tower. The hawks remain there for only a little while. And then they fly out to the river, leaving pigeons' heads for the Riverside maintenance men to clean up. When the hawks return, they fly in quietly—*unnoticed,* like the cats, the headless men, the ants, the ladies' masseur, the doorman with three bullets in his head, and most of the other offbeat wonders in this town without time.   32

Reading Critically

1. Our favorite specific detail in this essay is the brotherhood of Russian Bath Rubbers (paragraph 26). Our least favorite is the undefined "wise guys" (paragraph 9). List the five specific details that you most favor and the five you like least. Discuss your list with other members of the class who have read the essay. Where has Talese succeeded in using specific detail? Where has he failed?

2. Is Talese guilty of any unfair biases in this essay? Read paragraph 13 again. How does he characterize the people lined up for the early-morning theater? Do you see prejudiced judgments in other parts of the essay? How would you and your classmates characterize these people, or similar groups of people you might have seen in your town or city?

3. What function do the ants (paragraph 1) play in the essay? Are they necessary to some unstated point that Talese finds important? What purpose do the hawks (paragraph 32) serve? Is their function in the essay similar to that of the ants? With your classmates create a brief dialogue between the ants and the hawks. The subject: these absurd and funny humans.

4. Create another dialogue between the ants and hawks. This time, the subject: these annoying and dangerous humans.

Responding Through Writing

1. To get a good reading of a city, is it best to explore it in the middle of the day or, as Talese does, deep into the night? What important characteristics not only of New York, but of most cities and towns, are revealed only at night? Do a little exploring of your

town or city both by day and by night and write a short account in your notebook or journal comparing the two experiences.

2. Do you think that Talese focuses on trivial aspects of life in New York, and that he thus presents a distorted picture of life in that city? What kinds of events and people should be included in an essay like this one to give a more accurate picture of life in any town or city? Make up a "balanced" list and use it a the basis for writing an essay describing your town or city.

3. Even though this essay is somewhat dated, we have included it because many of Talese's examples are "timeless"; that is, the characters and incidents described here are essentially part of the metropolitan scene in any age. Using characteristics and incidents from your imagination, how would you rewrite the essay to "bring it up to date" but to still keep it "timeless"?

4. The first sentence of this essay is a splendid one: "New York is a city of things unnoticed." Try to develop an essay about your city or town by starting with the same sentence.

NAMELESS, TENNESSEE

WILLIAM LEAST HEAT MOON

William Least Heat Moon (b. 1939) is the tribal name of part-Sioux William Trogdon. Least Heat Moon graduated from the University of Missouri in 1961 and received a Ph.D. in literature there in 1973. He is best known for his best-selling Blue Highways: A Journey into America *(1982), a chronicle of his journey into the remote towns and cities of America. (The title of the book refers to the blue color used on road maps to mark secondary roads.) In* Blue Highways, *his talents as an observer bring to the reader a vivid portrait of the heart of America's land and people. Least Heat Moon also contributes articles to magazines including the* Atlantic Monthly *and* Esquire. *The following account was originally published in the* Atlantic Monthly *in November 1982.*

1   Nameless, Tennessee, was a town of maybe ninety people if you pushed it, a dozen houses along the road, a couple of barns, same number of churches, a general merchandise store selling Fire Chief gasoline, and a community center with a lighted volleyball court. Behind the center was an open-roof, rusting metal privy with PAINT ME on the door; in the hollow of a nearby oak lay a full pint of Jack Daniel's Black Label. From the houses, the odor of coal smoke.

Next to a red tobacco barn stood the general merchandise with   2
a poster of Senator Albert Gore, Jr., smiling from the window. I
knocked. The door opened partway. A tall, thin man said, "Closed
up. For good," and started to shut the door.

"Don't want to buy anything. Just a question for Mr. Thur-   3
mond Watts."

The man peered through the slight opening. He looked me   4
over. "What question would that be?"

"If this is Nameless, Tennessee, could he tell me how it got   5
that name?"

The man turned back into the store and called out, "Miss   6
Ginny! Somebody here wants to know how Nameless come to be
Nameless."

Miss Ginny edged to the door and looked me and my truck   7
over. Clearly, she didn't approve. She said, "You know as well as
I do, Thurmond. Don't keep him on the stoop in the damp to tell
him." Miss Ginny, I found out, was Mrs. Virginia Watts, Thurmond's wife.

I stepped in and they both began telling the story, adding a   8
detail here, the other correcting a fact there, both smiling at the
foolishness of it all. It seems the hilltop settlement went for years
without a name. Then one day the Post Office Department told
the people if they wanted mail up on the mountain they would
have to give the place a name you could properly address a letter
to. The community met; there were only a handful, but they
commenced debating. Some wanted patriotic names, some names
from nature, one man recommended in all seriousness his own
name. They couldn't agree, and they ran out of names to argue
about. Finally, a fellow tired of the talk; he didn't like the mail he
received anyway. "Forget the durn Post Office," he said. "This
here's a nameless place if I ever seen one, so leave it be." And
that's just what they did.

Watts pointed out the window. "We used to have signs on   9
the road, but the Halloween boys keep tearin' them down."

"You think Nameless is a funny name," Miss Ginny said. "I   10
see it plain in your eyes. Well, you take yourself up north a piece
to Difficult or Defeated or Shake Rag. Now them are silly names."

The old store, lighted only by three fifty-watt bulbs, smelled   11
of coal oil and baking bread. In the middle of the rectangular room,
where the oak floor sagged a little, stood an iron stove. To the right
was a wooden table with an unfinished game of checkers and a stool
made from an apple-tree stump. On shelves around the walls sat
earthen jugs with corncob stoppers, a few canned goods, and some

of the two thousand old clocks and clockworks Thurmond Watts
owned. Only one was ticking; the others he just looked at. I asked
how long he'd been in the store.

12   "Thirty-five years, but we closed the first day of the year.
We're hopin' to sell it to a churchly couple. Upright people. No
athians."

13   "Did you build this store?"

14   "I built this one, but it's the third general store on the ground.
I fear it'll be the last. I take no pleasure in that. Once you could
come in here for a gallon of paint, a pickle, a pair of shoes, and a
can of corn."

15   "Or horehound candy," Miss Ginny said. "Or corsets and
salves. We had cough syrups and all that for the body. In season,
we'd buy and sell blackberries and walnuts and chestnuts, before the
blight got them. And outside, Thurmond milled corn and sharpened
plows. Even shoed a horse sometimes."

16   "We could fix up a horse or a man or a baby," Watts said.

17   "Thurmond, tell him we had a doctor on the ridge in them
days."

18   "We had a doctor on the ridge in them days. As good as any
doctor alivin'. He'd cut a crooked toenail or deliver a woman. Dead
these last years."

19   "I got some bad ham meat one day," Miss Ginny said, "and
took to vomitin'. All day, all night. Hangin' on the drop edge of
yonder. I said to Thurmond, 'Thurmond, unless you want shut of
me, call the doctor.' "

20   "I studied on it," Watts said.

21   "You never did. You got him right now. He come over and
put three drops of iodeen in half a glass of well water. I drank it
down and the vomitin' stopped with the last swallow. Would you
think iodeen could do that?"

22   "He put Miss Ginny on one teaspoon of spirits of ammonia
in well water for her nerves. Ain't nothin' works better for her to
this day."

23   "Calms me like the hand of the Lord."

24   Hilda, the Wattses' daughter, came out of the backroom. "I
remember him," she said. "I was just a baby. Y'all were talkin' to
him, and he lifted me up on the counter and gave me a stick of Juicy
Fruit and a piece of cheese."

25   "Knew the old medicines," Watts said. "Only drugstore he
needed was a good kitchen cabinet. None of them anteebeeotics that
hit you worsen your ailment. Forgotten lore now, the old medicines, because they ain't profit in iodeen."

26   Miss Ginny started back to the side room where she and her

sister Marilyn were taking apart a duck-down mattress to make bolsters. She stopped at the window for another look at Ghost Dancing. "How do you sleep in that thing? Ain't you all cramped and cold?"

"How does the clam sleep in his shell?" Watts said in my defense. 27

"Thurmond, get the boy a piece of buttermilk pie afore he goes on." 28

"Hilda, get him some buttermilk pie." He looked at me. "You like good music?" I said I did. He cranked up an old Edison phonograph, the kind with the big morning-glory blossom for a speaker, and put on a wax cylinder. "This will be 'My Mother's Prayer,' " he said. 29

While I ate buttermilk pie, Watts served as disc jockey of Nameless, Tennessee. "Here's 'Mountain Rose.' " It was one of those moments that you know at the time will stay with you to the grave: the sweet pie, the gaunt man playing the old music, the coals in the stove glowing orange, the scent of kerosene and hot bread. "Here's 'Evening Rhapsody.' " The music was so heavily romantic we both laughed. I thought: It is for this I have come. 30

Feathered over and giggling, Miss Ginny stepped from the side room. She knew she was a sight. "Thurmond, give him some lunch. Still looks hungry." 31

Hilda pulled food off the woodstove in the backroom: home-butchered and canned whole-hog sausage, home-canned June apples, turnip greens, cole slaw, potatoes, stuffing, hot cornbread. All delicious. 32

Watts and Hilda sat and talked while I ate. "Wish you would join me." 33

"We've ate," Watts said. "Cain't beat a woodstove for flavorful cookin'." 34

He told me he was raised in a one-hundred-fifty-year-old cabin still standing in one of the hollows. "How many's left," he said, "that grew up in a log cabin? I ain't the last surely, but I must be climbin' on the list." 35

Hilda cleared the table. "You Watts ladies know how to cook." 36

"She's in nursin' school at Tennessee Tech. I went over for one of them football games last year there at Coevul." To say *Cookeville,* you let the word collapse in upon itself so that it comes out "Coevul." 37

"Do you like football?" I asked. 38

"Don't know. I was so high up in that stadium, I never opened my eyes." 39

40   Watts went to the back and returned with a fat spiral notebook that he set on the table. His expression had changed. "Miss Ginny's *Deathbook.*"

41   The thing startled me. Was it something I was supposed to sign? He opened it but said nothing. There were scads of names written in a tidy hand over pages incised to crinkliness by a ball-point. Chronologically, the names had piled up: wives, grandparents, a stillborn infant, relatives, friends close and distant. Names, names. After each, the date of *the* unknown finally known and transcribed. The last entry bore yesterday's date.

42   "She's wrote out twenty years' worth. Ever day she listens to the hospital report on the radio and puts the names in. Folks come by to check a date. Or they just turn through the books. Read them like a scrapbook."

43   Hilda said, "Like Saint Peter at the gates inscribin' the names."

44   Watts took my arm. "Come along." He led me to the fruit cellar under the store. As we went down, he said, "Always take a newborn baby upstairs afore you take him downstairs, otherwise you'll incline him downwards."

45   The cellar was dry and full of cobwebs and jar after jar of home-canned food, the bottles organized as a shopkeeper would: sausage, pumpkin, sweet pickles, tomatoes, corn relish, blackberries, peppers, squash, jellies. He held a hand out toward the dusty bottles. "Our tomorrows."

46   Upstairs again, he said, "Hope to sell the store to the right folk. I see now, though, it'll be somebody offen the ridge. I've studied on it, and maybe it's the end of our place." He stirred the coals. "This store could give a comfortable livin', but not likely get you rich. But just gettin' by is dice rollin' to people nowadays. I never did see my day guaranteed."

47   When it was time to go, Watts said, "If you find anyone along your way wants a good store—on the road to Cordell Hull Lake—tell them about us."

48   I said I would. Miss Ginny and Hilda and Marilyn came out to say goodbye. It was cold and drizzling again. "Weather to give a man the weary dismals," Watts grumbled. "Where you headed from here?"

49   "I don't know."

50   "Cain't get lost then."

51   Miss Ginny looked again at my rig. It had worried her from the first as it had my mother. "I hope you don't get yourself kilt in that durn thing gallivantin' around the country."

52   "Come back when the hills dry off," Watts said. "We'll go lookin' for some of them round rocks all sparkly inside."

I thought a moment. "Geodes?"   53
"Them's the ones. The country's properly full of them."   54

Reading Critically

1. Would you like to move to Nameless? What, specifically, would you gain by doing so? What would you give up? Don't forget to deal with the problem of "anteebeeotics" (paragraph 25) in your discussion.

2. The people of Nameless fear that their way of life will soon disappear. Do you know of any similar place where old-fashioned customs still exist? Should anything be done to maintain those customs, or should they be allowed to disappear in the name of progress? Discuss with your classmates.

3. The author uses local Tennessee dialect in his account of Nameless. In what ways does this technique help paint a picture of the town and its people? Discuss with your classmates.

4. What is the significance of the geodes at the end of the story? Is that significance real, symbolic, or both? How so?

Responding Through Writing

1. On a map of your state, trace a journey you would like to take in order to visit small, out-of-the-way places. In your notebook or journal write a brief account of what you would expect to find on your trip.

2. Imagine that on his journey Least Heat Moon visits the town or city where your college is located. Write for ten minutes indicating what you would tell him. Exchange your comments with

your classmates. Then write a brief account from Least Heat Moon's point of view.

3. Why is Miss Ginny's *Deathbook* popular reading in Nameless? Why do people read obituaries? Consult the obituaries in your local paper for a few days running. What do they tell you about life in your town or city over the past half-century? Write a general obituary for that half-century.

4. With your notebook or journal in hand, travel to some nearby community (or city district) whose name interests you and interview some of the people there about how the place got its name. Share with your classmates the results of your expedition.

THE MORNING AFTER, IN THE MORGUE

FRANCIS X. CLINES

After living in and writing about New York City as a reporter for the New York Times, *Francis X. Clines was assigned to London, England, where he now lives and about which he now writes. He is the author of* About New York: Sketches of the City *(1980), and frequently writes reviews and essays for the* New York Times Book Review. *He is considered one of the finest prose stylists among practicing journalists today. The following selection was originally published in the* New York Times *on December 6, 1977.*

Absolutely and forevermore, the people in the refrigerator had 1
found the end of animation. Indeed, the bearded man rolled out in
cold drawer No. 68 had collapsed into death while he was dancing
at a discotheque.

"That is not a bad way to die," the Chief Medical Examiner 2
says, looking down at the naked brown body's passive face.

He jokes gently in this stainless-steel staging area of the good 3
night. The medical examiner, Dr. Dominick J. DiMaio, is on his

morning rounds of inspecting people who turned up from life during the night.

4   It is a place of cold steel, pallid tile, and supine flesh. "Come on, Barbara, we have a flock of cases," he says to Mrs. Gordon, who takes his dictation down on what killed the people in the drawers.

5   It is hard to say what preserves decorum as the refrigerator doors are opened one after another by Sam Williams and the bodies are wheeled out in all their variety of smashed and punctured or perfectly whole and totally languid repose. Clothes help draw the line between the living and the dead. Dr. DiMaio's blue shirt sleeves are rolled up, his tie is loosened and his thin, dark-rimmed eyeglasses are windows of curiosity. He is bald with a white fringe of hair that seems ceremonial as he peers down at each corpse.

6   His rounds of the dead are repeatedly interrupted by phone calls and other business, and this morning there is a sensitive case involving the murder of a Brazilian citizen in a midtown hotel and a report to the Brazilian consulate.

7   "Hog-tied," Dr. DiMaio is saying, describing how the murderer pinioned that victim.

8   Only one is recalled and, right there by the bank of mortuary cabinets with its one open door and outthrust body, the doctor sends for the homicide ligatures of the old and the new "hog-tying" cases. Leather belts were employed in both murders, knotted as bindings. The doctor looks, he pokes. "The knots are different."

9   Immediately, he hands back the belts and shifts his attention to the body waiting at his elbow, a "well-developed, well-nourished white male," the doctor narrates as he lifts open an eyelid, opens the mouth for a glance, probes the abdomen. He looks over attendant paperwork and rules death is from cirrhosis of the liver and massive internal hemorrhage. Sam slides the man back into the bank like a dossier.

10   There is a small old lady in drawer No. 30 who obviously fell to her death. But the doctor doesn't entirely accept the police report of a drunken accident, no foul play. "Report says window sill was 30 inches up with a 13-inch opening. Look at her [size]. How the hell could she fall out? Send her up, Sam."

11   The latter is an order for an autopsy in which a body is taken apart and searched by a forensic pathologist for signs of unnatural, violent death. Not every body sent to the morgue is autopsied. The city doctors do not have the need or the time and budgetary wherewithal to be so totally thorough. Dr. DiMaio makes this point when he is interrupted by a phone call from an anxious private physician who has repeatedly requested a particular autopsy.

"Certainly not," Dr. DiMaio finally says into the phone.   12
"She's 73 years old in a nursing home, with a history of heart
condition, and you won't sign for her? Can you show foul play?"

The medical examiner's face takes on an extra biting look as   13
he adds, "Don't worry, doctor, this won't count against your death
record, if that's what you're worried about."

He snaps the phone back on the wall and returns to the   14
morning corpses, stepping for a moment onto the large floor-level
scale where the bodies are weighed. The arrow bounces up to 187
pounds.

"I ate too much yesterday," he says. Under the circumstances,   15
the remark seems a much-needed celebration of life, particularly
since the doctor is entering special mortuary room 24 where partially decomposed bodies are kept. Here death is perversely vivid
in surreal colors and odors and even the doctor, after 30 years of
this, grimaces and hurries a bit more. He checks two "floaters"—
bodies found in the river—and a wizened man who put a pistol to
his brain.

"Get me a knife," the doctor says to an aide, and right there   16
he probes for the bullet, a task no more remarkable to the doctor
than a bit of first aid, but one that begs a visitor to glance elsewhere—a conversation with Mrs. Gordon, perhaps.

"We take turns making the rounds with him," she says. "I   17
couldn't do it every day." Like other professionals at the morgue,
she describes the one certain trial of composure. "I can take anything
but a child. When I see a murdered child, that's it."

Dr. DiMaio enters the main autopsy room and the place is   18
literally buzzing with surgical saws as five of the eight steel tables
are occupied. The bodies face windows of opaque glass that flicker
almost theatrically with the shadows of falling snowflakes. Light
floods the room as pathologists uncap and open the bodies. It is more
mechanical than morbid as parts are catalogued and entities undone.

Dr. DiMaio is to do the autopsy on the Brazilian man, who   19
had been beaten and smothered. An impeccably tailored homicide
detective stands by, natty evidence that there is life before death. The
doctor makes small talk with him. "We are 50 [homicides] behind
last year, but our busy season is coming," he says as snowflakes
flicker past the window.

Reading Critically

1. Is it Clines's purpose simply to tell his audience about what goes on in a morgue, or is it his purpose to generalize about larger questions of life and death? Make two lists of questions that came to mind as you read the essay, one list on the specific operations of the morgue, the other on the larger issues of life and death. Compare your lists with those of your classmates.

2. Do you get the feeling, perhaps from the tone of the essay, that in some strange way the dead people in the morgue deserve to be there? What elements in the essay might lead a reader to get this feeling? Discuss with your classmates.

3. Discuss with your classmates whether you would like (or could stand) to work in a morgue, mortuary, or other place connected with death. Which specific elements of the job would be most revolting? Would any elements of the job be attractive? Don't be afraid to laugh: Not only is grim humor not out of place in this discussion, it may be necessary.

4. In paragraph 9, Clines describes how a corpse is slid back into the vault "like a dossier." What does this simile say about Clines's (and perhaps our) view of death? Discuss with your classmates the various psychological strategies people tend to use in order to deal with the fact of death.

Responding Through Writing

1. "That is not a bad way to die," says the Chief Medical Examiner when speaking of the man who collapsed while dancing in a discotheque (paragraph 2). Are there "good" ways and "bad" ways to die? What might some of them be? Which would you pick?

Which would you most avoid? In your notebook or journal, develop the first draft of an essay answering these questions.

2. How might a morgue in a small or medium-sized town differ from the New York morgue described in this essay? How would the histories of the dead people in the small-town morgue differ from the histories of the people mentioned here, especially regarding their manner of death? Write up one or two such case histories.

3. Curiously, there is little laughing or joking in this essay, the kind of grim humor you might expect to lighten up life in the face of death. Do you think the essay would have had greater appeal if Clines had lightened his tone or introduced a few examples we could laugh at? If so, rewrite a portion of the essay, introducing some grim humor.

4. List the descriptive details that you find most effective. Make one list of details about the dead and another list of details about the living. What do your lists tell you about Clines's strategy in selecting descriptive details? Is his purpose focused more on the living or on the dead? Rewrite a draft of a new essay, using the same subject matter but with the opposite focus.

SHOOTING AN ELEPHANT

GEORGE ORWELL

George Orwell, the pen name of Eric Blair (1903–1950), is best known for his novels Nineteen Eighty-Four *(1949) and* Animal Farm *(1945) and for his essays on language and politics, which appeared in publications including the* London Observer *and the* London Times. *Orwell was born in Bengal, India, and educated at Eton. A great traveler throughout his life, he worked as a dishwasher, private tutor, teacher, and part-time bookstore assistant, among other jobs during his travels, and fought for the Loyalist forces in the Spanish Civil War. He spent the years 1922 to 1927 serving in the British colonial police in Burma, during which the incident he describes here took place. Among Orwell's novels are* Down and Out in Paris and London *(1933),* Burmese Days *(1934), and* Keep the Aspidistra Flying *(1936); his nonfiction works include* The Road to Wigan Pier *(1937) and* Homage to Catalonia *(1938). Orwell once wrote that "when I sit down to write a book, I do not say to myself, 'I am going to produce a work of art.' I write it because there is some lie that I want to expose." Orwell died of tuberculosis at the age of 46 after living in seclusion on the island of Jura off the coast of Scotland. Two other selections by Orwell, "A Hanging" and "Politics and the English Language," are also included in this book. The following selection was originally published in* New Writing *magazine in the autumn of 1936.*

In Moulmein, in Lower Burma, I was hated by large numbers   1
of people—the only time in my life that I have been important
enough for this to happen to me. I was subdivisional police officer
of the town, and in an aimless, petty kind of way anti-European
feeling was very bitter. No one had the guts to raise a riot, but if
a European woman went through the bazaars alone somebody
would probably spit betel juice over her dress. As a police officer
I was an obvious target and was baited whenever it seemed safe to
do so. When a nimble Burman tripped me up on the football field
and the referee (another Burman) looked the other way, the crowd
yelled with hideous laughter. This happened more than once. In the
end the sneering yellow faces of young men that met me everywhere, the insults hooted after me when I was at a safe distance, got
badly on my nerves. The young Buddhist priests were the worst of
all. There were several thousands of them in the town and none of
them seemed to have anything to do except stand on street corners
and jeer at Europeans.

All this was perplexing and upsetting. For at that time I had   2
already made up my mind that imperialism was an evil thing and
the sooner I chucked up my job and got out of it the better.
Theoretically—and secretly, of course—I was all for the Burmese
and all against the oppressors, the British. As for the job I was doing,
I hated it more bitterly than I can perhaps make clear. In a job like
that you see the dirty work of Empire at close quarters. The
wretched prisoners huddling in the stinking cages of the lockups, the
grey, cowed faces of the long-term convicts, the scarred buttocks
of the men who had been flogged with bamboos—all these oppressed me with an intolerable sense of guilt. But I could get
nothing into perspective. I was young and ill-educated and I had
had to think out my problems in the utter silence that is imposed
on every Englishman in the East. I did not even know that the
British Empire is dying, still less did I know that it is a great deal
better than the younger empires that are going to supplant it. All
I knew was that I was stuck between my hatred of the empire I
served and my rage against the evil-spirited little beasts who tried
to make my job impossible. With one part of my mind I thought
of the British Raj as an unbreakable tyranny, as something clamped
down, in *saecula saeculorum,* upon the will of prostrate peoples; with

another part I thought that the greatest joy in the world would be to drive a bayonet into a Buddhist priest's guts. Feelings like these are the normal by-products of imperialism; ask any Anglo-Indian official, if you can catch him off duty.

3   One day something happened which in a roundabout way was enlightening. It was a tiny incident in itself, but it gave me a better glimpse than I had had before of the real nature of imperialism—the real motives for which despotic governments act. Early one morning the subinspector at a police station the other end of town rang me up on the phone and said that an elephant was ravaging the bazaar. Would I please come and do something about it? I did not know what I could do, but I wanted to see what was happening and I got on to a pony and started out. I took my rifle, an old .44 Winchester and much too small to kill an elephant, but I thought the noise might be useful *in terrorem.* Various Burmans stopped me on the way and told me about the elephant's doings. It was not, of course, a wild elephant, but a tame one which had gone "must." It had been chained up, as tame elephants always are when their attack of "must" is due, but on the previous night it had broken its chain and escaped. Its mahout, the only person who could manage it when it was in that state, had set out in pursuit, but had taken the wrong direction and was now twelve hours' journey away, and in the morning the elephant had suddenly reappeared in the town. The Burmese population had no weapons and were quite helpless against it. It had already destroyed somebody's bamboo hut, killed a cow and raided some fruit stalls and devoured the stock; also it had met the municipal rubbish van and, when the driver jumped out and took to his heels, had turned the van over and inflicted violences upon it.

4   The Burmese subinspector and some Indian constables were waiting for me in the quarter where the elephant had been seen. It was a very poor quarter, a labyrinth of squalid bamboo huts, thatched with palmleaf, winding all over a steep hillside. I remember that it was a cloudy, stuffy morning at the beginning of the rains. We began questioning the people as to where the elephant had gone and, as usual, failed to get any definite information. That is invariably the case in the East; a story always sounds clear enough at a distance, but the nearer you get to the scene of events the vaguer it becomes. Some of the people said that the elephant had gone in one direction, some said that he had gone in another, some professed not even to have heard of any elephant. I had almost made up my mind that the whole story was a pack of lies, when we heard yells a little distance away. There was a loud, scandalized cry of "Go

away, child! Go away this instant!" and an old woman with a switch in her hand came round the corner of a hut, violently shooing away a crowd of naked children. Some more women followed, clicking their tongues and exclaiming; evidently there was something that the children ought not to have seen. I rounded the hut and saw a man's dead body sprawling in the mud. He was an Indian, a black Dravidian coolie, almost naked, and he could not have been dead many minutes. The people said that the elephant had come suddenly upon him round the corner of the hut, caught him with its trunk, put its foot on his back and ground him into the earth. This was the rainy season and the ground was soft, and his face had scored a trench a foot deep and a couple of yards long. He was lying on his belly with arms crucified and head sharply twisted to one side. His face was coated with mud, the eyes wide open, the teeth bared and grinning with an expression of unendurable agony. (Never tell me, by the way, that the dead look peaceful. Most of the corpses I have seen looked devilish.) The friction of the great beast's foot had stripped the skin from his back as neatly as one skins a rabbit. As soon as I saw the dead man I sent an orderly to a friend's house nearby to borrow an elephant rifle. I had already sent back the pony, not wanting it to go mad with fright and throw me if it smelled the elephant.

The orderly came back in a few minutes with a rifle and five   5 cartridges, and meanwhile some Burmans had arrived and told us that the elephant was in the paddy fields below, only a few hundred yards away. As I started forward practically the whole population of the quarter flocked out of the houses and followed me. They had seen the rifle and were all shouting excitedly that I was going to shoot the elephant. They had not shown much interest in the elephant when he was merely ravaging their homes, but it was different now that he was going to be shot. It was a bit of fun to them, as it would be to an English crowd; besides they wanted the meat. It made me vaguely uneasy. I had no intention of shooting the elephant—I had merely sent for the rifle to defend myself if necessary—and it is always unnerving to have a crowd following you. I marched down the hill, looking and feeling a fool, with the rifle over my shoulder and an ever-growing army of people jostling at my heels. At the bottom, when you got away from the huts, there was a metalled road and beyond that a miry waste of paddy fields a thousand yards across, not yet ploughed but soggy from the first rains and dotted with coarse grass. The elephant was standing eight yards from the road, his left side towards us. He took not the slightest notice of the crowd's approach. He was tearing up bunches of grass, beating them against his knees to clean them and stuffing them into his mouth.

6   I had halted on the road. As soon as I saw the elephant I knew with perfect certainty that I ought not to shoot him. It is a serious matter to shoot a working elephant—it is comparable to destroying a huge and costly piece of machinery—and obviously one ought not to do it if it can possibly be avoided. And at that distance, peacefully eating, the elephant looked no more dangerous than a cow. I thought then and I think now that his attack of "must" was already passing off; in which case he would merely wander harmlessly about until the mahout came back and caught him. Moreover, I did not in the least want to shoot him. I decided that I would watch him for a little while to make sure that he did not turn savage again, and then go home.

7   But at that moment, I glanced round at the crowd that had followed me. It was an immense crowd, two thousand at the least and growing every minute. It blocked the road for a long distance on either side. I looked at the sea of yellow faces above the garish clothes—faces all happy and excited over this bit of fun, all certain that the elephant was going to be shot. They were watching me as they would watch a conjuror about to perform a trick. They did not like me, but with the magical rifle in my hands I was momentarily worth watching. And suddenly I realized that I should have to shoot the elephant after all. The people expected it of me and I had got to do it; I could feel their two thousand wills pressing me forward, irresistibly. And it was at this moment, as I stood there with the rifle in my hands, that I first grasped the hollowness, the futility of the white man's dominion in the East. Here was I, the white man with his gun, standing in front of the unarmed native crowd—seemingly the leading actor of the piece; but in reality I was only an absurd puppet pushed to and fro by the will of those yellow faces behind. I perceived in this moment that when the white man turns tyrant it is his own freedom that he destroys. He becomes a sort of hollow, posing dummy, the conventionalized figure of a sahib. For it is the condition of his rule that he shall spend his life in trying to impress the "natives," and so in every crisis he has got to do what the "natives" expect of him. He wears a mask, and his face grows to fit it. I had got to shoot the elephant. I had committed myself to doing it when I sent for the rifle. A sahib has got to act like a sahib; he has got to appear resolute, to know his own mind and do definite things. To come all that way, rifle in hand, with two thousand people marching at my heels, and then to trail feebly away, having done nothing—no, that was impossible. The crowd would

laugh at me. And my whole life, every white man's life in the East, was one long struggle not to be laughed at.

But I did not want to shoot the elephant. I watched him beating his bunch of grass against his knees, with that preoccupied grandmotherly air that elephants have. It seemed to me that it would be murder to shoot him. At that age I was not squeamish about killing animals, but I had never shot an elephant and never wanted to. (Somehow it always seems worse to kill a *large* animal.) Besides, there was the beast's owner to be considered. Alive, the elephant was worth at least a hundred pounds; dead, he would only be worth the value of his tusks, five pounds, possibly. But I had got to act quickly. I turned to some experienced-looking Burmans who had been there when we arrived, and asked them how the elephant had been behaving. They all said the same thing: He took no notice of you if you left him alone, but he might charge if you went too close to him.

It was perfectly clear to me what I ought to do. I ought to walk up to within, say, twenty-five yards of the elephant and test his behavior. If he charged, I could shoot; if he took no notice of me, it would be safe to leave him until the mahout came back. But also I knew that I was going to do no such thing. I was a poor shot with a rifle and the ground was soft mud into which one would sink at every step. If the elephant charged and I missed him, I should have about as much chance as a toad under a steamroller. But even then I was not thinking particularly of my own skin, only of the watchful yellow faces behind. For at that moment, with the crowd watching me, I was not afraid in the ordinary sense, as I would have been if I had been alone. A white man mustn't be frightened in front of "natives"; and so, in general, he isn't frightened. The sole thought in my mind was that if anything went wrong those two thousand Burmans would see me pursued, caught, trampled on, and reduced to a grinning corpse like that Indian up the hill. And if that happened it was quite probable that some of them would laugh. That would never do. There was only one alternative. I shoved the cartridges into the magazine and lay down on the road to get a better aim.

The crowd grew very still, and a deep, low, happy sigh, as of people who see the theatre curtain go up at last, breathed from innumerable throats. They were going to have their bit of fun after all. The rifle was a beautiful German thing with cross-hair sights. I did not then know that in shooting an elephant one would shoot to cut an imaginary bar running from ear-hole to ear-hole. I ought, therefore, as the elephant was sideways on, to have aimed straight at his ear-hole; actually I aimed several inches in front of this, thinking the brain would be further forward.

11   When I pulled the trigger I did not hear the bang or feel the kick—one never does when a shot goes home—but I heard the devilish roar of glee that went up from the crowd. In that instant, in too short a time, one would have thought, even for the bullet to get there, a mysterious, terrible change had come over the elephant. He neither stirred nor fell, but every line of his body had altered. He looked suddenly stricken, shrunken, immensely old, as though the frightful impact of the bullet had paralyzed him without knocking him down. At last, after what seemed a long time—it might have been five seconds, I dare say—he sagged flabbily to his knees. His mouth slobbered. An enormous senility seemed to have settled upon him. One could have imagined him thousands of years old. I fired again into the same spot. At the second shot he did not collapse but climbed with desperate slowness to his feet and stood weakly upright, with legs sagging and head drooping. I fired a third time. That was the shot that did for him. You could see the agony of it jolt his whole body and knock the last remnant of strength from his legs. But in falling he seemed for a moment to rise, for as his hind legs collapsed beneath him he seemed to tower upward like a huge rock toppling, his trunk reaching skywards like a tree. He trumpeted, for the first and only time. And then down he came, his belly towards me, with a crash that seemed to shake the ground even where I lay.

12   I got up. The Burmans were already racing past me across the mud. It was obvious that the elephant would never rise again, but he was not dead. He was breathing very rhythmically with long rattling gasps, his great mound of a side painfully rising and falling. His mouth was wide open. I could see far down into caverns of pale pink throat. I waited a long time for him to die, but his breathing did not weaken. Finally I fired my two remaining shots into the spot where I thought his heart must be. The thick blood welled out of him like red velvet, but still he did not die. His body did not even jerk when the shots hit him, the tortured breathing continued without a pause. He was dying, very slowly and in great agony, but in some world remote from me where not even a bullet could damage him further. I felt I had got to put an end to that dreadful noise. It seemed dreadful to see the great beast lying there, powerless to move and yet powerless to die, and not even to be able to finish him. I sent back for my small rifle and poured shot after shot into his heart and down his throat. They seemed to make no impression. The tortured gasps continued as steadily as the ticking of a clock.

In the end I could not stand it any longer and went away. I   13
heard later that it took him half an hour to die. Burmans were
bringing dahs and baskets even before I left, and I was told they had
stripped his body almost to the bones by the afternoon.

Afterwards, of course, there were endless discussions about the   14
shooting of the elephant. The owner was furious, but he was only
an Indian and could do nothing. Besides, legally I had done the right
thing, for a mad elephant has to be killed, like a mad dog, if its
owner fails to control it. Among the Europeans opinion was divided. The older men said I was right, the younger men said it was
a damn shame to shoot an elephant for killing a coolie, because the
elephant was worth more than any damn Coringhee coolie. And
afterwards I was very glad that the coolie had been killed; it put
me legally in the right and it gave me sufficient pretext for shooting
the elephant. I often wondered whether any of the others grasped
that I had done it solely to avoid looking a fool.

Reading Critically

1. Look up information on the British Empire, such as how
big it was at its greatest extent, approximately how long it lasted,
and when it declined. Then look up a definition of *colonialism.*
Now locate Burma on a map and find out how far it is from
England. In what way could this distance from England have
contributed to Orwell's feelings and ideas about colonialism?
Look up the definition or a description of a Coringhee coolie.
Why do the Europeans think the life of a coolie isn't worth the
life of an elephant? How is this sentiment consistent or inconsistent with your definition of colonialism? Discuss your ideas about
colonialism with your classmates.

2. If Orwell is such a bad shot, and if he knows his rifle ("an
old .44 Winchester") is "much too small to kill an elephant," why
does he take the gun with him? Why does he later send for an
elephant rifle? To what extent do Orwell's actions force him to kill
the elephant?

3. If the elephant is no longer dangerous, why does Orwell shoot it? In what way is Orwell "only an absurd puppet pushed to and fro"? Why is Orwell glad that the coolie had been killed? Isn't this position inconsistent with his belief that colonialism is wrong?

4. What similarities do you find between Orwell's descriptions of anti-European and anti-British sentiments and actions in this story and accounts of anti-American sentiments and actions in other countries today? Write a definition of *empire*. To what "younger empires" is Orwell referring when he states that the British Empire is "a great deal better than the younger empires that are going to supplant it"?

Responding Through Writing

1. Orwell is clearly using narration to make a point, not just tell a story. After reading paragraph 7, write one sentence summarizing Orwell's purpose in this story. Below this sentence, list the most important details in the story that develop Orwell's purpose.

2. Write a paragraph in which you summarize the information in paragraphs 2 and 3. How important is this information to the story? How could the information in these paragraphs have been presented less directly? Choose one paragraph in the story and rewrite it to include some of the information from these paragraphs.

3. In one sentence write what a hero is to you. Now list at least five different examples of people who fit your definition of a hero. Compare your definition and list with those of your classmates. According to your definition, is Orwell the hero of this story or just the narrator?

4. Write a list of the legal justifications Orwell gives for his actions at the conclusion of his story. In what way is Orwell's conclusion consistent with the second paragraph of the story? Write a paragraph or more in which you explain why Orwell's legal justifications for his actions are inadequate.

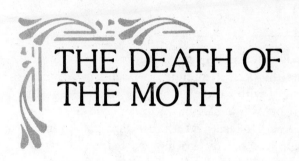

THE DEATH OF THE MOTH

VIRGINIA WOOLF

Virginia Woolf (1882–1941) received an unusually good education for a woman of her era. She and her husband, Leonard Woolf, were members of the Bloomsbury group, a loose association of writers and intellectuals living in London in the 1920s. In 1917 they founded the Hogarth Press, which was the first publisher of T. S. Eliot, Katherine Mansfield, and Gertrude Stein. Today, Woolf is still famous for her stream-of-consciousness writing and her ability to convey to the reader a character's sense of psychological isolation. A deep commitment to overcome the prejudices that women faced in her lifetime is also found in many of her works. Her novels include Mrs. Dalloway *(1925),* To the Lighthouse *(1927), and* Orlando *(1928). She is also widely hailed and admired for* A Room of One's Own *(1929), a discussion of the role of the woman artist. The following story first appeared in the collection* The Death of the Moth and Other Essays *(1942).*

Moths that fly by day are not properly to be called moths; they do not excite that pleasant sense of dark autumn nights and ivy-blossom which the commonest yellow-underwing asleep in the shadow of the curtain never fails to rouse in us. They are hybrid

1

creatures, neither gay like butterflies nor sombre like their own species. Nevertheless the present specimen, with his narrow hay-coloured wings, fringed with a tassel of the same colour, seemed to be content with life. It was a pleasant morning, mid-September, mild, benignant, yet with a keener breath than that of the summer months. The plough was already scoring the field opposite the window, and where the share had been, the earth was pressed flat and gleamed with moisture. Such vigour came rolling in from the fields and the down beyond that it was difficult to keep the eyes strictly turned upon the book. The rooks too were keeping one of their annual festivities; soaring round the tree tops until it looked as if a vast net with thousands of black knots in it had been cast up into the air; which, after a few moments sank slowly down upon the trees until every twig seemed to have a knot at the end of it. Then, suddenly, the net would be thrown into the air again in a wider circle this time, with the utmost clamour and vociferation, as though to be thrown into the air and settle slowly down upon the tree tops were a tremendously exciting experience.

2   The same energy which inspired the rooks, the ploughmen, the horses, and even, it seemed, the lean bare-backed downs, sent the moth fluttering from side to side of his square of the windowpane. One could not help watching him. One was, indeed, conscious of a queer feeling of pity for him. The possibilities of pleasure seemed that morning so enormous and so various that to have only a moth's part in life, and a day moth's at that, appeared a hard fate, and his zest in enjoying his meagre opportunities to the full, pathetic. He flew vigorously to one corner of his compartment, and, after waiting there a second, flew across to the other. What remained for him but to fly to a third corner and then to a fourth? That was all he could do, in spite of the size of the downs, the width of the sky, the far-off smoke of houses, and the romantic voice, now and then, of a steamer out at sea. What he could do he did. Watching him, it seemed as if a fibre, very thin but pure, of the enormous energy of the world had been thrust into his frail and diminutive body. As often as he crossed the pane, I could fancy that a thread of vital light became visible. He was little or nothing but life.

3   Yet, because he was so small, and so simple a form of the energy that was rolling in at the open window and driving its way through so many narrow and intricate corridors in my own brain and in those of other human beings, there was something marvellous as well as pathetic about him. It was as if someone had taken a tiny bead of pure life and decking it as lightly as possible with down and

feathers, had set it dancing and zigzagging to show us the true nature of life. Thus displayed one could not get over the strangeness of it. One is apt to forget all about life, seeing it humped and bossed and garnished and cumbered so that it has to move with the greatest circumspection and dignity. Again, the thought of all that life might have been had he been born in any other shape caused one to view his simple activities with a kind of pity.

After a time, tired by his dancing apparently, he settled on the   4
window ledge in the sun, and, the queer spectacle being at an end, I forgot about him. Then, looking up, my eye was caught by him. He was trying to resume his dancing, but seemed either so stiff or so awkward that he could only flutter to the bottom of the window-pane; and when he tried to fly across it he failed. Being intent on other matters I watched these futile attempts for a time without thinking, unconsciously waiting for him to resume his flight, as one waits for a machine, that has stopped momentarily, to start again without considering the reason of its failure. After perhaps a seventh attempt he slipped from the wooden ledge and fell, fluttering his wings, on to his back on the window sill. The helplessness of his attitude roused me. It flashed upon me that he was in difficulties; he could no longer raise himself; his legs struggled vainly. But, as I stretched out a pencil, meaning to help him to right himself, it came over me that the failure and awkwardness were the approach of death. I laid the pencil down again.

The legs agitated themselves once more. I looked as if for the   5
enemy against which he struggled. I looked out of doors. What had happened there? Presumably it was midday, and work in the fields had stopped. Stillness and quiet had replaced the previous animation. The birds had taken themselves off to feed in the brooks. The horses stood still. Yet the power was there all the same, massed outside, indifferent, impersonal, not attending to anything in particular. Somehow it was opposed to the little hay-coloured moth. It was useless to try to do anything. One could only watch the extraordinary efforts made by those tiny legs against an oncoming doom which could, had it chosen, have submerged an entire city, not merely a city, but masses of human beings; nothing, I knew had any chance against death. Nevertheless after a pause of exhaustion the legs fluttered again. It was superb this last protest, and so frantic that he succeeded at last in righting himself. One's sympathies, of course, were all on the side of life. Also, when there was nobody to care or to know, this gigantic effort on the part of an insignificant little moth, against a power of such magnitude, to retain what no one else

valued or desired to keep, moved one strangely. Again, somehow, one saw life, a pure bead. I lifted the pencil again, useless though I knew it to be. But even as I did so, the unmistakable tokens of death showed themselves. The body relaxed, and instantly grew stiff. The struggle was over. The significant little creature now knew death. As I looked at the dead moth, this minute wayside triumph of so great a force over so mean an antagonist filled me with wonder. Just as life had been strange a few minutes before, so death was now as strange. The moth having righted himself now lay most decently and uncomplainingly composed. O yes, he seemed to say, death is stronger than I am.

Reading Critically

1. When Woolf says that the moth is at once "marvellous" and "pathetic," is her purpose to talk simply about a moth or about larger elements of life? Which elements of life? Discuss with your classmates.

2. Why, in the end, does Woolf think it useless to try to help the moth? What larger meaning does her decision have? Would you or your classmates have tried to help?

3. What is the "pity" that Woolf speaks about at the end of paragraph 3? Is this sentimental pity for an insect, or is it a larger emotion having to do with human life as well? How would you characterize that emotion?

4. Have you or your classmates had experiences similar to Woolf's? Has something mundane like a dancing moth ever moved you to think of larger realities, such as life and death? Specify what it was that made you think that way, and discuss with your classmates.

Responding Through Writing

1. What is Woolf talking about when she says (paragraph 2), "The same energy which inspired the rooks, the ploughmen, the horses, and even, it seemed, the lean bare-backed downs, sent the moth fluttering from side to side of his square of the windowpane"? In your notebook or journal, write two or three paragraphs explaining the meaning of this comment and invent other examples to extend and develop it.

2. Woolf was a very self-consciously precise writer, a writer of pointed detail and great economy of words. How do these characteristics show forth in the story? Copy at least three examples of precise writing from this essay and comment briefly on each.

3. Woolf, a meticulous writer, sometimes makes grammatical "errors," as when she says (paragraph 2), "Watching him, it seemed. . . ." Would you correct her? Find some other grammatical errors in this essay and write out the corrections. Do your corrections help or hurt?

4. Why does the following sentence stand out (paragraph 3)? "It was as if someone had taken a tiny bead of pure life and decking it as lightly as possible with down and feathers, had set it dancing and zigzagging to show us the true nature of life." Try to rewrite this sentence making it more concise. Does your effort help or hurt?

THE LADY WITH THE DOG

ANTON CHEKHOV

Anton Chekhov (1860–1904) was born in Taganrog, Russia, where his father had built a fairly successful business. Both of Chekhov's parents were simple, semieducated religious people who enrolled Chekhov in Moscow University's medical school so that he would receive a proper education. While he was a student, Chekhov often submitted short pieces to various humor magazines in the area. Upon graduation, Chekhov chose a literary career over medicine and soon wrote his first play, Ivanov *(1887). More plays followed, including* The Seagull *(1896),* Uncle Vanya *(1899), and* The Cherry Orchard *(1904), establishing Chekhov as one of the greatest dramatists of modern times. He also wrote hundreds of short stories, including "Vanka" (1886), "The Doctor's Visit" (1898), and "The Betrothed" (1902). The following story was first published in a Russian magazine called* Russkaia mysi' *in 1899.*

1   People were telling one another that a newcomer had been seen on the promenade—a lady with a dog. Dmitri Dmitrich Gurov had been a fortnight in Yalta, and was accustomed to its ways, and he, too, had begun to take an interest in fresh arrivals. From his seat in

Vernet's outdoor café, he caught sight of a young woman in a toque, passing along the promenade; she was fair and not very tall; after her trotted a white Pomeranian.

Later he encountered her in the municipal park and in the square several times a day. She was always alone, wearing the same toque, and the Pomeranian always trotted at her side. Nobody knew who she was, and people referred to her simply as "the lady with the dog." 2

"If she's here without her husband, and without any friends," thought Gurov, "it wouldn't be a bad idea to make her acquaintance." 3

He was not yet forty but had a twelve-year-old daughter and two sons in high school. He had been talked into marrying in his second year at college, and his wife now looked nearly twice as old as he did. She was a tall woman with dark eyebrows, erect, dignified, imposing, and, as she said of herself, a "thinker." She was a great reader, omitted the "hard sign" at the end of words in her letters, and called her husband "Dimitry" instead of Dmitry; and though he secretly considered her shallow, narrow-minded, and dowdy, he stood in awe of her, and disliked being at home. He had first begun deceiving her long ago and he was now constantly unfaithful to her, and this was no doubt why he spoke slightingly of women, to whom he referred as *the lower race*. 4

He considered that the ample lessons he had received from bitter experience entitled him to call them whatever he liked, but without this "lower race" he could not have existed a single day. He was bored and ill-at-ease in the company of men, with whom he was always cold and reserved, but felt quite at home among women, and knew exactly what to say to them, and how to behave; he could even be silent in their company without feeling the slightest awkwardness. There was an elusive charm in his appearance and disposition which attracted women and caught their sympathies. He knew this and was himself attracted to them by some invisible force. 5

Repeated and bitter experience had taught him that every fresh intimacy, while at first introducing such pleasant variety into everyday life, and offering itself as a charming, light adventure, inevitably developed, among decent people (especially in Moscow, where they are so irresolute and slow to move), into a problem of excessive complication leading to an intolerably irksome situation. But every time he encountered an attractive woman he forgot all about this experience, the desire for life surged up in him, and everything suddenly seemed simple and amusing. 6

One evening, then, while he was dining at the restaurant in 7 the park, the lady in the toque came strolling up and took a seat at a neighboring table. Her expression, gait, dress, coiffure, all told him that she was from the upper classes, that she was married, that she was in Yalta for the first time, alone and bored. . . . The accounts of the laxity of morals among visitors to Yalta are greatly exaggerated, and he paid no heed to them, knowing that for the most part they were invented by people who would gladly have transgressed themselves, had they known how to set about it. But when the lady sat down at a neighboring table a few yards away from him, these stories of easy conquests, of excursions to the mountains, came back to him, and the seductive idea of a brisk transitory liaison, an affair with a woman whose very name he did not know, suddenly took possession of his mind.

8   He snapped his fingers at the Pomeranian and, when it trotted up to him, shook his forefinger at it. The Pomeranian growled. Gurov shook his finger again.

9   The lady glanced at him and instantly lowered her eyes.

10   "He doesn't bite," she said, and blushed.

11   "May I give him a bone?" he asked, and on her nod of consent added in friendly tones: "Have you been long in Yalta?"

12   "About five days."

13   "And I am dragging out my second week here."

14   Neither spoke for a few minutes.

15   "The days pass quickly, and yet one is so bored here," she said, not looking at him.

16   "It's the thing to say it's boring here. People never complain of boredom in godforsaken holes like Belyev or Zhizdra, but when they get here it's: 'Oh, the dullness! Oh, the dust!' You'd think they'd come from Granada to say the least."

17   She laughed. Then they both went on eating in silence, like complete strangers. But after dinner they left the restaurant together, and embarked upon the light, jesting talk of people free and contented, for whom it is all the same where they go, or what they talk about. They strolled along, remarking on the strange light over the sea. The water was a warm, tender purple, the moonlight lay on its surface in a golden strip. They said how close it was, after the hot day. Gurov told her he was from Moscow, that he was really a philologist, but worked in a bank; that he had at one time trained himself to sing in a private opera company, but had given up the idea; that he owned two houses in Moscow. . . . And from her he learned that she had grown up in Petersburg, but had gotten married in the town of S., where she had been living two years, that she would stay another month in Yalta, and that perhaps her husband,

who also needed a rest, would join her. She was quite unable to explain whether her husband was a member of the province council, or on the board of the *zemstvo,* and was greatly amused at herself for this. Further, Gurov learned that her name was Anna Sergeyevna.

Back in his own room he thought about her, and felt sure he 18 would meet her the next day. It was inevitable. As he went to bed he reminded himself that only a very short time ago she had been a schoolgirl, like his own daughter, learning her lessons, he remembered how much there was of shyness and constraint in her laughter, in her way of conversing with a stranger—it was probably the first time in her life that she found herself alone, and in a situation in which men could follow her and watch her, and speak to her, all the time with a secret aim she could not fail to divine. He recalled her slender, delicate neck, her fine gray eyes.

"And yet there's something pathetic about her," he thought to 19 himself as he fell asleep.

II

A week had passed since the beginning of their acquaintance. 20 It was a holiday. Indoors it was stuffy, but the dust rose in clouds out of doors, and people's hats blew off. It was a parching day and Gurov kept going to the outdoor café for fruit drinks and ices to offer Anna Sergeyevna. The heat was overpowering.

In the evening, when the wind had dropped, they walked to 21 the pier to see the steamer come in. There were a great many people strolling about the landing-place; some, bunches of flowers in their hands, were meeting friends. Two peculiarities of the smart Yalta crowd stood out distinctly—the elderly ladies all tried to dress very youthfully, and there seemed to be an inordinate number of generals about.

Owing to the roughness of the sea the steamer arrived late, 22 after the sun had gone down, and it had to maneuver for some time before it could get alongside the pier. Anna Sergeyevna scanned the steamer and passengers through her lorgnette, as if looking for someone she knew, and when she turned to Gurov her eyes were glistening. She talked a great deal, firing off abrupt questions and forgetting immediately what it was she had wanted to know. Then she lost her lorgnette in the crush.

The smart crowd began dispersing, features could no longer 23 be made out, the wind had quite dropped, and Gurov and Anna Sergeyevna stood there as if waiting for someone else to come off the steamer. Anna Sergeyevna had fallen silent, every now and then smelling her flowers, but not looking at Gurov.

24   "It's turned out a fine evening," he said. "What shall we do? We might go for a drive."

25   She made no reply.

26   He looked steadily at her and suddenly took her in his arms and kissed her lips, and the fragrance and dampness of the flowers closed round him, but the next moment he looked behind him in alarm—had anyone seen them?

27   "Let's go to your room," he murmured.

28   And they walked off together, very quickly.

29   Her room was stuffy and smelt of some scent she had bought in the Japanese shop. Gurov looked at her, thinking to himself: "How full of strange encounters life is!" He could remember carefree, good-natured women who were exhilarated by love-making and grateful to him for the happiness he gave them, however short-lived; and there had been others—his wife among them—whose caresses were insincere, affected, hysterical, mixed up with a great deal of quite unnecessary talk, and whose expression seemed to say that all this was not just lovemaking or passion, but something much more significant; then there had been two or three beautiful, cold women, over whose features flitted a predatory expression, betraying a determination to wring from life more than it could give, women no longer in their first youth, capricious, irrational, despotic, brainless, and when Gurov had cooled to these, their beauty aroused in him nothing but repulsion, and the lace trimming on their underclothes reminded him of fish-scales.

30   But here the timidity and awkwardness of youth and inexperience were still apparent; and there was a feeling of embarrassment in the atmosphere, as if someone had just knocked at the door. Anna Sergeyevna, "the lady with the dog," seemed to regard the affair as something very special, very serious, as if she had become a fallen woman, an attitude he found odd and disconcerting. Her features lengthened and drooped, and her long hair hung mournfully on either side of her face. She assumed a pose of dismal meditation, like a repentant sinner in some classical painting.

31   "It isn't right," she said. "You will never respect me anymore."

32   On the table was a watermelon. Gurov cut himself a slice from it and began slowly eating it. At least half an hour passed in silence.

33   Anna Sergeyevna was very touching, revealing the purity of a decent, naïve woman who had seen very little of life. The solitary candle burning on the table scarcely lit up her face, but it was obvious that her heart was heavy.

"Why should I stop respecting you?" asked Gurov. "You   34
don't know what you're saying."

"May God forgive me!" she exclaimed, and her eyes filled   35
with tears. "It's terrible."

"No need to seek to justify yourself."   36

"How can I justify myself? I'm a wicked, fallen woman, I   37
despise myself and have not the least thought of self-justification.
It isn't my husband I have deceived, it's myself. And not only now,
I have been deceiving myself for ever so long. My husband is no
doubt an honest, worthy man, but he's a flunky. I don't know what
it is he does at his office, but I know he's a flunky. I was only twenty
when I married him, and I was devoured by curiosity, I wanted
something higher. I told myself that there must be a different kind
of life I wanted to live, to live. . . . I was burning with curiosity
. . . you'll never understand that, but I swear to God I could no
longer control myself, nothing could hold me back, I told my
husband I was ill, and I came here. . . . And I started going about
like one possessed, like a madwoman . . . and now I have become
an ordinary, worthless woman, and everyone has the right to despise
me."

Gurov listened to her, bored to death. The naïve accents, the   38
remorse, all was so unexpected, so out of place. But for the tears
in her eyes, she might have been jesting or play-acting.

"I don't understand," he said gently. "What is it you want?"   39

She hid her face against his breast and pressed closer to him.   40

"Do believe me, I implore you to believe me," she said. "I love   41
all that is honest and pure in life, vice is revolting to me, I don't
know what I'm doing. The common people say they are snared by
the Devil. And now I can say that I have been snared by the Devil,
too."

"Come, come," he murmured.   42

He gazed into her fixed, terrified eyes, kissed her, and soothed   43
her with gentle affectionate words, and gradually she calmed down
and regained her cheerfulness. Soon they were laughing together
again.

When, a little later, they went out, there was not a soul on   44
the promenade, the town and its cypresses looked dead, but the sea
was still roaring as it dashed against the beach. A solitary fishing-
boat tossed on the waves, its lamp blinking sleepily.

They found a carriage and drove to Oreanda.   45

"I discovered your name in the hall, just now," said Gurov,   46
"written up on the board. Von Diederitz. Is your husband a German?"

47 "No. His grandfather was, I think, but he belongs to the Orthodox Church himself."

48 When they got out of the carriage at Oreanda they sat down on a bench not far from the church, and looked down at the sea, without talking. Yalta could be dimly discerned through the morning mist, and white clouds rested motionless on the summits of the mountains. Not a leaf stirred, the grasshoppers chirruped, and the monotonous hollow roar of the sea came up to them, speaking of peace, of the eternal sleep lying in wait for us all. The sea had roared like this long before there was any Yalta or Oreanda, it was roaring now, and it would go on roaring, just as indifferently and hollowly, when we had passed away. And it may be that in this continuity, this utter indifference to life and death, lies the secret of our ultimate salvation, of the stream of life on our planet, and of its never-ceasing movement towards perfection.

49 Side by side with a young woman, who looked so exquisite in the early light, soothed and enchanted by the sight of all this magical beauty—sea, mountains, clouds and the vast expanse of the sky—Gurov told himself that, when you came to think of it, everything in the world is beautiful really, everything but our own thoughts and actions, when we lose sight of the higher aims of life, and of our dignity as human beings.

50 Someone approached them—a watchman, probably—looked at them and went away. And there was something mysterious and beautiful even in this. The steamer from Feodosia could be seen coming towards the pier, lit up by the dawn, its lamps out.

51 "There's dew on the grass," said Anna Sergeyevna, breaking the silence.

52 "Yes. Time to go home."

53 They went back to the town.

54 After this they met every day at noon on the promenade, lunching and dining together, going for walks, and admiring the sea. She complained of sleeplessness, of palpitations, asked the same questions over and over again, alternately surrendering to jealousy and the fear that he did not really respect her. And often, when there was nobody in sight in the square or the park, he would draw her to him and kiss her passionately. The utter idleness, these kisses in broad daylight, accompanied by furtive glances and the fear of discovery, the heat, the smell of the sea, and the idle, smart, well-fed people continually crossing their field of vision, seemed to have given him a new lease of life. He told Anna Sergeyevna she was beautiful and seductive, made love to her with impetuous passion, and never left her side, while she was always pensive, always trying

to force from him the admission that he did not respect her, that he did not love her a bit, and considered her just an ordinary woman. Almost every night they drove out of town, to Oreanda, the waterfall, or some other beauty-spot. And these excursions were invariably a success, each contributing fresh impressions of majestic beauty.

All this time they kept expecting her husband to arrive. But a letter came in which he told his wife that he was having trouble with his eyes, and implored her to come home as soon as possible. Anna Sergeyevna made hasty preparations for leaving.

"It's a good thing I'm going," she said to Gurov. "It's the intervention of fate."

She left Yalta in a carriage, and he went with her as far as the railway station. The drive took nearly a whole day. When she got into the express train, after the second bell had been rung, she said:

"Let me have one more look at you. . . . One last look. That's right."

She did not weep, but was mournful, and seemed ill, the muscles of her cheeks twitching.

"I shall think of you . . . I shall think of you all the time," she said. "God bless you! Think kindly of me. We are parting forever, it must be so, because we ought never to have met. Good-bye—God bless you."

The train steamed rapidly out of the station, its lights soon disappearing, and a minute later even the sound it made was silenced, as if everything were conspiring to bring this sweet oblivion, this madness, to an end as quickly as possible. And Gurov, standing alone on the platform and gazing into the dark distance, listened to the shrilling of the grasshoppers and the humming of the telegraph wires, with a feeling that he had only just awakened. And he told himself that this had been just one more of the many adventures in his life, and that it, too, was over, leaving nothing but a memory. . . . He was moved and sad, and felt a slight remorse. After all, this young woman whom he would never again see had not been really happy with him. He had been friendly and affectionate with her, but in his whole behaviour, in the tones of his voice, in his very caresses, there had been a shade of irony, the insulting indulgence of the fortunate male, who was, moreover, almost twice her age. She had insisted in calling him good, remarkable, high-minded. Evidently he had appeared to her different from his real self, in a word he had involuntarily deceived her. . . .

There was an autumnal feeling in the air, and the evening was chilly.

63   "It's time for me to be going north, too," thought Gurov, as he walked away from the platform. "High time!"

III

64   When he got back to Moscow it was beginning to look like winter; the stoves were heated every day, and it was still dark when the children got up to go to school and drank their tea, so that the nurse had to light the lamp for a short time. Frost had set in. When the first snow falls, and one goes for one's first sleigh-ride, it is pleasant to see the white ground, the white roofs; one breathes freely and lightly, and remembers the days of one's youth. The ancient lime-trees and birches, white with hoarfrost, have a good-natured look, they are closer to the heart than cypresses and palms, and beneath their branches one is no longer haunted by the memory of mountains and the sea.

65   Gurov had always lived in Moscow, and he returned to Moscow on a fine frosty day, and when he put on his fur-lined overcoat and thick gloves, and sauntered down Petrovka Street, and when, on Saturday evening, he heard the church bells ringing, his recent journey and the places he had visited lost their charm for him. He became gradually immersed in Moscow life, reading with avidity three newspapers a day, while declaring he never read Moscow newspapers on principle. Once more he was caught up in a whirl of restaurants, clubs, banquets, and celebrations, once more glowed with the flattering consciousness that well-known lawyers and actors came to his house, that he played cards in the Medical Club opposite a professor.

66   He had believed that in a month's time Anna Sergeyevna would be nothing but a vague memory, and that hereafter, with her wistful smile, she would only occasionally appear to him in dreams, like others before her. But the month was now well over and winter was in full swing, and all was as clear in his memory as if he had parted with Anna Sergeyevna only the day before. And his recollections grew ever more insistent. When the voices of his children at their lessons reached him in his study through the evening stillness, when he heard a song, or the sounds of a music-box in a restaurant, when the wind howled in the chimney, it all came back to him: early morning on the pier, the misty mountains, the steamer from Feodosia, the kisses. He would pace up and down his room for a long time, smiling at his memories, and then memory turned into dreaming, and what had happened mingled in his imagination with what was going to happen. Anna Sergeyevna did not come to him

in his dreams, she accompanied him everywhere, like his shadow, following him everywhere he went. When he closed his eyes, she seemed to stand before him in the flesh, still lovelier, younger, tenderer than she had really been, and looking back, he saw himself, too, as better than he had been in Yalta. In the evenings she looked out at him from the bookshelves, the fireplace, the corner, he could hear her breathing, the sweet rustle of her skirts. In the streets he followed women with his eyes, to see if there were any like her. . . .

He began to feel an overwhelming desire to share his memories 67 with someone. But he could not speak of his love at home, and outside his home who was there for him to confide in? Not the tenants living in his house, and certainly not his colleagues at the bank. And what was there to tell? Was it love that he had felt? Had there been anything exquisite, poetic, anything instructive or even amusing about his relations with Anna Sergeyevna? He had to content himself with uttering vague generalizations about love and women, and nobody guessed what he meant, though his wife's dark eyebrows twitched as she said:

"The role of a coxcomb doesn't suit you a bit, Dimitry." 68

One evening, leaving the Medical Club with one of his card- 69 partners, a government official, he could not refrain from remarking:

"If you only knew what a charming woman I met in Yalta!" 70

The official got into his sleigh, and just before driving off, 71 turned and called out:

"Dmitry Dmitrich!" 72

"Yes?" 73

"You were quite right, you know—the sturgeon was just a 74 *leetle* off."

These words, in themselves so commonplace, for some reason 75 infuriated Gurov, seemed to him humiliating, gross. What savage manners, what people! What wasted evenings, what tedious, empty days! Frantic card-playing, gluttony, drunkenness, perpetual talk always about the same thing. The greater part of one's time and energy went on business that was no use to anyone, and on discussing the same thing over and over again, and there was nothing to show for it all but a stunted, earth-bound existence and a round of trivialities, and there was nowhere to escape to, you might as well be in a madhouse or a convict settlement.

Gurov lay awake all night, raging, and went about the whole 76 of the next day with a headache. He slept badly on the succeeding nights, too, sitting up in bed, thinking, or pacing the floor of his room. He was sick of his children, sick of the bank, felt not the slightest desire to go anywhere or talk about anything.

77   When the Christmas holidays came, he packed his things, telling his wife he had to go to Petersburg in the interests of a certain young man, and set off for the town of S. To what end? He hardly knew himself. He only knew that he must see Anna Sergeyevna, must speak to her, arrange a meeting, if possible.

78   He arrived at S. in the morning and engaged the best suite in the hotel, which had a carpet of gray military frieze, and a dusty inkpot on the table, surmounted by a headless rider, holding his hat in his raised hand. The hall porter told him what he wanted to know: von Diederitz had a house of his own in Staro-Goncharnaya Street. It wasn't far from the hotel, he lived on a grand scale, luxuriously, kept carriage-horses, the whole town knew him. The hall porter pronounced the name "Drideritz."

79   Gurov strolled over to Staro-Goncharnaya Street and discovered the house. In front of it was a long gray fence with inverted nails hammered into the tops of the palings.

80   "A fence like that is enough to make anyone want to run away," thought Gurov, looking at the windows of the house and the fence.

81   He reasoned that since it was a holiday, Anna's husband would probably be at home. In any case it would be tactless to embarrass her by calling at the house. And a note might fall into the hands of the husband, and bring about catastrophe. The best thing would be to wait about on the chance of seeing her. And he walked up and down the street, hovering in the vicinity of the fence, watching for his chance. A beggar entered the gate, only to be attacked by dogs, then, an hour later, the faint, vague sounds of a piano reached his ears. That would be Anna Sergeyevna playing. Suddenly the front door opened and an old woman came out, followed by a familiar white Pomeranian. Gurov tried to call to it, but his heart beat violently, and in his agitation he could not remember its name.

82   He walked on, hating the gray fence more and more, and now ready to tell himself irately that Anna Sergeyevna had forgotten him, had already, perhaps, found distraction in another—what could be more natural in a young woman who had to look at this accursed fence from morning to night? He went back to his hotel and sat on the sofa in his suite for some time, not knowing what to do, then he ordered dinner, and after dinner, had a long sleep.

83   "What a foolish, restless business," he thought, waking up and looking towards the dark windowpanes. It was evening by now. "Well, I've had my sleep out. And what am I to do in the night?"

84   He sat up in bed, covered by the cheap gray quilt, which

reminded him of a hospital blanket, and in his vexation he fell to taunting himself.

"You and your lady with a dog . . . there's adventure for you! 85 See what you get for your pains."

On his arrival at the station that morning he had noticed a 86 poster announcing in enormous letters the first performance at the local theatre of *The Geisha*. Remembering this; he got up and made for the theatre.

"It's highly probable that she goes to first nights," he told 87 himself.

The theatre was full. It was a typical provincial theatre, with 88 a mist collecting over the chandeliers, and the crowd in the gallery fidgeting noisily. In the first row of the stalls the local dandies stood waiting for the curtain to go up, their hands clasped behind them. There, in the front seat of the governor's box, sat the governor's daughter, wearing a boa, the governor himself hiding modestly behind the drapes, so that only his hands were visible. The curtain stirred, the orchestra took a long time tuning up their instruments. Gurov's eyes roamed eagerly over the audience as they filed in and occupied their seats.

Anna Sergeyevna came in, too. She seated herself in the third 89 row of the stalls, and when Gurov's glance fell on her, his heart seemed to stop, and he knew in a flash that the whole world contained no one nearer or dearer to him, no one more important to his happiness. This little woman, lost in the provincial crowd, in no way remarkable, holding a silly lorgnette in her hand, now filled his whole life, was his grief, his joy, all that he desired. Lulled by the sounds coming from the wretched orchestra, with its feeble, amateurish violinists, he thought how beautiful she was . . . thought and dreamed. . . .

Anna Sergeyevna was accompanied by a tall, round-shoul- 90 dered young man with small whiskers, who nodded at every step before taking the seat beside her and seemed to be continually bowing to someone. This must be her husband, whom, in a fit of bitterness, at Yalta, she had called a "flunky." And there really was something of a lackey's servility in his lanky figure, his side-whisk- ers, and the little bald spot on the top of his head. And he smiled sweetly, and the badge of some scientific society gleaming in his buttonhole was like the number on a footman's livery.

The husband went out to smoke in the first interval, and she 91 was left alone in her seat. Gurov, who had taken a seat in the stalls, went up to her and said in a trembling voice, with a forced smile: "How d'you do?"

She glanced up at him and turned pale, then looked at him 92 again in alarm, unable to believe her eyes, squeezing her fan and lorgnette in one hand, evidently struggling to overcome a feeling of faintness. Neither of them said a word. She sat there, and he stood beside her, disconcerted by her embarrassment, and not daring to sit down. The violins and flutes sang out as they were tuned, and there was a tense sensation in the atmosphere, as if they were being watched from all the boxes. At last she got up and moved rapidly towards one of the exits. He followed her and they wandered aimlessly along corridors, up and down stairs; figures flashed by in the uniforms of legal officials, high-school teachers and civil servants, all wearing badges; ladies, coats hanging from pegs flashed by; there was a sharp draft, bringing with it an odor of cigarette butts. And Gurov, whose heart was beating violently, thought:

93   "What on earth are all these people, this orchestra for? . . ."

94   The next minute he suddenly remembered how, after seeing Anna Sergeyevna off that evening at the station, he had told himself that all was over, and they would never meet again. And how far away the end seemed to be now!

95   She stopped on a dark narrow staircase over which was a notice bearing the inscription "To the upper circle."

96   "How you frightened me!" she said, breathing heavily, still pale and half-stunned. "Oh, how you frightened me! I'm almost dead! Why did you come? Oh, why?"

97   "But, Anna," he said, in low, hasty tones. "But, Anna. . . . Try to understand . . . do try. . . ."

98   She cast him a glance of fear, entreaty, love, and then gazed at him steadily, as if to fix his features firmly in her memory.

99   "I've been so unhappy," she continued, taking no notice of his words. "I could think of nothing but you the whole time, I lived on the thoughts of you. I tried to forget—why, oh, why did you come?"

100   On the landing above them were two schoolboys, smoking and looking down, but Gurov did not care, and, drawing Anna Sergeyevna towards him, began kissing her face, her lips, her hands.

101   "What are you doing, oh, what are you doing?" she said in horror, drawing back. "We have both gone mad. Go away this very night, this moment. . . . By all that is sacred, I implore you. . . . Somebody is coming."

102   Someone was ascending the stairs.

103   "You must go away," went on Anna Sergeyevna in a whisper. "D'you hear me, Dmitry Dmitrich? I'll come to you in Moscow. I have never been happy, I am unhappy now, and I shall never be happy—never! Do not make me suffer still more! I will come to

you in Moscow, I swear it! And now we must part! My dear one, my kind one, my darling, we must part."

She pressed his hand and hurried down the stairs, looking back 104 at him continually, and her eyes showed that she was in truth unhappy. Gurov stood where he was for a short time, listening, and when all was quiet, went to look for his coat, and left the theatre.

IV

And Anna Sergeyevna began going to Moscow to see him. 105 Every two or three months she left the town of S., telling her husband that she was going to consult a specialist on female diseases, and her husband believed her and did not believe her. In Moscow she always stayed at the Slavyanski Bazaar, sending a man in a red cap to Gurov the moment she arrived. Gurov went to her, and no one in Moscow knew anything about it.

One winter morning he went to see her as usual (the messenger 106 had been to him the evening before, but had not found him at home). His daughter was with him, for her school was on the way and he thought he might as well see her to it.

"It is forty degrees," said Gurov to his daughter, "and yet it 107 is snowing. You see it is only above freezing close to the ground, the temperature in the upper layers of the atmosphere is quite different."

"Why doesn't it ever thunder in winter, Papa?" 108

He explained this, too. As he was speaking, he kept reminding 109 himself that he was going to a rendezvous and that not a living soul knew about it, or, probably, ever would. He led a double life—one in public, in the sight of all whom it concerned, full of conventional truth and conventional deception, exactly like the lives of his friends and acquaintances, and another which flowed in secret. And, owing to some strange, possibly quite accidental chain of circumstances, everything that was important, interesting, essential, everything about which he was sincere and never deceived himself, everything that composed the kernel of his life, went on in secret, while everything that was false in him, everything that composed the husk in which he hid himself and the truth which was in him—his work at the bank, discussions at the club, his "lower race," his attendance at anniversary celebrations with his wife—was on the surface. He began to judge others by himself, no longer believing what he saw, and always assuming that the real, the only interesting life of every individual goes on as under cover of night, secretly. Every individual existence revolves around mystery, and perhaps that is the chief reason that all cultivated individuals insisted so strongly on the respect due to personal secrets.

110   After leaving his daughter at the door of her school Gurov set off for the Slavyanski Bazaar. Taking off his overcoat in the lobby, he went upstairs and knocked softly on the door. Anna Sergeyevna, wearing the gray dress he liked most, exhausted by her journey and by suspense, had been expecting him since the evening before. She was pale and looked at him without smiling, but was in his arms almost before he was fairly in the room. Their kiss was lingering, prolonged, as if they had not met for years.

111   "Well, how are you?" he asked. "Anything new?"

112   "Wait, I'll tell you in a minute. . . . I can't. . . ."

113   She could not speak, because she was crying. Turning away, she held her handkerchief to her eyes.

114   "I'll wait till she's had her cry out," he thought, and sank into a chair.

115   He rang for tea, and a little later, while he was drinking it, she was still standing there, her face to the window. She wept from emotion, from her bitter consciousness of the sadness of their life; they could only see one another in secret, hiding from people, as if they were thieves. Was not their life a broken one?

116   "Don't cry," he said.

117   It was quite obvious to him that this love of theirs would not soon come to an end, and that no one could say when this end would be. Anna Sergeyevna loved him ever more fondly, worshipped him, and there would have been no point in telling her that one day it must end. Indeed, she would not have believed him.

118   He moved over and took her by the shoulders, intending to fondle her with light words, but suddenly he caught sight of himself in the looking-glass.

119   His hair was already beginning to turn gray. It struck him as strange that he should have aged so much in the last few years. The shoulders on which his hands lay were warm and quivering. He felt a pity for this life, still so warm and exquisite, but probably soon to fade and droop like his own. Why did she love him so? Women had always believed him different from what he really was, had loved in him not himself but the man their imagination pictured him, a man they had sought for eagerly all their lives. And afterwards when they discovered their mistake, they went on loving him just the same. And not one of them had ever been happy with him. Time had passed, he had met one woman after another, become intimate with each, parted with each, but had never loved. There had been all sorts of things between them, but never love.

And only now, when he was gray-haired, had he fallen in love   120
properly, thoroughly, for the first time in his life.

He and Anna Sergeyevna loved one another as people who are   121
very close and intimate, as husband and wife, as dear friends love
one another. It seemed to them that fate had intended them for one
another, and they could not understand why she should have a
husband, and he a wife. They were like two migrating birds, the
male and the female, who had been caught and put into separate
cages. They forgave one another all that they were ashamed of in
the past and in the present, and felt that this love of theirs had
changed them both.

Formerly, in moments of melancholy, he had consoled himself   122
by the first argument that came into his head, but now arguments
were nothing to him, he felt profound pity, desired to be sincere,
tender.

"Stop crying, my dearest," he said. "You've had your cry, now   123
stop. . . . Now let us have a talk, let us try and think what we are
to do."

Then they discussed their situation for a long time, trying to   124
think how they could get rid of the necessity for hiding, deception,
living in different towns, being so long without meeting. How were
they to shake off these intolerable fetters?

"How? How?" he repeated, clutching his head. "How?"   125

And it seemed to them that they were within an inch of   126
arriving at a decision, and that then a new, beautiful life would
begin. And they both realized that the end was still far, far away,
and that the hardest, the most complicated part was only just beginning.

Reading Critically

1. Are there any people in your world whose names you do
not know and who you identify with phrases such as "the lady with
the dog"? In your college neighborhood is there a resident "guy
who hangs around the coffee shop" or a "lady with the mink coat
and too much makeup"? Do you suspect that these people might
lead secret lives as interesting as Chekhov's characters? Discuss with

your classmates some of the possible scenarios in the lives of at least two such people.

2. Why does Gurov want to meet the lady (paragraph 2)? Have you ever deliberately gone up to a total stranger and introduced yourself? What were your motives? What was the outcome? In paragraph 7 we learn that Gurov especially likes the idea of having an affair with "a woman whose very name he did not know." Why does he want this anonymity? Discuss with your classmates.

3. Discuss Gurov's behavior toward the end of the story. Do you find his behavior unusual or strange (e.g., following women who look like Anna, waiting outside Anna's house for a glimpse of her), or do you find these actions normal and in line with what people often do? Have you ever done similar things yourself? What do you think of Anna's reaction to Gurov's reappearance? Is her reaction "normal"? Would you have reacted in the same way? Why? Discuss with your classmates.

4. Why do Anna and Gurov realize at the story's end that to continue their affair will be "hard" and "complicated"? In what ways are their lives going to change? Why can't they simply pick up where they left off? If there must come a point in most relationships where things become "hard," are romantic affairs "worth it"? Discuss with your classmates.

Responding Through Writing

1. Gurov finds constant refreshment in life through a string of romantic experiences, all of which quickly burn out (paragraph 6). In your private journal or notebook write for fifteen or twenty minutes on why such experiences often burn out and why, knowing this, people still tend to want those experiences.

2. Gurov classifies into several different categories the women with whom he has had affairs (paragraph 2). In your private note-

book or journal, develop a classifying scheme of your own for friends, family members, classmates, lovers, or other people with whom you have had close relationships.

3. Gurov begins to see his public life as an empty sham (paragraphs 75 and 109), no better than being in a "madhouse or a convict settlement." Write a draft of an essay reacting to this statement in terms of your own life.

4. Why does Anna look upon her act of adultery as an "accomplishment"? Randomly list certain *private* "accomplishments" of your own and then in your private notebook or journal develop a narrative in reaction to one of them.

THE EAGLE

ALFRED, LORD TENNYSON

Alfred, Lord Tennyson (1809–1892) achieved great contemporary acclaim for expressing the spirit of Victorian England. For years Tennyson declined the offer of Queen Victoria to name him to the nobility. In 1850 he succeeded Wordsworth as England's poet laureate, and in 1884 he finally accepted Queen Victoria's offer and became Alfred, Lord Tennyson. "Ulysses" is considered his greatest poem, but other poems like "In Memoriam" and "Morte d'Arthur" compete strongly. The following poem, "The Eagle," was first published in 1851, in the seventh edition of Poems, *which was originally published in 1842.*

Fragment

He clasps the crag with crooked hands;
Close to the sun in lonely lands,
Ringed with the azure world, he stands.
The wrinkled sea beneath him crawls:
He watches from his mountain walls,
And like a thunderbolt he falls.

Reading Critically

1. What comparison does Tennyson imply between the eagle and human beings? Discuss with your classmates.

2. What abstract values does the eagle symbolize? Might it symbolize different things to different readers? How might various audiences respond in differing ways to the poem? Specify some of those audiences and discuss their probable reactions.

3. What does this poem suggest about the values of the age in which it was written? How do those values, especially with respect to achievement and "nobility of the spirit," differ from those of our own age? Is Tennyson's vision of the world out of place in the twentieth century? Is he too serious and optimistic for us? Should a critical response to the poem include a little laughter? A little scorn? Why, specifically? Discuss with your classmates.

4. Tennyson uses odd phrases. He has the sea "crawl" and thunderbolts merely "fall." Why does Tennyson choose these words when they obviously do not reflect reality? Can you and your classmates substitute better words and phrases?

Responding Through Writing

1. Is the final note of the poem one of triumph or of warning? Discuss in a few brief paragraphs.

2. Is this a poem about motion? Rewrite the poem removing the images associated with motion. What is left?

3. Could the poem be continued? Try to continue it for ten lines. What problems does your continuation present?

4. Why is it often more difficult to understand short poems rather than longer ones? Pick some longer poem by Tennyson for comparison with "The Eagle" and write an essay in answer to this question.

PART III

PROCESS ANALYSIS

A *process* is a series of acts or operations designed to bring about a desired result. A common form of process in writing is the recipe. By presenting a series of operations, the writer of a recipe enables a reader to achieve a desired result—a chocolate cake, Texas-style chili, fried chicken, or apple pie.

Analysis is the systematic division of any complex whole into its component parts, or pieces. As a child, you may have wanted to find out just what made a toy run, so you took it apart, you analyzed it—much to the consternation of your parents.

Process analysis is thus the step-by-step explanation of how something happened, how something is made, or how to do something. By breaking down a complex whole into its constituent parts, you can analyze the process by which that whole was created. For example, the business pages of newspapers and news magazines are filled with articles that use process analysis to determine how the stock market functions, how inflation occurs and how to control it, or how unemployment is created and how to reduce it. In short, economists are engaging in process analysis—the division of a complex whole into its components to examine the series of acts that brought about the end result.

Newspapers are filled with process analysis. From the sports pages through the business pages to the editorial pages, you can find articles examining how the local football team lost the big game, how to select good stocks for investment, or how the police department plans to combat the recent increase in burglaries. Other articles in a newspaper, especially the Sunday edition, cover a wide range of "how-to" subjects—how to lose weight, find a mate or a job, achieve happiness, get over an unhappy love affair, ask for a raise, fix your car, paint your house, cook a goat. Process analysis abounds in magazines as well; in fact, there are magazines entirely devoted to how-to subjects. In some cities, there are bookstores that sell nothing but how-to books. We have, it seems, an almost insatiable appetite for process analysis. As many writers and editors have discovered, process-analysis writing sells.

Purpose of Process Analysis

The primary purpose of all process analysis is to convey information. It is important, therefore, that you have in mind the exact purpose of your process analysis before you write. If your purpose is to give directions on how to change a flat tire, you should provide clear step-by-step directions for accomplishing that task and omit advice on what kind of tire to buy to avoid flats. If you do not have your purpose clearly in mind before you begin to write, your essay may wander and provide your readers with neither the directions nor the information they expected.

Remember Your Audience

It is important that you give careful consideration to your audience before you begin to write process analysis. It is not enough that you know why you are writing your essay (purpose); you must clearly know to whom you are writing. Picture your readers and ask yourself what they do and do not know about the subject of your process analysis. For example, a recipe for Béarnaise sauce would have more or fewer explanations of terms and techniques, depending on whether it was written for an audience of experienced chefs or for a class of students just learning how to cook. You could not assume much background knowledge on the part of beginning students, so you would have to define almost all your terms and explain carefully the cooking instruments required. Your audience, then, greatly affects the kind of process analysis you write, so be sure to consider your audience carefully.

Planning the Process Essay

Once you have determined the purpose of and audience for your essay, you can begin to plan the essay itself. Before writing, think through the process in specific detail, step by step. Next, list the steps of the process separately and in order. Then, before going further, ask yourself whether there are any steps the reader should be warned about in advance. For example, in a recipe for apple pie, your reader should first be given a list of the ingredients and all preparatory instructions, such as heating the oven to the proper temperature. In giving directions for changing a flat tire, list the necessary tools at the beginning; the time to assemble tools is before tire changing begins, not in the middle of the job. You must help your reader plan ahead. Again, if there is special background your reader needs before starting to change a tire, you should provide it before beginning the steps of the process.

Once you have given the preparatory information and the steps in the process, determine whether you need to provide additional explanation of special terms, processes, or techniques. If you do need to define the term *fricassee,* for example, where will you place the definition—in the list at the beginning of the recipe, in a footnote, or incorporated in the body of the recipe itself? Whatever method you choose, you must give your audience the information it needs to understand your process analysis.

Next, examine your list of steps and consider whether any should be subdivided into two or more steps. Perhaps a substep or two needs to be added to a major step in the process. Be sure that you have not assumed too much knowledge on the part of your audience and that you have not required too much to be done in one step: "After cleaning, stuffing, sewing, roasting, and basting the turkey, remove it from the oven and prepare the gravy."

Use Examples to Illustrate

Wherever possible, you should use examples to illustrate your steps. If necessary, you might even use charts, diagrams, or pictures. You can also use comparisons to illustrate your steps. All these devices help your reader with more specific, concrete illustrations of the steps required in the process. To bind your steps together in your essay, you should use transitional words and phrases like *first, second, next, then, after,* and *finally.* In other words, give clear markers when you are ending one step or stage in the process and beginning the next one. Without these signposts, your audience can easily become lost and confused.

Revising Your Essay

Finally, when your essay is finished, read it through carefully and make any necessary revisions. You should also check your final draft against the set of steps you listed before you started writing. If you changed any of the steps in the final draft, be sure the changes clarified the process and did not confuse it.

You must think carefully and specifically about your process analysis. You must think about the purpose of your essay, your audience, and how your purpose and audience will affect organization, content, and presentation. Only through careful planning, adequate attention to all elements, and thoughtful revision will you write a good essay. Be sure you do not skip any steps; shortcuts only lead to a badly written essay.

As you read the essays in this section, look for the elements we have discussed. Read these essays as a writer. Ask yourself if you would have written a particular essay that way and what changes you might want to make. Look for the stages or steps in the analysis and determine whether they are clearly listed and are adequate. Note, too, whether any terms are undefined or any directions obscure or confusing. In short, examine each essay as if you had written it yourself, decide whether you would revise it in any way, and determine why you would or would not revise it. Evaluate each essay in this section in terms of purpose, audience, adequate steps in the use of examples and illustrations, and adequate signposts for the reader.

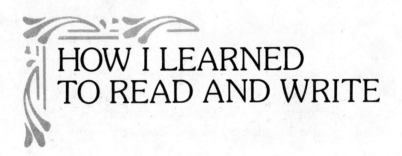

HOW I LEARNED
TO READ AND WRITE

FREDERICK DOUGLASS

Frederick Douglass (1817–1895) was born a slave in Talbot County, Maryland. In 1838 he escaped to the North, where he campaigned actively against slavery. After the Civil War, he became a leading figure in the campaign for black rights. He wrote three autobiographies at different times in his life. The first autobiography, and the most famous, is Narrative of the Life of Frederick Douglass, An American Slave, *published in Boston in 1875. Douglass wrote this autobiography when his experiences as a slave were still vivid in his memory. Ten years later he published* My Bondage and My Freedom, *and in 1881 he published* Life and Times of Frederick Douglass. *He served in a number of official offices, including secretary of the Santo Domingo Commission, marshal and recorder of the deeds of the District of Columbia, and minister of the United States to Haiti. The following excerpt is from his first autobiography.*

1   Very soon after I went to live with Mr. and Mrs. Auld, she very kindly commenced to teach me the A, B, C. After I had learned this, she assisted me in learning to spell words of three or four letters. Just at this point of my progress, Mr. Auld found out what was

going on, and at once forbade Mrs. Auld to instruct me further, telling her, among other things, that it was unlawful, as well as unsafe, to teach a slave to read. To use his own words, further, he said, "If you give a nigger an inch, he will take an ell. A nigger should know nothing but to obey his master—to do as he is told to do. Learning would *spoil* the best nigger in the world. Now," said he, "if you teach that nigger (speaking of myself) how to read, there would be no keeping him. It would forever unfit him to be a slave. He would at once become unmanageable, and of no value to his master. As to himself, it could do him no good, but a great deal of harm. It would make him discontented and unhappy." These words sank deep into my heart, stirred up sentiments within that lay slumbering, and called into existence an entirely new train of thought. It was a new and special revelation, explaining dark and mysterious things, with which my youthful understanding had struggled, but struggled in vain. I now understood what had been to me a most perplexing difficulty—to wit, the white man's power to enslave the black man. It was a grand achievement, and I prized it highly. From that moment, I understood the pathway from slavery to freedom. It was just what I wanted, and I got it at a time when I the least expected it. Whilst I was saddened by the thought of losing the aid of my kind mistress, I was gladdened by the invaluable instruction which, by the merest accident, I had gained from my master. Though conscious of the difficulty of learning without a teacher, I set out with high hope, and a fixed purpose, at whatever cost of trouble, to learn how to read. The very decided manner with which he spoke, and strove to impress his wife with the evil consequences of giving me instruction, served to convince me that he was deeply sensible of the truths he was uttering. It gave me the best assurance that I might rely with the utmost confidence on the results which, he said, would flow from teaching me to read. What he most dreaded, that I most desired. What he most loved, that I most hated. That which to him was a great evil, to be carefully shunned, was to me a great good, to be diligently sought; and the argument which he so warmly urged, against my learning to read, only served to inspire me with a desire and determination to learn. In learning to read, I owe almost as much to the bitter opposition of my master, as to the kindly aid of my mistress. I acknowledge the benefit of both. . . .

   I lived in Master Hugh's family about seven years. During this time, I succeeded in learning to read and write. In accomplishing this, I was compelled to resort to various stratagems. I had no regular teacher. My mistress, who had kindly commenced to instruct me, had, in compliance with the advice and direction of her husband, not only ceased to instruct, but had set her face against my being instructed by any one else. It is due, however, to my mistress to say of her, that she did not adopt this course of treatment immediately. She at first lacked the depravity indispensable to shutting me up in mental darkness. It was at least necessary for her to have some training in the exercise of irresponsible power, to make her equal to the task of treating me as though I were a brute.

3   My mistress was, as I have said, a kind and tender-hearted woman; and in the simplicity of her soul she commenced, when I first went to live with her, to treat me as she supposed one human being ought to treat another. In entering upon the duties of a slaveholder, she did not seem to perceive that I sustained to her the relation of a mere chattel, and that for her to treat me as a human being was not only wrong, but dangerously so. Slavery proved as injurious to her as it did to me. When I went there, she was a pious, warm, and tender-hearted woman. There was no sorrow or suffering for which she had not a tear. She had bread for the hungry, clothes for the naked, and comfort for every mourner that came within her reach. Slavery soon proved its ability to divest her of these heavenly qualities. Under its influence, the tender heart became stone, and the lamblike disposition gave way to one of tiger-like fierceness. The first step in her downward course was in her ceasing to instruct me. She now commenced to practise her husband's precepts. She finally became even more violent in her opposition than her husband himself. She was not satisfied with simply doing as well as he had commanded; she seemed anxious to do better. Nothing seemed to make her more angry than to see me with a newspaper. She seemed to think that here lay the danger. I have had her rush at me with a face made all up of fury, and snatch from me a newspaper, in a manner that fully revealed her apprehension. She was an apt woman; and a little experience soon demonstrated, to her satisfaction, that education and slavery were incompatible with each other.

4   From this time I was most narrowly watched. If I was in a separate room any considerable length of time, I was sure to be suspected of having a book, and was at once called to give an account of myself. All this, however, was too late. The first step had been taken. Mistress, in teaching me the alphabet, had given me the *inch,* and no precaution could prevent me from taking the *ell.*

5   The plan which I adopted, and the one by which I was most successful, was that of making friends of all the little white boys whom I met in the street. As many of these as I could, I converted into teachers. With their kindly aid, obtained at different times and

in different places, I finally succeeded in learning to read. When I was sent on errands, I always took my book with me, and by going one part of my errand quickly, I found time to get a lesson before my return. I used also to carry bread with me, enough of which was always in the house, and to which I was always welcome; for I was much better off in this regard than many of the poor white children in our neighborhood. This bread I used to bestow upon the hungry little urchins, who, in return, would give me that more valuable bread of knowledge. I am strongly tempted to give the names of two or three of those little boys, as a testimonial of the gratitude and affection I bear them; but prudence forbids;—not that it would injure me, but it might embarrass them; for it is almost an unpardonable offence to teach slaves to read in this Christian country. It is enough to say of the dear little fellows, that they lived on Philpot Street, very near Durgin and Bailey's shipyard. I used to talk this matter of slavery over with them. I would sometimes say to them, I wished I could be as free as they would be when they got to be men. "You will be free as soon as you are twenty-one, *but I am a slave for life!* Have not I as good a right to be free as you have?" These words used to trouble them; they would express for me the liveliest sympathy, and console me with the hope that something would occur by which I might be free.

I was now about twelve years old, and the thought of being *a slave for life* began to bear heavily upon my heart. Just about this time, I got hold of a book entitled "The Columbian Orator." Every opportunity I got, I used to read this book. Among much of other interesting matter, I found in it a dialogue between a master and his slave. The slave was represented as having run away from his master three times. The dialogue represented the conversation which took place between them, when the slave was retaken the third time. In this dialogue, the whole argument in behalf of slavery was brought forward by the master, all of which was disposed of by the slave. The slave was made to say some very smart as well as impressive things in reply to his master—things which had the desired though unexpected effect; for the conversation resulted in the voluntary emancipation of the slave on the part of the master.

In the same book, I met with one of Sheridan's mighty speeches on and in behalf of Catholic emancipation. These were choice documents to me. I read them over and over again with unabated interest. They gave tongue to interesting thoughts of my own soul, which had frequently flashed through my mind, and died away for want of utterance. The moral which I gained from the dialogue was the power of truth over the conscience of even a slaveholder. What I got from Sheridan was a bold denunciation of slavery, and a powerful vindication of human rights. The reading of these documents enabled me to utter my thoughts, and to meet the arguments brought forward to sustain slavery; but while they relieved me of one difficulty, they brought on another even more painful than the one of which I was relieved. The more I read, the more I was led to abhor and detest my enslavers. I could regard them in no other light than a band of successful robbers, who had left their homes, and gone to Africa, and stolen us from our homes, and in a strange land reduced us to slavery. I loathed them as being the meanest as well as the most wicked of men. As I read and contemplated the subject, behold! that very discontentment which Master Hugh had predicted would follow my learning to read had already come, to torment and sting my soul to unutterable anguish. As I writhed under it, I would at times feel that learning to read had been a curse rather than a blessing. It had given me a view of my wretched condition, without the remedy. It opened my eyes to the horrible pit, but to no ladder upon which to get out. In moments of agony, I envied my fellow-slaves for their stupidity. I have often wished myself a beast. I preferred the condition of the meanest reptile to my own. Any thing, no matter what, to get rid of thinking! It was this everlasting thinking of my condition that tormented me. There was no getting rid of it. It was pressed upon me by every object within sight or hearing, animate or inanimate. The silver trump of freedom had roused my soul to eternal wakefulness. Freedom now appeared, to disappear no more forever. It was heard in every sound, and seen in every thing. It was ever present to torment me with a sense of my wretched condition. I saw nothing without seeing it, I heard nothing without hearing it, and felt nothing without feeling it. It looked from every star, it smiled in every calm, breathed in every wind, and moved in every storm.

8   I often found myself regretting my own existence, and wishing myself dead; and but for the hope of being free, I have no doubt but that I should have killed myself, or done something for which I should have been killed. While in this state of mind, I was eager to hear any one speak of slavery. I was a ready listener. Every little while, I could hear something about the abolitionists. It was some time before I found what the word meant. It was always used in such connections as to make it an interesting word to me. If a slave ran away and succeeded in getting clear, or if a slave killed his master, set fire to a barn, or did any thing very wrong in the mind of a slaveholder, it was spoken of as the fruit of *abolition*. Hearing the word in this connection very often, I set about learning what

it meant. The dictionary afforded me little or no help. I found it was "the act of abolishing"; but then I did not know what was to be abolished. Here I was perplexed. I did not dare to ask any one about its meaning, for I was satisfied that it was something they wanted me to know very little about. After a patient waiting, I got one of our city papers, containing an account of the number of petitions from the north, praying for the abolition of slavery in the District of Columbia, and of the slave trade between the States. From this time I understood the words *abolition* and *abolitionist,* and always drew near when that word was spoken, expecting to hear something of importance to myself and fellow-slaves. The light broke in upon me by degrees. I went one day down on the wharf of Mr. Waters; and seeing two Irishmen unloading a scow of stone, I went, unasked, and helped them. When we had finished, one of them came to me and asked, "Are ye a slave for life?" I told him that I was. The good Irishman seemed to be deeply affected by the statement. He said to the other that it was a pity so fine a little fellow as myself should be a slave for life. He said it was a shame to hold me. They both advised me to run away to the north; that I should find friends there, and that I should be free. I pretended not to be interested in what they said, and treated them as if I did not understand them; for I feared they might be treacherous. White men have been known to encourage slaves to escape, and then, to get the reward, catch them and return them to their masters. I was afraid that these seemingly good men might use me so; but I nevertheless remembered their advice, and from that time I resolved to run away. I looked forward to a time at which it would be safe for me to escape. I was too young to think of doing so immediately; besides, I wished to learn how to write, as I might have occasion to write my own pass. I consoled myself with the hope that I should one day find a good chance. Meanwhile, I would learn to write.

The idea as to how I might learn to write was suggested to me by being in Durgin and Bailey's ship-yard, and frequently seeing the ship carpenters, after hewing, and getting a piece of timber ready for use, write on the timber the name of that part of the ship for which it was intended. When a piece of timber was intended for the larboard side, it would be marked thus—"L." When a piece was for the starboard side, it would be marked thus—"S." A piece for the larboard side forward, would be marked thus—"L. F." When a piece was for starboard side forward, it would be marked thus —"S. F." For larboard aft, it would be marked thus—"L. A." For starboard aft, it would be marked thus—"S. A." I soon learned the names of these letters, and for what they were intended when placed upon a piece of timber in the ship-yard. I immediately commenced copying them, and in a short time was able to make the four letters named. After that, when I met with any boy who I knew could write, I would tell him I could write as well as he. The next word would be, "I don't believe you. Let me see you try it." I would then make the letters which I had been so fortunate as to learn, and ask him to beat that. In this way I got a good many lessons in writing, which it is quite possible I should never have gotten in any other way. During this time, my copy-book was the board fence, brick wall, and pavement; my pen and ink was a lump of chalk. With these, I learned mainly how to write. I then commenced and continued copying the Italics in Webster's Spelling Book, until I could make them all without looking on the book. By this time, my little Master Thomas had gone to school, and learned how to write, and had written over a number of copy-books. These had been brought home, and shown to some of our near neighbors, and then laid aside. My mistress used to go to class meeting at the Wilk Street meeting-house every Monday afternoon, and leave me to take care of the house. When left thus, I used to spend this time writing in the spaces left in Master Thomas's copy-book, copying what he had written. I continued to do this until I could write a hand very similar to that of Master Thomas. Thus, after a long, tedious effort for years, I finally succeeded in learning how to write.

Reading Critically

1. Why do you think it was illegal to teach slaves to read and write? What does such a law suggest about the nature of slavery and also about the benefits the ability to read and write gives an individual? What does Douglass mean in paragraph 1 when he says that "from that moment, I understood the pathway from slavery to freedom"? How could knowing how to read and write help set Douglass free?

2. Look up the word *abolition* and find out what this word meant in relation to slavery in Douglass's day. Why does Douglass

find little help in the dictionary when he looks up *abolition?* What was an *abolitionist* in his day?

3. What was Douglass's chief purpose in learning to read and write? Before you answer, consider the implicit comments on slaves, slavery, and learning that Douglass makes and the judgments about slaveholders he makes. Discuss your reaction with your classmates.

4. Look up information on slavery in an encyclopedia or similar reference book and prepare a report that includes such information as how long slavery was practiced in the United States, how many slaves there were in the United States at any given time, and in what ways a slave could become a free person. Discuss your report with your classmates.

Responding Through Writing

1. Given his experiences as a slave, you might expect Douglass to be angry and outraged, but clearly he is not. How would you characterize the tone of his autobiography? What restraint in tone does Douglass exercise? What does this tone contribute to the purpose of his autobiography? Choose one paragraph in this selection and rewrite it with a tone of anger or outrage. Then discuss your paragraph with your classmates. What does the change in tone contribute to the selection? What does it take away from it?

2. How does Douglass learn to write the alphabet? How does he learn to write sentences? Except for only the most basic help, Douglass essentially taught himself to read and write. Does this mean that he was an exceptionally intelligent man, or might it suggest something about how motivation influences any person who wants to learn? If you are keeping a journal or a notebook in this course, write in it for five to ten minutes about a time you learned something on your own. Discuss why you learned it, how difficult it was to learn, and what you gained from the experience.

3. Douglass wrote his autobiography over 100 years ago. For whom did Douglass write his autobiography, the general public or a more specific audience? Cite evidence from this selection to support your answer. Write a paragraph in which you describe Douglass's audience, especially on the basis of what Douglass thought his audience knew and did not know about slavery, and the condition and treatment of slaves.

4. In addition to chronological order, how has Douglass organized his essay? Suggest one other way Douglass could have organized his essay, and then write an introductory paragraph for it in which you introduce that principle of organization. In what ways is your proposed pattern of organization more effective or less effective than Douglass's?

ON KEEPING
A NOTEBOOK

JOAN DIDION

Essayist, novelist, journalist, playwright, and screenwriter, Joan Didion (b. 1934) has been praised for her "surgical prose." A graduate of the University of California at Berkeley, Didion has become famous for her interior monologues and observations of social relationships. Her most famous collections of essays are Slouching Towards Bethlehem *(1968) and* The White Album *(1979). Author of several novels, Didion has also written two nonfiction books,* Salvador *(1983) and* Miami *(1987), which detail the social conditions in those respective locales. With her husband, John Gregory Dunne, Didion has cowritten four screenplays, the most famous of which is* A Star Is Born *(1976). The following essay first appeared in* Holiday *magazine in 1966.*

" 'That woman Estelle,' " the note reads, " 'is partly the reason 1
why George Sharp and I are separated today.' *Dirty crepe-de-Chine
wrapper, hotel bar, Wilmington RR, 9:45 a.m. August Monday morning.*"

Since the note is in my notebook, it presumably has some 2
meaning to me. I study it for a long while. At first I have only the
most general notion of what I was doing on an August Monday

morning in the bar of the hotel across from the Pennsylvania Railroad station in Wilmington, Delaware (waiting for a train? missing one? 1960? 1961? why Wilmington?), but I do remember being there. The woman in the dirty crepe-de-Chine wrapper had come down from her room for a beer, and the bartender had heard before the reason why George Sharp and she were separated today. "Sure," he said, and went on mopping the floor, "You told me." At the other end of the bar is a girl. She is talking, pointedly, not to the man beside her but to a cat lying in the triangle of sunlight cast through the open door. She is wearing a plaid silk dress from Peck & Peck, and the hem is coming down.

3   Here is what it is: the girl has been on the Eastern Shore, and now she is going back to the city, leaving the man beside her, and all she can see ahead are the viscous summer sidewalks and the 3 A.M. long-distance calls that will make her lie awake and then sleep drugged through all the steaming mornings left in August (1960? 1961?). Because she must go directly from the train to lunch in New York, she wishes that she had a safety pin for the hem of the plaid silk dress, and she also wishes that she could forget about the hem and the lunch and stay in the cool bar that smells of disinfectant and malt and make friends with the woman in the crepe-de-Chine wrapper. She is afflicted by a little self-pity, and she wants to compare Estelles. That is what that was all about.

4   Why did I write it down? In order to remember, of course, but exactly what was it I wanted to remember? How much of it actually happened? Did any of it? Why do I keep a notebook at all? It is easy to deceive oneself on all those scores. The impulse to write things down is a peculiarly compulsive one, inexplicable to those who do not share it, useful only accidentally, only secondarily, in the way that any compulsion tries to justify itself. I suppose that it begins or does not begin in the cradle. Although I have felt compelled to write things down since I was five years old, I doubt that my daughter ever will, for she is a singularly blessed and accepting child, delighted with life exactly as life presents itself to her, unafraid to go to sleep and and unafraid to wake up. Keepers of private notebooks are a different breed altogether, lonely and resistant rearrangers of things, anxious malcontents, children afflicted apparently at birth with some presentiment of loss.

5   My first notebook was a Big Five tablet, given to me by my mother with the sensible suggestion that I stop whining and learn to amuse myself by writing down my thoughts. She returned the tablet to me a few years ago; the first entry is an account of a woman who believed herself to be freezing to death in the Arctic night, only

to find, when day broke, that she had stumbled onto the Sahara Desert, where she would die of the heat before lunch. I have no idea what turn of a five-year-old's mind could have prompted so insistently "ironic" and exotic a story, but it does reveal a certain predilection for the extreme which has dogged me into adult life; perhaps if I were analytically inclined I would find it a truer story than any I might have told about Donald Johnson's birthday party or the day my cousin Brenda put Kitty Litter in the Aquarium.

So the point of my keeping a notebook has never been, nor   6
is it now, to have an accurate factual record of what I have been doing or thinking. That would be a different impulse entirely, an instinct for reality which I sometimes envy but do not possess. At no point have I ever been able successfully to keep a diary; my approach to daily life ranges from the grossly negligent to the merely absent, and on those few occasions when I have tried dutifully to record a day's events, boredom has so overcome me that the results are mysterious at best. What is this business about "shopping, typing piece, dinner with E, depressed"? Shopping for what? Typing what piece? Who is E? Was this "E" depressed, or was I depressed? Who cares?

In fact I have abandoned altogether that kind of pointless   7
entry; instead I tell what some would call lies. "That's simply not true," the members of my family frequently tell me when they come up against my memory of a shared event. "The party was *not* for you, the spider was *not* a black widow, *it wasn't that way at all.*" Very likely they are right, for not only have I always had trouble distinguishing between what happened and what merely might have happened, but I remain unconvinced that the distinction, for my purposes, matters. The cracked crab that I recall having for lunch the day my father came home from Detroit in 1945 must certainly be embroidery, worked into the day's pattern to lend verisimilitude; I was ten years old and would not now remember the cracked crab. The day's events did not turn on cracked crab. And yet it is precisely that fictitious crab that makes me see the afternoon all over again, a home movie run all too often, the father bearing gifts, the child weeping, an exercise in family love and guilt. Or that is what it was to me. Similarly, perhaps it never did snow that August in Vermont; perhaps there never were flurries in the night wind, and maybe no one else felt the ground hardening and summer already dead even as we pretended to bask in it, but that was how it felt to me, and it might as well have snowed, could have snowed, did snow.

How it felt to me: that is getting closer to the truth about a   8
notebook. I sometimes delude myself about why I keep a notebook,

imagine that some thrifty virtue derives from preserving everything observed. See enough and write it down, I tell myself, and then some morning when the world seems drained of wonder, some day when I am only going through the motions of doing what I am supposed to do, which is write—on that bankrupt morning I will simply open my notebook and there it will all be, a forgotten account with accumulated interest, paid passage back to the world out there: dialogue overheard in hotels and elevators and at the hat-check counter in Pavillon (one middle-aged man shows his hat check to another and says, "That's my old football number"); impressions of Bettina Aptheker and Benjamin Sonnenberg and Teddy ("Mr. Acapulco") Stauffer; careful *aperçus* about tennis bums and failed fashion models and Greek shipping heiresses, one of whom taught me a significant lesson (a lesson I could have learned from F. Scott Fitzgerald, but perhaps we all must meet the very rich for ourselves) by asking, when I arrived to interview her in her orchid-filled sitting room on the second day of a paralyzing New York blizzard, whether it was snowing outside.

9   I imagine, in other words, that the notebook is about other people. But of course it is not. I have no real business with what one stranger said to another at the hat-check counter in Pavillon; in fact I suspect that the line "That's my old football number" touched not my own imagination at all, but merely some memory of something once read, probably "The Eighty-Yard Run." Nor is my concern with a woman in a dirty crepe-de-Chine wrapper in a Wilmington bar. My stake is always, of course, in the unmentioned girl in the plaid silk dress. *Remember what it was to be me:* that is always the point.

10   It is a difficult point to admit. We are brought up in the ethic that others, any others, all others, are by definition more interesting than ourselves; taught to be diffident, just this side of self-effacing. ("You're the least important person in the room and don't forget it," Jessica Mitford's governess would hiss in her ear on the advent of any social occasion; I copied that into my notebook because it is only recently that I have been able to enter a room without hearing some such phrase in my inner ear.) Only the very young and the very old may recount their dreams at breakfast, dwell upon self, interrupt with memories of beach picnics and favorite Liberty lawn dresses and the rainbow trout in a creek near Colorado Springs. The rest of us are expected, rightly, to affect absorption in other people's favorite dresses, other people's trout.

11   And so we do. But our notebooks give us away, for how-

ever dutifully we record what we see around us, the common denominator of all we see is always, transparently, shamelessly, the implacable "I." We are not talking here about the kind of notebook that is patently for public consumption, a structural conceit for binding together a series of graceful *pensées;* we are talking about something private, about bits of the mind's string too short to use, an indiscriminate and erratic assemblage with meaning only for its maker.

And sometimes even the maker has difficulty with the meaning. There does not seem to be, for example, any point in my knowing for the rest of my life that, during 1964, 720 tons of soot fell on every square mile of New York City, yet there it is in my notebook, labeled "FACT." Nor do I really need to remember that Ambrose Bierce liked to spell Leland Stanford's name "£eland $tanford" or that "smart women almost always wear black in Cuba," a fashion hint without much potential for practical application. And does not the relevance of these notes seem marginal at best?:

> In the basement museum of the Inyo County Courthouse in Independence, California, sign pinned to a mandarin coat: "This MANDARIN COAT was often worn by Mrs. Minnie S. Brooks when giving lectures on her TEAPOT COLLECTION."

> Redhead getting out of car in front of Beverly Wilshire Hotel, chinchilla stole, Vuitton bags with tags reading:
>
> MRS LOU FOX
> HOTEL SAHARA
> VEGAS

Well, perhaps not entirely marginal. As a matter of fact, Mrs. Minnie S. Brooks and her MANDARIN COAT pull me back into my own childhood, for although I never knew Mrs. Brooks and did not visit Inyo County until I was thirty, I grew up in just such a world, in houses cluttered with Indian relics and bits of gold ore and ambergris and the souvenirs my Aunt Mercy Farnsworth brought back from the Orient. It is a long way from that world to Mrs. Lou Fox's world, where we all live now, and is it not just as well to remember that? Might not Mrs. Minnie S. Brooks help me to remember what I am? Might not Mrs. Lou Fox help me to remember what I am not?

14   But sometimes the point is harder to discern. What exactly did I have in mind when I noted down that it cost the father of someone I know $650 a month to light the place on the Hudson in which he lived before the Crash? What use was I planning to make of this line by Jimmy Hoffa: "I may have my faults, but being wrong ain't one of them"? And although I think it interesting to know where the girls who travel with the Syndicate have their hair done when they find themselves on the West Coast, will I ever make suitable use of it? Might I not be better off just passing it on to John O'Hara? What is a recipe for sauerkraut doing in my notebook? What kind of magpie keeps this notebook? *"He was born the night the Titanic went down."* That seems a nice enough line, and I even recall who said it, but is it not really a better line in life than it could ever be in fiction?

15   But of course that is exactly it: not that I should ever use the line, but that I should remember the woman who said it and the afternoon I heard it. We were on her terrace by the sea, and we were finishing the wine left from lunch, trying to get what sun there was, a California winter sun. The woman whose husband was born the night the *Titanic* went down wanted to rent her house, wanted to go back to her children in Paris. I remember wishing that I could afford the house, which cost $1,000 a month. "Someday you will," she said lazily. "Someday it all comes." There in the sun on her terrace it seemed easy to believe in someday, but later I had a low-grade afternoon hangover and ran over a black snake on the way to the supermarket and was flooded with inexplicable fear when I heard the checkout clerk explaining to the man ahead of me why she was finally divorcing her husband. "He left me no choice," she said over and over as she punched the register. "He has a little seven-month-old baby by her, he left me no choice." I would like to believe that my dread then was for the human condition, but of course it was for me, because I wanted a baby and did not then have one and because I wanted to own the house that cost $1,000 a month to rent and because I had a hangover.

16   It all comes back. Perhaps it is difficult to see the value in having one's self back in that kind of mood, but I do see it; I think we are well advised to keep on nodding terms with the people we used to be, whether we find them attractive company or not. Otherwise they turn up unannounced and surprise us, come hammering on the mind's door at 4 A.M. of a bad night and demand to

know who deserted them, who betrayed them, who is going to make amends. We forget all too soon the things we thought we could never forget. We forget the loves and the betrayals alike, forget what we whispered and what we screamed, forget who we were. I have already lost touch with a couple of people I used to be; one of them, a seventeen-year-old, presents little threat, although it would be of some interest to me to know again what it feels like to sit on a river levee drinking vodka-and-orange-juice and listening to Les Paul and Mary Ford and their echoes sing "How High the Moon" on the car radio. (You see I still have the scenes, but I no longer perceive myself among those present, no longer could even improvise the dialogue.) The other one, a twenty-three-year-old, bothers me more. She was always a good deal of trouble, and I suspect she will reappear when I least want to see her, skirts too long, shy to the point of aggravation, always the injured party, full of recriminations and little hurts and stories I do not want to hear again, at once saddening me and angering me with her vulnerability and ignorance, an apparition all the more insistent for being so long banished.

It is a good idea, then, to keep in touch, and I suppose that 17 keeping in touch is what notebooks are all about. And we are all on our own when it comes to keeping those lines open to ourselves: your notebook will never help me, nor mine you. *"So what's new in the whiskey business?"* What could that possibly mean to you? To me it means a blonde in a Pucci bathing suit sitting with a couple of fat men by the pool at the Beverly Hills Hotel. Another man approaches, and they all regard one another in silence for a while. "So what's new in the whiskey business?" one of the fat men finally says by way of welcome, and the blonde stands up, arches one foot and dips it in the pool, looking all the while at the cabaña where Baby Pignatari is talking on the telephone. That is all there is to that, except that several years later I saw the blonde coming out of Saks Fifth Avenue in New York with her California complexion and a voluminous mink coat. In the harsh wind that day she looked old and irrevocably tired to me, and even the skins in the mink coat were not worked the way they were doing them that year, not the way she would have wanted them done, and there is the point of the story. For a while after that I did not like to look in the mirror, and my eyes would skim the newspapers and pick out only the deaths, the cancer victims, the premature coronaries, the suicides, and I stopped riding the Lexington Avenue IRT because I noticed for the first time that all the strangers I had seen for years—the man with the seeing-eye dog, the spinster who read the classified pages every day, the fat girl who always got off with me at Grand Central—looked older than they once had.

18   It all comes back. Even that recipe for sauerkraut: even that brings it back. I was on Fire Island when I first made that sauerkraut, and it was raining, and we drank a lot of bourbon and ate the sauerkraut and went to bed at ten, and I listened to the rain and the Atlantic and felt safe. I made the sauerkraut again last night and it did not make me feel any safer, but that is, as they say, another story.

Reading Critically

1. Why is the story about the woman who wakes up in the Sahara Desert a better notebook entry than "Donald Johnson's birthday party or the day my cousin Brenda put Kitty Litter in the Aquarium"? What general point is Didion trying to make about the craft of writing by using these examples? Discuss with your classmates.

2. If you are confused or a bit put off by the first four paragraphs, be patient until you finish paragraph 9 and realize who the girl in the plaid silk dress is. In this connection, why can keeping a journal help you remember "what it was to be me"? Do you wish you had kept a journal during your high school years? How would that journal have helped you "remember what it was to be me"?

3. Carry your notebook or journal with you for three days and note "facts" you observe or read about, as Didion does in paragraphs 11–15. What does your assembled collection of three day's worth of "facts" say about yourself and your perceptions? Discuss with your classmates.

4. What good advice have you gleaned from Didion on the subject of keeping a notebook or journal? Discuss with your classmates.

Responding Through Writing

1. As an experiment, fill at least two pages of your private notebook or journal every day, alternating days between "facts" and "imagination." On "fact" days try to stick to literal descriptions of what you do and observe. On the other days use your actions and observations as springboards for imaginative—or argumentative—writing. What did you learn from this experiment about the dividing line between "facts" and imagination?

2. Try for a period of at least three days to fill your notebook or journal with nothing but "lies," as Didion does in paragraph 3. What does this experiment tell you about the nature of writing?

3. Consult any edition of the Wednesday *New York Times* and read the "Metropolitan Diary" column on page 2 of the Living Section. Almost all "Metropolitan Diary" columns contain pieces of overheard dialogue. Using these pieces as your cue, write up at least five pieces of overheard dialogue in your notebook or journal.

4. Let a few weeks go by; then go back to question 1 and reread the lists of "facts" you developed in response to that question. Pick the four or five facts that evoke memories for you, and write a few paragraphs on each (see Didion's paragraphs 17 and 18).

STICKY FINGERS

DAVID FINKLE

David Finkle is a free-lance writer who lives and works in New York. In addition to frequent book reviews for the New York Times *and the* New York Times Book Review, *he also writes on a great variety of subjects for publications including* Variety *and* New York Woman. *Often, he writes about subjects that generally receive little attention or scrutiny; the following article on shoplifters and shoplifting in New York is a case in point, revealing that "the act of shoplifting is born of thrill, not necessity." It first appeared in* New York Woman *in 1987.*

1   "I looked through my closet the other day and counted nineteen dresses, skirts, and blouses I'd shoplifted. This doesn't include apparel I keep in my chest of drawers, things like underwear. Nor does it include articles I have stolen that have since been given as gifts, handed down to friends, or discarded."

2   The speaker is Martha Alcott (not—and it will become increasingly clear why—her real name), who isn't confessing but boasting. Boasting because she is one of a population of New York women so far eluding the appropriate census takers. She is a long-time shoplifter without a police record or even a signed statement in a department store file. She is an effervescent, quite pretty woman, born to a middle-class family in one of Manhattan's bedroom towns.

Martha has a college degree, is single, and has held a number of responsible jobs that she chose to leave rather than the other way around.

It is difficult to know just how many women Martha represents   3
and what percentage they account for of the $25 billion the National Retail Merchants Association (NRMA) estimates that stores nation-wide lose annually to shoplifters.

What I suspect but can't prove is that she is indicative of a large   4
group, and the reason I say this is because I happen to know a fair number of them. Why, I can't say, but some years ago first this woman with whom I was acquainted and then another and then another began to confide in me—quite possibly not exclusively—that she occasionally or, in some cases, regularly stole from local Manhattan stores.

While I was convinced that I wasn't necessarily a magnet for   5
the larcenous, I was equally convinced that I was onto a story, and at that point I began to ask other women. Much more often than not the responses I got were affirmative. If the woman hadn't actually shoplifted, she knew someone else who had shoplifted, taken a blouse or two, pocketed a bikini, five-finger discounted a nightgown.

Eventually I ran across Martha Alcott, who was like all the   6
others in that she had no financial need to shoplift and unlike them in that she volunteered to tell me her whole, unvarnished story for publication.

"The art of shoplifting is born of thrill, not necessity. I get dressed   7
up and venture—with an empty wallet—to either Bonwit's, Saks, Berg-dorf Goodman, or Bendel's. They have now put white tags on just about everything in Bendel's, but lingerie is still a possibility there, since there are some fabrics you just can't put a white tag on. White plastic inventory tags are a definite bust for shoplifters, and thank goodness all the stores have not seen fit to employ them. Bonwit's is still wide open. I only shoplift in stores which have a laid-back feeling, where the security is relaxed. I would never attempt shoplifting in Bloomingdale's, for instance, because I'm sure they're looking for it."

Bloomingdale's is not talking when it comes to shoplifting.   8
"It's one of the things we won't touch," a spokesperson says before ringing off. Evidently someone at Bloomingdale's did talk for the record a few years ago, and the result was a noticeable increase in thefts. Macy's isn't talking either and will allow no one in an authoritative position to comment on the long-bandied rumor that 7 percent of Macy's first-floor merchandise is pilfered annually. No department store will discuss the subject—possibly because no de-

partment store wants to encourage a crime for which it is unlikely, according to a recent story in *The New York Times,* that there will be heavy convictions, especially among middle- and upper-class thieves.

9   *"I stick to the stores I know, the more expensive stores, for two reasons. First, why not the best? And, second, as long as I am capable of conducting myself in the manner of a wealthy patron, the risk factor is substantially less. I always wear something that people will notice, that looks nice and makes me look as if I belong in the store. I never attempt heists in jeans, especially in New York. I might consider doing it in jeans that are obviously high-fashion jeans. When I get to the store, I never know what I want—well, on rare occasions when I've needed underwear, I go straight to the underwear department. I haven't bought underwear in years and have an inexhaustible collection of nightgowns. But usually I browse. When I see what I want, I go into the fitting room and stuff it in my bag."*

10   The owner of a chain of upscale clothing boutiques reluctantly agrees to acknowledge, anonymously, that shoplifting by customers is a "dreadful" problem. "Customers figure if they're buying two expensive blouses, they deserve to get one free," she says, and she also observes, "When the professional is out to get you, there is nothing you can do"—nothing, despite the Knogo and Sensamatic tags many stores have resorted to. Tags may have slowed shoplifting, but they have not wiped it out. And the boutique owner stresses that the cost of tagging is high—tags are about a dollar or a dollar and a half apiece, and there's the cost of paying an employee to affix them. Security guards cost this owner $150,000 annually. "When I analyze it," she says, woefully, "I sometimes think I should just let them steal."

11   *"The wardrobe of a confirmed shoplifter is dominated by crushable materials. We have trained eyes that can cruise racks and automatically separate those pieces that will fit in the purse from those that will not. I browse around, by the way, with a large bag, but no one would ever think that it was large enough to contain very much. You'd never think there was anything in it. Oh, and a special detail is: if your purse is open when you go into a fitting room, it must be open when you exit."*

12   Because retailers are so tight-lipped about shoplifting, NRMA has only been able to put together sketchy statistics—nothing approximating profiles of shoplifters as to class and income. NRMA has reason to believe, however, that merchandise stock shortages are about 2 percent (actually 1.98 percent) of annual retail sales, and that 31 percent of this figure is accounted for by external theft (as differentiated from internal theft and other forms of inventory

disappearance). To combat this, NRMA distributed a highly specific loss prevention checklist and also sells and rents advisory films and tapes. NRMA figures are supplemented by the National Coalition to Prevent Shoplifting. The organization, now defunct, ran its most recent thorough survey in 1979, when the estimated value of sho-plifted merchandise was $16 billion, which, the Coalition noted, was in contrast to bank robbery losses of a mere $47.5 million. The Coalition also discovered that in 1979 New York State ranked second in the country with $1.243 billion in merchandise loss (California was the first), and 45 percent of the shoplifting activity took place during the Christmas season. The Coalition also found that approximately five cents of every consumer dollar spent goes to cover merchandise loss.

Commercial Service Systems, Inc., a loss prevention and market research firm in Van Nuys, California, has figures that show 45 percent of shoplifters are female. This means that although males account for more than half the total number of shoplifters, shoplifting is the crime with the largest percentage of women, in contrast, to 37 percent involved in white collar crime or 8 percent in violent crime. 13

"Attitude is the whole thing. I know I'm going to succeed, so I succeed. Being sure of yourself is essential—not in a bitchy way, but in a way that intimidates people. Also I try to think of an explanation that will keep me out of trouble if I get caught, although I don't dwell on this, since thinking about getting caught brings negative feelings to the endeavor. Confusion also brings handcuffs. I am not daring someone to catch me, and I think if I started taking things I need instead of the things I want, the desperation would show. 14

"Basically, I can say I am guilt-free. If I thought shoplifting was hurting somebody, I wouldn't do it. It has to do with my personal politics. It's my way of attacking the people who are keeping the money from everyone else. I am ripping off the military-industrial complex I learned about in college." 15

Psychiatrists are very precise about making a distinction between shoplifting and kleptomania. "When we talk about shoplifting," explains Dr. Naomi Goldstein, a forensic psychiatrist, "we are not talking about kleptomania, which is a relatively rare disorder." The Diagnostic and Statistics Manual claims that kleptomania is a proper diagnosis when there is "a recurrent failure to resist impulses to steal objects that are not for immediate use or their monetary value." 16

Neither Goldstein nor other psychiatrists or psychotherapists will venture one definition of the middle- or upper-class shoplifter. 17

"You can speculate," says Goldstein, who, in her post, has seen hundreds of shoplifters of different backgrounds. "You can say it's for the thrill or to challenge the system. Sometimes we see first episodes of shoplifting in depressed middle-aged or older women."

18   "There's no one explanation," concurs Dr. Janet Markowitz, who is director of the Staten Island Clinic of the Jewish Board of Family and Children's Services, and who sees a number of shoplifters in her private practice. "It's difficult to know what is being played out—loneliness, anomie, feeling unneeded, a sense of shame—but the closest I can come is that shoplifting arises from a feeling of not being given to."

19   *"There is no formula to shoplifting. Every situation is different. Like sometimes I know whether I have to take many things or just one thing into the dressing room. I'm making decisions every minute. You have to be ready to change your plans at any time. You have to steer clear of the salespeople with a curt, efficient 'Yes, I'm being helped' or get them to like you and leave you alone. If someone insists on helping me, I accept their help then tell them I've decided not to buy anything. You have to look around the department and see whether it's very quiet. Are there lots of people standing around doing nothing? On the other hand, it doesn't have to be busy. If I think anybody is observing me a little too carefully, I go to another store, or I forget it for the day and just enjoy the shopping, since I love shopping anyway."*

20   Naomi Goldstein says it appears that there are three groups of middle- and upper-class women who shoplift—women in their twenties, thirties, and forties; older women; and young girls. According to Goldstein, older women might turn to shoplifting after sustaining severe loss or changes such as the death of a husband—they're depressed and don't know how to alleviate it. She believes this is a phase soon passed through. Young girls, she says, are busy experimenting, perhaps like the fourteen-year-old in Donald Barthelme's story "Paradise," who steals a "lip gloss called Penumbra." Goldstein even mentions that private schools, like Dalton, might be encountering the problem. Dalton, however, hasn't, says spokesperson Selma Blackburn, who reports that there is an ethics course in the curriculum, but no incidents of shoplifting have been reported by local merchants, and no disciplinary action has had to be taken.

21   *"I started stealing at college when an affluent sorority sister showed me how to stuff booty into a shopping bag from another store; and though since that time I've never been caught, I have had one disheartening comedown. I couldn't take a particular job I wanted because it necessitated taking a lie detector test. I'm confident I can deal with humans fairly*

effectively, but I balk at the idea of challenging a machine. My favorite heists? I have no favorites. Whenever I steal something, I've taken something for nothing, and that's just as exciting every time. Well, I did have one heady day and took two $100 blouses at Bonwit's. I had taken them into the fitting room, tried them on, loved them, and had to have them. So I stuffed them in my bag and walked right out of there, standing around for a while, of course. I always stand around. I never leave right away. An extra thrill for vets like me is having a nice chat with a salesperson—whether it's in a department store or a small boutique—after your bag has been loaded with their merchandise. By the way, I knew those two blouses would be missed at the end of the day, because they were one of a kind. That was part of the pleasure. Sounds like the Pink Panther, doesn't it? I should leave a glove."

Statutes 217 and 218 of New York General Business Law say that a "peace officer, owner, employee, or agent" of a store may stop a customer on reasonable grounds and for a reasonable time if a felony is suspected. " 'Reasonable grounds' shall include, but not be limited to, knowledge that a person has concealed possession of an unpurchased merchandise of a retail mercantile establishment. 'Reasonable time' shall mean the time necessary to permit the person detained to make a statement or to refuse to make a statement, and then the time necessary to examine the employees and records of the merchandise establishment relative to the ownership of the merchandise." A customer may be stopped "on or in the immediate vicinity of the premises of a retail establishment for the purpose of investigation or questioning as to the ownership of any merchandise." 22

Civil suits on the books involve local merchants like Lord & Taylor, Abraham & Strauss, Alexander's, and Bloomingdale's. Most of these suits have to do with charges of false arrest and a finding in one, where Bloomingdale's was the defendant, says, "The right to detain a person . . . does not include the right to fingerprint or photograph him . . . a defendant who engages in such conduct acts unreasonably, and this constitutes false imprisonment as a matter of the law." 23

"Wearing-out is an interesting little variation on the basic lift. Mostly I do it when the store people are so busy or unsuspecting that the situation is crying out for a blatant gesture. I've worn out plastic headbands, belts, underwear (but hardly ever), handbags, and sunglasses. 24

"My most audacious lift was a white jacket I stole right on the floor at Bonwit's. I really wanted it, and it just wasn't the kind of garment you'd go into the dressing-room to try on. So I took a big chance and stashed it right behind a rack. There was another shopper standing not too far 25

away from me, and I'll never know whether she saw me or not. All these years, I've never noticed anyone else shoplifting, by the way."

26   Stores have to be extremely careful about whom they apprehend because of the possibility of false arrest charges. A few years back a woman was stopped in a Lord & Taylor in a mall in Ridgewood, New Jersey. She was accused of hiding two items in a dumpster in order to return later and steal them. She was tried and convicted. She appealed, and her conviction was overturned. The appellate judge, after reading the transcript of the trial, decided that the store employees who testified had lost sight of their suspect long enough for it to be possible that they'd mistaken another customer—the plaintiff—for her. Lord & Taylor eventually agreed to give the woman, who maintained that she had suffered severe psychological damage as a result of the arrest and conviction, a settlement of $17,000.

27   *"Another variation is the exchange without a sales slip. It helps if the garment has a store label, of course. You make it look like this is an everyday occurrence. You don't act desperate. I tell myself I am not leaving the store until I get a merchandise voucher at least. I think up different stories, sometimes saying the item I am exchanging was a gift. That's a good one, because you don't have a receipt, and there has to be a logical explanation. So far I have had remarkable success. Once I received cash by mistake during the Christmas rush for a garment with no sales slip. My family fared very well that holiday.*

28   *"I have taken friends with me, but it is not a good idea, and most people decline the invitation anyway. Which brings me to the subject of hot gifts. Most people would feel so bad that you'd spent that much money that you have to tell them. Nothing has ever been refused—few are that principled—but I have been chastised unpleasantly. I have lavished hot gifts on the family but never of the obviously out-of-my-price-range type."*

29   Every once in a while a reporter covers a story where immersing him- or herself in the enterprise being covered provides a clearer understanding of the subject. It occurred to me that this story could be one. But it's uncomfortable, I can tell you, for a male reporter to hang around a lingerie department for very long, particularly with the intention possibly to steal. What became apparent to me, nonetheless, after casing the lingerie department at Bloomingdale's for even a very short time, is how easy it would be—or seem to be—to pocket some crushable item or, on wandering into the men's department, to place an open carryall on the floor and then drop a tie into it while pretending to be putting it back on the rack. Once the simplicity—or seeming simplicity—of such a tie heist struck

me, it was tough, believe me, to stifle the urge to go through with it, to feel my heart pound faster, to imagine myself rapidly but not conspicuously traveling at least a block before taking a relaxed and victorious breath.

Did I or didn't I?   30

"Clothes are hideously and criminally expensive so that only a   31 *privileged few can afford those of quality. Also since I have been in New York City, I have been especially conscious of the fact that people treat you according to how you are dressed. So I certainly don't want my lack of funds, when there is a lack, begetting me subclass treatment. The people I'm hurting don't feel guilty about what they're doing. My beliefs are that prices are going up, but not because I'm pilfering. Do I have any tips for stores to stop people like me? Are you crazy?"*

Reading Critically

1. What drives well-off and moderately well-off people like "Martha Alcott" to shoplift? If you know anybody who has shop-lifted, have they done it out of need or for a "thrill"? Does shoplift-ing share some of the characteristics of other behavior, drinking and gambling, for example? Discuss with your classmates.

2. Doesn't advertising encourage shoplifting? After all, are we not all constantly bombarded with images suggesting that to be successful we must wear the right clothes, tell time by the right watch, and run in the right running shoes? Which forms of adver-tisement, and which particular ads, would be most likely to tempt people to shoplift? Bring some examples to class and discuss this question with your classmates.

3. Do you find it surprising that almost half the nation's yearly shoplifting takes place during the Christmas season? What do you suspect are the reasons? What other seasons of the year are likely to be prime shoplifting periods?

4. Why does "Martha Alcott" enjoy talking with salespeople after she steals things from their departments? What does this reveal about her character and about our tendencies toward flirting with danger? Have you ever acted on similar tendencies? Discuss with your classmates.

Responding Through Writing

1. Why do you think "Martha Alcott" boasts about shoplifting? Do you know people who boast about antisocial behavior? What underlies that kind of boasting? If she really wants to boast, shouldn't she lift items with higher price tags: diamond rings and Rolex watches? Write a short character sketch of "Martha Alcott."

2. Have you or people you know ever shoplifted anything? Oh, come now, not even a grape in the supermarket? How do you feel about those actions in retrospect? Just for the sake of argument make a list of items you think you could easily shoplift. Write a paragraph or two indicating how you would go about doing so. Write another paragraph indicating your probable reactions on being caught.

3. Note how Finkle alternates analysis of why people shoplift with narratives about actual shoplifting incidents taken from "Martha Alcott." Sketch out an essay of your own on shoplifting or some other petty criminal behavior using the same technique.

4. In a short essay of your own, answer Finkle's question, "Did I or didn't I?" Use evidence from the essay itself to develop your answer.

ON WAITRESSING

IRENE OPPENHEIM

After graduating with a B.A. degree in English from San Francisco State University in 1971, Irene Oppenheim began her career with the San Francisco Bay Guardian *as a dance critic, but was soon writing theater and dance reviews, feature pieces and essays for publications such as* Dance Magazine, City Magazine, New West, *and the* Village Voice. *She has also written several plays that have been produced in the United States and Europe. Oppenheim also writes articles about her own life and daily adventures. The following essay was first published in* The Threepenny Review *in the summer of 1986.*

In September of 1985 I needed a job that would give me a regular income for a few months. I hadn't worked as a waitress for more than a decade, and at first didn't consider that a possibility. But as I searched for more demure employment, I found that one after another of my interviewers would glance at my resume, sadly mumble something about "all that writing," and proceed, making as much eye-contact as I'd permit, to ask "sincerely" about my intentions, naming anything less than full commitment a form of deceit. Unable to assuage their concern with a convincingly forthright response, I soon found myself applying for work at Canter's, a sprawling twenty-four-hour-a-day Jewish (though non-kosher)

1

baker, delicatessen, and restaurant which for the past forty-five years has been dishing up kishka and knishes in the Fairfax district of Los Angeles. I knew that neither of my most recent waitress references would check out—Herb of Herb's Hamburgers in San Francisco had thrown down his spatula some years ago and gone to work in a hardware store, while the Sand Dollar Cafe in Stinson Beach had changed owners, so no one there would remember just how deftly I could sling hash. I told all this to Jackie Canter who, in her early twenties, is among a number of Canter relations working in the family business. She hesitated, but I was hired anyway.

2   While I don't wish to discredit my powers of persuasion, getting hired at Canter's was hardly a difficult affair. The "Help Wanted" sign in Canter's front window was a faded, permanent fixture. And in the two months I ultimately worked at the restaurant, the volume of employee comings and goings was never less than impressive. There were, however, exceptions to this transitoriness, and some among the large Canter crew had been with the restaurant for ten, twenty, or even thirty years. These were mostly older women who remained through a combination of loyalty, age, narrow skills, and inertia. The younger people tended to find the work too demanding and the income increasingly unreliable. Canter's heyday had been in the pre-McDonalds, pre-cholesterol days of the 1950s and 60s. And while the erosion was gradual, it was clear that the combination of fast food and *nouvelle cuisine* was steadily reducing Canter's corned beef/pastrami/chopped liver clientele. Despite trendy additions to the menu, such as an avocado melt sandwich (not bad) and the steamed vegetable plate (not good), there were now many quiet afternoons when the older waitresses, wiping off ketchup bottles and filling napkin holders to pass the time, would tell you about the days when the lines for Canter's stretched right down from the door to the corner of Beverly Boulevard.

3   Canter's could still get enormously busy—on holidays, for instance, or weekend nights. Sometimes for no reason at all the place would suddenly be mobbed. But it all had become unpredictable. And while this unpredictability made the owners niggardly and anxious, its more immediate toll was on the waiters and waitresses, who were almost totally dependent on customer tips. Canter's is a "union house," which means that for sixteen dollars a month the workers are covered by a not-too-respected grievance procedure and a well-loved medical/dental plan. The pay for waiting on tables, however, remains $3.37 per hour (two cents above minimum wage),

so at Canter's, as with most restaurants, any real money has to come from tips.

Until a few years ago these tips were untaxed, which made   4
waitressing a tough but reasonably lucrative profession. Now tips
have to be regularly declared, and through a complicated process
that involves the IRS taking eight percent of a restaurant's gross
meal receipts and dividing that amount up among the number of
food servers, a per-employee tip figure is arrived at, and any waiter
who declares less than that may very well be challenged. In some
restaurants the management automatically deducts the estimated
amount from the paychecks. At Canter's each individual makes a
weekly declaration. But in either case there's great bitterness among
the table waiters about the way the tax is estimated. In every
restaurant, for instance, some shifts are far more profitable than
others, a subtlety the IRS doesn't take into account. There's also a
built-in bias toward "class" operations where the bills are high and
the tips generally run fifteen to twenty percent, while at Canter's
with its soup and sandwich fare, ten percent or less is the norm. Also,
waitresses and waiters volubly and resentfully claim that others in
service professions, such as porters, cab drivers, or hairdressers, are
left to make simple declarations, without the income of the business
being involved.

Where it is possible, most restaurant workers under-declare   5
their tips and simply hope they can get away with it. But a few of
them at Canter's had been called in each year, and the more canny
of the waitresses told me I should keep a daily tally of all my checks
in case the IRS claimed I'd made not just more than I'd declared,
but more than I really took in. What all this meant in terms of an
actual paycheck was that, after meal deductions, regular taxes, and
taxes declared on my tips, my average check for a forty-hour week
was $74.93 or, in the first week of the month, when union fees were
due, $58.93. Whatever else I took home was in the form of tips,
and if business wasn't good these could become an unnervingly
scarce commodity.

Still, most waitresses at Canter's made more than they would   6
as bank tellers, store clerks, or non-managerial office workers. And
even for those whose options were somewhat less grim, waitressing
was not without its alluring aspects. The range of tips—which,
depending on how many customers of what kind you got on a shift,
might be as low as twelve dollars or as high as eighty—gave the
job a gambling flavor which appealed to some. (Gambling, in fact,
was rather a big item at Canter's. More than a few of the waitresses

played as much bingo as paying their rent allowed, while the kitchen help would, almost every day, pool their money and purchase long strings of lottery tickets, with any winnings divided among the buyers.) Others among the waitresses worked there because they preferred the restaurant's physical demands to the boredom of paper work, and several were performers or students who took advantage of the night hours and flexible scheduling. But no one was really happy to be at Canter's. It simply wasn't a very happy place.

7   I've never worked anywhere that had more rules than Canter's. The staff bulletin board was so crammed with admonitions that the overflow had to be taped to the adjacent wall. The topics of these missives varied. One sign, for example, warned that bags and purses might be checked on the way out for purloined food; another that those who didn't turn up for their shifts on holidays such as Christmas (Canter's is open every day of the year except Rosh Hashanah and Yom Kippur) would be automatically dismissed; a third firmly stated that no food substitutions were permitted, which meant that it was against regulations to give a customer who requested it a slice of tomato instead of a pickle. When working on the floor, one encountered even more elaborate rules. All ice cream, juice, or bakery items, for instance, had to be initialed on your check by that shift's hostess, lest you serve something without writing it down. To further complicate matters, orders for deli sandwiches had to be written on a slip of paper along with your waitress number (mine was #35), and these slips were then matched against your checks to make sure, for example, that if you ordered two pastrami sandwiches the customer had paid for two. I was castigated by Jackie one day for—along with the more major infraction of not charging fifty cents extra for a slice of cheese—charging ten cents too little for a cup of potato salad. It seems like a small thing, said Jackie (I concurred), but then she added grimly that little mistakes like mine with the potato salad cost the restaurant many thousands of dollars each year. I was tempted to point out that undoubtedly an equal number of errors were made in the restaurant's favor. But I held my tongue, knowing by then that, in the face of a documented Canter's money loss, anything that could be construed as less than acute remorse would only serve to bring my checks under even closer scrutiny.

8   The waitresses were generally good to each other, though such camaraderie didn't often run deep and rarely extended to any auxiliary personnel such as the bus boys. These were constantly (and mostly unjustly) suspected of stealing tips from the tables and thereby adding to their required tips from the waitresses (I'm not

sure exactly what this came to per individual bus boy, but every waitress contributed about twenty dollars a week which was divided up among the bus boys). At one time Canter's bus boy positions had been filled by strapping immigrant Jewish boys from places such as Bulgaria and Lithuania. But now the bus boys were almost all Mexican, as were the cooks, and a troublesome plate of blintzes or latkes would be garnished by a storm of Spanish curses. In the back kitchen, too, where they made the soups and mixed together enormous vats of tuna salad, the workers were mostly Spanish-speaking. Things in the back kitchen were usually less frantic than in the front, and the back kitchen guys would smile and try to make conversation as you negotiated your way over the wooden floor slats to the bathroom or the time clock. From the deli and kitchen men, however, surliness was a virtual constant, with their black moods frequently exacerbated into anger by such things as the restaurant's awkward design and organization. It was required, for example, that a waitress serving a cheddar cheese omelette first write a slip for the cheese, which had to be sliced and picked up at the front deli counter, and then, after writing another slip for the kitchen, hand-carry the cheese back to the grill. When the place got busy, tempers also ran short among the waitresses themselves, who would swear at the always recalcitrant toasters, at the bagels (or lack of them), or at each other, as fast movers stumbled into slower ones. But in the arena of churlishness the waitresses never came close to competing with the hardworking deli men. Brandishing knives and hunks of meat with a rhythmic skill and an admirable—even graceful—economy of movement, they set the tone at Canter's. And I remember a time when, having made a mistake, I said to one of the deli men, by way of apology, that I'd try to improve. "Don't try," he snarled back. "Do."

One of the more graphic symbols of Canter's changing times 9 was the uniform closet. The male waiters—a relative novelty at Canter's—were allowed to work in a black-pants/white-shirt combo, with some of them opting to appear in the "I Love Canter's" T-shirt available for eight dollars (*their* eight dollars) at the front cash register.

The women could get "I Love Canter's" stenciled free on the 10 off-work shirt of their choice, but their on-the-job dress code was more severe. No one's memory reached back to a time when Canter's waitresses had worn anything other than cream-colored outfits with a single brown stripe running down from each shoulder. There were many of these lined up in the uniform closet. In most cases the uniforms were well-worn, with underarms stained an irreparable gray and hems which had been let up or down more than once. But their dominant characteristic was size. Most of the available uniforms could have doubled as small tents. And no matter how many pins or tucks you employed, material would billow out over your tightly pulled apron strings, an irrepressible tribute to the amplitude of your predecessors.

11   Although there was a locker room at Canter's it was deemed dangerous for reasons I never explored, and I always arrived with my uniform already on. At first I'd worked various shifts—twelve P.M. to eight P.M., eight P.M. to four A.M.—but finally was assigned to days, primarily because I was considered easy-going and the day shift had a contentious reputation. My first task was to relieve Pauline at the counter. She went on duty at six A.M., and technically I was to relieve her at nine A.M. when my shift began. Though the management preferred you didn't clock it in, the rules at Canter's required you to be on the floor fifteen minutes before your shift time, and I'd generally show up around 8:40, which would give Pauline a chance to finish off her checks and put together her own breakfast—usually a mixture of Frosted Flakes and Wheaties put together from the little boxes kept on display right near the coffee machine.

12   There was nothing contentious about Pauline. She was a slow, heavy woman in her early sixties. She was having tooth problems during the time I knew her. But her feet were also troublesome, and she'd made long knife cuts in the front of her white shoes so that, defying the beige of her nylons, the flesh of each foot pushed out rosy-pink between the slits. Pauline had been working at Canter's for twenty-five years, and was the only one of the waitresses left who had her name machine-embroidered onto her uniform. The rest of us were given pins with our first names punched out on a black dymo label. But Pauline's was sewn right in, so you knew she represented a different, less transient era at the restaurant. You could tell by watching her, too, by the deliberate way she moved, that this was a place she was intimately familiar with.

13   Only one part of the counter was open in the morning. It sat around fourteen people and included, as part of the station, three adjacent two-person booths as well as any take-out coffee orders. Almost everyone hated working the counter because the turnover could be impossibly fast and the tips were always small. On the other hand, the counter didn't involve as much running around as the other stations, and Pauline preferred it. She'd move as though she were doing a little dance, reaching toward the coffee machine,

and then the toaster, and then scooping up packets of strawberry jam (strawberry was the only jam flavor Canter's served), with a steady elegance that belied her girth—a factor substantial enough to make it virtually unfeasible for both of us to work behind the counter at once.

Pauline was always glad to see me, for the half-hour's rest I   14
represented would be the longest break she'd have until getting off work at two P.M. I liked Pauline too, and we got along well, but the counter was another matter. Generally two kinds of people showed up at the counter: those who were alone and in a hurry to get somewhere else, and a group of "regulars" for whom time was not a consideration. This latter group was dominated by retired men who met at Canter's punctually each day to have windy discussions which would begin focused on a single topic—such as how people on welfare should be prevented from buying lottery tickets—that would gradually merge into a broader lament about the disintegration of the neighborhood, the city, the nation, and onward. From my standpoint, both these counter groups meant trouble: those who were alone tended to be impatient, while those who came in every day expected special treatment which included remembering details about their preferences (water without ice, or a cherry danish heated with soft butter on the side), and they'd become belligerent if these idiosyncrasies were forgotten or if they felt some mere counter itinerant were getting better service. But there were other regulars too, lonely souls who were not part of the clique. As you stopped for a moment to write out their check, they'd start to tell you about painful cataracts or distant children. I remember one woman who liked her single piece of rye toast burnt almost black. She'd occasionally whisper, so that I had to bend down to hear her, that she was short of cash, and would ask to borrow a dollar from me to pay the bill. I'd always do it. And next day the loan would be stealthily but triumphantly repaid, the dollar slipped into my hand or pocket with a conspiratorial smile as though this act of trust and complicity had secretly bonded us together.

My Canter's career was to come to an unfortunately abrupt   15
end. A restaurant as large as Canter's was bound to have "walk-outs" who'd leave without paying their checks, and I'd had a few. There was one obese woman who asked me a couple of times if she could pay with a credit card (Canter's didn't accept them) and then left me a tip before managing to get away without paying for her hamburger and coke. Another man had me take his bacon and eggs back to the kitchen twice for repairs; he left me a tip too, but the

eggs and bacon went unpaid for. Though there was an element of disgrace in having a walk-out, these small incidents were too common for much of a fuss to be made. But one busy Saturday I had a party of seven who each ordered around ten dollars worth of food and then made a calculated escape while I was in the back adding up their check. Jackie sat me down at the staff table and grimly said that while she didn't blame me for what happened, she did want me to know that it was the largest walk-out loss in the history of Canter's. Nothing was mentioned about my leaving, though Jackie did say that from this point on she wanted me immediately to report to her or the hostess any of my customers who seemed suspicious. I worked the rest of my shift, but everyone I served began to look vaguely suspicious. And with my reputation securely if infamously etched into Canter's history, it seemed time to move on.

Reading Critically

1. Since it is likely that at least one person in your class has been a waitress or waiter, ask that person to discuss his or her experiences in light of Oppenheim's essay.

2. Why do waiters and waitresses so resent having to pay taxes (paragraph 3)? Should they get a special tax break, in your opinion? Which other groups in society argue for special tax breaks for themselves? (By the way, note that Oppenheim [paragraph 5] does not reveal the amount of her tips.) Discuss with your classmates.

3. Discuss with your classmates at least two or three job-related rules from your own experience that you thought at the time were absurd. On reflection, do you still hold the same opinion of those rules?

4. Have you met people, like the men in paragraph 14, who constantly complain about the state of society? What subjects do

chronic complainers usually complain about? Do you agree with any of those chronic complaints?

Responding Through Writing

1. Write a short account in your notebook or journal about some difficult work situation you have experienced. Then write a letter to your former employer, indicating how the situation might be improved (you don't have to send the letter).

2. Is there anyone from your working past whom you strongly dislike? Write a letter to that person, describing what he or she did to you and what you think of him or her (you don't have to send the letter).

3. Are jobs more transitory now than in the recent past (see paragraph 12)? Are professional people likely to switch from one career to another? Write a list of at least five different jobs you would like to have in the future. Write a few paragraphs in which you try to determine what those jobs have in common.

4. Write a list of details about some particular job you have had in the past. Then use those details to develop the draft of an essay describing that job.

I WAS A SLAVE
TO ART

ADAM GOPNIK

Adam Gopnik is widely known for his column, "The Art World," in
The New Yorker, *in which he writes about art news. His pieces have
also appeared in such magazines as* The New Republic, Art in America, *and* Harper's. *Before becoming an art critic, Gopnik was a student
who worked at the Frick Art Reference Library where it was his job "to
find the death dates of artists who the head librarian has decided should
be dead. . . . The claw of the head librarian gets us all in the end." The
following selection was originally published in* Harper's *in 1983.*

1   I am a student at the Institute of Fine Arts, and I work part
time at the Frick Art Reference Library. It is my job to find the
death dates of artists who the head librarian has decided should be
dead. Any artist who was born before 1911 and whose main entry
card in our authority file does not include a death date is presumed by the head librarian to have passed on, unfairly, while the
Frick Art Reference Library was looking the other way. She takes
these cards out of the file (in library parlance this is called placing
the cards "above the rod") and puts them on my desk. If I can
find the artist's death date in a necrology or biographical dictio-

nary, I retype the card and include this date. Then someone else puts it back in the card catalogue. If I can also find an obituary notice for the artist in a back issue of the *Times,* I cut it out and paste it on the back of the card. This is the only part of the job I like, since the paste smells like paste and I get to do the cutting with blunt-edge scissors. At first I liked rooting for the elderly artists to outlast the head librarian. But now I know that even if no death notice turns up for the artist his card stays above the rod all the same until one does. The claw of the head librarian gets us all in the end.

While I search for the remains of dead artists, the woman who 2 works at the desk next to mine, whose name is Miss Chernik, is busy researching and producing what the head librarian refers to as "mounts." A mount is a black-and-white photograph of a painting, glued to a sheet of construction paper. When Miss Chernik makes a mount of a seventeenth-century Dutch flower painting, for instance—and mounts of seventeenth-century Dutch flower paintings are Miss Chernik's speciality—she first cuts out a photograph of this sort of painting from a monograph or catalogue, and then types everything she can find out about its iconography and provenance onto one side of a sheet of heavy gray construction paper. Then she glues the photograph to the other side of the paper and gives it to the head librarian to file. Miss Chernik's mounts are used by those art historians who enjoy thinking about seventeenth-century Dutch flower painting while looking at black-and-white photographs glued to gray construction paper.

Miss Chernik seems to be in her mid-fifties, and I think she 3 comes originally from someplace in Eastern Europe—she will not say exactly where. We hardly spoke at all until one day last winter I brought in the catalogue from the Guggenheim Museum's show of Russian avant-garde art from the George Costakis collection. We began to talk about the show, and I soon discovered that Miss Chernik knows more about the Russian avant-garde than anyone else I have ever met. While she is supposed to be working on the masters of Dutch flower painting, she tells me long, scabrous stories about the stormy careers and sad ends of the gods of the Russian avant-garde: how Chasnik abandoned a wife and two children for nonobjective painting, how Malevich conspired to prevent the construction of Tatlin's monument after a struggle for the person of the future Mrs. Malevich, how Kandinsky loved only Kliun, who loved only Rozanova, who loved only her art.

Miss Chernik clams up when you ask her about her past, so 4 I do not know how reliable any of this is. I suspect that her father was a minor member of Tatlin's circle who at one time or another fled to Paris—Miss Chernik speaks excellent French. She has told me that she once registered in the Ph.D. program at the Institute of Fine Arts—she was going to write her dissertation on Kliun—but it came to nothing. There is a lot more of the diarist (John Aubrey) than the art historian (Erwin Panofsky) about Miss Chernik's historical method, so perhaps this is not really so surprising.

5   The other morning I was in the stacks on the fifth floor, looking for a book that both Miss Chernik and I needed, when the strange machine that summons staff members from the stacks to answer telephone calls began to hum. This machine is interesting to watch but very hard to describe: it is really a system of six machines, one on every floor of the library, each one consisting of a long scroll of paper with an electric stylus mounted above it, and looking a bit like a seismograph laid flat. This system was manufactured sometime in the late Twenties, when the library was built, and it reproduces human script in much the way that a telephone reproduces the human voice. Whatever you write on the scroll of paper with the electric stylus will be perfectly reproduced by all five other machines in the library, right down to the way you cross your *t*s and dot your *i*s. We use these machines to call staff members from the stacks when a telephone call comes for them on the sixth floor, where all the desks are. I am not sure why the library does not have an intercom system like every other library, but I think the head librarian suspects that all this electric telephony may be no more than a passing fancy, and she does not intend to see the Frick Art Reference Library caught with all its eggs in one basket; when AT&T goes down, the Frick Art Reference Library is not going down with it.

6   Also, this procedure is so cumbersome and time-consuming that it effectively prevents staff members from getting any outside calls at all. By the time you have watched the message form on the writing machine, ascended in the elevator, and gotten to the phone booth on the sixth floor, whoever is calling you has usually hung up. The phone booth on the sixth floor of the Frick Art Reference Library, by the way, is almost as interesting as the machines that copy handwriting: there is an old pay phone, a big framed photograph of Mr. Henry Clay Frick visiting a foxhole during the Great War, another framed photograph of Mr. Frick playing golf in plus fours, and two notices written in big block letters: RESTRICT ALL PHONE CALLS TO THREE MINUTES and, labeling a small vial, ALCOHOL: DISINFECT PHONE AFTER USE. I always disinfect the phone after I use

it, since I am afraid of catching some romantic wasting disease of
the last century that has lingered on at the end of the telephone
receivers at the Frick Art Reference Library—consumption or neu-
ralgia or scarlet fever. Miss Chernik tells me that her "blood boils"
every time she has to go into the phone booth and look at the two
framed photographs of Mr. Frick. Miss Chernik also thinks that we
are burdened with the six machines that copy handwriting because
Mr. Frick had a financial interest in them. "If the Fricks had owned
Western Union," she has said to me, "all of us would be working
in Morse code." Miss Chernik has the old revolutionary's habit of
referring every questionable decision of the trustees who administer
the Frick collection and library to the personal malice of the Frick
family.

The six machines that copy handwriting have, apparently, been   7
working almost perfectly in the fifty years since they were first
installed, but on the morning that I went up into the stacks to look
for the book we needed, the machine on the fifth floor began to
behave erratically. I watched as it wrote my name perfectly, repro-
ducing a hand that I recognized as Miss Chernik's. Then it suddenly
began to vibrate wildly, describing violent peaks and valleys before
subsiding into small cursive hooks and circles in the lower right-
hand corner. When it was finished, what it had produced looked
a lot like a painting by Cy Twombly, the American abstract artist.
At first I thought that Miss Chernik was just being puckish—
although she is far from a puckish woman—and so after I came
upstairs and answered the phone I began to joke with her about it.
She seemed puzzled, and when I explained to her what had happened she showed me that she had written out a completely conventional message (CALL ON SIX), which the fifth-floor machine had
somehow scrambled. I went downstairs to the third floor and told
the head librarian, whose name is Miss Sawyer, that there was
something wrong with the machine on the fifth floor.

"It's drawing pictures that look like Cy Twomblys," I told   8
her.

She called her assistant, Miss Christie, and we all went upstairs   9
to examine the machine on Five. Miss Sawyer looked over what the
machine had done, and then told Miss Christie to go back upstairs
to Six and send another message. Miss Christie walked toward the
elevator and then turned back.

"Who shall I say is calling?" she asked politely.   10

"Just write, TESTING, TESTING," Miss Sawyer snapped back.   11

Miss Christie went upstairs and we waited, in anxious silence,   12
until the machine began to hum and the electric stylus began to

write. This time it produced nothing recognizable at all, nothing that looked the least bit like TESTING, TESTING, just long, broken, vertical strokes, like the marks in a De Kooning drawing. It occurred to me that similar scrambled messages were probably appearing at that moment on four other machines in the library, and I think that this occurred to Miss Sawyer, too, because she looked a bit shaken.

13   "This machine is out of order," she announced, and she took out a felt-tipped pen and wrote OUT OF ORDER: DO NOT USE on the scroll of paper, in the same hand that had once penned LIMIT ALL PHONE CALLS and DISINFECT AFTER USE.

14   "What will we do if we get phone calls while we're in the stacks?" I asked her.

15   Miss Sawyer thought this over. "We will install a temporary courier system," she said finally. She looked me in the eye. *"You* will be the temporary courier," she announced, and then she went downstairs to telephone Mr. Rotan, the only repairman left in New York who knows anything about the six machines that copy handwriting.

16   It turned out, however, that Mr. Rotan was down with pleurisy and wouldn't be able to come for at least a week. I served as temporary courier all day Monday and on Tuesday afternoon (I have classes Tuesday mornings) but I think that having me pound up and down the stairs calling people to the phone violated Miss Sawyer's sense of library decorum, so on Wednesday morning she turned all the writing machines back on and gave them another chance. They worked perfectly all morning: "CALL ON SIX," "QUERY ON THREE FOR MISS EVETTS," "MISS CHERNIK SEE MISS SAWYER ON THREE." They even got the funny way Miss Sawyer does her Qs right. But then after lunch they got sly and lyrical: breaking off in the middle of sentences to do figure eights and calligraphic spirals, writing legible-looking script that turned out to be nonsense when you examined it closely, interrupting dogged reproduction to take off on flights of graphic fancy, in general turning from mimesis to the expressive gesture. By three o'clock the machines had settled into a vein of restful, almost wholly satisfying abstract draftsmanship, something on the order of the drawings of Philip Guston in the mid-Fifties.

17   I was at school all day Thursday, but Miss Chernik tells me that Miss Sawyer, who is nothing if not persistent, decided to try again. This time, Miss Chernik went on, the machines were downright subversive, alternating unpredictably between letter-perfect reproduction and extravagant abstraction. On Thursday the ma-

chines seemed to be going through a period something like the one
Malevich went through in 1919, when, according to Miss Chernik,
he would occasionally turn out conventional perspective miniatures
in the midst of his nonobjective researches, just to show that he
could do it if he chose.

Miss Chernik began to tear off and collect some of the ma-   18
chine's stronger designs, both the intended original message and its
five strange consequences. She pointed out that, motivated by God
only knew what simple mechanical failure, these machines were still
uniquely advancing the cause of modernism, combining the sheer
gestural bravura of the best American painting with the concern for
mechanical reproduction that had always characterized the Russian
avant-garde. On Friday afternoon, Miss Chernik and I spent the last
two hours of the work week gluing the best of the machine's work
to sheets of gray construction paper, with all that we knew about
their peculiar provenance neatly typed out on the other side. "It is
like *Potemkin*," Miss Chernik commented as we made these mounts.
"The menials lead, and the intellectuals follow."

On Monday morning, Mr. Rotan finally appeared. He went   19
to examine the machine on the sixth floor.

"What's gotten into this machine?" he asked Miss Chernik,   20
with a wan, pleurisy-laden smile.

"The zeitgeist," she answered calmly.   21

Mr. Rotan worked the machines over for an hour, and since   22
that morning they have retreated back into dutiful mimesis, prescribed realism. This has been a tremendous disappointment to Miss
Chernik and me. Miss Chernik, though, knows how to handle it;
she is hoarding her collection, polishing her memories, waiting for
the thaw. She has been through all this before.

Reading Critically

1. Is Gopnik's central purpose simply to describe the processes
of the library where he works, or is it to criticize the ways in which
those processes are carried out? Can you cite points throughout the
essay where Gopnik uses just the right touch of sarcasm to achieve
his purpose? Note the phrase "above the rod" in the first paragraph,
for example, and the phrase "remains of dead artists" in the second.

Does Gopnik's sarcasm ever become too obvious or heavy? Discuss with your classmates.

2. Consult a reference work (encyclopedia, biographical dictionary) and read the entry on Henry Clay Frick. How does your knowledge of Frick's life help you to understand this essay? For example, do you now see reasons for Miss Chernik's reactions as described in paragraph 6?

3. Why do Gopnik and Miss Chernik mount the productions of the handwriting machine? What does their action say about their opinion of abstract art? Do you and your classmates agree with that opinion?

4. What is Gopnik's real message in the first paragraph when he says, "The claw of the head librarian gets us all in the end"? For what audience is this message intended?

Responding Through Writing

1. Do you know any people like Miss Sawyer? Have you ever had fun at such a person's expense? Write a short sketch of the person in question.

2. Note the ways in which Gopnik makes his job sound unappealing. If you have ever had an unappealing job, write the draft of a short essay in your journal or notebook describing that job. Try to use some of Gopnik's techniques.

3. In a short essay, try to use sly humor like Gopnik's to criticize some of the beauracratic processes at your college.

4. Have you ever felt yourself enslaved by a job? Draw up a list of the jobs you have had and pick the two or three that were most dehumanizing. Write a few paragraphs in your notebook or journal about what those jobs had in common.

THE LADY WITH THE PET DOG

JOYCE CAROL OATES

Joyce Carol Oates (b. 1938) published her first short story "In the Old World" in 1959, when she was a student at Syracuse University. The piece won the college fiction prize sponsored by Mademoiselle *magazine. In fact, Oates has won the O. Henry Prize so often that a special award has been designated for her. She has published over 17 novels, including* Expensive People *(1968),* Marya: A Life *(1986),* American Appetites *(1988), and* The Assignation *(1988), and over a dozen books of short stories including* By the North Gate *(1963)* Night-Side *(1977) and* Last Days *(1984). Oates is currently a professor of English at Princeton University. The following story first appeared in* Partisan Review *in the spring of 1972 and is also contained in a collection of short stories entitled* Marriages and Infidelities *(1972).*

Strangers parted as if to make way for him. There he stood.   1
He was there in the aisle, a few yards away, watching her.

She leaned forward at once in her seat, her hand jerked up to   2
her face as if to ward off a blow—but then the crowd in the aisle

hid him, he was gone. She pressed both hands against her cheeks. He was not there; she had imagined him.

3   "My God," she whispered.

4   She was alone. Her husband had gone out to the foyer to make a telephone call; it was intermission at the concert, a Thursday evening.

5   Now she saw him again, clearly. He was standing there. He was staring at her. Her blood rocked in her body, draining out of her head . . . she was going to faint. . . . They stared at each other. They gave no sign of recognition. Only when he took a step forward did she shake her head *no—no—*keep away. It was not possible.

6   When her husband returned she was staring at the place where her lover had been standing. Her husband leaned forward to interrupt that stare.

7   "What's wrong?" he said. "Are you sick?"

8   Panic rose in her in long shuddering waves. She tried to get to her feet, panicked at the thought of fainting here, and her husband took hold of her. She stood like an aged woman, clutching the seat before her.

9   At home he helped her up the stairs and she lay down. Her head was like a large piece of crockery that had to be held still, it was so heavy. She was still panicked. She felt it in the shallows of her face, behind her knees, in the pit of her stomach. It sickened her, it made her think of mucus, of something thick and gray congested inside her, stuck to her, that was herself and yet not herself, a poison.

10   She lay with her knees drawn up toward her chest, her eyes hotly open, while her husband spoke to her. She imagined that other man saying, *Why did you run away from me?* Her husband was saying other words. She tried to listen to them. He was going to call the doctor, he said, and she tried to sit up. "No, I'm all right now," she said quickly. The panic was like lead inside her, so thickly congested. How slow love was to drain out of her, how fluid and sticky it was inside her head!

11   Her husband believed her. No doctor. No threat. Grateful, she drew her husband down to her. They embraced, not comfortably. For years now they had not been comfortable together, in their intimacy and at a distance, and now they struggled gently as if the paces of this dance were too rigorous for them. It was something they might have known once, but had now outgrown. The panic in her thickened at this double betrayal: she drew her husband to

her, she caressed him wildly, she shut her eyes to think about that other man.

A crowd of men and women parting, unexpectedly, and there   12
he stood—there he stood—she kept seeing him, and yet her vision blotched at the memory. It had been finished between them six months before, but he had come out here . . . and she had escaped him, now she was lying in her husband's arms, in his embrace, her face pressed against his. It was a kind of sleep, this lovemaking. She felt herself falling asleep, her body falling from her. Her eyes shut.

"I love you," her husband said fiercely, angrily.   13

She shut her eyes and thought of that other man, as if betraying   14
him would give her life a center.

"Did I hurt you? Are you—?" her husband whispered.   15

Always this hot flashing of shame between them, the shame of   16
her husband's near-failure, the clumsiness of his love. . . .

"You didn't hurt me," she said.   17

II

They had said goodbye six months before. He drove her from   18
Nantucket, where they had met, to Albany, New York, where she visited her sister. The hours of intimacy in the car had sealed something between them, a vow of silence and impersonality: she recalled the movement of the highways, the passing of other cars, the natural rhythms of the day hypnotizing her toward sleep while he drove. She trusted him; she could sleep in his presence. Yet she could not really fall asleep in spite of her exhaustion, and she kept jerking awake, frightened, to discover that nothing had changed— still the stranger who was driving her to Albany, still the highway, the sky, the antiseptic odor of the rented car, the sense of rhythm behind the rhythm of the air that might unleash itself at any second. Everywhere on this highway, at this moment, there were men and women driving together, bonded together—what did that mean, to be together? What did it mean to enter into a bond with another person?

No, she did not really trust him; she did not really trust men.   19
He would glance at her with his small cautious smile and she felt a declaration of shame between them.

Shame.   20

In her head she rehearsed conversations. She said bitterly,   21
"You'll be relieved when we get to Albany. Relieved to get rid of me." They had spent so many days talking, confessing too much,

driven to a pitch of childish excitement, laughing together on the beach, breaking into that pose of laughter that seems to eradicate the soul, so many days of this that the silence of the trip was like the silence of a hospital—all these surface noises, these rattles, and hums, but an interior silence, a befuddlement. She said to him in her imagination, "One of us should die." Then she leaned over to touch him. She caressed the back of his neck. She said aloud, "Would you like me to drive for a while?"

22   They stopped at a "picnic area" where other cars were stopped—couples, families—and walked together, smiling at their good luck. He put his arm around her shoulders and she sensed how they were in a posture together, a man and a woman forming a posture, a figure, that someone might sketch and show to them. She said slowly. "I don't want to go back. . . ."

23   Silence. She looked up at him. His face was heavy with her words, as if she had pulled at his skin with her fingers. Children ran nearby and distracted him—yes, he was a father too, his children ran like that, they tugged at his skin with their light, busy fingers.

24   "Are you so unhappy?" he said.

25   "I'm not unhappy, back there. I'm nothing. There's nothing to me," she said.

26   They stared at each other. The sensation between them was intense, exhausting. She thought that this man was her Savior, that he had come to her at a time in her life when her life demanded completion, an end, a permanent fixing of all that was troubled and shifting and deadly. And yet it was absurd to think this. No person could save another. So she drew back from him and released him.

27   A few hours later they stopped at a gas station in a small city. She went to the women's restroom, having to ask the attendant for a key, and when she came back her eye jumped nervously onto the rented car—why? did she think he might have driven off without her?—onto the man, her friend, standing in conversation with the young attendant. Her friend was as old as her husband, over forty, with lanky, sloping shoulders, a full body, his hair thick, a dark burnished red, a festive color that made her eye twitch a little—and his hands were always moving, always those rapid conversational circles, going nowhere, gestures that were a little aggressive and apologetic at once.

28   She put her hand on his arm, a claim. He turned to her and smiled and she felt that she loved him, that everything in her life had forced her to this moment and that she had no choice about it.

29   They sat in the car for two hours in Albany, in the parking lot of a Howard Johnson's restaurant, talking, trying to figure out

their past. There was no future. They concentrated on the past, the several days behind them, lit up with a hot, dazzling August sun, like explosions that already belonged to other people, to strangers. Her face was faintly reflected in the green-tinted curve of the windshield, but she could not have recognized that face. She began to cry; she told herself: *"I am not here, this will pass, this is nothing."* Still, she could not stop crying. What if a policeman ran up to the car and accused this man of molesting her? The muscles of her face were springy, like a child's, unpredictable muscles. He stroked her arms, her shoulders, trying to comfort her. "This is so hard . . . this is impossible . . . ," he said. She felt panic for the world outside this car, all that was not herself and this man, and at the same time she understood that she was free of him, as people are free of other people; she would leave him soon, safely, and within a few days he would have fallen into the past, the impersonal past. . . . What if someone, an ordinary husband and father, were to notice them in this car, were to run over and accuse her friend of upsetting her? She was much younger, she was girlish and frightened, she was not really here in this car saying these things. . . .

"I'm so ashamed of myself!" she said finally.

She returned to her husband and saw that another woman, a shadow woman, had taken her place—noiseless and convincing, like a dancer, performing certain difficult steps. Her husband folded her in his arms and talked to her of his own loneliness, his worries about his business, his health, his mother, kept tranquilized and mute in a nursing home, and her spirit detached itself from her and drifted about the rooms of the large house she lived in with her husband, a shadow woman delicate and imprecise. There was no boundary to her, no edge. Alone, she took hot baths and sat exhausted in the steaming water, wondering at her perpetual exhaustion. All that winter she noticed the limp, languid weight of her arms, her veins bulging slightly with the pressure of her extreme weariness. *This is fate,* she thought, to be here and not there, to be one person and not another, a certain man's wife and not the wife of another man. The long, slow pain of this certainty rose in her, but it never became clear; it was baffling and imprecise. She could not be serious about it: she kept congratulating herself on her own good luck, to have escaped so easily, to have freed herself. So much love had gone into the first several years of her marriage that there wasn't much left, now, for another man. . . . She was certain of that. But the bath water made her dizzy, all that perpetual heat, and one day in January she drew a razor blade lightly across the inside of her arm, near the elbow, to see what would happen.

30
31

32   Afterward she wrapped a small towel around it, to stop the bleeding. The towel soaked through. She wrapped a bath towel around that and walked through the empty rooms of her home, not very worried, hardly aware of the stubborn seeping of blood. There was no boundary to her in this house, no precise limit. She could flow out like her own blood and come to no end.

33   Her husband telephoned her when he would be staying late at the plant. He talked to her always about his plans, his problems, his business friends, his future. It was obvious that he had a future. As he spoke she nodded to encourage him, and her heartbeat quickened with the memory of her own, personal shame, the shame of this man's particular, private wife. One evening at dinner he leaned forward and put his head in his arms, and fell asleep, like a child. She sat at the table with him for a while, watching him. His hair had gone gray, almost white, at the temples—no one would guess that he was so quick, so careful a man, still fairly young about the eyes. She put her hand on his head, lightly, as if to prove to herself that he was real. He slept, exhausted.

34   One evening they went to a concert and she looked up to see her lover there, in the crowded aisle, in this city, watching her. He was standing there, with his overcoat on, watching her. She went cold. That morning the telephone had rung while her husband was still home, and she had heard him answer it, heard him hang up—it must have been a wrong number—and when the telephone rang again, at nine-thirty, she had been afraid to answer it for some reason. She had left home to be out of the range of that ringing, but now, in this public place, in this busy auditorium, she found herself staring at that man, unable to make any sign to him, any gesture of recognition.

35   He would have come to her but she shook her head. No. Stay away.

36   Her husband helped her out of the row of seats, saying, "Excuse us, please. Excuse us," so that strangers got to their feet, quickly, alarmed, to let them pass. Was that woman about to faint? What was wrong?

37   At home she felt the blood drain slowly back into her head. Her husband embraced her hips, pressing his face against her, in that silence that belonged to the earliest days of their marriage. She thought, *He will drive it out of me.* He made love to her and she was back in the auditorium again, sitting alone now that the concert was over. The stage was empty; the heavy velvet curtains had not been drawn; the musicians' chairs were empty, everything was silent and expectant; in the aisle her lover stood and smiled at her— Her

husband was impatient. He was apart from her, working on her, operating on her; and then, stricken, he whispered, "Did I hurt you?"

The telephone rang the next morning. Dully, sluggishly, she answered it. She recognized his voice at once—that "Anna?" with its lifting of the second syllable, questioning and apologetic and making its claim. "Yes, what do you want?" she said. 38

"Just to see you. Please—?" 39

"I can't." 40

"Anna, I'm sorry, I didn't mean to upset you—" 41

"I can't see you." 42

"Just for a few minutes—I have to talk to you—" 43

"But why, why now? Why now?" she said. 44

She heard her voice rising, but she could not stop it. He began to talk again, drowning her out. She remembered his rapid conversation. She remembered his gestures, the witty energetic circling of his hands. 45

"How are you? Please don't hang up!" he cried. 46

"I can't—I don't want to go through it again—" 47

"I'm not going to hurt you. Just tell me how you are." 48

"Everything is the same." 49

"Everything is the same with me." 50

She looked up at the ceiling, shyly. "Your wife? Your children?" 51

"The same." 52

"Your son?" 53

"He's fine." 54

"I'm glad to hear that. I—" 55

"Is it still the same with you, your marriage? Tell me what you feel. What are you thinking?" 56

"I don't know. . . ." 57

She remembered his intense, eager words, the movement of his hands, that impatient precise fixing of the air by his hands, the jabbing of his fingers. 58

"Do you love me?" he said. 59

She could not answer. 60

"I'll come over to see you," he said. 61

"No," she said. 62

What will come next, what will happen? 63

Flesh hardening on his body, aging. Shrinking. He will grow old, but not soft like her husband. They are two different types: he is nervous, lean, energetic, wise. She will grow thinner as the tension radiates out from her backbone, wearing down her flesh. Her collar- 64 bones will jut out of her skin. Her husband, caressing her in their bed, will discover that she is another woman—she is not there with him—instead she is rising in an elevator in a downtown hotel, carrying a book as a prop, or walking quickly away from that hotel, her head bent and filled with secrets. Love, what to do with it . . . ? Useless as moths' wings, as moths' flutterings . . . She feels the flutterings of silky, crazy wings in her chest.

65   He flew out to visit her every several weeks, staying at a different hotel each time. He telephoned her, and she drove down to park in an underground garage at the very center of the city.

66   She lay in his arms while her husband talked to her, miles away, one body fading into another. He will grow old, his body will change, she thought, pressing her cheek against the back of one of these men. If it was her lover, they were in a hotel room: always the propped-up little booklet describing the hotel's many services, with color photographs of its cocktail lounge and dining room and coffee shop. Grow old, leave me, die, go back to your neurotic wife and your sad, ordinary children, she thought, but still her eyes closed gratefully against his skin and she felt how complete their silence was, how they had come to rest in each other.

67   "Tell me about your life here. The people who love you," he said, as he always did.

68   One afternoon they lay together for four hours. It was her birthday and she was intoxicated with her good fortune, this prize of the afternoon, this man in her arms! She was a little giddy, she talked too much. She told him about her parents, about her husband. . . . "They were all people I believed in, but it turned out wrong. Now, I believe in you. . . ." He laughed as if shocked by her words. She did not understand. Then she understood. "But I believe truly in you. I can't think of myself without you," she said. He spoke of his wife, her ambitions, her intelligence, her use of the children against him, her use of his younger son's blindness, all of his words gentle and hypnotic and convincing in the late-afternoon peace of this hotel room . . . and she felt the terror of laughter, threatening laughter. Their words, like their bodies, were aging.

69   She dressed quickly in the bathroom, drawing her long hair up around the back of her head, fixing it as always, anxious that everything be the same. Her face was slightly raw, from his face. The rubbing of his skin. Her eyes were too bright, wearily bright. Her hair was blond but not so blond as it had been that summer in the white Nantucket air.

70   She ran water and splashed it on her face. She blinked at the water. Blind. Drowning. She thought with satisfaction that soon,

soon, he would be back home, in that house on Long Island she had never seen, with that woman she had never seen, sitting on the edge of another bed, putting on his shoes. She wanted nothing except to be free of him. Why not be free? *Oh,* she thought suddenly, *I will follow you back and kill you. You and her and the little boy. What is there to stop me?*

She left him. Everyone on the street pitied her, that look of absolute zero.   71

III

A man and a child, approaching her. The sharp acrid smell of   72
fish. The crashing of waves. Anna pretended not to notice the father with his son—there was something strange about them. That frank, silent intimacy, too gentle, the man's bare feet in the water and the boy a few feet away, leaning away from his father. He was about nine years old and still his father held his hand.

A small yipping dog, a golden dog, bounded near them.   73

Anna turned shyly back to her reading; she did not want to   74
have to speak to these neighbors. She saw the man's shadow falling over her legs, then over the pages of her book, and she had the idea that he wanted to see what she was reading. The dog nuzzled her; the man called him away.

She watched them walk down the beach. She was relieved that   75
the man had not spoken to her.

She saw them in town later that day, the two of them red-   76
haired and patient, now wearing sandals, walking with that same look of care. The man's white shorts were soiled and a little baggy. His pullover shirt was a faded green. His face was broad, the cheekbones wide, spaced widely apart, the eyes stark in their sockets, as if they fastened onto objects for no reason, ponderous and edgy. The little boy's face was pale and sharp; his lips were perpetually parted.

Anna realized that the child was blind.   77

The next morning, early, she caught sight of them again. For   78
some reason she went to the back door of her cottage. She faced the sea breeze eagerly. Her heart hammered. . . . She had been here, in her family's old house, for three days, alone, bitterly satisfied at being alone, and now it was a puzzle to her how her soul strained to fly outward, to meet with another person. She watched the man with his son, his cautious, rather stooped shoulders above the child's small shoulders.

The man was carrying something, it looked like a notebook.   79

He sat on the sand, not far from Anna's spot of the day before, and the dog rushed up to them. The child approached the edge of the ocean, timidly. He moved in short jerky steps, his legs stiff. The dog ran around him. Anna heard the child crying out a word that sounded like "Ty"—it must have been the dog's name—and then the man joined in, his voice heavy and firm.

80   "Ty . . ."

81   Anna tied her hair back with a yellow scarf and went down to the beach.

82   The red-haired man glanced around at her. He smiled. She stared past him at the waves. To talk to him or not to talk—she had the freedom of that choice. For a moment she felt that she had made a mistake, that the child and the dog would not protect her, that behind this man's ordinary, friendly face there was a certain arrogant maleness—then she relented, she smiled shyly.

83   "A nice house you've got there," the man said.

84   She nodded her thanks.

85   The man pushed his sunglasses up on his forehead. Yes, she recognized the eyes of the day before—intelligent and nervous, the sockets pale, untanned.

86   "Is that your telephone ringing?" he said.

87   She did not bother to listen. "It's a wrong number," she said.

88   Her husband calling: she had left home for a few days, to be alone.

89   But the red-haired man, settling himself on the sand, seemed to misinterpret this. He smiled in surprise, one corner of his mouth higher than the other. He said nothing. Anna wondered: _What is he thinking?_ The dog was leaping about her, panting against her legs, and she laughed in embarrassment. She bent to pet it, grateful for its busyness. "Don't let him jump up on you," the man said. "He's a nuisance."

90   The dog was a small golden retriever, a young dog. The blind child, standing now in the water, turned to call the dog to him. His voice was shrill and impatient.

91   "Our house is the third one down—the white one," the man said.

92   She turned, startled. "Oh, did you buy it from Dr. Patrick? Did he die?"

93   "Yes, finally . . ."

94   Her eyes wandered nervously over the child and the dog. She felt the nervous beat of her heart out to the very tips of her fingers, the fleshy tips of her fingers: little hearts were there, pulsing. _What_

is he thinking? The man had opened his notebook. He had a piece of charcoal and he began to sketch something.

Anna looked down at him. She saw the top of his head, his 95
thick red hair, the freckles on his shoulders, the quick, deft movement of his hand. Upside down, Anna herself being drawn. She
smiled in surprise.

"Let me draw you. Sit down," he said. 96

She knelt awkwardly a few yards away. He turned the page 97
of the sketchpad. The dog ran to her and she sat, straightening out
her skirt beneath her, flinching from the dog's tongue. "Ty!" cried
the child. Anna sat, and slowly the pleasure of the moment began
to glow in her; her skin flushed with gratitude.

She sat there for nearly an hour. The man did not talk much. 98
Back and forth the dog bounded, shaking itself. The child came to
sit near them, in silence. Anna felt that she was drifting into a kind
of trance, while the man sketched her, half a dozen rapid sketches,
the surface of her face given up to him. "Where are you from?"
the man asked.

"Ohio. My husband lives in Ohio." 99

She wore no wedding band. 100

"Your wife—" Anna began. 101

"Yes?" 102

"Is she here?" 103

"Not right now." 104

She was silent, ashamed. She had asked an improper question. 105
But the man did not seem to notice. He continued drawing her, bent
over the sketchpad. When Anna said she had to go, he showed her
the drawings—one after another of her, Anna, recognizably Anna,
a woman in her early thirties, her hair smooth and flat across the
top of her head, tied behind by a scarf. "Take the one you like best,"
he said, and she picked one of her with the dog in her lap, sitting
very straight, her brows and eyes clearly defined, her lips girlishly
pursed, the dog and her dress suggested by a few quick irregular
lines.

"Lady with pet dog," the man said, smiling oddly. 106

She spent the rest of that day reading, nearer her cottage. It 107
was not really a cottage—it was a two-story house, large and
ungainly and weathered. It was mixed up in her mind with her
family, her own childhood, and she glanced up from her book,
perplexed, as if waiting for one of her parents or her sister to come
up to her. Then she thought of the man with the red hair, the man
with the blind child, the man with the dog, and she could not

concentrate on her reading. Someone—probably her father—had marked a passage that must be important, but she kept reading and rereading it: *We try to discover in things, endeared to us on that account, the spiritual glamour which we ourselves have cast upon them; we are disillusioned, and learn that they are in themselves barren and devoid of the charm which they owed, in our minds, to the association of certain ideas. . . .*

108 She thought again of the man on the beach. She laid the book aside and thought of him: his eyes, his aloneness, his drawings of her.

109 They began seeing each other after that. He came to her front door in the evening, without the child; he drove her into town for dinner. She was shy and extremely pleased. The darkness of the expensive restaurant released her; she heard herself chatter; she leaned forward and seemed to be offering her face up to him, listening to him. He talked about his work on a Long Island newspaper and she seemed to be listening to him, as she stared at his face, arranging her own face into the expression she had seen in that charcoal drawing. Did he see her like that, then?—girlish and withdrawn and patrician? She felt the weight of his interest in her, a force that fell upon her like a blow. A repeated blow. Of course he was married, he had children—of course she was married, permanently married. This flight from her husband was not important. She had left him before, to be alone; it was not important. Everything in her was slender and delicate and not important.

110 They walked for hours after dinner, looking at the other strollers, the weekend visitors, the tourists, the couples like themselves. Surely they were mistaken for a couple, a married couple. *This is the hour in which everything is decided,* Anna thought. They had both had several drinks and they talked a great deal. Anna found herself saying too much, stopping and starting giddily. She put her hand to her forehead, feeling faint.

111 "It's from the sun—you've had too much sun," he said.

112 At the door to her cottage, on the front porch, she heard herself asking him shyly if he would like to come in. She allowed him to lead her inside, to close the door. *This is not important,* she thought clearly, *he doesn't mean it, he doesn't love me, nothing will come of it.* She was frightened, yet it seemed to her necessary to give in: she had to leave Nantucket with that act completed, an act of adultery, an accomplishment she would take back to Ohio and to her marriage.

113 Then, incredibly, she heard herself asking: "Do you . . . do you love me?"

114 "You're so beautiful!" he said, amazed.

115 She felt this beauty, shy and glowing and centered in her eyes.

He stared at her. In this large, drafty house, alone together, they were like accomplices, conspirators. She could not think: how old was she? which year was this? They had done something unforgivable together, and the knowledge of it was tugging at their faces. A cloud seemed to pass over her. She felt herself smiling shrilly.

Afterward, a peculiar raspiness, a dryness of breath. He was   116
silent. She felt a strange, idle fear, a sense of the danger outside this room and this old, comfortable bed—a danger that would not recognize her as the lady in that drawing, the lady with the pet dog. There was nothing to say to this man, this stranger. She felt the beauty draining out of her face, her eyes fading.

"I've got to be alone," she told him.   117

He left, and she understood that she would not see him again.   118
She stood by the window of the room, watching the ocean. A sense of shame overpowered her: it was smeared everywhere on her body, the smell of it, the richness of it. She tried to recall him and his face was confused in her memory: she would have to shout to him across a jumbled space, she would have to wave her arms wildly. *You love me! You must love me!* But she knew he did not love her, and she did not love him; he was a man who drew everything up into himself, like all men, walking away, free to walk away, free to have his own thoughts, free to envision her body, all the secrets of her body. . . . And she lay down again in the bed, feeling how heavy this body had become, her insides heavy with shame, the very backs of her eyelids coated with shame.

"This is the end of one part of my life," she thought.   119

But in the morning the telephone rang. She answered it. It was   120
her lover: they talked brightly and happily. She could hear the eagerness in his voice, the love in his voice, that same still, sad amazement—she understood how simple life was, there were no problems.

They spent most of their time on the beach, with the child and   121
the dog. He joked and was serious, at the same time. He said once, "You have defined my soul for me," and she laughed to hide her alarm. In a few days it was time for her to leave. He got a sitter for the boy and took the ferry with her to the mainland, then rented a car to drive her up to Albany. She kept thinking: *Now something will happen. It will come to an end.* But most of the drive was silent and hypnotic. She wanted him to joke with her, to say again that she had defined his soul for him, but he drove fast, he was serious, she distrusted the hawkish look of his profile—she did not know him at all. At a gas station she splashed her face with cold water. Alone in the grubby little restroom, shaky and very much alone. In such places are women totally alone with their bodies. The body

grows heavier, more evil, in such silence. . . . On the beach everything had been noisy with sunlight and gulls and waves: here, as if run to earth, everything was cramped and silent and dead.

122 She went outside, squinting. There he was, talking with the station attendant. She could not think as she returned to him whether she wanted to live or not.

123 She stayed in Albany for a few days, then flew home to her husband. He met her at the airport, near the luggage counter, where her three pieces of pale brown luggage were brought to him on a conveyor belt, to be claimed by him. He kissed her on the cheek. They shook hands, a little embarrassed. She had come home again.

124 "How will I live out the rest of my life?" she wondered.

125 In January her lover spied on her: she glanced up and saw him, in a public place, in the DeRoy Symphony Hall. She was paralyzed with fear. She nearly fainted. In this faint she felt her husband's body, loving her, working its love upon her, and she shut her eyes harder to keep out the certainty of his love—sometimes he failed at loving her, sometimes he succeeded, it had nothing to do with her or her pity or her ten years of love for him, it had nothing to do with a woman at all. It was a private act accomplished by a man, a husband or a lover, in communion with his own soul, his manhood.

126 Her husband was forty-two years old now, growing slowly into middle age, getting heavier, softer. Her lover was about the same age, narrower in the shoulders, with a full, solid chest, yet lean, nervous. She thought, in her paralysis, of men and how they love freely and eagerly so long as their bodies are capable of love, love for a woman: and then, as love fades in their bodies, it fades from their souls and they become immune and immortal and ready to die.

127 Her husband was a little rough with her, as if impatient with himself. "I love you," he said fiercely, angrily. And then, ashamed, he said, "Did I hurt you . . . ?"

128 "You didn't hurt me," she said.

129 Her voice was too shrill for their embrace.

130 While he was in the bathroom she went to her closet and took out that drawing of the summer before. There she was, on the beach at Nantucket, a lady with a pet dog, her eyes large and defined, the dog in her lap hardly more than a few snarls, a few coarse soft lines of charcoal . . . her dress smeared, her arms oddly limp . . . her hands not well drawn at all. . . . She tried to think: did she love the man who had drawn this? did he love her? The fever in her husband's body had touched her and driven her temperature up, and now she stared at the drawing with a kind of lust, fearful of seeing an ugly soul in that woman's face, fearful of seeing the face suddenly

through her lover's eyes. She breathed quickly and harshly, staring at the drawing.

And so, the next day, she went to him at his hotel. She wept, 131 pressing against him, demanding of him, "What do you want? Why are you here? Why don't you let me alone?" He told her that he wanted nothing. He expected nothing. He would not cause trouble.

"I want to talk about last August," he said. 132

"We are both married permanently," she said. 133

She was hypnotized by his gesturing hands, his nervousness, his 134 obvious agitation. He kept saying, "I understand. I understand that. I am making no claims upon you."

They became lovers again. 135

He called room service for something to drink and they sat side 136 by side on his bed, looking through a copy of *The New Yorker*, laughing at the cartoons. It was so peaceful in this room, so complete. They were on a holiday. It was a secret holiday. Four-thirty in the afternoon, on a Friday, an ordinary Friday: a secret holiday.

"I won't bother you again," he said. 137

He flew back to see her again in March, and in late April. He 138 telephoned her from his hotel—a different hotel each time—and she came down to him at once. She rose to him in various elevators, she knocked on the doors of various rooms, she stepped into his embrace, breathless and guilty and already angry with him, pleading with him. One morning in May, when he telephoned, she pressed her forehead against the door frame and could not speak. He kept saying, "What's wrong? Can't you talk? Aren't you alone?" She felt that she was going insane. Her head would burst. Why, why did he love her, why did he pursue her? Why did he want her to die?

She went to him in the hotel room. A familiar room: had they 139 been here before? "Everything is repeating itself. Everything is stuck," she said. He framed her face in his hands and said that she looked thinner—was she sick? what was wrong? She shook herself free. He, her lover, looked about the same. There was a small, angry pimple on his neck. He stared at her, eagerly and suspiciously. Did she bring bad news?

"So you love me? You love me?" she asked. 140

"Why are you so angry?" 141

"I want to be free of you. The two of us free of each other." 142

"That isn't true—you don't want that—" 143

He embraced her. She was wild with that old, familiar passion 144 for him, her body clinging to his, her arms not strong enough to hold him. Ah, what despair!—what bitter hatred she felt!—she needed this man for her salvation, he was all she had to live for, and yet she could not believe in him. He embraced her thighs, her hips, kissing her, pressing his warm face against her, and yet she could not believe in him, not really. She needed him in order to live, but he was not worth her love, he was not worth her dying. . . . She promised herself this: when she got back home, when she was alone, she would draw the razor more deeply across her arm.

145   The telephone rang and he answered it: a wrong number.

146   "Jesus," he said.

147   They lay together, still. She imagined their posture like this, the two of them one figure, one substance; and outside this room and this bed there was a universe of disjointed, separate things, blank things, that had nothing to do with them. She would not be Anna out there, the lady in the drawing. He would not be her lover.

148   "I love you so much . . ." she whispered.

149   "Please don't cry! We have only a few hours, please. . . ."

150   It was absurd, their clinging together like this. She saw them as pressing mutely together. Helpless substance, so heavy and warm and doomed. It was absurd that any human being should be so important to another human being. She wanted to laugh: a laugh might free them both.

151   She could not laugh.

152   Some time later he said, as if they had been arguing, "Look. It's you. You're the one who doesn't want to get married. You lie to me—"

153   "Lie to you?"

154   "You love me but you won't marry me, because you want something left over . . . something not finished. . . . All your life you can attribute your misery to me, to our not being married— you are using me—"

155   "Stop it! You'll make me hate you!" she cried.

156   "You can say to yourself that you're miserable because of *me*. We will never be married, you will never be happy, neither one of us will ever be happy—"

157   "I don't want to hear this!" she said.

158   She pressed her hands flat against her face.

159   She went to the bathroom to get dressed. She washed her face and part of her body, quickly. The fever was in her, in the pit of her belly. She would rush home and strike a razor across the inside of her arm and free that pressure, that fever.

160   The impatient bulging of her veins: an ordeal over.

161   The demand of the telephone's ringing: that ordeal over.

162   The nuisance of getting the car and driving home, in all that five o'clock traffic: an ordeal too much for a woman of her size.

163   The movement of this stranger's body in hers: over, finished.

164   Now, dressed, a little calmer, they held hands and talked. They

had to talk swiftly, to get all their news in: he did not trust the people who worked for him, he had faith in no one, his wife had moved to a textbook publishing company and was doing well, she had inherited a Ben Shahn painting from her father and wanted to "touch it up a little"—she was crazy!—his blind son was at another school, doing fairly well, in fact his children were all doing fairly well in spite of the stupid mistake of their parents' marriage—and what about her? what about her life? She told him in a rush the one thing he wanted to hear: that she lived with her husband lovelessly, the two of them polite strangers, sharing a bed, lying side by side in the night in that bed, bodies out of which souls had fled. There was no longer even any shame between them.

"And what about me? Do you feel shame with me still?" he   165
asked her anxiously.

She did not answer. She kissed him and prepared to leave. The   166
last five minutes had been so good, so fine, that she felt strangely happy. It was like the first day of their meeting on the beach, Anna self-conscious and exhilarated by this red-haired man's presence. Only to exist in the same world with him!—did she really want any more? And it seemed to her, suddenly, that their love might possibly come to a conclusion. They would marry, perhaps. Or break off their relationship. They would come to rest permanently in each other, pressed permanently together, or they would grow old and forget each other and be free forever. . . .

"You look so beautiful. You look so happy," he said, as if   167
jealous at this life inside her, this radiance he could not share. What, was it beginning all over again? Their love beginning again, in spite of them? "Why do you look so happy? Why?"

"Do I look happy?" she said, startled. "I don't know—I can't   168
help myself."

Reading Critically

1. Before responding to any of these questions, read Anton Chekhov's "The Lady with the Dog" (p. 108). Why does Oates choose to begin her own story at the point where Chekhov has the lover reappear, rather than begin where Chekhov begins? How does she change Chekhov's chronology? Do her changes make the story

more interesting? In what way does she change the point of view from the Chekhov story? What are the consequences of that change for the story's development? Would you say that where Chekhov's story is written from a male point of view, Oates's is written from a female point of view? Or is that an oversimplification? Discuss with your classmates.

2. Why does Anna think that she will give her life a center by betraying her lover? Have you ever thought that by giving up an illicit relationship or other "bad" behavior you would "find a center" or become happy? What are the flaws in this line of reasoning? Discuss with your classmates.

3. Both Anna's husband and lover are considerably older than she. What makes older men attractive to younger women, and younger women to older men? Do you know of cases illustrating the opposite? Discuss with your classmates.

4. Why does Anna *need* her lover? What does he provide in her life that her husband doesn't give her? Do you think that if Anna had a happy marriage she would still want a lover? Is there any need for a lover when one is happily married? Discuss with your classmates.

Responding Through Writing

1. At one point, Anna asks, "What did it mean to enter into a bond with another person?" In your private notebook or journal, make two entries, each describing a different kind of bond you have had with another person.

2. Why does Anna make those half-hearted attempts at suicide? Nothing in her life seems so terrible as to warrant those attempts. Why does she ultimately reject suicide as a solution? Respond with a few minutes of writing in your journal or notebook.

3. Were you surprised at the shift in chronology that takes place at the beginning of Part III? Write the draft of a narrative about some period in your own life, using the same kind of narrative chronology shift.

4. Scan the story once more, picking out the small details that Oates uses to intensify Anna's perceptions (the folds in her skirt in her picture with the dog, the hotel booklet that she sees when in bed with her lover). Pick some interesting moment in your own life and list the concrete details that come to mind as you think about that moment. Focus especially on seemingly minor details. Then use those details to write a description of that moment.

STOPPING BY WOODS ON A SNOWY EVENING

ROBERT FROST

Although Robert Frost (1874–1963) is identified as the quintessential "New England" poet, he was born in San Francisco. After the death of his father when Frost was ten, his mother moved to Lawrence, Massachusetts. Frost attended Dartmouth College briefly but quit school and took a variety of jobs, including working as a bobbin boy in a clothing mill in Lawrence. He married in 1895 and two years later enrolled at Harvard, but he dropped out after two years and, in 1899 bought a farm in Derry, New Hampshire, where he lived for most of his life. Although he began to write poetry in 1894, he did not gain critical acclaim until he published A Boy's Will *in 1913; this volume was followed by* North of Boston *in 1914, while he was living in England. He received the Pulitzer Prize in 1924, 1931, 1937, and 1942 and the Poetry Society of America medal in 1941. In 1950 the U.S. Senate passed a unanimous resolution honoring him. Frost has been praised as the poet of the commonplace who sees more in ordinary things than most people see. The following poem was originally published in his collection* New Hampshire *(1924).*

Whose woods these are I think I know.
His house is in the village though;
He will not see me stopping here
To watch his woods fill up with snow.   4

My little horse must think it queer
To stop without a farmhouse near
Between the woods and frozen lake
The darkest evening of the year.   8

He gives his harness bells a shake
To ask if there is some mistake.
The only other sound's the sweep
Of easy wind and downy flake.   12

The woods are lovely, dark and deep.
But I have promises to keep,
And miles to go before I sleep,
And miles to go before I sleep.   16

Reading Critically

1. Which elements of the poem suggest death? What else, other than death, might these same elements suggest? What does this ambiguity contribute to the poem?

2. Although Frost once said that he never intended that the poem be about death, many people still interpret the poem as being about the inevitability of death. Discuss with your classmates why this statement by Frost does not mean that the poem is therefore definitely not about death.

3. To what extent is this poem about life, not death? How would you argue that the poem isn't about death at all, that it suggests instead that you pause and quietly examine your life every once in a while?

4. Why do you think the title of the poem is "Stopping by Woods" and not "Stopping by *a* Woods" or "Stopping by *the* Woods"? To what extent does the title affect your interpretation of the poem? How would your interpretation of the poem change if it had no title? How important are titles for poems? Discuss with your classmates other possible titles for this poem.

Responding Through Writing

1. Read this poem aloud, paying special attention to the last stanza, especially the last two lines. (Be sure you read the poem according to its punctuation.) What effect is achieved by repeating the third line? What does this effect contribute to the theme of the poem? Read the last stanza aloud without the last line. What effect is lost? Write a paragraph in which you explain which reading you preferred and why. Discuss your paragraph with your classmates.

2. Why does the narrator say that his horse "must think it queer / To stop without a farmhouse near"? Surely he doesn't care what his horse thinks. Write a few sentences explaining the real purpose of these lines.

3. Go through the poem and write a list of all the words and images that create its mood of calm and quiet. Compare your list with the lists drawn up by your classmates.

4. Based upon your answers to the questions above, and your discussions with your classmates, write the first draft of an essay in which you discuss whether this poem is about death or life. Your classmates are the audience for your essay. Present your draft to them for discussion, and revise your essay based upon this discussion.

PART IV

CLASSIFICATION

The Purpose of Classification

When you began the process of picking the college you now attend, you probably did so by using the principles of classification. Unless you simply picked your college randomly (it's been known to happen), you probably began the selection process by listing (at least mentally) the *kinds* of college you wanted to attend. Did you want a big school or a small one, a state school or a private school, a school that emphasized liberal arts and sciences or one that emphasized professional programs, a school in an urban setting or a school off in the farmlands? Each time you asked those questions, you were employing principles of classification; that is, you were placing items into distinct groups *for a particular purpose.* If you used those principles well, you classified the colleges in question according to a single standard at a time (size, academic programs, location, and so on), and you tried not to let those standards overlap. Above all, you chose standards that fit your purpose, standards that reflected your principal reasons for attending a college.

Making a Classification Exhaustive

If you used the principles of classification well when picking a college, you probably made an *exhaustive* classification. That is, you judged each choice against *every* standard of classification that was important to your purpose for choosing a college. Many people fail to make exhaustive classifications and thus do not meet their purpose. You may know of people who chose a particular college because it had nice dormitories and was in a pleasant rural setting. When they arrived there, however, they learned that they couldn't complete a strong major in their field of choice, or that the weather in the winter was unbearably cold for them, or that they didn't like the number of large lecture-format classes they were required to take. Those individuals had failed to take classification far enough. As soon as they classified their prospective choices according to one or two principles, they prematurely stopped. Their sad results emphasize the need to be as exhaustive as your purpose requires when making classifications.

While a classification should be as exhaustive as it needs to be for your purpose, it would be a silly exercise to make every classification "totally" exhaustive. In picking a college you would probably not want to classify your prospective choices according to their plumbing and heating systems or the sizes of their endowments. You would instead pick those standards of classification that mattered to you, and you would exhaust those, starting with the most important. If you intended to major in journalism, an obvious first concern would be the presence or absence of a good journalism department. Your second concern would probably be an active college newspaper. Your next concern might be good writing courses. You would go on until you had exhausted your concerns; the areas for exploration would likely become less and less significant, and at the point that you felt your purposes for classifying had been adequately met, you would stop.

Looping Back to Subclassify

Rather than going on endlessly, adding minor or even pointless categories to your classification, you might loop back in the process and make subclassifications. If a good journalism department were a major concern, subclassifications might consider whether the journalism faculty was full-time or part-time, whether distinguished journalists appeared as visiting professors, or whether the department had an intern program with a respectable newspaper. Looping back and making subclassifications adds organization to your list of priorities.

The Problem of Overlapping

The process of making a useful classification need not be rigid. Rarely are useful classifications *made* through the outlines or branching tree diagrams that many rhetoric books suggest. On the contrary, those outlines and tree diagrams are usually the *result* of a process in which there is much overlapping of categories. If you are sometimes puzzled by the fact that a subcategory could easily be a major category, or vice versa, or that some of your categories and subcategories seem to overlap *slightly,* do not worry. Returning to our example of selecting a journalism department, you could list the qualities of the faculty either as a subcategory of the journalism department or as a major classification in itself.

The important point is not to get bogged down in artificial rules once you have seen to it that your major categories are as distinct as possible. There will inevitably be some overlapping. Above all, do not let your purpose become obscured for the sake of "symmetry," "order," or "balance." Remember that your aim is not to write some abstract piece of classification that looks nice, but to meet some concrete purpose.

Keeping to Logical and Distinct Standards of Classification

If some overlapping develops in your classification, make sure that it is not illogical. The greatest danger is that you will fail to keep logically distinct categories separate as you move through the process of classifying, or that you will move so quickly from one category to another that they will become blurred together. It is remarkably easy to allow your classification to become muddled. To continue with our choosing-a-college example, you can rapidly move from thinking (or writing) about one college in terms of its fine academic program, to another in terms of its wonderful location, to another in terms of its winning football team, and so forth. It may be appealing to think about the best each college has to offer, but if you have no main principle of selection, and hence no distinct standard by which to classify, your thinking will end in a mishmash and your final choice is likely to be made at random. Decide on your purpose (stated as narrowly as possible), assign standards of classification that help you achieve that purpose, and then determine how each college meets those standards, one standard at a time.

Relationships Between Classification and Comparison–Contrast

Classification and comparison–contrast are two techniques in thinking and writing that are very closely linked. Every rational comparison implies a classification. In the introduction to the next section of this book, "Comparison and Contrast," you will find some suggestions for developing the results of classification in essays that compare or contrast. It might be worth your while at least to skim that introduction now, since it stresses some of the basic and functional aspects of both comparison and, by implication, of classification.

FOUR KINDS
OF CHANCE

JAMES H. AUSTIN

James H. Austin (b. 1925) is a specialist in neurology who has been praised both as a professional scientist and for his writing skills in making complex scientific issues comprehensible to laypersons. Educated at Brown University and Harvard Medical School, he is the author of Chase, Chance, and Creativity: The Lucky Art of Novelty *(1978) and is professor of neurology at the Medical School of the University of Colorado. Austin has concentrated his energies on brain research and has received the American Association of Neuropathologists Prize for his work. Austin's writings deal in large part with the role of chance in scientific discovery. The following selection was first published in the* Saturday Review *in 1974.*

What is chance? Dictionaries define it as something fortuitous   1
that happens unpredictably without discernible human intention.
Chance is unintentional and capricious, but we needn't conclude
that chance is immune from human intervention. Indeed, chance
plays several distinct roles when humans react creatively with one
another and with their environment.

We can readily distinguish four varieties of chance if we   2
consider that they each involve a different kind of motor activity

and a special kind of sensory receptivity. The varieties of chance also involve distinctive personality traits and differ in the way one particular individual influences them.

3   Chance I is the pure blind luck that comes with no effort on our part. If, for example, you are sitting at a bridge table of four, it's "in the cards" for you to receive a hand of all 13 spades, but it will come up only once in every 6.3 trillion deals. You will ultimately draw this lucky hand—with no intervention on your part—but it does involve a longer wait than most of us have time for.

4   Chance II evokes the kind of luck Charles Kettering had in mind when he said: "Keep on going and the chances are you will stumble on something, perhaps when you are least expecting it. I have never heard of anyone stumbling on something sitting down."

5   In the sense referred to here, Chance II is not passive, but springs from an energetic, generalized motor activity. A certain basal level of action "stirs up the pot," brings in random ideas that will collide and stick together in fresh combinations, lets chance operate. When someone, *anyone,* does swing into motion and keeps on going, he will increase the number of collisions between events. When a few events are linked together, they can then be exploited to have a fortuitous outcome, but many others, of course, cannot. Kettering was right. Press on. Something will turn up. We may term this the Kettering Principle.

6   In the two previous examples, a unique role of the individual person was either lacking or minimal. Accordingly, as we move on to Chance III, we see blind luck, but in camouflage. Chance presents the clue, the opportunity exists, but it would be missed except by that one person uniquely equipped to observe it, visualize it conceptually, and fully grasp its significance. Chance III involves a special receptivity and discernment unique to the recipient. Louis Pasteur characterized it for all time when he said: "Chance favors only the prepared mind."

7   Pasteur himself had it in full measure. But the classic example of his principle occurred in 1928, when Alexander Fleming's mind instantly fused at least five elements into a conceptually unified nexus. His mental sequences went something like this: (1) I see that a mold has fallen by accident into my culture dish; (2) the staphylococcal colonies residing near it failed to grow; (3) the mold must have secreted something that killed the bacteria; (4) I recall a similar experience once before; (5) if I could separate this new "something" from the mold, it could be used to kill staphylococci that cause human infections.

Actually, Fleming's mind was exceptionally well prepared for   8
the penicillin mold. Six years earlier, while he was suffering from
a cold, his own nasal drippings had found their way into a culture
dish, for reasons not made entirely clear. He noted that nearby
bacteria were killed, and astutely followed up the lead. His observations led him to discover a bactericidal enzyme present in nasal
mucus and tears, called lysozyme. Lysozyme proved too weak to be
of medical use, but imagine how receptive Fleming's mind was to
the penicillin mold when it later happened on the scene!

One word evokes the quality of the operations involved in the   9
first three kinds of chance. It is *serendipity*. The term describes the
facility for encountering unexpected good luck, as the result of:
accident (Chance I), general exploratory behavior (Chance II), or
sagacity (Chance III). The word itself was coined by the English-
man-of-letters Horace Walpole, in 1754. He used it with reference
to the legendary tales of the Three Princes of Serendip (Ceylon),
who quite unexpectedly encountered many instances of good fortune on their travels. In today's parlance, we have usually watered
down *serendipity* to mean the good luck that comes solely by
accident. We think of it as a result, not an ability. We have tended
to lose sight of the element of sagacity, by which term Walpole
wished to emphasize that some distinctive personal receptivity is
involved.

There remains a fourth element in good luck, an unintentional   10
but subtle personal prompting of it. The English Prime Minister
Benjamin Disraeli summed up the principle underlying Chance IV
when he noted that "we make our fortunes and we call them fate."
Disraeli, a politician of considerable practical experience, appreciated that we each shape our own destiny, at least to some
degree. One might restate the principle as follows: *Chance favors the
individualized action.*

In Chance IV the kind of luck is peculiar to one person, and   11
like a personal hobby, it takes on a distinctive individual flavor. This
form of chance is one-man-made, and it is as personal as a signature.
. . . Chance IV has an elusive, almost miragelike, quality. Like a
mirage, it is difficult to get a firm grip on, for it tends to recede as
we pursue it and advance as we step back. But we still accept a
mirage when we see it, because we vaguely understand the basis for
the phenomenon. A strongly heated layer of air, less dense than
usual, lies next to the earth, and it bends the light rays as they pass
through. The resulting image may be magnified as if by a telescopic
lens in the atmosphere, and real objects, ordinarily hidden far out
of sight over the horizon, are brought forward and revealed to the

eye. What happens in a mirage then, and in this form of chance, not only appears farfetched but indeed is farfetched.

12   About a century ago, a striking example of Chance IV took place in the Spanish cave of Altamira.[1] There, one day in 1879, Don Marcelino de Sautuola was engaged in his hobby of archaeology, searching Altamira for bones and stones. With him was his daughter, Maria, who had asked him if she could come along to the cave that day. The indulgent father had said she could. Naturally enough, he first looked where he had always found heavy objects before, on the *floor* of the cave. But Maria, unhampered by any such preconceptions, looked not only at the floor but also all around the cave with the open-eyed wonder of a child! She looked up, exclaimed, and then he looked up, to see incredible works of art on the cave ceiling! The magnificent colored bison and other animals they saw at Altamira, painted more than 15,000 years ago, might lead one to call it "the Sistine Chapel of Prehistory." Passionately pursuing his interest in archaeology, de Sautuola, to his surprise, discovered man's first paintings. In quest of science, he happened upon Art.

13   Yes, a dog did "discover" the cave, and the initial receptivity was his daughter's, but the pivotal reason for the cave paintings' discovery hinged on a long sequence of prior events originating in de Sautuola himself. For when we dig into the background of this amateur excavator, we find he was an exceptional person. Few Spaniards were out probing into caves 100 years ago. The fact that he—not someone else—decided to dig that day in the cave of Altamira was the culmination of his passionate interest in his hobby. Here was a rare man whose avocation had been to educate himself from scratch, as it were, in the science of archaeology and cave exploration. This was no simple passive recognizer of blind luck when it came his way, but a man whose unique interests served as an active creative thrust—someone whose own actions and personality would focus the events that led circuitously but inexorably to the discovery of man's first paintings.

14   Then, too, there is a more subtle manner. How do you give full weight to the personal interests that imbue your child with your own curiosity, that inspire her to ask to join you in your own musty hobby, and that then lead you to agree to her request at the critical moment? For many reasons, at Altamira, more than the special receptivity of Chance III was required—this was a different domain, that of the personality and its actions.

---

1. The cave had first been discovered some years before by an enterprising hunting dog in search of game. Curiously, in 1932 the French cave of Lascaux was discovered by still another dog.

A century ago no one had the remotest idea our caveman   15
ancestors were highly creative artists. Weren't their talents rather
minor and limited to crude flint chippings? But the paintings at
Altamira, like a mirage, would quickly magnify this diminutive
view, bring up into full focus a distant, hidden era of man's prehistory, reveal sentient minds and well-developed aesthetic sen-
sibilities to which men of any age might aspire. And like a mirage, the events at Altamira grew out of de Sautuola's heated
personal quest and out of the invisible forces of chance we know
exist yet cannot touch. Accordingly, one may introduce the term
altamirage to identify the quality underlying Chance IV. Let us
define it as the facility for encountering unexpected good luck as
the result of highly individualized action. Altamirage goes well
beyond the boundaries of serendipity in its emphasis on the role of
personal action in chance.

Chance IV is favored by distinctive, if not eccentric, hobbies,   16
personal life-styles, and modes of behavior peculiar to one individual, usually invested with some passion. The farther apart these
personal activities are from the area under investigation, the more
novel and unexpected will be the creative product of the encounter.

Reading Critically

1. To what extent do you believe in luck? Cite some examples
where "just plain luck" saved the day for you. Then discuss these
examples with your classmates. Was "luck" the only factor involved? To what extent do education and training come into play
in most people's "luck"?

2. Austin speculates in paragraph 3 about the possibility of
drawing the ultimate hand in cards: "You will ultimately draw this
lucky hand . . . but it does involve a longer wait than most of us
have time for." Evidently he means that, given enough time, absolutely everything that could happen to you, would happen to you.
Discuss this possibility in terms of reincarnation. Would you choose
to live again and again until "everything" happened to you, good
and bad?

3. Do you think that wars happen mainly by chance? If so, is a nuclear war inevitable? Can anything at all be done to stop it? Is the human race totally at the mercy of chance? Discuss these questions with your classmates.

4. What is the central standard of classification in this essay? What does it have to do with the difference between randomness and human intent? Which elements are common to the four kinds of chance? Which elements are different? Can you and your classmates reach consensus on these questions?

Responding Through Writing

1. In a short series of paragraphs, discuss the differences between Chance I and the remaining kinds of chance Austin describes.

2. What is Austin's purpose in introducing the story of the Altamira cave in the last part of the essay? As part of Austin's audience, do you have any difficulty connecting this example with Austin's attempt to define Chance IV? Would another example have been better, more immediate? Rewrite the first part of the essay using an example of your own.

3. Austin begins his classification essay with a definition of chance (paragraph 1). The remainder of the essay shows why this "dictionary" definition is incomplete and unsatisfactory. Choose two or three other dictionary definitions and write a paragraph for each one, showing why it is not entirely accurate.

4. Austin says that "Chance IV is favored by distinctive, if not eccentric, hobbies" (paragraph 16). Have you ever come upon "chance" discoveries as a result of hobbies or pastimes? Write a short essay indicating how this happened.

SALUTATION DISPLAYS

DESMOND MORRIS

Desmond Morris (b. 1928), through his studies in zoology and animal behavior, has attempted to describe modern society in terms of innate animal behavior patterns. Though his premise, that analogues to human social institutions are found in animal behavior, has been challenged, the stimulating and entertaining style of, for example, The Naked Ape: A Zoologist's Study of the Human Animal *(1967), has brought much scientific material to a wide audience. Morris has written on animal behavior from juvenile to scholarly levels, sometimes as coauthor with his wife, Ramona Morris. His most recent works include* Catwatching *(1987),* Dogwatching *(1987), and* Catlore *(1988). The following essay is from his 1977 book,* Manwatching.

A Salutation Display demonstrates that we wish people well, or, at the very least, that we wish them no harm. It transmits signals of friendliness or the absence of hostility. It does this at peak moments—when people are arriving on the scene, departing from it, or dramatically changing their social role. We salute their comings, their goings and their transformations, and we do it with rituals of greeting, farewell and celebration.

2   Whenever two friends meet after a long separation, they go through a special Greeting Ritual. During the first moments of the reunion they amplify their friendly signals to super-friendly signals. They smile and touch, often embrace and kiss, and generally behave more intimately and expansively than usual. They do this because they have to make up for lost time—lost friendship time. While they have been apart it has been impossible for them to send the hundreds of small, minute-by-minute friendly signals to each other that their relationship requires, and they have, so to speak, built up a backlog of these signals.

3   This backlog amounts to a gestural debt that must be repaid without delay, as an assurance that the bond of friendship has not waned but has survived the passage of time spent apart—hence the gushing ceremonies of the reunion scene, which must try to pay off this debt in a single outburst of activity.

4   Once the Greeting Ritual is over, the old relationship between the friends is now re-established and they can continue with their amicable interactions as before. Eventually, if they have to part for another long spell, there will be a Separation Ritual in which the super-friendly signals will once again be displayed. This time they have the function of leaving both partners with a powerful dose of befriendedness, to last them through the isolated times to come.

5   In a similar way, if people undergo a major change in social role, we again offer them a massive outpouring of friendliness, because we are simultaneously saying farewell to their old self and greeting their new self. We do this when boy and girl become man and wife, when man and wife become father and mother, when prince becomes king, when candidate becomes president, and when competitor becomes champion.

6   We have many formal procedures for celebrating these occasions, both the physical arrivals and departures and the symbolic comings and goings of the social transformations. We celebrate birthdays, christenings, comings-of-age, weddings, coronations, anniversaries, inaugurations, presentations, and retirements. We give house-warmings, welcoming parties, farewell dinners, and funerals. In all these cases we are, in essence, performing Salutation Displays.

7   The grander the occasion, the more rigid and institutional are the procedures. But even our more modest, private, two-person rituals follow distinct sets of rules. We seem to be almost incapable of beginning or ending any kind of encounter without performing some type of salutation. This is even true when we write a letter to someone. We begin with "Dear Mr. Smith" and end "Yours

faithfully," and the rules of salutation are so compelling that we do this even when Mr. Smith is far from dear to us and we have little faith in him.

Similarly we shake hands with unwelcome guests and express 8 regret at their departure, although we are glad to see the back of them. All the more reason, then, that our genuine greetings and farewells should be excessively demonstrative.

Social greetings that are planned and anticipated have a distinc- 9 tive structure and fall into four separate phases:

1. The Inconvenience Display. To show the strength of our 10 friendliness, we "put ourselves out" to varying degrees. We demonstrate that we are taking trouble. For both host and guest, this may mean "dressing up." For the guest it may mean a long journey. For the host it also entails a bodily shift from the center of his home territory. The stronger the greeting, the greater the inconvenience. The Head of State drives to the airport to meet the important arrival. The brother drives to the airport to greet his sister returning from abroad. This is the maximum form of bodily displacement that a host can offer. From this extreme there is a declining scale of inconvenience, as the distance traveled by the host decreases. He may only go as far as the local station or bus depot. Or he may move no farther than his front drive, emerging from his front door after watching through the window for the moment of arrival. Or he may wait for the bell to ring and then only displace himself as far as his doorway or front hall. Or he may allow a child or servant to answer the door and remain in his room, the very center of his territory, awaiting the guest who is then ushered into his presence. The minimal Inconvenience Display he can offer is to stand up when the guest enters the room, displacing himself vertically but not horizontally. Only if he remains seated as the guest enters and approaches him, can he be said to be totally omitting Phase One of a planned social greeting. Such omissions are extremely rare today and some degree of voluntary inconvenience is nearly always demonstrated. If, because of some accident or delay, it is unavoidably omitted, there are profuse apologies for its absence when the meeting finally takes place.

At the time of farewell, the Inconvenience Display is repeated 11 in much the same form. "You know your own way out" is the lowest level of expression here. Beyond that, there is an increasing displacement from territorial base, with the usual social level being "I will see you to the door." A slightly more intense form involves going outside the house and waiting there until the departing figures have vanished from sight. And so on, with the full expression being an accompaniment to the station or airport.

12   2. The Distant Display. The main moment of greeting is when body contact is made, but before this comes the moment of first sighting. As soon as host and guest have identified each other, they signify this fact with a recognition response. Doorstep meetings tend to curtail this phase, because contact can be made almost immediately the door is opened, but in most other greeting situations the Distance Display is prominently demonstrated. It consists of six visual elements: (1) the Smile; (2) the Eyebrow Flash; (3) the Head Tilt; (4) the Hail; (5) the Wave; and (6) the Intention Embrace.

13   The first three of these almost always occur, and they are performed simultaneously. At the moment of recognition, the head tilts back, the eyebrows arch up, and the face breaks into a large smile. The Head Tilt and the Eyebrow Flash may be very brief. They are elements of surprise. Combined with the smile, they signal a "pleasant surprise" at seeing the friend. This basic pattern may or may not be augmented by an arm movement. The simplest such action is the Hail—the raising of one hand. A more intense version, typical of long-distance greetings, is the Wave, and a still more intense expression is the Intention Embrace, in which the arms are stretched out towards the friend, as if the greeter cannot wait to perform the contact-embrace that is about to take place. A flamboyant specialty sometimes added is the Thrown or Blown Kiss, again anticipating the contact to come.

14   As before, the same actions are repeated during the farewell Separation Ritual, but with Intention Embraces less likely and Thrown or Blown Kisses more likely.

15   Of these Distant Displays, the Smile, Head Tilt, and Eyebrow Flash appear to be worldwide. They have been observed in remote native tribes that had never previously encountered white men. The raising of an arm in some form of Hail or Wave salute is also extremely widespread. The exact form of the arm movement may vary from culture to culture, but the existence of *some* kind of arm action appears to be global for mankind. The action seems to stem, like the Intention Embrace, from an urge to reach out and touch the other person. In the Hail, the arm is raised up rather than reached out, because this makes it more conspicuous from a distance, but the movement is essentially a stylized version of touching the distant friend. More "historical" explanations, such as that the hand is raised to show it is empty of weapons or that it is thrust up to mime the

action of offering the owner's sword, and therefore his allegiance, may be true in certain specific contexts, but the action is too widespread and too general for this interpretation to stand for all cases of Hailing.

The Wave takes three main forms: the Vertical Wave, the Hidden-palm Wave, and the Lateral Wave. In the Vertical Wave, the palm faces the friend and the hand moves repeatedly up and down. This appears to be the "primitive" form of waving. In origin, it seems to be a vacuum patting action, the hand patting the friend's body at a distance, again in anticipation of the friend's embrace to come. The Hidden-palm Wave, seen mainly in Italy, is also a patting action, but with the hand moving repeatedly towards the waver himself. To non-Italians, this looks rather like beckoning, but it is basically another form of vacuum embracing. The Lateral Wave, common all over the world, consists of showing the palm to the friend and then moving it rhythmically from side to side. This appears to be an improved form of the other waves. The modification is essentially one of increasing the visibility and conspicuousness of the patting action. In turning it into a lateral movement, it loses its embracing quality, but gains dramatically in visual impact from a distance. It can be further exaggerated by extending it to full arm-waving, or even double-arm-waving.

3. The Close Display. As soon as the Distant Display has been performed, there is an approach interval and then the key moment of actual body contact. At full intensity this consists of a total embrace, bringing both arms around the friend's body, with frontal trunk contact and head contact. There is much hugging, squeezing, patting, cheek-pressing, and kissing. This may be followed by intense eye contact at close range, cheek-clasping, mouth-kissing, hair-stroking, laughing, even weeping, and, of course, continued smiling.

From this uninhibited display, there is a whole range of body-contacts of decreasing strength, right down to the formal handshake. The precise intensity will depend on: (1) the depth of the prior relationship; (2) the length of the separation; (3) the privacy of the greeting context; (4) the local, cultural display-rules and traditions; and (5) the changes that have taken place during the separation.

Most of these conditions are obvious enough, but the last deserves comment. If the friend is known to have been through some major emotional experience—an ordeal such as imprisonment, illness, or disaster, or a great success such as an award, a victory, or an honor—there will be a much more intense greeting and stronger embracing. This is because the Salutation Display is simultaneously a greeting and a celebration and is, in effect, double-strength.

20   Different cultures have formalized the close greeting performance in different ways. In all cases, the basis of the display is the full embrace, but when this is simplified, different parts of it are retained in different places. In some cultures, the head-to-head element becomes nose-rubbing, cheek-mouthing, or face-pressing. In others, there is a stylized mutual cheek-kiss, with the lips stopping short of contact. In others again, there is kissing between men—in France and Russia, for example—while in many cultures, male-to-male kissing is omitted as supposedly effeminate.

21   While these cultural variations are, of course, of interest, they should not be allowed to obscure the fact that they are all variations on a basic theme—the body embrace. This is the fundamental, global, human contact action, the one we all know as babies, infants, and growing children, and to which we return whenever the rules permit and we wish to demonstrate feelings of attachment for another individual.

22   4. The "Grooming" Display. Following the initial body contacts, we move into the final stage of the greeting ceremony, which is similar to the social grooming performances of monkeys and apes. We do not pick at one another's fur, but instead we display "Grooming Talk"—inane comments that mean very little in themselves, but which demonstrate vocally our pleasure at the meeting. "How are you?" "How nice of you to come," "Did you have a good journey?" "You are looking so well," "Let me take your coat," and so on. The answers are barely heard. All that is important is to pay compliments and to receive them. To show concern and to show pleasure. The precise verbal content and the intelligence of the questions is almost irrelevant. This Grooming Display is sometimes augmented by helping with clothing, taking off coats, and generally fussing with creature comforts. On occasion there is an additional Gift Display on the part of the guest, who brings some small offering as a further, material form of salutation.

23   After the Grooming Display is over, the friends leave the special site of the greeting and move on to resume their old, familiar, social interactions. The Salutation Display is complete and has performed its important task.

24   By contrast, unplanned greetings are far less elaborate. When we see a friend in the street, or somewhere away from home, we give the typical Distant Display—a smile and a wave—and perhaps no more. Or we approach and add a Close Display, usually a rather abbreviated embrace, but more usually a mere handshake. As we

part, we again display, often turning for a final Distant Signal, as we move off.

Introductory Greetings take yet another form. If we are meet- 25
ing someone for the first time, we omit the Distant Display, simply because we are not recognizing an old friend. We do, however, offer a minor form of Close Display, nearly always a handshake, and we smile at the new acquaintance and offer him a Grooming Display of friendly chatter and concern. We treat him, in fact, as though he were a friend already, not a close one but a friend none the less, and in so doing we bring him into our orbit and initiate a social relationship with him.

As a species of primate, we are remarkably rich in greetings 26
and farewells. Other primates do show some simple greeting rituals, but we exceed them all, and we also show farewell displays which they seem to lack entirely. Looking back into our ancestry, there seems to have been a good reason for this development. Most primates move around in a fairly close-knit group. Occasionally, they may drift apart and then, on reuniting, will give small gestures of greeting. But they rarely part deliberately, in a purposeful way, so they have no use for Separation Displays. Early man established himself as a hunting species, with the male hunting group leaving for a specific purpose at a specific time, and then returning to the home base with the kill. For millions of years, therefore, we have needed Salutation Displays, both in the form of farewells, as the group split up in its major division-of-labor, and in the form of greetings, when they came together again. And the importance of success or failure on the hunt meant that these were not trivial, but vital moments in the communal life of the primeval tribe. Little wonder that today we are such a salutatory species.

Reading Critically

1. Is politeness always a sign of positive feeling? How can you be both polite and unfriendly at the same time? Describe a time when you were polite to someone you really didn't like. Why were you polite? Given such situations, discuss with your classmates what the real meaning of politeness is.

2. In paragraph 24 Morris says that there are great differences between planned and unplanned greetings. Give one example of a planned greeting and one example of an unplanned greeting. What are the differences between the two kinds of greetings?

3. In what ways can "salutation displays" be unfriendly? Discuss with your classmates some unfriendly salutations and the situations in which they occur.

4. What are "inconvenience displays"? After reading paragraph 10, list a few examples of such displays, then compare your examples with those of your classmates. Which displays mentioned by other students have you never encountered? What does the range of response in your class suggest about the origin and meaning of "inconvenience displays" and "salutation displays"?

Responding Through Writing

1. In paragraph 18 Morris lists the conditions necessary for bodily contact during a greeting. Write the first draft of a short essay about a time someone wanted to shake your hand, hug you, or engage in some other social bodily contact but you didn't. Explain why you didn't and what message you were trying to send to the other person by your actions.

2. Morris ends his essay with the remark that human beings "are remarkably rich in greetings and farewells." He thus leaves you with the suggestion that much more could be said on his topic. Write the first draft of an essay in which you classify additional examples of greetings and farewells. After discussing your draft with your classmates, revise your essay.

3. Read paragraphs 10, 12, 17, and 22, and then list the classifications of "salutation displays" Morris makes. (Make sure you leave room on your list so you can add more information to it.)

Then rearrange the list and add whatever subdivisions you think are needed.

4. To your new list, add each of the examples Morris uses. Which classifications and subdivisions have examples and which do not? Add some new examples to the list.

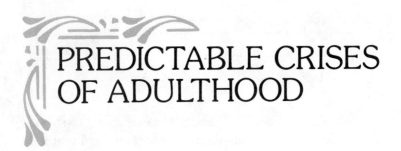

PREDICTABLE CRISES OF ADULTHOOD

GAIL SHEEHY

Gail Sheehy (b. 1937) received a B.S. degree from the University of Vermont in 1958, after which she entered graduate study at Columbia University. She began her writing career as fashion editor for the Rochester (N.Y.) Democrat and Chronicle, *and as a feature writer for the* New York Herald Tribune, New York *magazine, and a number of other magazines. She is the author of the novel* Lovesounds *(1970), a book about people who get divorced for "no good reason." Her remaining works tend to be sociological investigations:* Panthermania: The Clash of Black Against Black in One American City *(1971);* Speed Is of the Essence *(1971), a study of the use and effects of amphetamines;* Hustling: Prostitution in Our Wide Open Society *(1973); and* Passages: Predictable Crises of Adult Life *(1976), a popularization of psychological theories developed by Daniel Levinson, Erik Erikson, Roger Gould, and others. The following essay appeared in* New York *magazine in 1974.*

1   We are not unlike a particularly hardy crustacean. The lobster grows by developing and shedding a series of hard, protective shells.

Each time it expands from within, the confining shell must be sloughed off. It is left exposed and vulnerable until, in time, a new covering grows to replace the old.

With each passage from one stage of human growth to the   2
next we, too, must shed a protective structure. We are left exposed and vulnerable—but also yeasty and embryonic again, capable of stretching in ways we hadn't known before. These sheddings may take several years or more. Coming out of each passage, though, we enter a longer and more stable period in which we can expect relative tranquility and a sense of equilibrium regained. . . .

As we shall see, each person engages the steps of development   3
in his or her own characteristic *step-style*. Some people never complete the whole sequence. And none of us "solves" with one step—by jumping out of the parental home into a job or marriage, for example—the problems in separating from the caregivers of childhood. Nor do we "achieve" autonomy once and for all by converting our dreams into concrete goals, even when we attain those goals. The central issues or tasks of one period are never fully completed, tied up, and cast aside. But when they lose their primacy and the current life structure has served its purpose, we are ready to move on to the next period.

Can one catch up? What might look to others like listlessness,   4
contrariness, a maddening refusal to face up to an obvious task may be a person's own unique detour that will bring him out later on the other side. Developmental gains won can later be lost—and rewon. It's plausible, though it can't be proven, that the mastery of one set of tasks fortifies us for the next period and the next set of challenges. But it's important not to think too mechanistically. Machines work by units. The bureaucracy (supposedly) works step by step. Human beings, thank God, have an individual inner dynamic that can never be precisely coded.

Although I have indicated the ages when Americans are likely   5
to go through each stage, and the differences between men and women where they are striking, do not take the ages too seriously. The stages are the thing, and most particularly the sequence.

Here is the briefest outline of the developmental ladder.   6

Pulling Up Roots

Before 18, the motto is loud and clear: "I have to get away   7
from my parents." But the words are seldom connected to action. Generally still safely part of our families, even if away at school,

we feel our autonomy to be subject to erosion from moment to moment.

8   After 18, we begin Pulling Up Roots in earnest. College, military service, and short-term travels are all customary vehicles our society provides for the first round trips between family and a base of one's own. In the attempt to separate our view of the world from our family's view, despite vigorous protestations to the contrary—"I know exactly what I want!"—we cast about for any beliefs we can call our own. And in the process of testing those beliefs we are often drawn to fads, preferably those most mysterious and inaccessible to our parents.

9   Whatever tentative memberships we try out in the world, the fear haunts us that we are really kids who cannot take care of ourselves. We cover that fear with acts of defiance and mimicked confidence. For allies to replace our parents, we turn to our contemporaries. They become conspirators. So long as their perspective meshes with our own, they are able to substitute for the sanctuary of the family. But that doesn't last very long. And the instant they diverge from the shaky ideals of "our group," they are seen as betrayers. Rebounds to the family are common between the ages of 18 and 22.

10   The tasks of this passage are to locate ourselves in a peer group role, a sex role, an anticipated occupation, an ideology or world view. As a result, we gather the impetus to leave home physically and the identity to *begin* leaving home emotionally.

11   Even as one part of us seeks to be an individual, another part longs to restore the safety and comfort of merging with another. Thus one of the most popular myths of this passage is: We can piggyback our development by attaching to a Stronger One. But people who marry during this time often prolong financial and emotional ties to the family and relatives that impede them from becoming self-sufficient.

12   A stormy passage through the Pulling Up Roots years will probably facilitate the normal progression of the adult life cycle. If one doesn't have an identity crisis at this point, it will erupt during a later transition, when the penalties may be harder to bear.

The Trying Twenties

13   The Trying Twenties confront us with the question of how to take hold in the adult world. Our focus shifts from the interior turmoils of late adolescence—"Who am I?" "What is truth?"—and

we become almost totally preoccupied with working out the externals. "How do I put my aspirations into effect?" "What is the best way to start?" "Where do I go?" "Who can help me?" "How did *you* do it?"

In this period, which is longer and more stable compared with the passage that leads to it, the tasks are as enormous as they are exhilarating: To shape a Dream, that vision of ourselves which will generate energy, aliveness, and hope. To prepare for a lifework. To find a mentor if possible. And to form the capacity for intimacy, without losing in the process whatever consistency of self we have thus far mustered. The first test structure must be erected around the life we choose to try. 14

Doing what we "should" is the most pervasive theme of the twenties. The "shoulds" are largely defined by family models, the press of the culture, or the prejudices of our peers. If the prevailing cultural instructions are that one should get married and settle down behind one's own door, a nuclear family is born. If instead the peers insist that one should do one's own thing, the 25-year-old is likely to harness himself onto a Harley-Davidson and burn up Route 66 in the commitment to have no commitments. 15

One of the terrifying aspects of the twenties is the inner conviction that the choices we make are irrevocable. It is largely a false fear. Change is quite possible, and some alteration of our original choices is probably inevitable. 16

Two impulses, as always, are at work. One is to build a firm, safe structure for the future by making strong commitments, to "be set." Yet people who slip into a ready-made form without much self-examination are likely to find themselves *locked in.* 17

The other urge is to explore and experiment, keeping any structure tentative and therefore easily reversible. Taken to the extreme, these are people who skip from one trial job and one limited personal encounter to another, spending their twenties in the *transient* state. 18

Although the choices of our twenties are not irrevocable, they do set in motion a Life Pattern. Some of us follow the lock-in pattern, others the transient pattern, the wunderkind pattern, the caregiver pattern, and there are a number of others. Such patterns strongly influence the particular questions raised for each person during each passage. . . . 19

Buoyed by powerful illusions and belief in the power of the will, we commonly insist in our twenties that what we have chosen to do is the one true course in life. Our backs go up at the merest 20 hint that we are like our parents, that two decades of parental training might be reflected in our current actions and attitudes.

21   "Not me," is the motto, "I'm different."

Catch-30

22   Impatient with devoting ourselves to the "shoulds," a new vitality springs from within as we approach 30. Men and women alike speak of feeling too narrow and restricted. They blame all sorts of things, but what the restrictions boil down to are the outgrowth of career and personal choices of the twenties. They may have been choices perfectly suited to that stage. But now the fit feels different. Some inner aspect that was left out is striving to be taken into account. Important new choices must be made, and commitments altered or deepened. The work involves great change, turmoil, and often crisis—a simultaneous feeling of rock bottom and the urge to bust out.

23   One common response is the tearing up of the life we spent most of our twenties putting together. It may mean striking out on a secondary road toward a new vision or converting a dream of "running for president" into a more realistic goal. The single person feels a push to find a partner. The woman who was previously content at home with children chafes to venture into the world. The childless couple reconsiders children. And almost everyone who is married, especially those married for seven years, feels a discontent.

24   If the discontent doesn't lead to a divorce, it will, or should, call for a serious review of the marriage and of each partner's aspirations in their Catch-30 condition. The gist of that condition was expressed by a 29-year-old associate with a Wall Street law firm:

25   "I'm considering leaving the firm. I've been there four years now; I'm getting good feedback, but I have no clients of my own. I feel weak. If I wait much longer, it will be too late, too close to that fateful time of decision on whether or not to become a partner. I'm success-oriented. But the concept of being 55 years old and stuck in a monotonous job drives me wild. It drives me crazy now, just a little bit. I'd say that 85 percent of the time I thoroughly enjoy my work. But when I get a screwball case, I come away from court saying, 'What am I doing here?' It's a *visceral* reaction that I'm wasting my time. I'm trying to find some way to make a social contribution or a slot in city government. I keep saying, 'There's something more.' "

26   Besides the push to broaden himself professionally, there is a

wish to expand his personal life. He wants two or three more children. "The concept of a home has become very meaningful to me, a place to get away from troubles and relax. I love my son in a way I could not have anticipated. I never could live alone."

Consumed with the work of making his own critical life-steering decisions, he demonstrates the essential shift at this age: an absolute requirement to be more self-concerned. The self has new value now that his competency has been proved.

His wife is struggling with her own age-30 priorities. She wants to go to law school, but he wants more children. If she is going to stay home, she wants him to make more time for the family instead of taking on even wider professional commitments. His view of the bind, of what he would most like from his wife, is this:

"I'd like not to be bothered. It sounds cruel, but I'd like not to have to worry about what she's going to do next week. Which is why I've told her several times that I think she should do something. Go back to school and get a degree in social work or geography or whatever. Hopefully that would fulfill her, and then I wouldn't have to worry about her line of problems. I want her to be decisive about herself."

The trouble with his advice to his wife is that it comes out of concern with *his* convenience, rather than with *her* development. She quickly picks up on this lack of goodwill: He is trying to dispose of her. At the same time, he refuses her the same latitude to be "selfish" in making an independent decision to broaden her horizons. Both perceive a lack of mutuality. And that is what Catch-30 is all about for the couple.

Rooting and Extending

Life becomes less provisional, more rational and orderly in the early thirties. We begin to settle down in the full sense. Most of us begin putting down roots and sending out new shoots. People buy houses and become very earnest about climbing career ladders. Men in particular concern themselves with "making it." Satisfaction with marriage generally goes downhill in the thirties (for those who have remained together) compared with the highly valued, vision-supporting marriage of the twenties. This coincides with the couple's reduced social life outside the family and the in-turned focus on raising their children.

The Deadline Decade

In the middle of the thirties we come upon a crossroads. We have reached the halfway mark. Yet even as we are reaching our prime, we begin to see there is a place where it finishes. Time starts to squeeze.

33   The loss of youth, the faltering of physical powers we have always taken for granted, the fading purpose of stereotyped roles by which we have thus far identified ourselves, the spiritual dilemma of having no absolute answers—any or all of these shocks can give this passage the character of crisis. Such thoughts usher in a decade between 35 and 45 that can be called the Deadline Decade. It is a time of both danger and opportunity. All of us have the chance to rework the narrow identity by which we defined ourselves in the first half of life. And those of us who make the most of the opportunity will have a full-out authenticity crisis.

34   To come through this authenticity crisis, we must reexamine our purposes and reevaluate how to spend our resources from now on. "Why am I doing all this? What do I really believe in?" No matter what we have been doing, there will be parts of ourselves that have been suppressed and now need to find expression. "Bad" feelings will demand acknowledgment along with the good.

35   It is frightening to step off onto the treacherous footbridge leading to the second half of life. We can't take everything with us on this journey through uncertainty. Along the way, we dis- cover that we are alone. We no longer have to ask permission because we are the providers of our own safety. We must learn to give ourselves permission. We stumble upon feminine or mascu- line aspects of our natures that up to this time have usually been masked. There is grieving to be done because an old self is dying. By taking in our suppressed and even our unwanted parts, we prepare at the gut level for the reintegration of an identity that is ours and ours alone—not some artificial form put together to please the culture or our mates. It is a dark passage at the begin- ning. But by disassembling ourselves, we can glimpse the light and gather our parts into a renewal.

36   Women sense this inner crossroads earlier than men do. The time pinch often prompts a woman to stop and take an all-points survey at age 35. Whatever options she has already played out, she feels a "my last chance" urgency to review those options she has set aside and those that aging and biology will close off in the *now foreseeable* future. For all her qualms and confusion about where to start looking for a new future, she usually enjoys an exhilaration of release. Assertiveness begins rising. There are so many firsts ahead.

37   Men, too, feel the time push in the mid-thirties. Most men respond by pressing down harder on the career accelerator. It's "my

last chance" to pull away from the pack. It is no longer enough to be the loyal junior executive, the promising young novelist, the lawyer who does a little *pro bono* work on the side. He wants now to become part of top management, to be recognized as an established writer, or an active politician with his own legislative program. With some chagrin, he discovers that he has been too anxious to please and too vulnerable to criticism. He wants to put together his own ship.

During this period of intense concentration on external advancement, it is common for men to be unaware of the more difficult, gut issues that are propelling them forward. The survey that was neglected at 35 becomes a crucible at 40. Whatever rung of achievement he has reached, the man of 40 usually feels stale, restless, burdened, and unappreciated. He worries about his health. He wonders, "Is this all there is?" He may make a series of departures from well-established lifelong base lines, including marriage. More and more men are seeking second careers in midlife. Some become self-destructive. And many men in their forties experience a major shift of emphasis away from pouring all their energies into their own advancement. A more tender, feeling side comes into play. They become interested in developing an ethical self.

Renewal or Resignation

Somewhere in the mid-forties, equilibrium is regained. A new stability is achieved, which may be more or less satisfying.

If one has refused to budge through the midlife transition, the sense of staleness will calcify into resignation. One by one, the safety and supports will be withdrawn from the person who is standing still. Parents will become children; children will become strangers; a mate will grow away or go away; the career will become just a job—and each of these events will be felt as an abandonment. The crisis will probably emerge again around 50. And although its wallop will be greater, the jolt may be just what is needed to prod the resigned middle-ager toward seeking revitalization.

On the other hand . . .

If we have confronted ourselves in the middle passage and found a renewal of purpose around which we are eager to build a more authentic life structure, these may well be the best years. Personal happiness takes a sharp turn upward for partners who can now accept the fact: "I cannot expect *anyone* to fully understand me." Parents can be forgiven for the burdens of our childhood.

Children can be let go without leaving us in collapsed silence. At 50, there is a new warmth and mellowing. Friends become more important than ever, but so does privacy. Since it is so often proclaimed by people past midlife, the motto of this stage might be "No more bullshit."

Reading Critically

1. Through which of the stages described by Sheehy do you think your life is passing now? Discuss with your classmates how someone might be in one of Sheehy's stages chronologically but in another stage in terms of the developments in his or her life.

2. What does Sheehy mean in paragraph 2 when she says, "We are left exposed and vulnerable—but also yeasty and embryonic again. . . ."? Be sure you can define *yeasty* and *embryonic.*

3. With your classmates, sort yourselves into one of the age groups listed by Sheehy. If you have older classmates, discuss with them whether they think they have passed through the stages of growth as described by Sheehy. In what ways do you and your classmates agree or disagree with her description of the concerns of those in the "Pulling Up Roots" stage of development?

4. What does Sheehy mean when she says that "none of us 'solves' with one step—by jumping out of the parental home into a job or marriage, for example—the problems in separating from the caregivers of childhood" (paragraph 2)? What does this lack of a single-step solution imply as the central problem each of us will face for the rest of our lives? According to Sheehy, can we ever hope to reach a lasting state of happiness or contentment in our lives? What does she suggest is the source of our continuing discontent during our lives?

Responding Through Writing

1. If you are keeping a journal or notebook, write in it about your reactions to the "Pulling Up Roots" stage of development. Do you believe everyone passes through such a stage? Are you in this stage? Passing through it? Already through it? How important do you think this stage is for young people? Write as much as you can in ten minutes.

2. Write a list of each of the stages of development Sheehy discusses. Besides chronology, list the other bases Sheehy uses to classify her stages of development. How does Sheehy classify the stages? Write an alternative classification of your own.

3. Using the information you gained in answering both questions 1 and 2 above, write the first draft of an essay in which you classify the various ways young people today "pull up roots" and begin to establish their own identities.

4. Look up a description of *crustacean* and list the distinguishing aspects of a crustacean. Write a definition of *metaphor*. Now write a paragraph in which you explain how the metaphor of the crustacean was appropriate for clarifying the different stages of growth. In a second paragraph discuss whether or not this metaphor helped you understand the different stages of growth. Where in the essay (besides the first two paragraphs) does Sheehy use this metaphor?

BLACK WASN'T BEAUTIFUL

MARY MEBANE

Mary Mebane (b. 1933) holds a Ph.D. from the University of North Carolina and is professor of English at the University of South Carolina in Columbia. In 1982 the National Endowment for the Arts recognized her talent and awarded her a Creative Writing Fellowship. In the same year, she received the Distinguished Alumna Award from the University of North Carolina in Chapel Hill. Mebane's work focuses on the post-1960 experience of blacks in the South. She says, "It is my belief that the black folk are the most creative, viable people that America has produced. They just don't know it." Mebane is the author of a two-act play, Take a Sad Song *(1975), and has also written her autobiography in two books,* Mary *(1981), from which the following selection was taken, and* Mary Wayfarer *(1983). In the epilogue to* Mary, *Mebane writes, "Writing, the gulf stream of my life, has saved me."*

1   In the fall of 1951 during my first week at North Carolina College, a black school in Durham, the chairman's wife, who was indistinguishable from a white woman, stopped me one day in the hall. She wanted to see me, she said.

2   When I went to her office, she greeted me with a big smile.

"You know," she said, "you made the highest mark on the verbal part of the examination." She was referring to the examination that the entire freshman class took upon entering the college. In spite of her smile, her eyes and tone of voice were saying, "How could this black-skinned girl score higher on the verbal than some of the students who've had more advantages than she? It must be some sort of fluke." I felt it, but I managed to smile my thanks and back off. For here at North Carolina College, social class and color were the primary criteria used in deciding status. The faculty assumed light-skinned students were more intelligent, and they were always a bit nonplussed when a dark-skinned student did well, especially if she was a girl.

I don't know whether African men recently transported to the   3
New World considered themselves handsome or, more important, whether they considered African women beautiful in comparison with native American Indian women or immigrant European women. But one thing I know for sure: by the 20th century, really black skin on a woman was considered ugly in this country. In the 1950s this was particularly true among those who were exposed to college. Black skin was to be disguised at all costs. Since a black face is rather hard to disguise, many women took refuge in ludicrous makeup.

I observed all through elementary and high school, in various   4
entertainments, the girls were placed on the stage in order of color. And very black ones didn't get into the front row. If they were past caramel-brown, to the back row they would go. Nobody questioned the justice of this—neither the students nor the teachers.

Oddly enough, the lighter-skinned black male did not seem to   5
feel so much prejudice toward the black black woman. It was no accident, I felt, that Mr. Harrison, the eighth-grade teacher, who was reddish-yellow himself, once protested to the science and math teacher about the fact that he always assigned sweeping duties to Doris and Ruby, two black black girls. Mr. Harrison said to them one day in the other teacher's presence, "You must be some bad girls. Every day I come down here you all are sweeping." The science and math teacher got the point and didn't ask them to sweep any more. Uneducated black males, too, sometimes related very well to the black black woman. They had been less indoctrinated by the white society around them.

Because of the stigma attached to having dark skin, a black   6
black woman had to do many things to find a place for herself. One possibility was to attach herself to a light-skinned woman, hoping that some of the magic would rub off on her. A second was to make

herself sexually available, hoping thereby to attract a mate. Third, she could resign herself to a more chaste life-style—either (for the professional woman) teaching and work in established churches or (for the uneducated woman) domestic work and zealous service in "holy and sanctified" churches.

7   Lucy had chosen the first route. Lucy was short, skinny, short-haired and black black, and thus unacceptable. So she made her choice. She selected Patricia, the lightest-skinned girl in the school, as her friend and followed her around. Patricia and her friends barely tolerated Lucy, but Lucy smiled and doggedly hung on, hoping that those who noticed Patricia might notice her also. Though I felt shame for her behavior, even then I understood.

8   A fourth avenue open to the black black woman is excellence in a career. Since in the South the field most accessible to such women is education, a great many of them prepared to become teachers. But here, too, the black black woman had problems. Grades weren't given to her lightly in school, nor were promotions on the job. She had to pass examinations with flying colors or be left behind. She had to be overqualified for a job because otherwise she didn't stand a chance of getting it—and she was competing only with other blacks.

9   The black woman's training would pay off in the 1970s. With the arrival of integration, the black black woman would find, paradoxically enough, that her skin color in an integrated situation was not the handicap it had been in an all-black situation. But it wasn't until the middle and late 1960s, when the post-1945 genera-tion of black males arrived in college that I noticed any change in the situation at all. *He* wore an Afro and *she* wore an Afro, and sometimes the only way you could tell them apart was when his Afro was taller than hers. Black had become beautiful. It was then that the dread I felt at dealing with the college-educated black male began to ease. Even now, though, when I have occasion to engage in any transaction with a college-educated black man, I gauge his age. If I guess he was born after 1945, I feel confident that the transaction will turn out all right. If he probably was born before 1945, my stomach tightens, I find myself taking shallow breaths, and I try to state my business and escape as soon as possible.

10   When the grades for the first quarter at North Carolina Col-lege came out, I had the highest average in the freshman class. The chairman's wife called me into her office again. We did a replay of the same scene we had played during the first week of the term. She complimented me on my grades. Then she reached into a drawer and pulled out a copy of the freshman English final examination. She asked me to take the exam over again.

At first I couldn't believe what she was saying. I had taken the   11
course under another teacher; and it was so incredible to her that
I should have made the highest score in the class that she was trying
to test me again personally. For a few moments I knew rage so
intense that I wanted to take my fists and start punching her. I have
seldom hated anyone so deeply. I handed the examination back to
her and walked out.

Reading Critically

1. You are classified regularly during your life—the Internal
Revenue Service classifies you, credit card companies classify you,
insurance companies classify you, teachers classify you by giving
you a grade. Discuss a time you think you were classified unfairly.
How did you feel? What were the effects of that classification?
Discuss with your classmates why you think people will probably
never stop classifying each other.

2. Why do people classify other people? What classifications
do you find yourself making, perhaps unconsciously, in relation to
people's physical characteristics? Discuss with your classmates why
it seems surprising that members of a minority would classify each
other according to physical characteristics.

3. How surprised were you when you read the first two
paragraphs of this essay? Is color discrimination supposed to exist
within a race of people? What other ethnic groups can you name
that practice the same kind of within-group discrimination? What
do you think this kind of discrimination reveals about the nature
of discrimination and prejudice?

4. What classification is central to this essay? On what characteristic is it based? What subclassifications does Mebane make in
paragraph 6? What is the basis for these subclassifications? Write a
list of these classifications and subclassifications.

Responding Through Writing

1. Who is the audience for this essay? What evidence can you cite in the essay that indicates the intended audience? What surprise is there for the audience in paragraphs 1 and 2? Assume that the audience for this essay will be white, suburban, middle-class college students. Write an introduction to the essay for that audience.

2. Although Mebane uses classification as the principle basis for organizing and developing her essay, she also uses chronological development, especially in paragraphs 4 through 9. Discuss how she might have organized her essay solely on the basis of classification. What would she have had to change in the essay? Write an outline of this essay organized only on the basis of classification.

3. Write a one-sentence definition of *irony*. What irony is there in paragraph 9? What is Mebane indirectly saying about the character of prejudice in this paragraph?

4. Mebane uses two personal experiences to begin and end her essay. What do these personal experiences have in common? Why doesn't Mebane conclude her essay with a different kind of personal experience? Write a different conclusion for the essay, one that will either replace the present conclusion, or one that can follow it. What effect does your conclusion have on the rest of the essay?

LOSING PEOPLE

ANNE TAYLOR FLEMING

Anne Taylor Fleming is a free-lance writer living in Los Angeles who frequently contributes to the New York Times *and the* New York Times Magazine. *In 1975 she authored* The First Time, *a book that details the accounts of various celebrities' loss of virginity. Her essays focus on those small aspects of life that carry great meaning. Writing about something as ordinary as her new telephone-address book, she observes that it "would last a lifetime and outlast the lifetimes of at least half the people whose names I would write in it. . . . people I had loved, people who had been at the very center of my life when I was young." The following article appeared in the* New York Times *on April 6, 1980.*

For Christmas, I was given a new telephone-address book of sleek caramel-colored leather, made in France, that smells like the inside of a fancy imported car. My name is embossed in gold in the lower right-hand corner. It is the first address book I have had with my name on it. The books I had before were like the ones from school days, small and plastic, and I usually bent them and tore them and finally lost them, feeling nothing when I did. This one, I think, will outlast me; its beauty seems so invincible. Having it, owning it, holding it in my hands makes me feel greedy and giddy and almost elegant. I cannot imagine harming it. I wipe my hands before touching it; then, as if it were a mirror, I wipe its surface clear of my handprints with a cuff or sleeve. I carry it as I move from room to room, imagining myself, brave and lovely, pulling it from my shoulder bag while leaning against a dusty window in some seedy telephone booth in some foreign city.

2   The problem with the book is that I have not been able to use it; as yet, I have not made a single entry in it. I had anticipated with such pleasure the process of transferring the names from my old book to my new. I bought new pens, three of them, with the finest felt tips to write the names in my new book. I practiced my printing. I counted the lines on each page, the number of pages for each letter, discovering that I had room for 400 A's and 60 X's. Then, ready, I sat before the book as if I were sitting down to a meal.

3   I skimmed through the A's in my old book, deciding whom to transfer to the new book and whom not to transfer, a simple clerical chore, I thought. Not so. Each name caught me up. I could not get out of the A's. There was my friend from high school who sometimes uses her own name, sometimes that of her husband. Should I put her in my new book under the name I first knew and loved her by, the name I had heard her called a thousand times in a thousand study halls, or should I wait and list her later by her married name? After all, I mused, we were grown-ups now, over 30, married, men's names after our own. It had all gone too fast. I wanted her here under the A's, under her own name. But who was I to make that judgment?

4   Then there was my sister, listed by her first name. Brothers and sisters, however old, never seem to have more than first names. Yet again, I thought, my sister and I are grown, I will give her a last name finally. I turned to the M's to enter her—her married name is Moore—but I couldn't do it. To me she was only that one name, that two-syllable first name I could hear my pleading child's voice using when I had done something awful to her and she had locked me out of her room, and I pounded, saying her name over and over, to get through that door and back into her heart.

5   I turned back to the A's, my page still empty. I set the new book aside for a moment. I went on through the old book, bumping into the names of people I hardly knew anymore, old classmates who in that frantic hour before graduation insisted on leaving their names in my book, knowing I would never call—just as I knew and they knew they would never call me. If I left them there in the old book and didn't bring them into the new, they would be gone forever, lost from my memory. Should I take them with me into my new book, knowing that I would never see them again? That was silly. Yet I was reluctant to abandon them. I thumbed on, finding names of cousins I barely knew, telephone numbers of

people I had met at parties and never seen again. Half the impulse was to retain everybody, simply copy the old book verbatim, no questions asked, no memories aborted. The other half of the impulse was to purge, to clean out, moving only the best of best of friends into my beautiful new book, leaving behind anyone who had ever hurt me, even slightly, as if not transferring their names would somehow keep them from ever hurting me again.

By the time I was midway through the old book, I had not   6
crossed off a single name nor made a single entry in the new one. The new book was, I realized, intimidating in its loveliness, more intimidating in its implication of permanence. Leather, my name in gold, it would last a lifetime and outlast the lifetimes of at least half the people whose names I would write in it. So later, much later, carrying it still, I would see names and addresses of people I had loved, people who had been at the very center of my life when I was young.

Reading Critically

1. Why does Fleming say in paragraph 5 that she couldn't just go through the old telephone book and copy the names of current friends into the new book and delete the names of old friends? What do these acts of copying and deleting do to Fleming's life? Discuss with your classmates.

2. How many people do you know in this class? How many will you remember after this class is over at the end of the semester? How do you choose which people to keep in your life and in your memory? How does keeping a journal or diary help you keep people in your life and in your memory?

3. Have you ever gone through your telephone, address, or similar book and crossed out names? If you have never gone through such a book, describe another experience that gave you the sense of loss that Fleming describes. From where does that sense of loss come, according to Fleming?

4. How can you lose people as you go through life? In what sense are they lost? In what way does keeping a telephone book record your life? In what other ways do you record your life? Bring an old address book to class and discuss how you may have "discarded" friends. What similarities do you find between your "discards" and those of your classmates?

Responding Through Writing

1. Cite evidence from the essay that indicates whether Fleming has a definite audience for her essay, or whether she is just talking to herself. Write a paragraph in which you describe the audience of this essay. How can anyone who does not keep a telephone or address book appreciate this essay?

2. Examine Fleming's sentence structure and note the wide variety of sentences she uses. Note, for example, the opening sentence of the essay, which is followed by two relatively simple sentences. Again, in paragraph 3 she begins with a rather long sentence followed by a fragment. What does she achieve by such sentence variety? Rewrite the long sentence opening the essay and the long sentence beginning paragraph 3 as short, simple sentences. What effect is lost with this rewriting? What, if anything, is gained by this rewriting?

3. Do you think paragraphs 1 and 5 are too long, out of balance with the rest of the paragraphs in the essay? Rewrite these paragraphs, breaking them up into shorter paragraphs. Compare your revisions with those written by your classmates. Which version do you like better?

4. After reading paragraph 6 again, especially the last sentence, write a sentence in which you state Fleming's purpose in this essay. Why does Fleming wait until the last paragraph in her essay to state her purpose?

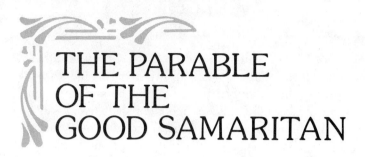

THE PARABLE
OF THE
GOOD SAMARITAN

LUKE

Like the three other Evangelists (Matthew, Mark, and John), Luke is someone about whom we know very little beyond the fact that he wrote one of the gospels. The quality of his Greek, however, suggests that he was an educated man and had the abilities of a scholar and an aim to be factually accurate. His purpose in writing the gospel, as he indicated to the Greek official Theophilus, was to provide "a careful investigation that you may have certitude." We do know that Luke relied heavily on the writings of Mark, but not as heavily as did Matthew, and that he probably also wrote sections of Acts of the Apostles. *Popular legend has it that Luke was a physician, but of this there is no proof. Luke's gospel has perhaps been best characterized by Dante, who called Luke "scriba de mansuetudinis Christi" (the writer of the mercy of Christ). It is only in the Gospel of Luke, for example, that we find the parable of the prodigal son and Jesus's promise that the "good" thief will enter paradise.*

And behold, a certain lawyer stood up, and tempted him, saying, "Master, what shall I do to inherit eternal life?" He said unto him, "What is written in the law? how readest thou?" And he answering, said, "Thou shalt love the Lord thy God with all thy heart, and with all thy soul, and with all thy strength, and with all thy mind, and thy neighbour as thyself." And he said unto him, "Thou hast answered right: this do, and thou shalt live." But he willing to justify himself, said unto Jesus, "And who is my neighbour?" And Jesus answering, said, "A certain man went down from Jerusalem to Jericho, and fell among thieves, which stripped him of his raiment, and wounded him, and departed, leaving him half dead. And by chance there came down a certain priest that way, and when he saw him, he passed by on the other side. And likewise a Levite, when he was at the place, came and looked on him, and passed by on the other side. But a certain Samaritan, as he journeyed, came where he was; and when he saw him, he had compassion on him, and went to him, and bound up his wounds, pouring in oil and wine, and set him on his own beast, and brought him to an inn, and took care of him. And on the morrow when he departed, he took out two pence, and gave them to the host, and said unto him, 'Take care of him, and whatsoever thou spendest more, when I come again I will repay thee.' Which now of these three, thinkest thou, was neighbour unto him that fell among the thieves?" And he said, "He that showed mercy on him." Then said Jesus unto him, "Go, and do thou likewise."

Reading Critically

1. Of what significance is it that the Samaritan takes personal care of the man who was robbed and does not simply spend money to see that the man is taken care of? What does this aspect of the parable say about differences between "personal" and "corporate" charity?

2. If you were to try to love *everyone* as you love yourself, wouldn't "love" become meaningless? Isn't it better to care intensely about a few people (family, close friends) than to care in a diluted way about the whole world? Discuss this question with your classmates.

3. Why is it appropriate that the parable should start with a question from a lawyer?

4. In what sense is this parable an essay in classification, in definition? What standards of classification does Luke implicitly employ?

Responding Through Writing

1. What application does this parable have to the situations of homeless people? Do we typically treat the homeless as our "neighbors"? Is being a "neighbor" as easy as the parable makes it seem? Write your reaction to these questions in your journal or notebook.

2. Can you rewrite the parable using contemporary references? Let's say, for example, that you have a moderate income and some credit cards, and that you come upon a homeless person sleeping on the steps of a local hotel. What do you do? Write a few paragraphs in your journal or notebook in response to this question.

3. Does the archaic language of the text lend dignity and stateliness to the parable, or does it make the message obscure? Rewrite the parable in contemporary English. Does the meaning seem to change?

4. What indirect message is there in the fact that religious officials (a priest and a Levite) pass by a half-dead man? Using this example as your cue, write an essay employing examples that illustrate contemporary hypocrisy toward the poor and destitute.

A MISCELLANY OF CHARACTERS THAT WILL NOT APPEAR

JOHN CHEEVER

John Cheever (1912–1982) has been praised for his humor, candor, and originality. His first short story, "Expelled" (1930), appeared in the New Republic *and recounted the 17-year-old Cheever's expulsion from the Thayer Academy for smoking and laziness. To earn money after being thrown out of school, Cheever wrote short stories and essays for various magazines. It was not long before he was recognized, and in 1942 Cheever's first collection of stories,* The Way Some People Live, *was published. His first novel,* The Wapshot Chronicle *(1957), won Cheever the National Book Award for 1958. His other novels include* Bullet Park *(1969),* Falconer *(1977), and* Oh What a Paradise It Seems *(1982). His most famous collection of short stories,* The Stories of John Cheever *(1978), earned him a Pulitzer Prize for fiction and the American Book Award. The following story is contained in that collection and was first published in* The New Yorker *in November 1960.*

1. The pretty girl at the Princeton–Dartmouth Rugby game. She wandered up and down behind the crowd that was ranged along the foul line. She seemed to have no date, no particular companion

but to be known to everyone. Everyone called her name (Florrie), everyone was happy to see her, and, as she stopped to speak with friends, one man put his hand flat on the small of her back, and at this touch (in spite of the fine weather and the green of the playing field) a dark and thoughtful look came over his face, as if he felt immortal longings. Her hair was a fine dark gold, and she pulled a curl down over her eyes and peered through it. Her nose was a little too quick, but the effect was sensual and aristocratic, her arms and legs were round and fine but not at all womanly, and she squinted her violet eyes. It was the first half, there was no score, and Dartmouth kicked the ball offside. It was a muffed kick, and it went directly into her arms. The catch was graceful; she seemed to have been chosen to receive the ball and stood there for a second, smiling, bowing, observed by everyone, before she tossed it charmingly and clumsily back into play. There was some applause. Then everyone turned their attention from Florrie back to the field, and a second later she dropped to her knees, covering her face with her hands, recoiling violently from the excitement. She seemed very shy. Someone opened a can of beer and passed it to her, and she stood and wandered again along the foul line and out of the pages of my novel because I never saw her again.

2. All parts for Marlon Brando.

3. All scornful descriptions of American landscapes with ruined tenements, automobile dumps, polluted rivers, jerry-built ranch houses, abandoned miniature golf links, cinder deserts, ugly hoardings, unsightly oil derricks, diseased elm trees, eroded farmlands, gaudy and fanciful gas stations, unclean motels, candlelit tearooms, and streams paved with beer cans, for these are not, as they might seem to be, the ruins of our civilization but are the temporary encampments and outposts of the civilization that we—you and I—shall build.

4. All such scenes as the following: "Clarissa stepped into the room and then _____." Out with this and all other explicit descriptions of sexual commerce, for how can we describe the most exalted experience of our physical lives, as if—jack, wrench, hubcap, and nuts—we were describing the changing of a flat tire?

5. All lushes. For example: The curtain rises on the copy office of a Madison Avenue advertising agency, where X, our principal character, is working out the exploitation plans for a new brand of rye whiskey. On a drafting table to the right of his fruitwood desk is a pile of suggestions from the art department. Monarchal and baronial crests and escutcheons have been suggested for the label. For advertising there is a suggested scene of

plantation life where the long-gone cotton aristocracy drink whiskey on a magnificent porch. X is not satisfied with this and examines next a watercolor of pioneer America. How fresh, cold, and musical is the stream that pours through the forest. The tongues of the brook speak into the melancholy silence of a lost wilderness, and what is that in the corner of the blue sky but a flight of carrier pigeons. On a rock in the foreground a wiry young man, in rude leather clothing and a coonskin hat, is drinking rye from a stone jug. This prospect seems to sadden X, and he goes on to the next suggestion, which is that one entertain with rye; that one invite to one's house one exploded literary celebrity, one unemployed actress, the grandniece of a President of the United States, one broken-down bore, and one sullen and wicked literary critic. They stand grouped around an enormous bottle of rye. This picture disgusts X, and he goes on to the last, where a fair young couple in evening dress stand at dusk on a medieval battlement (aren't those the lights and towers of Siena in the distance?) toasting what must be a seduction of indescribable prowess and duration in the rye that is easy on your dollar.

6   X is not satisfied. He turns away from the drafting table and walks toward his desk. He is a slender man of indiscernible age, although time seems to have seized upon his eye sockets and the scruff of his neck. This last is seamed and scored as wildly as some disjointed geodetic survey. There is a cut as deep as a saber scar running diagonally from the left to the right of his neck with so many deep and numerous branches and tributaries that the effect is discouraging. But it is in his eyes that the recoil of time is most noticeable. Here we see, as on a sandy point we see the working of two tides, how the powers of his exaltation and his misery, his lusts and his aspirations, have stamped a wilderness of wrinkles onto the dark and pouchy skin. He may have tired his eyes looking at Vega through a telescope or reading Keats by a dim light, but his gaze seems hangdog and impure. These details would lead you to believe that he was a man of some age, but suddenly he drops his left shoulder very gracefully and shoots the cuff of his silk shirt as if he were eighteen—nineteen at the most. He glances at his Italian calendar watch. It is ten in the morning. His office is soundproofed and preternaturally still. The voice of the city comes faintly to his high window. He stares at his dispatch case, darkened by the rains of England, France, Italy, and Spain. He is in the throes of a grueling melancholy that makes the painted walls of his office (pale yellow and pale blue) seem like fabrications of paper put up to conceal the volcanos and floodwaters that are the terms of his misery. He seems to be approaching the moment of his death, the moment of his

conception, some critical point in time. His head, his shoulders, and his hands begin to tremble. He opens his dispatch case, takes out a bottle of rye, gets to his knees, and thirstily empties the bottle.

He is on the skids, of course, and we will bother with only one more scene. After having been fired from the office where we last saw him he is offered a job in Cleveland, where the rumors of his weakness seem not to have reached. He has gone to Cleveland to settle the arrangements and rent a house for his family. Now they are waiting at the railroad station for him to return with good news. His pretty wife, his three children, and the two dogs have all come down to welcome Daddy. It is dusk in the suburb where they live. They are, by this time, a family that have received more than their share of discouragements, but in having been recently denied the common promises and rewards of their way of life—the new car and the new bicycle—they have discovered a melancholy but steady quality of affection that has nothing to do with acquisitions. They have glimpsed, in their troubled love for Daddy, the thrill of a destiny. The local rattles into view. A soft spray of golden sparks falls from the brake box as the train slows and halts. They all feel, in the intensity of their anticipation, nearly incorporeal. Seven men and two women leave the train, but where is Daddy? It takes two conductors to get him down the stairs. He has lost his hat, his necktie, and his topcoat, and someone has blacked his right eye. He still holds the dispatch case under one arm. No one speaks, no one weeps as they get him into the car and drive him out of our sight, out of our jurisdiction and concern. Out they go, male and female, all the lushes; they throw so little true light on the way we live.

6. And while we are about it, out go all those homosexuals who have taken such a dominating position in recent fiction. Isn't it time that we embraced the indiscretion and inconstancy of the flesh and moved on? The scene this time is Hewitt's Beach on the afternoon of the Fourth of July. Mrs. Ditmar, the wife of the Governor, and her son Randall have carried their picnic lunch up the beach to a deserted cove, although the American flag on the clubhouse can be seen flying beyond the dunes. The boy is sixteen, well formed, his skin the fine gold of youth, and he seems to his lonely mother so beautiful that she admires him with trepidation. For the last ten years her husband, the Governor, has neglected her in favor of his intelligent and pretty executive secretary. Mrs. Ditmar has absorbed, with the extraordinary commodiousness of human nature, a nearly daily score of wounds. Of course she loves her son. She finds nothing of her husband in his appearance. He has the best qualities of *her* family, she thinks, and she is old enough to think that such things as a slender foot and fine hair are marks

of breeding, as indeed they may be. His shoulders are square. His body is compact. As he throws a stone into the sea, it is not the force with which he throws the stone that absorbs her but the fine grace with which his arm completes the circular motion once the stone has left his hand—as if every gesture he made were linked, one to the other. Like any lover, she is immoderate and does not want the afternoon with him to end. She does not dare wish for an eternity, but she wishes the day had more hours than is possible. She fingers her pearls in her worn hands, and admires their sea lights, and wonders how they would look against his golden skin.

9   He is a little bored. He would rather be with men and girls his own age, but his mother has supported him and defended him so he finds some security in her company. She has been a staunch and formidable protector. She can and has intimidated the headmaster and most of the teachers at his school. Offshore he sees the sails of the racing fleet and wishes briefly that he were with them, but he refused an invitation to crew and has not enough self-confidence to skipper, so in a sense he chose to be alone on the beach with his mother. He is timid about competitive sports, about the whole appearance of organized society, as if it concealed a force that might tear him to pieces; but why is this? Is he a coward, and is there such a thing? Is one born a coward, as one is born dark or fair? Is his mother's surveillance excessive; has she gone so far in protecting him that he has become vulnerable and morbid? But considering how intimately he knows the depth of her unhappiness, how can he forsake her until she has found other friends?

10   He thinks of his father with pain. He has tried to know and love his father, but all their plans come to nothing. The fishing trip was canceled by the unexpected arrival of the Governor of Massachusetts. At the ball park a messenger brought him a note saying that his father would be unable to come. When he fell out of the pear tree and broke his arm, his father would undoubtedly have visited him in the hospital had he not been in Washington. He learned to cast with a fly rod, feeling that, cast by cast, he might work his way into the terrain of his father's affection and esteem, but his father had never found time to admire him. He can grasp the power of his own disappointment. This emotion surrounds him like a mass of energy, but an energy that has no wheels to drive, no stones to move. These sad thoughts can be seen in his posture. His shoulders droop. He looks childish and forlorn, and his mother calls him to her.

11   He sits in the sand at her feet, and she runs her fingers through his light hair. Then she does something hideous. One wants to look away but not before we have seen her undo her pearls and fasten

them around his golden neck. "See how they shine," says she, doing the clasp as irrevocably as the manacle is welded to the prisoner's shin.

Out they go; out they go; for, like Clarissa and the lush, they shed too little light.   12

7. In closing—in closing, that is, for this afternoon (I have to go to the dentist and then have my hair cut), I would like to consider the career of my laconic old friend Royden Blake. We can, for reasons of convenience, divide his work into four periods. First there were the bitter moral anecdotes—he must have written a hundred— that proved that most of our deeds are sinful. This was followed, as you will remember, by nearly a decade of snobbism, in which he never wrote of characters who had less than sixty-five thousand dollars a year. He memorized the names of the Groton faculty and the bartenders at "21." All of his characters were waited on hand and foot by punctilious servants, but when you went to his house for dinner you found the chairs held together with picture wire, you ate fried eggs from a cracked plate, the doorknobs came off in your hand, and if you wanted to flush the toilet you had to lift the lid off the water tank, roll up a sleeve, and reach deep into the cold and rusty water to manipulate the valves. When he had finished with snobbism, he made the error I have mentioned in Item 4 and then moved on into his romantic period, where he wrote "The Necklace of Malvio d'Alfi" (with that memorable scene of child-birth on a mountain pass), "The Wreck of the S.S. *Lorelei*," "The King of the Trojans," and "The Lost Girdle of Venus," to name only a few. He was quite sick at the time, and his incompetence seemed to be increasing. His work was characterized by everything that I have mentioned. In his pages one found alcoholics, scarifying de-scriptions of the American landscape, and fat parts for Marlon Brando. You might say that he had lost the gift of evoking the perfumes of life: sea water, the smoke of burning hemlock, and the breasts of women. He had damaged, you might say, the ear's inner-most chamber, where we hear the heavy noise of the dragon's tail moving over the dead leaves. I never liked him, but he was a colleague and a drinking companion, and when I heard, in my home in Kitzbühel, that he was dying, I drove to Innsbruck and took the express to Venice, where he then lived. It was in the late autumn. Cold and brilliant. The boarded-up palaces of the Grand Canal— gaunt, bedizened, and crowned—looked like the haggard faces of that grade of nobility that shows up for the royal weddings in Hesse. He was living in a *pensione* on a back canal. There was a high tide, the reception hall was flooded, and I got to the staircase over an arrangement of duckboards. I brought him a bottle of Turinese gin   13

and a package of Austrian cigarettes, but he was too far gone for these, I saw when I sat down in a painted chair (broken) beside his bed. "I'm working," he exclaimed. "I'm working. I can see it all. Listen to me!"

14   "Yes," I said.

15   "It begins like this," he said, and changed the level of his voice to correspond, I suppose, to the gravity of his narrative. "The Transalpini stops at Kirchbach at midnight," he said, looking in my direction to make sure that I had received the full impact of this poetic fact.

16   "Yes," I said.

17   "Here the passengers for Vienna continue on," he said sonorously, "while those for Padua must wait an hour. The station is kept open and heated for their convenience, and there is a bar where one may buy coffee and wine. One snowy night in March, three strangers at this bar fell into a conversation. The first was a tall, bald-headed man, wearing a sable-lined coat that reached to his ankles. The second was a beautiful American woman going to Isvia to attend funeral services for her only son, who had been killed in a mountain-climbing accident. The third was a white-haired, heavy Italian woman in a black shawl, who was treated with great deference by the waiter. He bowed from the waist when he poured her a glass of cheap wine, and addressed her as 'Your Majesty.' Avalanche warnings had been posted earlier in the day . . ." Then he put his head back on the pillow and died—indeed, these were his dying words, and the dying words, it seemed to me, of generations of storytellers, for how could this snowy and trumped-up pass, with its trio of travelers, hope to celebrate a world that lies spread out around us like a bewildering and stupendous dream?

Reading Critically

1. Who is Marlon Brando? What does Cheever mean (paragraph 2) when he says that there will be no parts for Brando in his stories or novels? What kinds of parts would those be? What do you learn about Cheever's views on writing from this statement? Discuss with your classmates.

2. In what ways is Cheever's long description of the "lush" in paragraphs 5 to 7 a parody of bad writing? What parts of this passage do you find overdrawn and pathetically sentimental? Why is excess sentimentality a bad quality in writing? Discuss with your classmates.

3. What is Cheever's purpose in paragraphs 8 to 12 in describing the young boy and his mother? In what way is this passage a parody of badly written stories about adolescent development? Discuss with your classmates.

4. Why has Cheever deliberately loaded paragraphs 13 to 17 with absurdly obscure references? What is the effect of the repeated phrase, " 'Yes,' I said"?

Responding Through Writing

1. At the next sporting event that you attend, bring a pad and pen and do a short character sketch of a person who interests you, just as Cheever has done for the girl in paragraph 1.

2. In your private notebook or journal try, if you care to, to complete the sentence regarding Clarissa in paragraph 4.

3. Rewrite the story of the "lush" (paragraphs 5 to 7) in such a way that you think Cheever might *want* to have it appear in one of his stories.

4. Rewrite either paragraphs 8 to 12 or 13 to 17 according to the directions in the previous item.

MENDING WALL

ROBERT FROST

*Although Robert Frost (1874–1963) is identified as the quintessential
"New England" poet, he was born in San Francisco. After the death of
his father when Frost was ten, his mother moved to Lawrence, Massachusetts. Frost attended Dartmouth College briefly, but he quit school and took
a variety of jobs, including working as a bobbin boy in a clothing mill
in Lawrence. He married in 1895. Two years later he enrolled at Harvard
but dropped out after two years, and in 1900 he bought a farm in Derry,
New Hampshire, where he lived for most of his life. Although he began
to write poetry in 1894, he did not gain critical acclaim until he published*
A Boy's Will *in 1913, followed by* North of Boston *in 1914 while
he was living in England. He received the Pulitzer Prize in 1924, 1931,
1937, and 1942 and the Poetry Society of America medal in 1941. In
1950 the U.S. Senate passed a unanimous resolution honoring him. Frost
has been praised as the poet of the commonplace who sees more than most
people do in ordinary things. Frost's poems "Stopping by Woods on a
Snowy Evening" and "The Road Not Taken" are also included in this
book. The following poem was originally published in* North of Boston.

Something there is that doesn't love a wall,
That sends the frozen-ground-swell under it,
And spills the upper boulders in the sun;

And makes gaps even two can pass abreast.
The work of hunters is another thing: 5
I have come after them and made repair
Where they have left not one stone on a stone,
But they would have the rabbit out of hiding,
To please the yelping dogs. The gaps I mean,
No one has seen them made or heard them made,   10
But at spring-mending time we find them there.
I let my neighbor know beyond the hill;
And on a day we meet to walk the line
And set the wall between us once again.
We keep the wall between us as we go.   15
To each the boulders that have fallen to each.
And some are loaves and some so nearly balls
We have to use a spell to make them balance:
"Stay where you are until our backs are turned!"
We wear our fingers rough with handling them.   20
Oh, just another kind of outdoor game,
One on a side. It comes to little more:
There where it is we do not need the wall:
He is all pine and I am apple orchard.
My apple trees will never get across   25
And eat the cones under his pines, I tell him.
He only says, "Good fences make good neighbors."
Spring is the mischief in me, and I wonder
If I could put a notion in his head:
"*Why* do they make good neighbors? Isn't it   30
Where there are cows? But here there are no cows.
Before I built a wall I'd ask to know
What I was walling in or walling out,
And to whom I was like to give offense.
Something there is that doesn't love a wall,   35
That wants it down." I could say "Elves" to him,
But it's not elves exactly, and I'd rather
He said it for himself. I see him there
Bringing a stone grasp firmly by the top
In each hand, like an old-stone savage armed.   40
He moves in darkness as it seems to me,
Not of woods only and the shade of trees.
He will not go behind his father's saying,
And he likes having thought of it so well
He says again, "Good fences make good neighbors."   45

Reading Critically

1. The title of this poem is ambiguous, with at least two meanings. The title can be interpreted to mean that the two people in the poem are mending the wall, or it can mean that the wall is mending something. In what way can a wall "mend"? What might be broken that a wall can mend? In what way do good fences make good neighbors? Why does the neighbor merely repeat the phrase and not explain or defend it?

2. What exactly are the narrator of the poem and his neighbor doing besides fixing a broken stone fence that divides their properties? Why does the narrator of the poem argue that the wall is unnecessary? What counterarguments does his neighbor offer? What does the narrator mean when he says, "Something there is that doesn't love a wall"? How does this attitude compare with the attitude of his neighbor?

3. What does the narrator mean when he says his neighbor "will not go behind his father's saying"? Is the neighbor a person who does things without thinking? What might be another explanation for his steadfast belief in the benefits of having a wall between the properties?

4. The narrator says that fixing the wall is "just another kind of outdoor game, One on a side. It comes to little more." What in the poem suggests that this casual comment does not reflect the narrator's true position? What is that position?

Responding Through Writing

1. Read this poem aloud, paying attention to its conversational quality. How has Frost achieved this quality in the poem?

Note the words he uses, especially in the passages enclosed in quotation marks. Write a paragraph in which you explain the effect Frost achieves by making the poem seem so conversational.

2. What does the narrator mean when he says in line 15 that "We keep the wall between us as we go"? Does this line suggest a division between the narrator and his neighbor? Write a list of the other places in the poem that describe the relationship between the two men. Now write a paragraph in which you describe the relationship you think the two neighbors have, discussing whether you think they are good neighbors to each other.

3. Write the first draft of an essay in which you discuss what a neighbor is, according to the two men in this poem. If you think the two men have different ideas on what constitutes a good neighbor, you will have to discuss both ideas of a good neighbor. Your audience for this essay is your classmates. Discuss your draft with your classmates, and based upon this discussion revise your essay.

4. Write one sentence in which you state the theme of this poem. Discuss your sentence with your classmates. What agreement and disagreement is there among you? If possible, state the theme of the poem in one sentence on which you all agree.

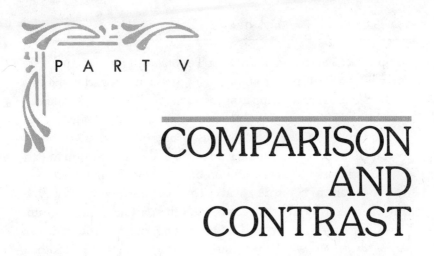

PART V

COMPARISON AND CONTRAST

The process of comparison and contrast is a fundamental and daily human activity. As children we contrasted the size of our piece of pie with the size of the piece our big brother got. As we grew, we continued to use comparison and contrast in both trivial and serious situations—this sweater or that sweater, this movie or that movie, this college or that college? The process of comparison and contrast pervades our lives, so much so that we are often unaware that we are using it—which bag of fruit to select, what clothes to wear, which car to buy?

In the introduction to the previous section, we discussed how you would use the techniques of classification to go about choosing a college. At some point in that process you would have narrowed down your choices to two or three colleges. It is at that point that your purpose would move from classification to comparison and contrast. Whereas you started out by testing a large number of colleges against several standards of classification, your purpose would now shift to a direct comparison of the two or three colleges that seemed the best according to the two or three standards of comparison you deemed the most important. Your aim would no longer be to be exhaustive but to zero in and directly compare according to precisely formulated criteria.

In making a comparison there are several principles to keep in mind and various organizational options to choose from. These are discussed below.

Use a Logical Standard of Comparison

If you go out to buy a car, you might compare a Chevrolet with a Ford, or a Ford with a Toyota, but you would certainly not compare a Chevrolet, a Ford, or a Toyota with a fire engine. Fire engines are a class apart from passenger cars, and comparing the two is like the proverbial comparing of apples and oranges. While this example may seem obvious, the failure to choose a single, logical standard when making comparisons is one of the most common logical fallacies. Some examples are given in the introduction to Part IV, "Classification." To expand on one of those examples, let's say that you want to compare two colleges: In your research you find that one has a fine football team; the other, a fine debating team. This information might well be interesting, but to write it up *by way of comparison* would be pointless. Trying to measure a football team against a debating team is indeed like comparing apples and oranges. Again, the fallacy here may seem obvious to you, but how many times have you come across comparisons where this fallacy was operating but not so immediately noticeable? "Come to Podunk University, the Oxford of the Ozarks," reads the brochure with glossy pictures of lakes, fraternity houses, and smiling cheerleaders. Podunk may indeed be a great place to spend four years, but lakes, fraternities, and cheerleading are not logical standards for a comparison with Oxford. Similarly, it is not uncommon to find large spreads in business magazines lauding the virtues of various regions, and even countries, as potential sites for factories and office complexes. The smart businessperson comparing these sites will ignore distracting standards of classification (pretty scenery, interesting ruined castles, plentitude of giraffes) and concentrate on one logical standard of comparison at a time. He or she will compare western Massachusetts and eastern Nebraska—or Kenya and Senegal—on the basis of standards like access to roads and airports, literacy of the population, tax advantages, and other norms that directly relate to his or her business's needs. The same person comparing the same two places as potential sites for a vacation would use different standards: hotel facilities, beaches, and, indeed, perhaps even plentitude of giraffes.

Developing a Comparison: Methods of Organization

Once you have chosen a standard of comparison, you will want to apply it to the two or more items to be compared. After this is done, you may decide that your comparison is complete, or you may want to choose one or more *related* standards of comparison to apply to the *same items.* How do you organize all these comparisons into a coherent essay?

There are three basic methods of organizing a comparison-and-contrast essay: the *block method,* the *point-by-point method,* and the *similarities-and-differences method.*

Using the Block Method

Using the block method, you discuss one item according to one or more standards of comparison and then discuss a second item *according to those very same standards in the same order.* In most cases you should devote approximately the same amount of discussion to each standard of comparison. Sometimes, however, one standard of comparison will be more important than the others. If in comparing beach resorts, for example, your chief interest is scuba diving, you would be likely to give more space to that topic than to comparisons of pool facilities or hotel restaurants.

The Point-by-Point Method

Using the point-by-point method, you organize your discussion not by the items to be compared, but by the standards of comparison that you intend to apply to those items. Instead of discussing resort X according to scuba opportunities, pool facilities, and hotel restaurants, and then doing the same for hotel $Y,$ as you would do using the block method, you would discuss scuba opportunities at both hotels, then pool facilities, and so on.

The Similarities-and-Differences Method

Using the similarities-and-differences method, you first list all the similarities between the two subjects (both resorts have good pool facilities and restaurants), then all the differences (they differ markedly in scuba opportunities). Alternatively, you can list the differences first and then the similarities, as Bruce Catton does in "Grant and Lee: A Study in Contrasts" (p. 260).

Table 1 shows the three methods. The sample assignment used here is a comparison of fast-food restaurants according to three standards: food quality, price, and service.

Of course, this table is simplified. In the point-by-point method, for example, you might very well want to discuss more than just two points of comparison and contrast between your subjects. Also, in the block method, your discussion of each subject might well be more than one paragraph long. But this table should help you decide the basic pattern of organization for your comparison-and-contrast essay.

Which Method Is Best?

Of the three methods for organizing a comparison-and-contrast essay, the point-by-point method is perhaps the most commonly used. This method allows you to discuss several points of comparison between two subjects without requiring your reader to keep in mind *all* the points of comparison at any one time. Thus, as a rule, the point-by-point method seems to work well when there

TABLE 1. METHODS OF COMPARISON AND CONTRAST

Block Method	Point-by-Point Method	Similarities/ Differences Method
Introduction	Introduction	Introduction
Discuss McDonald's according to food quality, price, and service.	Discuss food quality at McDonald's and Wendy's.	Discuss similarities between McDonald's and Wendy's, choosing among food quality, prices, and service.
Discuss Wendy's according to food quality, price, and service.	Discuss prices at McDonald's and Wendy's.	Discuss differences between McDonald's and Wendy's, choosing among food quality, prices, and service.
	Discuss service at McDonald's and Wendy's.	
Conclusion	Conclusion	Conclusion

are several points of comparison, while the block method works well when there are only a few. We would use the point-by-point method, for example, to compare colleges, but the block method to compare two college courses. The similarities-and-differences method is best used when there are wide differences or close similarities between the objects of comparison. This method would be ideally suited to a comparison, for example, between American football and British rugby.

Purpose and Audience

In choosing the appropriate method of comparison and contrast, you need to consider your subject matter, your purpose, and your audience. Put yourself in the reader's place. How much does your reader know about the subjects you are comparing and contrasting? You need to determine whether your audience knows both subjects in the comparison, neither subject, or only one of the subjects. If your reader has some knowledge about both subjects (two baseball teams, for example), you can discuss the similarities and differences briefly and concentrate instead on your reasons for making the comparison. If your reader knows something about only one of your subjects (baseball but not cricket, for example), you should begin with the familiar subject (baseball) before discussing the unfamiliar one (cricket). If your reader knows nothing about either, you will want to preface your comparison with some general explanations.

Whatever approach you take, remember that audiences have certain general expectations. In a comparison-and-contrast essay, readers expect a certain balance in treatment of the two or more subjects compared. This does not mean that you must devote exactly equal amounts of space to each subject, but it does mean that you should meet your readers' expectations for balance and proportion.

Combining Methods of Comparison

After you have mastered the three methods individually, you will soon discover the benefits of combining methods in one essay.

For example, you may begin an essay using the block method to establish broad similarities and differences between your subjects and then shift to the point-by-point method in order to discuss comparisons between the two subjects in more detail. Mastering the three methods individually allows you the freedom and flexibility to combine two of the methods to suit your purpose and audience better.

Making Outlines

In using comparison and contrast, it is necessary that you thoughtfully and carefully develop a strategy before you write. You may begin, of course, with any of the typical prewriting exercises that your instructor is likely to ask you to use: freewriting, brainstorming, clustering, etc. However, once you have done so, you should try consciously to organize your material. Unlike narrative, descriptive, and other kinds of writing where outlines may tend to "get in the way," comparison and contrast relies heavily on outlining before you write your first draft. For that first draft, at least, choose one of the three methods described above, outline an organizational plan according to that method, and write your draft by sticking to that plan. By doing so you are likely to establish a sense of clarity that will come through to the reader whatever the twists, turns, and experiments of your succeeding drafts.

GRANT AND LEE: A STUDY IN CONTRASTS

BRUCE CATTON

As a boy growing up in a small town in Michigan, Bruce Catton (1889–1978) listened to harrowing stories from many veterans of the Civil War. "I grew up surrounded by the traditions of that war," he said. But it was not until his fifties, after a full career as a journalist for Boston, Cleveland, and Washington newspapers, that he began to write about the Civil War. Catton won both the Pulitzer Prize for history and the National Book Award for A Stillness at Appomattox *(1953) and also received a nonfiction award for* The Coming Fury *(1961). He was presented with the Presidential Freedom Medal in 1977 and wrote his seventeenth and final novel,* The Bold and Magnificent Dream, *in 1978, the year of his death. His other works include* The War Lords of Washington *(1948),* Terrible Swift Sword *(1963), and* Never Call Retreat *(1965). The following essay first appeared in the 1956 book,* The American Story, *a collection of historical essays edited by Earl Schenk Miers.*

When Ulysses S. Grant and Robert E. Lee met in the parlor of a modest house at Appomattox Court House, Virginia, on April

9, 1865 to work out the terms for the surrender of Lee's Army of Northern Virginia, a great chapter in American life came to a close, and a great new chapter began.

2   These men were bringing the Civil War to its virtual finish. To be sure, other armies had yet to surrender, and for a few days the fugitive Confederate government would struggle desperately and vainly, trying to find some way to go on living now that its chief support was gone. But in effect it was all over when Grant and Lee signed the papers. And the little room where they wrote out the terms was the scene of one of the poignant, dramatic contrasts in American history.

3   They were two strong men, these oddly different generals, and they represented the strengths of two conflicting currents that, through them, had come into final collision.

4   Back of Robert E. Lee was the notion that the old aristocratic concept might somehow survive and be dominant in American life.

5   Lee was tidewater Virginia, and in his background were family, culture, and tradition . . . the age of chivalry transplanted to a New World which was making its own legends and its own myths. He embodied a way of life that had come down through the age of knighthood and the English country squire. America was a land that was beginning all over again, dedicated to nothing much more complicated than the rather hazy belief that all men had equal rights, and should have an equal chance in the world. In such a land Lee stood for the feeling that it was somehow of advantage to human society to have a pronounced inequality in the social structure. There should be a leisure class, backed by ownership of land; in turn, society itself should be keyed to the land as the chief source of wealth and influence. It would bring forth (according to this ideal) a class of men with a strong sense of obligation to the community; men who lived not to gain advantage for themselves, but to meet the solemn obligations which had been laid on them by the very fact that they were privileged. From them the country would get its leadership; to them it could look for the higher values—of thought, of conduct, of personal deportment—to give it strength and virtue.

6   Lee embodied the noblest elements of this aristocratic ideal. Through him, the landed nobility justified itself. For four years, the Southern states had fought a desperate war to uphold the ideals for which Lee stood. In the end, it almost seemed as if the Confederacy fought for Lee; as if he himself was the Confederacy . . . the best thing that the way of life for which the Confederacy stood could ever have to offer. He had passed into legend before Appomattox.

Thousands of tired, underfed, poorly clothed Confederate soldiers, long-since past the simple enthusiasm of the early days of the struggle, somehow considered Lee the symbol of everything for which they had been willing to die. But they could not quite put this feeling into words. If the Lost Cause, sanctified by so much heroism and so many deaths, had a living justification, its justification was General Lee.

Grant, the son of a tanner on the Western frontier, was everything Lee was not. He had come up the hard way, and embodied nothing in particular except the eternal toughness and sinewy fiber of the men who grew up beyond the mountains. He was one of a body of men who owed reverence and obeisance to no one, who were self-reliant to a fault, who cared hardly anything for the past but who had a sharp eye for the future.   7

These frontier men were the precise opposites of the tidewater aristocrats. Back of them, in the great surge that had taken people over the Alleghenies and into the opening Western country, there was a deep, implicit dissatisfaction with a past that had settled into grooves. They stood for democracy, not from any reasoned conclusion about the proper ordering of human society, but simply because they had grown up in the middle of democracy and knew how it worked. Their society might have privileges, but they would be privileges each man had won for himself. Forms and patterns meant nothing. No man was born to anything, except perhaps to a chance to show how far he could rise. Life was competition.   8

Yet along with this feeling had come a deep sense of belonging to a national community. The Westerner who developed a farm, opened a shop or set up in business as a trader, could hope to prosper only as his own community prospered—and his community ran from the Atlantic to the Pacific and from Canada down to Mexico. If the land was settled, with towns and highways and accessible markets, he could better himself. He saw his fate in terms of the nation's own destiny. As its horizons expanded, so did his. He had, in other words, an acute dollars-and-cents stake in the continued growth and development of his country.   9

And that, perhaps, is where the contrast between Grant and Lee becomes most striking. The Virginia aristocrat, inevitably, saw himself in relation to his own region. He lived in a static society which could endure almost anything except change. Instinctively, his first loyalty would go to the locality in which that society existed. He would fight to the limit of endurance to defend it, because in defending it he was defending everything that gave his own life its deepest meaning.   10

11   The Westerner, on the other hand, would fight with an equal tenacity for the broader concept of society. He fought so because everything he lived by was tied to growth, expansion, and a constantly widening horizon. What he lived by would survive or fall with the nation itself. He could not possibly stand by unmoved in the face of an attempt to destroy the Union. He would combat it with everything he had, because he could only see it as an effort to cut the ground out from under his feet.

12   So Grant and Lee were in complete contrast, representing two diametrically opposed elements in American life. Grant was the modern man emerging; beyond him, ready to come on the stage, was the great age of steel and machinery, of crowded cities and a restless, burgeoning vitality. Lee might have ridden down from the old age of chivalry, lance in hand, silken banner fluttering over his head. Each man was the perfect champion of his cause, drawing both his strengths and his weaknesses from the people he led.

13   Yet it was not all contrast, after all. Different as they were—in background, in personality, in underlying aspiration—these two great soldiers had much in common. Under everything else, they were marvelous fighters. Furthermore, their fighting qualities were really very much alike.

14   Each man had, to begin with, the great virtue of utter tenacity and fidelity. Grant fought his way down the Mississippi Valley in spite of acute personal discouragement and profound military handicaps. Lee hung on in the trenches at Petersburg after hope itself had died. In each man there was an indomitable quality . . . the born fighter's refusal to give up as long as he can still remain on his feet and lift his two fists.

15   Daring and resourcefulness they had, too; the ability to think faster and move faster than the enemy. These were the qualities which gave Lee the dazzling campaigns of Second Manassas and Chancellorsville and won Vicksburg for Grant.

16   Lastly, and perhaps greatest of all, there was the ability, at the end, to turn quickly from war to peace once the fighting was over. Out of the way these two men behaved at Appomattox came the possibility of a peace of reconciliation. It was a possibility not wholly realized, in the years to come, but which did, in the end, help the two sections to become one nation again . . . after a war whose bitterness might have seemed to make such a reunion wholly impossible. No part of either man's life became him more than the part he played in their brief meeting in the McLean house at Appomattox. Their behavior there put all succeeding generations of

Americans in their debt. Two great Americans, Grant and Lee—very different, yet under everything very much alike. Their encounter at Appomattox was one of the great moments of American history.

Reading Critically

1. Catton sees Grant and Lee as representatives of two traditions in conflict. Briefly outline what these two traditions are, according to Catton. What does Catton suggest has happened to these two traditions as a result of the Civil War? Discuss with your classmates which tradition you would like to be a part of, and why.

2. Discuss with your classmates whether Catton seems to favor either of the men he is describing, or whether his account is completely objective. Discuss also whether Catton seems to favor either of the traditions he says the two men represent. Cite specific evidence from the essay to support your position.

3. Catton says in paragraph 1 that with the signing of the surrender a "great chapter in American life came to a close, and a great new chapter began." Look up an account of the developments that occurred in the United States immediately after the end of the Civil War and prepare a report for class discussion. Pay close attention to the westward expansion of the country during this period.

4. What does Catton mean when he describes Lee as "tidewater Virginia"? Where is the tidewater area of Virginia located? Look up a description of this area. Cite one similar description that is used today to describe a rich and privileged person, perhaps a person from Park Avenue, New York, or Beverly Hills, California. Read the society page of a major newspaper and take notes on how people

in "high society" are described. Compare your notes with your classmates'. What words and phrases are commonly used to describe the people discussed in the society pages?

Responding Through Writing

1. What background does Catton assume about his audience? Make a list of the assumptions Catton makes that cause problems for you in reading the essay. Compare your list with your classmates' lists. What problems do you think a foreign student would have in reading this essay? Write an introduction that will help a foreign student understand this essay.

2. Under the headings "Grant" and "Lee," list the points of comparison and contrast that Catton discusses for each man.

3. Why, in an essay entitled "Grant and Lee," does Catton begin his comparison and contrast with a discussion of Lee? What advantages and disadvantages would there be in starting with Grant? If Grant were discussed first, how would Catton have to change the conclusion of his essay where he talks about the past and future of the country? Consider an essay discussing Grant first and then Lee. Write a concluding paragraph for that essay, and compare your concluding paragraph with Catton's. In what ways are the two paragraphs different?

4. Write the first drafts of two introductions for two essays. The first essay concentrates on Grant as the outstanding general of the Civil War, while the second essay concentrates on Lee as the outstanding general. Both essays are intended for your classmates as the audience.

COMPARING THE WORK ETHICS: JAPAN AND AMERICA

WILLIAM OUCHI

William Ouchi (b. 1943) is a professor in the Graduate School of Management at UCLA. He received his MBA from Stanford University and his Ph.D. in business administration from the University of Chicago. He is a consultant to major American corporations, many of which have adopted the style of business management he calls "Theory Z Management." As a theorist and consultant, Ouchi is especially concerned with today's competition between American and Japanese businesses for the worldwide market. He is the author of The M-Form Society: How American Teamwork Can Recapture the Competitive Edge *(1984)* and Theory Z: How American Businesses Can Meet the Japanese Challenge *(1981), which was a national best-seller and from which the following essay is excerpted.*

Perhaps the most difficult aspect of the Japanese for Westerners   1
to comprehend is the strong orientation to collective values, particularly a collective sense of responsibility. Let me illustrate with an anecdote about a visit to a new factory in Japan owned and operated

by an American electronics company. The American company, a particularly creative firm, frequently attracts attention within the business community for its novel approaches to planning, organizational design, and management systems. As a consequence of this corporate style, the parent company determined to make a thorough study of Japanese workers and to design a plant that would combine the best of East and West. In their study they discovered that Japanese firms almost never make use of individual work incentives, such as piecework or even individual performance appraisal tied to salary increases. They concluded that rewarding individual achievement and individual ability is always a good thing.

2   In the final assembly area of their new plant, long lines of young Japanese women wired together electronic products on a piece-rate system: the more you wired, the more you got paid. About two months after opening, the head foreladies approached the plant manager. "Honorable plant manager," they said humbly as they bowed, "we are embarrassed to be so forward, but we must speak to you because all of the girls have threatened to quit work this Friday." (To have this happen, of course, would be a great disaster for all concerned.) "Why," they wanted to know, "can't our plant have the same compensation system as other Japanese companies? When you hire a new girl, her starting wage should be fixed by her age. An eighteen-year-old should be paid more than a sixteen-year-old. Every year on her birthday, she should receive an automatic increase in pay. The idea that any of us can be more productive than another must be wrong, because none of us in final assembly could make a thing unless all of the other people in the plant had done their jobs right first. To single one person out as being more productive is wrong and is also personally humiliating to us." The company changed its compensation system to the Japanese model.

3   Another American company in Japan had installed a suggestion system much as we have in the United States. Individual workers were encouraged to place suggestions to improve productivity into special boxes. For an accepted idea the individual received a bonus amounting to some fraction of the productivity savings realized from his or her suggestion. After a period of six months, not a single suggestion had been submitted. The American managers were puzzled. They had heard many stories of the inventiveness, the commitment, and the loyalty of Japanese workers, yet not one suggestion to improve productivity had appeared.

4   The managers approached some of the workers and asked why the suggestion system had not been used. The answer: "No one can

come up with a work improvement idea alone. We work together, and any ideas that one of us may have are actually developed by watching others and talking to others. If one of us was singled out for being responsible for such an idea, it would embarrass all of us." The company changed to a group suggestion system, in which workers collectively submitted suggestions. Bonuses were paid to groups which would save bonus money until the end of the year for a party at a restaurant or, if there was enough money, for family vacations together. The suggestions and productivity improvements rained down on the plant.

One can interpret these examples in two quite different ways. Perhaps the Japanese commitment to collective values is an anachronism that does not fit with modern industrialism but brings economic success despite that collectivism. Collectivism seems to be inimical to the kind of maverick creativity exemplified in Benjamin Franklin, Thomas Edison, and John D. Rockefeller. Collectivism does not seem to provide the individual incentive to excel which has made a great success of American enterprise. Entirely apart from its economic effects, collectivism implies a loss of individuality, a loss of the freedom to be different, to hold fundamentally different values from others.

The second interpretation of the examples is that the Japanese collectivism is economically efficient. It causes people to work well together and to encourage one another to better efforts. Industrial life requires interdependence of one person on another. But a less obvious but far-reaching implication of the Japanese collectivism for economic performance has to do with accountability.

In the Japanese mind, collectivism is neither a corporate or individual goal to strive for nor a slogan to pursue. Rather, the nature of things operates so that nothing of consequence occurs as a result of individual effort. Everything important in life happens as a result of teamwork or collective effort. Therefore, to attempt to assign individual credit or blame to results is unfounded. A Japanese professor of accounting, a brilliant scholar trained at Carnegie–Mellon University who teaches now in Tokyo, remarked that the status of accounting systems in Japanese industry is primitive compared to those in the United States. Profit centers, transfer prices, and computerized information systems are barely known even in the largest Japanese companies, whereas they are a commonplace in even small United States organizations. Though not at all surprised at the difference in accounting systems, I was not at all sure that the Japanese were primitive. In fact, I thought their system a good deal more efficient than ours.

8   Most American companies have basically two accounting systems. One system summarizes the overall financial state to inform stockholders, bankers, and other outsiders. That system is not of interest here. The other system, called the managerial or cost accounting system, exists for an entirely different reason. It measures in detail all of the particulars of transactions between departments, divisions, and key individuals in the organization, for the purpose of untangling the interdependencies between people. When, for example, two departments share one truck for deliveries, the cost accounting system charges each department for part of the cost of maintaining the truck and driver, so that at the end of the year, the performance of each department can be individually assessed, and the better department's manager can receive a larger raise. Of course, all of this information processing costs money, and furthermore may lead to arguments between the departments over whether the costs charged to each are fair.

9   In a Japanese company a short-run assessment of individual performance is not wanted, so the company can save the considerable expense of collecting and processing all of that information. Companies still keep track of which department uses a truck how often and for what purposes, but like-minded people can interpret some simple numbers for themselves and adjust their behavior accordingly. Those insisting upon clear and precise measurement for the purpose of advancing individual interests must have an elaborate information system. Industrial life, however, is essentially integrated and interdependent. No one builds an automobile alone, no one carries through a banking transaction alone. In a sense the Japanese value of collectivism fits naturally into an industrial setting, whereas the Western individualism provides constant conflicts. The image that comes to mind is of Chaplin's silent film "Modern Times" in which the apparently insignificant hero played by Chaplin successfully fights against the unfeeling machinery of industry. Modern industrial life can be aggravating, even hostile, or natural: all depends on the fit between our culture and our technology.

· · ·

10   The *shinkansen* or "bullet train" speeds across the rural areas of Japan giving a quick view of cluster after cluster of farmhouses surrounded by rice paddies. This particular pattern did not develop purely by chance, but as a consequence of the technology peculiar to the growing of rice, the staple of the Japanese diet. The growing of rice requires the construction and maintenance of an irrigation system, something that takes many hands to build. More impor-

tantly, the planting and the harvesting of rice can only be done efficiently with the cooperation of twenty or more people. The "bottom line" is that a single family working alone cannot produce enough rice to survive, but a dozen families working together can produce a surplus. Thus the Japanese have had to develop the capacity to work together in harmony, no matter what the forces of disagreement or social disintegration, in order to survive.

Japan is a nation built entirely on the tips of giant, suboceanic volcanoes. Little of the land is flat and suitable for agriculture. Terraced hillsides make use of every available square foot of arable land. Small homes built very close together further conserve the land. Japan also suffers from natural disasters such as earthquakes and hurricanes. Traditionally homes are made of light construction materials, so a house falling down during a disaster will not crush its occupants and also can be quickly and inexpensively rebuilt. During the feudal period until the Meiji restoration of 1868, each feudal lord sought to restrain his subjects from moving from one village to the next for fear that a neighboring lord might amass enough peasants with which to produce a large agricultural surplus, hire an army and pose a threat. Apparently bridges were not commonly built across rivers and streams until the late nineteenth century, since bridges increased mobility between villages. 11

Taken all together, this characteristic style of living paints the picture of a nation of people who are homogeneous with respect to race, history, language, religion, and culture. For centuries and generations these people have lived in the same village next door to the same neighbors. Living in close proximity and in dwellings which gave very little privacy, the Japanese survived through their capacity to work together in harmony. In this situation, it was inevitable that the one most central social value which emerged, the one value without which the society could not continue, was that an individual does not matter. 12

To the Western soul this is a chilling picture of society. Subordinating individual tastes to the harmony of the group and knowing that individual needs can never take precedence over the interests of all is repellent to the Western citizen. But a frequent theme of Western philosophers and sociologists is that individual freedom exists only when people willingly subordinate their self-interests to the social interest. A society composed entirely of self-interested individuals is a society in which each person is at war with the other, a society which has no freedom. This issue, constantly at the heart of understanding society, comes up in every century, and in every society, whether the writer be Plato, Hobbes, or B. F. Skinner. The question of understanding which contemporary insti- 13 tutions lie at the heart of the conflict between automatism and totalitarianism remains. In some ages, the kinship group, the central social institution, mediated between these opposing forces to preserve the balance in which freedom was realized; in other times the church or the government was most critical. Perhaps our present age puts the work organization as the central institution.

14   In order to complete the comparison of Japanese and American living situations, consider flight over the United States. Looking out of the window high over the state of Kansas, we see a pattern of a single farmhouse surrounded by fields, followed by another single homestead surrounded by fields. In the early 1800s in the state of Kansas there were no automobiles. Your nearest neighbor was perhaps two miles distant; the winters were long, and the snow was deep. Inevitably, the central social values were self-reliance and independence. Those were the realities of that place and age that children had to learn to value.

15   The key to the industrial revolution was discovering that non-human forms of energy substituted for human forms could increase the wealth of a nation beyond anyone's wildest dreams. But there was a catch. To realize this great wealth, non-human energy needed huge complexes called factories with hundreds, even thousands of workers collected into one factory. Moreover, several factories in one central place made the generation of energy more efficient. Almost overnight, the Western world was transformed from a rural and agricultural country to an urban and industrial state. Our technological advance seems to no longer fit our social structure: in a sense, the Japanese can better cope with modern industrialism. While Americans still busily protect our rather extreme form of individualism, the Japanese hold their individualism in check and emphasize cooperation.

Reading Critically

1. "A society composed entirely of self-interested individuals," writes Ouchi in paragraph 13, "is a society in which each person is at war with the other, a society which has no freedom." State at least three ways in which individuals in our society are at

war with each other, then state at least three ways in which individuals cooperate with each other. Discuss your opinions with
your classmates.

2. In paragraph 5 Ouchi suggests that the Japanese system
"seems to be inimical to the kind of maverick creativity exemplified
in Benjamin Franklin, Thomas Edison, and John D. Rockefeller."
After defining *inimical* and *maverick,* look up accounts of Franklin,
Edison, and Rockefeller. What did each man do that was so creative? How did each man work? Based upon your research, discuss
with your classmates ways in which each man worked collectively
with others, as well as individually.

3. Read paragraph 11 again, then look up at least two accounts of Japan and prepare a report that describes the country
today. Discuss your report with your classmates, concentrating on
the ways in which Japan is similar to the United States and the ways
in which Japan differs from the United States. Which of these
similarities and differences does Ouchi find most significant? Which
do you think are most significant? What do you think these similarities and differences suggest about future relations between the two
countries?

4. Look up a summary of the plot of Charlie Chaplin's *Modern
Times* and report to your classmates. (If possible, watch a videotape
of the movie and report on that.) How does this movie illustrate
Ouchi's contention that Western individualism provides constant
conflicts between workers and modern industry? List two or three
other examples (from books, movies, television programs, or other
sources) of similar conflicts between the individual and modern
industrial processes. Compare your examples with those of your
classmates.

Responding Through Writing

1. If you are keeping a journal or notebook in this course,
write in it for five to ten minutes describing a job you have had.

Discuss whether you were encouraged to work as an individual or as part of a team, and which way you would prefer to work. Compare your notes with those of your classmates.

2. Write a paragraph in which you describe the audience for Ouchi's essay. Discuss your paragraph with your classmates. How many different audiences do all of you see for this essay? What evidence in the essay can you cite to support your description of the essay's audience?

3. The first six paragraphs of this essay are an introduction. Write a one-paragraph introduction replacing these six paragraphs. How does this change affect the essay? Compare your introductory paragraph with those written by your classmates.

4. Write one sentence stating the purpose of this essay. (Before you write your sentence, read paragraph 15 again.) Compare your sentence with those written by your classmates. As a group, write a sentence that you all agree states the essay's purpose.

AMERICAN SPACE, CHINESE PLACE

YI-FU TUAN

Born in 1930 in Tientsin, China, Yi-Fu Tuan came to the United States at 21 and later became a citizen. A geography professor who has taught in Canada, England, and Hawaii, Tuan is also a student of Eastern and Western cultures. His writings include such diverse books as China *(1969),* The Hydrological Cycle and the Wisdom of God: A Theme in Geoteleology *(1968),* Landscapes of Fear *(1981), and his tenth and most recent novel,* The Good Life *(1986). In* Space and Place: The Perspective of Experience *(1977) Tuan writes, "I try to develop my material from a single perspective—namely that of experience." In an epilogue to the same work, he adds, "Much of human experience is difficult to articulate, however, and we are far from feeling or aesthetic response." Tuan is currently the John Kirkland Wright Professor of Geography at the University of Wisconsin–Madison. The following selection was first published in 1974 in* Harper's *magazine.*

Americans have a sense of space, not of place. Go to an   1
American home in exurbia, and almost the first thing you do is drift
toward the picture window. How curious that the first compliment

you pay your host inside his house is to say how lovely it is outside his house! He is pleased that you should admire his vistas. The distant horizon is not merely a line separating earth from sky, it is a symbol of the future. The American is not rooted in his place, however lovely: his eyes are drawn by the expanding space to a point on the horizon, which is his future.

2   By contrast, consider the traditional Chinese home. Blank walls enclose it. Step behind the spirit wall and you are in a courtyard with perhaps a miniature garden around a corner. Once inside his private compound you are wrapped in an ambiance of calm beauty, an ordered world of buildings, pavement, rock, and decorative vegetation. But you have no distant view: nowhere does space open out before you. Raw nature in such a home is experienced only as weather, and the only open space is the sky above. The Chinese is rooted in his place. When he has to leave, it is not for the promised land on the terrestrial horizon, but for another world altogether along the vertical, religious axis of his imagination.

3   The Chinese tie to place is deeply felt. Wanderlust is an alien sentiment. The Taoist classic *Tao Te Ching* captures the ideal of rootedness in place with these words: "Though there may be another country in the neighborhood so close that they are within sight of each other and the crowing of cocks and barking of dogs in one place can be heard in the other, yet there is no traffic between them; and throughout their lives the two peoples have nothing to do with each other." In theory if not in practice, farmers have ranked high in Chinese society. The reason is not only that they are engaged in a "root" industry of producing food but that, unlike pecuniary merchants, they are tied to the land and do not abandon their country when it is in danger.

4   Nostalgia is a recurrent theme in Chinese poetry. An American reader of translated Chinese poems may well be taken aback—even put off—by the frequency, as well as the sentimentality, of the lament for home. To understand the strength of this sentiment, we need to know that the Chinese desire for stability and rootedness in place is prompted by the constant threat of war, exile, and the natural disasters of flood and drought. Forcible removal makes the Chinese keenly aware of their loss. By contrast, Americans move, for the most part, voluntarily. Their nostalgia for home town is really longing for a childhood to which they cannot return: in the meantime the future beckons and the future is "out there," in open space. When we criticize American rootlessness, we tend to forget that it is a result of ideals we admire, namely, social mobility and

optimism about the future. When we admire Chinese rootedness, we forget that the word "place" means both a location in space and position in society: to be tied to place is also to be bound to one's station in life, with little hope of betterment. Space symbolizes hope; place, achievement and stability.

Reading Critically

1. Read the quotation in paragraph 3 from the *Tao Te Ching* that talks about geographically close neighbors living, as it were, in different worlds having nothing to do with each other. Does an atmosphere of polite indifference prevail in American neighborhoods? Why is it that we can live next door or down the block from people and have nothing to do with them? Discuss with your classmates.

2. Do you accept Tuan's basic premise that Chinese look inward while Americans look outward? What evidence from your personal experience, as well as from Chinese or American history, literature, and art, can you use to answer this question? If you have little knowledge of Chinese culture, answer this question by comparing American culture to some other culture about which you know, perhaps the culture of one of your classmates.

3. Tuan says that for Americans, "nostalgia for home town is really longing for a childhood to which they cannot return. . . ." Is this an accurate statement in terms of your own life? Discuss with your classmates the place and power of nostalgia in American life.

4. At various points in the essay (between paragraphs 1 and 2, in paragraph 4, at the middle) Tuan uses the phrase "by contrast" to indicate a transition from American to Chinese viewpoints, or vice versa. How useful are transitional words and phrases in essays that compare and contrast? Is there any danger in using too few or

too many of them? Where else in the essay could Tuan have used the phrase "by contrast"? Why do you think he sometimes chose not to use an explicitly transitional phrase?

Responding Through Writing

1. Do you think that Tuan's view of American life (and perhaps of Chinese life) is based on stereotypes? How many people, after all, have homes with picture windows? And how many of those picture windows open to grand vistas (rather than to another picture window across the street)? Write a letter to Tuan describing the characteristics of a "typical" American home.

2. Would most readers think this essay too short? Or would they think that its brevity helps to drive home its central point? If you were to make the essay three times as long as it is, how would you do so? What kinds of examples would you add? Where would you add them? Would you have to change the basic structure of the essay as a whole? Answer these questions and then either extend Tuan's discussion or write an extended discussion comparing an aspect of American culture with a parallel aspect of some other culture.

3. How do the words *place* and *space* operate in the essay, especially at the end? Do these words accurately characterize either Chinese or American perspectives, or do they confuse and mislead the reader? Can writers ever become the "prisoners" of their own metaphors? Has that ever happened to you as a writer? Write a brief response indicating how metaphors can mislead.

4. This essay is a fine example of comparison and contrast done according to the point-by-point method (p. 255). How would you rewrite the essay by the block method? Which method seems better suited to the subject matter?

ONE PERSON'S FACTS ARE ANOTHER'S FICTION

SYDNEY J. HARRIS

Syndey Harris (1917–1986) was well-known for his syndicated column "Strictly Personal" and for his many books, including A Majority of One, For the Time Being, *and his last,* Clearing the Ground *(1986). Born in London, he eventually moved to Chicago where he attended school, and worked as a reporter, feature writer, public relations staff writer, drama critic, teacher, and magazine editor. The following essay is part of his collection of syndicated newspaper columns,* Strictly Personal *(1977).*

Journalism, like history, is supposed to rely on "facts." But what are facts? They are just the building-blocks of truth, and since no one has the time or space to use *all* the blocks, we have to select those we think most important. That's where the rub comes in.

Suppose I were an early American historian, recording the career of one of our Founding Fathers. Here is what I might say:

"He early opposed the Stamp Act and other British restrictions. When his ship, *Liberty,* was confiscated and burned, he became a martyr and was elected to the Massachusetts legislature. He was a member and president of the Continental Congress. His name appears first on the Declaration of Independence. After the Revolution, he was elected governor of Massachusetts."

4   Now let's suppose I were a British historian, recording the same career.

5   This is what I might say:

6   "Son of a poor clergyman whose father died when he was nine, he was favored by a rich uncle who sent him to Harvard. When he was still in his 20s, his uncle died and without working a day he inherited the greatest fortune ever amassed in New England.

7   "He wore lavender suits and rode in bright yellow coaches. He loved dancing, card parties, wine and all festivities. He was lazy and unpunctual. John Adams called him a 'leaky vessel,' who betrayed state secrets. He was the greatest smuggler on the continent, who yearned to be Commander in Chief of the continental Army, and was mortified when George Washington was nominated."

8   Of course you have recognized the eminent name of John Hancock. Everything said about him in both these versions is perfectly true and factual. But history, and much more journalism, must condense these facts. Which shall be left in, and which left out? What balance shall be struck? How much of the positive facts are "veneration"; how much of the negative facts are "depreciation"?

9   What is said about Hancock depends, in large part, upon the historian's bias, perspective, and sense of values. He cannot put everything in (unless he is writing a full biography of the man), and anything he leaves out inevitably distorts the total portrait. Everything that is written is "selective."

10   Ponder on this the next time you demand that a story be "objective." All we have a right to ask is that the historian—or journalist—tries to be as honest as he can, and does not deliberately distort. Beyond this, one man's patriot is all too often another man's smuggler.

Thinking Critically

1. Harris says that writers ought to strike a proper "balance" (paragraphs 8 and 9) among the facts. Do you agree? Should historians of World War II seek to strike a proper balance when writing about the Holocaust, for example? Does truth always lie in the middle? Discuss with your classmates.

2. In reading the two accounts of John Hancock, did you feel more interested in one piece than in the other? Was the negative, less typical piece the more interesting? Why? With your classmates, try to construct a positive sketch of a "bad" character (e.g., Charles Manson) and a negative sketch of a "good" character (e.g., *Star Trek*'s Captain Kirk or Captain Picard).

3. Can you and your classmates cite any "factual" descriptions in today's news that you think might be just "slightly" distorted? As an exercise, read and discuss the "same" story in two widely differing newspapers (e.g., the *New York Times* versus the *New York Post*). How have the two writers dealt with the presumed facts? To what extent is each story factual?

4. What does Harris's essay say about the difference between subjective and objective opinions? Can any opinion ever be entirely objective? Discuss with your classmates.

Responding Through Writing

1. Select some prominent person from today's news and do for him or her what Harris does for John Hancock: that is, write *two* descriptions of the person, one from a positive perspective, the other from a negative perspective. In *both* descriptions use only facts.

2. If recent wars had turned out differently, would journalists and historians have since taken a different slant on the events in those wars? How might the attack on Pearl Harbor and the atomic bombing of Hiroshima and Nagasaki be typically described (using the same facts, of course) if the Japanese had won? In your notebook, write a few paragraphs along these lines.

3. Contemporary news stories tend to focus on outrageous behavior. As an exercise, see if, using selected facts in a news story, you can construct a brief written account of an event so that unreasonable actions seem reasonable, or vice versa. Use, for example, an airline hijacking or a case of government corruption.

4. Pretend that you have a contract from a publisher to write a short history of the past 12 months. Which events would you focus on? How would you go about attempting to be objective? Write a list of at least 20 items, and then go back and delete at least half. Then write a paragraph or two indicating why you chose to highlight some "facts" and ignore others.

ARIA

RICHARD RODRIGUEZ

Richard Rodriguez was born in San Francisco in 1944 to Spanish-speaking Mexican immigrant parents. Rodriguez did not begin to speak English until grammar school, but he eventually attended Stanford University, Columbia University, and The Warburg Institute in London, and he received his Ph.D. in English literature from the University of California at Berkeley. His prize-winning memoir, Hunger of Memory *(1982), tells of his experiences in assimilating into American culture while still identifying with his Mexican heritage. Rodriguez contributes to magazines including* Change, The Saturday Review, The American Scholar, *and* Harper's, *often writing about affirmative action and bilingual education. The following narrative originally appeared in* The American Scholar *in 1981.*

I remember to start with that day in Sacramento—a California now nearly thirty years past—when I first entered a classroom, able to understand some fifty stray English words.

The third of four children, I had been preceded to a neighborhood Roman Catholic school by an older brother and sister. But neither of them had revealed very much about their classroom experiences. Each afternoon they returned, as they left in the morning, always together, speaking in Spanish as they climbed the five steps of the porch. And their mysterious books, wrapped in shopping-bag paper, remained on the table next to the door, closed firmly behind them.

3   An accident of geography sent me to a school where all my classmates were white, many the children of doctors and lawyers and business executives. All my classmates certainly must have been uneasy on that first day of school—as most children are uneasy—to find themselves apart from their families in the first institution of their lives. But I was astonished.

4   The nun said, in a friendly but oddly impersonal voice, 'Boys and girls, this is Richard Rodriguez.' (I heard her sound out: *Rich-heard Road-ree-guess.*) It was the first time I had heard anyone name me in English. 'Richard,' the nun repeated more slowly, writing my name down in her black leather book. Quickly I turned to see my mother's face dissolve in a watery blur behind the pebbled glass door.

5   Many years later there is something called bilingual education—a scheme proposed in the late 1960s by Hispanic-American social activists, later endorsed by a congressional vote. It is a program that seeks to permit non-English-speaking children, many from lower-class homes, to use their family language as the language of school. (Such is the goal its supporters announce.) I hear them and am forced to say no: It is not possible for a child—any child—ever to use his family's language in school. Not to understand this is to misunderstand the public uses of schooling and to trivialize the nature of intimate life—a family's 'language.'

6   Memory teaches me what I know of these matters; the boy reminds the adult. I was a bilingual child, a certain kind—socially disadvantaged—the son of working-class parents, both Mexican immigrants.

7   In the early years of my boyhood, my parents coped very well in America. My father had steady work. My mother managed at home. They were nobody's victims. Optimism and ambition led them to a house (our home) many blocks from the Mexican south side of town. We lived among *gringos* and only a block from the biggest, whitest houses. It never occurred to my parents that they couldn't live wherever they chose. Nor was the Sacramento of the fifties bent on teaching them a contrary lesson. My mother and father were more annoyed than intimidated by those two or three neighbors who tried initially to make us unwelcome. ('Keep your brats away from my sidewalk!') But despite all they achieved,

perhaps because they had so much to achieve, any deep feeling of ease, the confidence of 'belonging' in public was withheld from them both. They regarded the people at work, the faces in crowds, as very distant from us. They were the others, *los gringos.* That term was interchangeable in their speech with another, even more telling, *los americanos.*

I grew up in a house where the only regular guests were my 8 relations. For one day, enormous families of relatives would visit and there would be so many people that the noise and the bodies would spill out to the backyard and front porch. Then, for weeks, no one came by. (It was usually a salesman who rang the doorbell.) Our house stood apart. A gaudy yellow in a row of white bungalows. We were the people with the noisy dog. The people who raised pigeons and chickens. We were the foreigners on the block. A few neighbors smiled and waved. We waved back. But no one in the family knew the names of the old couple who lived next door; until I was seven years old, I did not know the names of the kids who lived across the street.

In public, my father and mother spoke a hesitant, accented, not 9 always grammatical English. And they would have to strain—their bodies tense—to catch the sense of what was rapidly said by *los gringos.* At home they spoke Spanish. The language of their Mexican past sounded in counterpoint to the English of public society. The words would come quickly, with ease. Conveyed through those sounds was the pleasing, soothing, consoling reminder of being at home.

During those years when I was first conscious of hearing, my 10 mother and father addressed me only in Spanish; in Spanish I learned to reply. By contrast, English *(inglés),* rarely heard in the house, was the language I came to associate with *gringos.* I learned my first words of English overhearing my parents speak to strangers. At five years of age, I knew just enough English for my mother to trust me on errands to stores one block away. No more.

I was a listening child, careful to hear the very different sounds 11 of Spanish and English. Wide-eyed with hearing, I'd listen to sounds more than words. First, there were English *(gringo)* sounds. So many words were still unknown that when the butcher or the lady at the drugstore said something to me, exotic polysyllabic sounds would bloom in the midst of their sentences. Often the speech of people in public seemed to me very loud, booming with confidence. The man behind the counter would literally ask, 'What can I do for you?' But by being so firm and so clear, the sound of his voice said that he was a *gringo;* he belonged in public society.

12   I would also hear then the high nasal notes of middle-class American speech. The air stirred with sound. Sometimes, even now, when I have been traveling abroad for several weeks, I will hear what I heard as a boy. In hotel lobbies or airports, in Turkey or Brazil, some Americans will pass, and suddenly I will hear it again—the high sound of American voices. For a few seconds I will hear it with pleasure, for it is now the sound of *my* society—a reminder of home. But inevitably—already on the flight headed for home—the sound fades with repetition. I will be unable to hear it anymore.

13   When I was a boy, things were different. The accent of *los gringos* was never pleasing nor was it hard to hear. Crowds at Safeway or at bus stops would be noisy with sound. And I would be forced to edge away from the chirping chatter above me.

14   I was unable to hear my own sounds, but I knew very well that I spoke English poorly. My words could not stretch far enough to form complete thoughts. And the words I did speak I didn't know well enough to make into distinct sounds. (Listeners would usually lower their heads, better to hear what I was trying to say.) But it was one thing for *me* to speak English with difficulty. It was more troubling for me to hear my parents speak in public: their high-whining vowels and guttural consonants; their sentences that got stuck with 'eh' and 'ah' sounds; the confused syntax; the hesitant rhythm of sounds so different from the way *gringos* spoke. I'd notice, moreover, that my parents' voices were softer than those of *gringos* we'd meet.

15   I am tempted now to say that none of this mattered. In adulthood I am embarrassed by childhood fears. And, in a way, it didn't matter very much that my parents could not speak English with ease. Their linguistic difficulties had no serious consequences. My mother and father made themselves understood at the county hospital clinic and at government offices. And yet, in another way, it mattered very much—it was unsettling to hear my parents struggle with English. Hearing them, I'd grow nervous, my clutching trust in their protection and power weakened.

16   There were many times like the night at a brightly lit gasoline station (a blaring white memory) when I stood uneasily, hearing my father. He was talking to a teenaged attendant. I do not recall what they were saying, but I cannot forget the sounds my father made as he spoke. At one point his words slid together to form one word—sounds as confused as the threads of blue and green oil in the puddle next to my shoes. His voice rushed through what he had left to say. And, toward the end, reached falsetto notes, appealing

to his listener's understanding. I looked away to the lights of passing automobiles. I tried not to hear anymore. But I heard only too well the calm, easy tones in the attendant's reply. Shortly afterward, walking toward home with my father, I shivered when he put his hand on my shoulder. The very first chance that I got, I evaded his grasp and ran on ahead into the dark, skipping with feigned boyish exuberance.

But then there was Spanish. *Español:* my family's language. 17
Español: the language that seemed to me a private language. I'd hear strangers on the radio and in the Mexican Catholic church across town speaking in Spanish, but I couldn't really believe that Spanish was a public language, like English. Spanish speakers, rather, seemed related to me, for I sensed that we shared—through our language— the experience of feeling apart from *los gringos.* It was thus a ghetto Spanish that I heard and I spoke. Like those whose lives are bound by a barrio, I was reminded by Spanish of my separateness from *los otros, los gringos* in power. But more intensely than for most barrio children—because I did not live in a barrio—Spanish seemed to me the language of home. (Most days it was only at home that I'd hear it.) It became the language of joyful return.

A family member would say something to me and I would feel 18
myself specially recognized. My parents would say something to me and I would feel embraced by the sounds of their words. Those sounds said: *I am speaking with ease in Spanish. I am addressing you in words I never use with* los gringos. *I recognize you as someone special, close, like no one outside. You belong with us. In the family.*

(Ricardo.) 19

At the age of five, six, well past the time when most other 20
children no longer easily notice the difference between sounds uttered at home and words spoken in public, I had a different experience. I lived in a world magically compounded of sounds. I remained a child longer than most; I lingered too long, poised at the edge of language—often frightened by the sounds of *los gringos,* delighted by the sounds of Spanish at home. I shared with my family a language that was startlingly different from that used in the great city around us.

For me there were none of the gradations between public and 21
private society so normal to a maturing child. Outside the house was public society; inside the house was private. Just opening or closing the screen door behind me was an important experience. I'd rarely leave home all alone or without reluctance. Walking down the sidewalk, under the canopy of tall trees, I'd warily notice the— suddenly—silent neighborhood kids who stood warily watching

me. Nervously, I'd arrive at the grocery store to hear there the sounds of the *gringo*—foreign to me—reminding me that in this world so big, I was a foreigner. But then I'd return. Walking back toward our house, climbing the steps from the sidewalk, when the front door was open in summer, I'd hear voices beyond the screen door talking in Spanish. For a second or two, I'd stay, linger there, listening. Smiling, I'd hear my mother call out, saying in Spanish (words): 'Is that you, Richard?' All the while her sounds would assure me: *You are home now; come closer; inside. With us.*

22   *'Si,'* I'd reply.

23   Once more inside the house I would resume (assume) my place in the family. The sounds would dim, grow harder to hear. Once more at home, I would grow less aware of that fact. It required, however, no more than the blurt of the doorbell to alert me to listen to sounds all over again. The house would turn instantly still while my mother went to the door. I'd hear her hard English sounds. I'd wait to hear her voice return to soft-sounding Spanish, which assured me, as surely as did the clicking tongue of the lock on the door, that the stranger was gone.

24   Plainly, it is not healthy to hear such sounds so often. It is not healthy to distinguish public words from private sounds so easily. I remained cloistered by sounds, timid and shy in public, too dependent on voices at home. And yet it needs to be emphasized: I was an extremely happy child at home. I remember many nights when my father would come back from work, and I'd hear him call out to my mother in Spanish, sounding relieved. In Spanish, he'd sound light and free notes he never could manage in English. Some nights I'd jump up just at hearing his voice. With *mis hermanos* I would come running into the room where he was with my mother. Our laughing (so deep was the pleasure!) became screaming. Like others who know the pain of public alienation, we transformed the knowledge of our public separateness and made it consoling—the reminder of intimacy. Excited, we joined our voices in a celebration of sounds. *We are speaking now the way we never speak out in public. We are alone—together,* voices sounded, surrounded to tell me. Some nights, no one seemed willing to loosen the hold sounds had on us. At dinner, we invented new words. (Ours sounded Spanish, but made sense only to us.) We pieced together new words by taking, say, an English verb and giving it Spanish endings. My mother's instructions at bedtime would be lacquered with mock-urgent tones. Or a word like *si* would become, in several notes, able to convey added measures of feeling. Tongues explored the edges of words, especially the fat vowels. And we happily sounded that military

drum roll, the twirling roar of the Spanish *r*. Family language: my family's sounds. The voices of my parents and sisters and brother. Their voices insisting: *You belong here. We are family members. Related. Special to one another. Listen!* Voices singing and sighing, rising, straining, then surging, teeming with pleasure that burst syllables into fragments of laughter. At times it seemed there was steady quiet only when, from another room, the rustling whispers of my parents faded and I moved closer to sleep.

Reading Critically

1. When Rodriguez says in paragraph 5, "It is not possible for a child—any child—ever to use his family's language in school," is he talking only about the "family" languages of minorities, or does this statement apply to native speakers of English as well? How is a family language different from a public or school language? Are these family and public language interchangeable? Discuss with your classmates.

2. If you have lived in an environment where a language other than your native language was dominant, discuss with your classmates your experiences in trying to learn the new language. Were the native speakers of the new language helpful or hostile? In what ways do your experiences parallel those of Rodriguez? In what ways are they different?

3. What is your reaction to Rodriguez's stand on bilingual education? Are you surprised at his view? Do you agree with his position? Why or why not? Discuss with your classmates.

4. Do you think that English should be the only language used for public purposes in the United States? Why or why not? Discuss with your classmates.

Responding Through Writing

1. In developing his essay, Rodriguez first writes a short narrative about a personal event and then comments on the wider implications that the event suggests. In your notebook or journal, try to use the same technique to write about some important social issue.

2. Pretend you are Rodriguez and write a letter to your neighbors discussing your reactions to their language.

3. Pretend you are Rodriguez's father or mother and write a letter to him discussing the role that Spanish and English will play in his life. Give him some specific advice. Discuss this letter with your classmates.

4. If you speak English as a second language, write for ten minutes in your notebook or journal, giving your reaction to Rodriguez's essay. Use your native language. Let a few hours go by and do the same, only this time in English. In what ways does the content of your responses differ?

NOT POOR, JUST BROKE

DICK GREGORY

Dick Gregory (b. 1932), track star, comic, historian, civil rights spokesperson, political analyst, and political candidate, grew up in St. Louis, Missouri. In his youth, Gregory used his comedic talent to rebut racial slurs, a tactic that threw off his attackers and also won him respect. He gradually learned to use his fresh style and quick wit professionally, for social satire in general. However, Gregory's serious concern for solving social problems soon led him to alternate continually between the comedian's stage and participation in the civil rights movement. In 1968 he ran for president of the United States as the candidate of the Peace and Freedom Party. The same concerns for social justice also led him to begin his writing career. Gregory's concise style and sharp images make reading his works a pleasure, especially since his real-life experiences are often more exciting than fiction. His books include From the Back of the Bus *(1962),* No More Lies: The Myth and Reality of American History *(1971),* Dick Gregory's Political Primer *(1971),* Up from Nigger *(1976), and* Dick Gregory's Bible Tales *(1978). The following is an excerpt from Gregory's autobiography,* Nigger *(1964), a million-copy best-seller.*

1   Like a lot of Negro kids, we never would have made it without our Momma. When there was no fatback to go with the beans, no socks to go with the shoes, no hope to go with tomorrow, she'd smile and say: "We ain't poor; we're just broke." Poor is a state of mind you never grow out of, but being broke is just a temporary condition. She always had a big smile, even when her legs and feet swelled from high blood pressure and she collapsed across the table with sugar diabetes. You have to smile twenty-four hours a day, Momma would say. If you walk through life showing the aggravation you've gone through, people will feel sorry for you, and they'll never respect you. She taught us that man has two ways out in life—laughing or crying. There's more hope in laughing. A man can fall down the stairs and lie there in such pain and horror that his own wife will collapse and faint at the sight. But if he can just hold back his pain for a minute she might be able to collect herself and call the doctor. It might mean the difference between his living to laugh again or dying there on the spot.

2   So you laugh; so you smile. Once a month the big gray relief truck would pull up in front of our house and Momma would flash that big smile and stretch out her hands. "Who else you know in this neighborhood gets this kind of service?" And we could all feel proud when the neighbors, folks who weren't on relief, folks who had Daddies in their houses, would come by the back porch for some of those hundred pounds of potatoes, for some sugar and flour and salty fish. We'd stand out there on the back porch and hand out the food like we were in charge of helping poor people, and then we'd take the food they brought us in return.

3   And Momma came home one hot summer day and found we'd been evicted, thrown out into the streetcar zone with our orange-crate chairs and secondhand lamps. She flashed that big smile and dried our tears and bought some penny Kool-Aid. We stood out there and sold drinks to thirsty people coming off the streetcar, and we thought nobody knew we were kicked out—figured they thought we *wanted* to be there. And Momma went off to talk the landlord into letting us back in on credit.

4   But I wonder about my Momma sometimes, and all other Negro mothers who got up at 6 A.M. to go to the white man's house with sacks over their shoes because it was so wet and cold. I wonder

how they made it. They worked very hard for the man, they made his breakfast, and they scrubbed his floors and diapered his babies. They didn't have too much time for us.

I wonder about my Momma, who walked out of a white   5
woman's clean house at midnight and came back to her own where the lights had been out for three months, and the pipes were frozen, and the wind came in through the cracks. She'd have to make deals with the rats: leave some food out for them so they wouldn't gnaw on the doors or bite the babies. The roaches, they were just like part of the family.

I wonder how she felt telling those white kids she took care   6
of to brush their teeth after they ate, to wash their hands after they peed. She could never tell her own kids because there wasn't soap or water back home.

I wonder how my Momma felt when we came home from   7
school with a list of vitamins and pills and cod liver oils the school nurse said we had to have. Momma would cry all night, and then go out and spend most of the rent money for pills. A week later, the white man would come for his eighteen dollars rent and Momma would plead with him to wait until tomorrow. She had lost her pocketbook. The relief check was coming. The white folks had some money for her. Tomorrow. I'd be hiding in the coal closet because there was only supposed to be two kids in the flat, and I could hear the rent man curse my Momma and call her a liar. And when he finally went away, Momma put the sacks on her shoes and went off to the rich white folks' house to dress the rich white kids so their mother could take them to a special baby doctor.

Momma had to take us to Homer G. Phillips, the free hospital,   8
the city hospital for Negroes. We'd stand in line and wait for hours, smiling and Uncle Tomming every time a doctor or a nurse passed by. We'd feel good when one of them smiled back and didn't look as though we were dirty and had no right coming down there. All the doctors and nurses at Homer G. Phillips were Negro, too.

I remember one time when a doctor in white walked up and   9
said: "What's wrong with him?" as if he didn't believe that anything was.

Momma looked at me and looked at him and shook her head.   10
"I sure don't know, Doctor, but he cried all night long. Held his stomach."

"Bring him in and get his damned clothes off."   11

I was so mad the way he was talking to my Momma that I   12
bit down too hard on the thermometer. It broke in my mouth. The doctor slapped me across my face.

13   "Both of you go stand in the back of the line and wait your turn."

14   My Momma had to say: "I'm sorry, Doctor," and go to the back of the line. She had five other kids at home and she never knew when she'd have to bring another down to the City Hospital.

15   And those rich white folks Momma was so proud of. She'd sit around with the other women and they'd talk about how good their white folks were. They'd lie about how rich they were, what nice parties they gave, what good clothes they wore. And how they were going to be remembered in their white folks' wills. The next morning the white lady would say, "We're going on vacation for two months, Lucille; we won't be needing you until we get back." Damn. Two-month vacation without pay.

16   I wonder how my Momma stayed so good and beautiful in her soul when she worked seven days a week on swollen legs and feet, how she kept teaching us to smile and laugh when the house was dark and cold and she never knew when one of her hungry kids was going to ask about Daddy.

17   I wonder how she kept from teaching us hate when the social worker came around. She was a nasty woman with a pinched face who said, "We have reason to suspect you are working, Miss Gregory, and you can be sure I'm going to check on you. We don't stand for welfare cheaters."

18   Momma, a welfare cheater. A criminal who couldn't stand to see her kids go hungry, or grow up in slums and end up mugging people in dark corners. I guess the system didn't want her to get off relief, the way it kept sending social workers around to be sure Momma wasn't trying to make things better.

19   I remember how that social worker would poke around the house, wrinkling her nose at the coal dust on the chilly linoleum floor, shaking her head at the bugs crawling over the dirty dishes in the sink. My Momma would have to stand there and make like she was too lazy to keep her own house clean. She could never let on that she spent all day cleaning another woman's house for two dollars and carfare. She would have to follow that nasty woman around those drafty three rooms, keeping her fingers crossed that the telephone hidden in the closet wouldn't ring. Welfare cases weren't supposed to have telephones.

20   But Momma figured that some day the Gregory kids were going to get off North Taylor Street and into a world where they would have to compete with kids who grew up with telephones in their houses. She didn't want us to be at a disadvantage. She couldn't explain that to the social worker. And she couldn't explain that

while she was out spoon-feeding somebody else's kids, she was worrying about her own kids, that she could rest her mind by picking up the telephone and calling us—to find out if we had bread for our baloney or baloney for our bread, to see if any of us had gotten run over by the streetcar while we played in the gutter, to make sure the house hadn't burnt down from the papers and magazines we stuffed in the stove when the coal ran out.

But sometimes when she called there would be no answer. 21 Home was a place to be only when all other places were closed.

I never learned hate at home, or shame. I had to go to school 22 for that. I was about seven years old when I got my first big lesson. I was in love with a little girl named Helene Tucker, a light-complected little girl with pigtails and nice manners. She was always clean and she was smart in school. I think I went to school then mostly to look at her. I brushed my hair and even got me a little old handkerchief. It was a lady's handkerchief, but I didn't want Helene to see me wipe my nose on my hand. The pipes were frozen again; there was no water in the house, but I washed my socks and shirt every night. I'd get a pot, and go over to Mister Ben's grocery store, and stick my pot down into his soda machine. Scoop out some chopped ice. By evening the ice melted to water for washing. I got sick a lot that winter because the fire would go out at night before the clothes were dry. In the morning I'd put them on, wet or dry, because they were the only clothes I had.

Everybody's got a Helene Tucker, a symbol of everything you 23 want. I loved her for her goodness, her cleanliness, her popularity. She'd walk down my street and my brothers and sisters would yell, "Here comes Helene," and I'd rub my tennis sneakers on the back of my pants and wish my hair wasn't so nappy and the white folks' shirt fit me better. I'd run out on the street. If I knew my place and didn't come too close, she'd wink at me and say hello. That was a good feeling. Sometimes I'd follow her all the way home, and shovel the snow off her walk and try to make friends with her Momma and her aunts. I'd drop money on her stoop late at night on my way back from shining shoes in the taverns. And she had a Daddy, and he had a good job. He was a paper hanger.

I guess I would have gotten over Helene by summertime, 24 but something happened in that classroom that made her face hang in front of me for the next twenty-two years. When I played the drums in high school it was for Helene, and when I started standing behind microphones and heard applause I wished Helene could hear it, too. It wasn't until I was twenty-nine years old and married and making money that I finally got her out of my system.

Helene was sitting in that classroom when I learned to be ashamed of myself.

25   It was on a Thursday. I was sitting in the back of the room, in a seat with a chalk circle drawn around it. The idiot's seat, the troublemaker's seat.

26   The teacher thought I was stupid. Couldn't spell, couldn't read, couldn't do arithmetic. Just stupid. Teachers were never interested in finding out that you couldn't concentrate because you were so hungry, because you hadn't had any breakfast. All you could think about was noontime; would it ever come? Maybe you could sneak into the cloakroom and steal a bite of some kid's lunch out of a coat pocket. A bite of something. Paste. You can't really make a meal of paste, or put it on bread for a sandwich, but sometimes I'd scoop a few spoonfuls out of the paste jar in the back of the room. Pregnant people get strange tastes. I was pregnant with poverty. Pregnant with dirt and pregnant with smells that made people turn away, pregnant with cold and pregnant with shoes that were never bought for me, pregnant with five other people in my bed and no Daddy in the next room, and pregnant with hunger. Paste doesn't taste too bad when you're hungry.

27   The teacher thought I was a troublemaker. All she saw from the front of the room was a little black boy who squirmed in his idiot's seat and made noises and poked the kids around him. I guess she couldn't see a kid who made noises because he wanted someone to know he was there.

28   It was on a Thursday, the day before the Negro payday. The eagle always flew on Friday. The teacher was asking each student how much his father would give to the Community Chest. On Friday night, each kid would get the money from his father, and on Monday he would bring it to the school. I decided I was going to buy me a Daddy right then. I had money in my pocket from shining shoes and selling papers, and whatever Helene Tucker pledged for her Daddy I was going to top it. And I'd hand the money right in. I wasn't going to wait until Monday to buy me a Daddy.

29   I was shaking, scared to death. The teacher opened her book and started calling out names alphabetically.

30   "Helene Tucker?"

31   "My Daddy said he'd give two dollars and fifty cents."

32   "That's very nice, Helene. Very, very nice indeed."

33   That made me feel pretty good. It wouldn't take too much to top that. I had almost three dollars in dimes and quarters in my pocket. I stuck my hand in my pocket and held onto the money,

waiting for her to call my name. But the teacher closed her book after she called everybody else in the class.

I stood up and raised my hand.   34

"What is it now?"   35

"You forgot me."   36

She turned toward the blackboard. "I don't have time to be   37
playing with you, Richard."

"My Daddy said he'd . . ."   38

"Sit down, Richard; you're disturbing the class."   39

"My Daddy said he'd give . . . fifteen dollars."   40

She turned around and looked mad. "We are collecting this   41
money for you and your kind, Richard Gregory. If your Daddy can
give fifteen dollars you have no business being on relief."

"I got it right now, I got it right now, my Daddy gave it to   42
me to turn in today, my Daddy said. . . ."

"And furthermore," she said, looking right at me, her nostrils   43
getting big and her lips getting thin and her eyes opening wide, "we
know you don't have a Daddy."

Helene Tucker turned around, her eyes full of tears. She felt   44
sorry for me. Then I couldn't see her too well because I was crying,
too.

"Sit down, Richard."   45

And I always thought the teacher kind of liked me. She always   46
picked me to wash the blackboard on Friday, after school. That was
a big thrill; it made me feel important. If I didn't wash it, come
Monday the school might not function right.

"Where are you going, Richard?"   47

I walked out of school that day, and for a long time I didn't   48
go back very often. There was shame there.

Now there was shame everywhere. It seemed like the whole   49
world had been inside that classroom; everyone had heard what the
teacher had said; everyone had turned around and felt sorry for me.
There was shame in going to the Worthy Boys' Annual Christmas
Dinner for you and your kind, because everybody knew what a
worthy boy was. Why couldn't they just call it the Boys' Annual
Dinner; why'd they have to give it a name? There was shame in
wearing the brown and orange and white plaid mackinaw the
welfare gave to 3,000 boys. Why'd it have to be the same for
everybody so when you walked down the street the people could
see you were on relief? It was a nice warm mackinaw and it had
a hood, and my Momma beat me and called me a little rat when
she found out I stuffed it in the bottom of a pail full of garbage
way over on Cottage Street. There was shame in running over to

Mister Ben's at the end of the day and asking for his rotten peaches; there was shame in asking Mrs. Simmons for a spoonful of sugar; there was shame in running out to meet the relief truck. I hated that truck, full of food for you and your kind. I ran into the house and hid when it came. And then I started to sneak through alleys, to take the long way home so the people going into White's Eat Shop wouldn't see me. Yeah, the whole world heard the teacher that day; we all know you don't have a Daddy.

50   It lasted for a while, this kind of numbness. I spent a lot of time feeling sorry for myself. And then one day I met this wino in a restaurant. I'd been out hustling all day, shining shoes, selling newspapers, and I had googobs of money in my pocket. Bought me a bowl of chili for fifteen cents, and a cheeseburger for fifteen cents, and a Pepsi for five cents, and a piece of chocolate cake for ten cents. That was a good meal. I was eating when this old wino came in. I love winos because they never hurt anyone but themselves.

51   The old wino sat down at the counter and ordered twenty-six cents worth of food. He ate it like he really enjoyed it. When the owner, Mister Williams, asked him to pay the check, the old wino didn't lie or go through his pocket like he suddenly found a hole.

52   He just said, "Don't have no money."

53   The owner yelled, "Why in hell you come in here and eat my food if you don't have no money? That food cost me money."

54   Mister Williams jumped over the counter and knocked the wino off his stool and beat him over the head with a pop bottle. Then he stepped back and watched the wino bleed. Then he kicked him. And he kicked him again.

55   I looked at the wino with blood all over his face and I went over. "Leave him alone, Mister Williams. I'll pay the twenty-six cents."

56   The wino got up, slowly, pulling himself up to the stool, then up to the counter, holding on for a minute until his legs stopped shaking so bad. He looked at me with pure hate. "Keep your twenty-six cents. You don't have to pay, not now. I just finished paying for it."

57   He started to walk out, and as he passed me, he reached down and touched my shoulder. "Thanks, sonny, but it's too late now. Why didn't you pay it before?"

58   I was pretty sick about that. I waited too long to help another man.

59   I remember a white lady who came to our door once around Thanksgiving time. She wore a woolly, green bonnet around her head, and she smiled a lot.

"Is your mother home, little boy?"   60

"No, she ain't."   61

"May I come in?"   62

"What do you want, ma'am?"   63

She didn't stop smiling once, but she sighed a little when she   64
bent down and lifted up a big yellow basket. The kind I saw around
church that were called Baskets for the Needy.

"This is for you."   65

"What's in there?"   66

"All sorts of good things," she said, smiling. "There's candy   67
and potatoes and cake and cranberry sauce and"—she made a funny
little face at me by wrinkling up her nose—"and a great big fat
turkey for Thanksgiving dinner."

"Is it cooked?"   68

"A big fat juicy turkey, all plucked clean for you. . . ."   69

"Is it cooked?"   70

"No, it's not. . . ."   71

"We ain't got nothing in the house to cook it with, lady."   72

I slammed the door in her face. Wouldn't that be something,   73
to have a turkey like that in the house with no way to cook it? No
gas, no electricity, no coal. Just a big fat juicy raw turkey.

I remember Mister Ben, the grocery-store man, a round little   74
white man with funny little tufts of white hair on his head and
sad-looking eyes. His face was kind of gray-colored, and the skin
was loose and shook when he talked.

"Momma want a loaf of bread, Mister Ben, fresh bread."   75

"Right away, Richard," he'd say and get the bread he bought   76
three days old from the bakeries downtown. It was the only kind
he had for his credit-book customers. He dropped it on the counter.
Clunk.

I'd hand him the credit book, that green tablet with the picture   77
of the snuff can on it, to write down how much we owed him. He'd
lick the tip of that stubby pencil he kept behind his ear. Six cents.

"How you like school, Richard?"   78

"I like school fine, Mister Ben."   79

"Good boy, you study, get smart."   80

I'd run home to Momma and tell her that the bread wasn't   81
fresh bread, it was stale bread. She'd flash the big smile.

"Oh, that Mister Ben, he knew I was fixin to make toast."   82

The peaches were rotten and the bread wasn't fresh and some-   83
times the butter was green, but when it came down to the nitty-
gritty you could always go to Mister Ben. Before a Jewish holiday
he'd take all the food that was going to spoil while the store was

shut and bring it over to our house. Before Christmas he'd send over some meat even though he knew it was going on the tablet and he might never see his money. When the push came to the shove and every hungry belly in the house was beginning to eat on itself, Momma could go to Mister Ben and always get enough for some kind of dinner.

84   But I can remember three days in a row I went into Mister Ben's and asked him to give me a penny Mr. Goodbar from the window.

85   Three days in a row he said: "Out, out, or I'll tell your Momma you been begging."

86   One night I threw a brick through his window and took it.

87   The next day I went into Mister Ben's to get some bread for Momma and his skin was shaking and I heard him tell a lady, "I can't understand why should anybody break my window for a penny piece of candy, a lousy piece of candy, all they got to do is ask, that's all, and I give."

Reading Critically

1. What is the difference between being "poor" and being "broke"? To what extent is being poor essentially "a state of mind"? Discuss with your classmates.

2. Is Gregory's mother a welfare cheater (paragraph 17)? If so, is her "cheating" justified? Discuss the ambiguities of "cheating" in related areas of life (taxes, work-study, etc.).

3. Discuss with your classmates the predicament of Gregory's mother whose need to work left little time for the children. To what extent is this a problem faced by people today?

4. Do children benefit or suffer from a mother's need to work? Discuss the support systems that society does (or could) provide for working mothers.

Responding Through Writing

1. Are all poor working mothers confronted by essentially similar experiences, or do domestic workers have to face particularly difficult psychological experiences in taking care of other people's children? How must Gregory's mother feel when she tells her employer's children to wash well while knowing that her own children don't even have soap? Put yourself in her position and write for five minutes just letting your thoughts flow on this subject.

2. Do you agree that people have "two ways out in life— laughing or crying"? Can you cite examples of both ways from your own experience? Write a short essay comparing and contrasting these two ways.

3. Why are Gregory's mother and her friends proud of their "rich white folks" (paragraph 15)? To what extent does their identification with their employers heighten their own self-esteem? To what extent is that identification self-deceptive? Sketch the draft of a short essay exploring and comparing both sides of this problem.

4. Gregory says, "Everybody's got a Helene Tucker, a symbol of everything you want" (paragraph 23). What other symbols does Gregory use throughout the essay to communicate his ideas? Start with the paste and the eagle in the last few paragraphs and list these symbols, then see whether you can come up with a parallel list of symbols that might work as well in Gregory's essay.

ONCE MORE TO THE LAKE

E. B. WHITE

E. B. White (1899–1985) is perhaps best known for his collaboration with William Strunk, Jr. (his former English composition teacher at Cornell University), in the creation of what probably is the most quoted style manual of all time: Elements of Style. *White spent most of his life as a journalist and essayist, principally for* Harper's *and* The New Yorker. *His writings are collected in many volumes, including* The Second Tree from the Corner *(1954) and* The Points of My Compass *(1962). He is also remembered by many of today's adults for his children's stories, the most famous of which is* Charlotte's Web *(1952). The E. B. stands for Elwyn Brooks. The following story first appeared in* Harper's *magazine in 1939 in a regular column White wrote called "One Man's Meat."*

August 1941

1   One summer, along about 1904, my father rented a camp on a lake in Maine and took us all there for the month of August. We all got ringworm from some kittens and had to rub Pond's Extract

on our arms and legs night and morning, and my father rolled over in a canoe with all his clothes on; but outside of that the vacation was a success and from then on none of us ever thought there was any place in the world like that lake in Maine. We returned summer after summer—always on August 1 for one month. I have since become a salt-water man, but sometimes in summer there are days when the restlessness of the tides and the fearful cold of the sea water and the incessant wind that blows across the afternoon and into the evening make me wish for the placidity of a lake in the woods. A few weeks ago this feeling got so strong I bought myself a couple of bass hooks and a spinner and returned to the lake where we used to go, for a week's fishing and to revisit old haunts.

I took along my son, who had never had any fresh water up   2
his nose and who had seen lily pads only from train windows. On the journey over to the lake I began to wonder what it would be like. I wondered how time would have marred this unique, this holy spot—the coves and streams, the hills that the sun set behind, the camps and the paths behind the camps. I was sure that the tarred road would have found it out, and I wondered in what other ways it would be desolated. It is strange how much you can remember about places like that once you allow your mind to return into the grooves that lead back. You remember one thing, and that suddenly reminds you of another thing. I guess I remembered clearest of all the early mornings, when the lake was cool and motionless, remembered how the bedroom smelled of the lumber it was made of and of the wet woods whose scent entered through the screen. The partitions in the camp were thin and did not extend clear to the top of the rooms, and as I was always the first up I would dress softly so as not to wake the others, and sneak out into the sweet outdoors and start out in the canoe, keeping close along the shore in the long shadows of the pines. I remembered being very careful never to rub my paddle against the gunwale for fear of disturbing the stillness of the cathedral.

The lake had never been what you would call a wild lake.   3
There were cottages sprinkled around the shores, and it was in farming country although the shores of the lake were quite heavily wooded. Some of the cottages were owned by nearby farmers, and you would live at the shore and eat your meals at the farmhouse. That's what our family did. But although it wasn't wild, it was a fairly large and undisturbed lake and there were places in it that, to a child at least, seemed infinitely remote and primeval.

I was right about the tar: it led to within half a mile of the   4 shore. But when I got back there, with my boy, and we settled into a camp near a farmhouse and into the kind of summertime I had known, I could tell that it was going to be pretty much the same as it had been before—I knew it, lying in bed the first morning smelling the bedroom and hearing the boy sneak quietly out and go off along the shore in a boat. I began to sustain the illusion that he was I, and therefore, by simple transposition, that I was my father. This sensation persisted, kept cropping up all the time we were there. It was not an entirely new feeling, but in this setting it grew much stronger. I seemed to be living a dual existence. I would be in the middle of some simple act, I would be picking up a bait box or laying down a table fork, or I would be saying something and suddenly it would be not I but my father who was saying the words or making the gesture. It gave me a creepy sensation.

5   We went fishing the first morning. I felt the same damp moss covering the worms in the bait can, and saw the dragonfly alight on the tip of my rod as it hovered a few inches from the surface of the water. It was the arrival of this fly that convinced me beyond any doubt that everything was as it always had been, that the years were a mirage and that there had been no years. The small waves were the same, chucking the rowboat under the chin as we fished at anchor, and the boat was the same boat, the same color green and the ribs broken in the same places, and under the floorboards the same fresh water leavings and débris—the dead hellgrammite, the wisps of moss, the rusty discarded fishhook, the dried blood from yesterday's catch. We stared silently at the tips of our rods, at the dragonflies that came and went. I lowered the tip of mine into the water, tentatively, pensively dislodging the fly, which darted two feet away, poised, darted two feet back, and came to rest again a little farther up the rod. There had been no years between the ducking of this dragonfly and the other one—the one that was part of memory. I looked at the boy, who was silently watching his fly, and it was my hands that held his rod, my eyes watching. I felt dizzy and didn't know which rod I was at the end of.

6   We caught two bass, hauling them in briskly as though they were mackerel, pulling them over the side of the boat in a business-like manner without any landing net, and stunning them with a blow on the back of the head. When we got back for a swim before lunch, the lake was exactly where we had left it, the same number of inches from the dock, and there was only the merest suggestion of a breeze. This seemed an utterly enchanted sea, this lake you could leave to its own devices for a few hours and come back to, and find

that it had not stirred, this constant and trustworthy body of water. In the shallows, the dark, water-soaked sticks and twigs, smooth and old, were undulating in clusters on the bottom against the clean ribbed sand, and the track of the mussel was plain. A school of minnows swam by, each minnow with its small individual shadow, doubling the attendance, so clear and sharp in the sunlight. Some of the other campers were in swimming, along the shore, one of them with a cake of soap, and the water felt thin and clear and unsubstantial. Over the years there had been this person with the cake of soap, this cultist, and here he was. There had been no years.

Up to the farmhouse to dinner through the teeming dusty 7 field, the road under our sneakers was only a two-track road. The middle track was missing, the one with the marks of the hooves and the splotches of dried, flaky manure. There had always been three tracks to choose from in choosing which track to walk in; now the choice was narrowed down to two. For a moment I missed terribly the middle alternative. But the way led past the tennis court, and something about the way it lay there in the sun reassured me; the tape had loosened along the backline, the alleys were green with plantains and other weeds, and the net (installed in June and removed in September) sagged in the dry noon, and the whole place steamed with midday heat and hunger and emptiness. There was a choice of pie for dessert, and one was blueberry and one was apple, and the waitresses were the same country girls, there having been no passage of time, only the illusion of it as in a dropped curtain— the waitresses were still fifteen; their hair had been washed, that was the only difference—they had been to the movies and seen the pretty girls with the clean hair.

Summertime, oh, summertime, pattern of life indelible with 8 fade-proof lake, the wood unshatterable, the pasture with the sweet-fern and the juniper forever and ever, summer without end; this was the background, and the life along the shore was the design, the cottages with their innocent and tranquil design, their tiny docks with the flagpole and the American flag floating against the white clouds in the blue sky, the little paths over the roots of the trees leading from camp to camp and the paths leading back to the outhouses and the can of lime for sprinkling, and at the souvenir counters at the store the miniature birchbark canoes and the post-cards that showed things looking a little better than they looked. This was the American family at play, escaping the city heat, wondering whether the newcomers in the camp at the head of the cove were "common" or "nice," wondering whether it was true that the people who drove up for Sunday dinner at the farmhouse were turned away because there wasn't enough chicken.

9   It seemed to me, as I kept remembering all this, that those times and those summers had been infinitely precious and worth saving. There had been jollity and peace and goodness. The arriving (at the beginning of August) had been so big a business in itself, at the railway station the farm wagon drawn up, the first smell of the pine-laden air, the first glimpse of the smiling farmer, and the great importance of the trunks and your father's enormous authority in such matters, and the feel of the wagon under you for the long ten-mile haul, and at the top of the last long hill catching the first view of the lake after eleven months of not seeing this cherished body of water. The shouts and cries of the other campers when they saw you, and the trunks to be unpacked, to give up their rich burden. (Arriving was less exciting nowadays, when you sneaked up in your car and parked it under a tree near the camp and took out the bags and in five minutes it was all over, no fuss, no loud wonderful fuss about trunks.)

10   Peace and goodness and jollity. The only thing that was wrong now, really, was the sound of the place, an unfamiliar nervous sound of the outboard motors. This was the note that jarred, the one thing that would sometimes break the illusion and set the years moving. In those other summertimes all motors were inboard; and when they were at a little distance, the noise they made was a sedative, an ingredient of summer sleep. They were one-cylinder and two-cylinder engines, and some were make-and-break and some were jump-spark, but they all made a sleepy sound across the lake. The one-lungers throbbed and fluttered, and the twin-cylinder ones purred and purred, and that was a quiet sound, too. But now the campers all had outboards. In the daytime, in the hot mornings, these motors made a petulant, irritable sound; at night in the still evening when the afterglow lit the water, they whined about one's ears like mosquitoes. My boy loved our rented outboard, and his great desire was to achieve single-handed mastery over it, and authority, and he soon learned the trick of choking it a little (but not too much), and the adjustment of the needle valve. Watching him I would remember the things you could do with the old one-cylinder engine with the heavy flywheel, how you could have it eating out of your hand if you got really close to it spiritually. Motorboats in those days didn't have clutches, and you would make a landing by shutting off the motor at the proper time and coasting in with a dead rudder. But there was a way of reversing them, if you learned the trick, by

cutting the switch and putting it on again exactly on the final dying revolution of the flywheel, so that it would kick back against compression and begin reversing. Approaching a dock in a strong following breeze, it was difficult to slow up sufficiently by the ordinary coasting method, and if a boy felt he had complete mastery over his motor, he was tempted to keep it running beyond its time and then reverse it a few feet from the dock. It took a cool nerve, because if you threw the switch a twentieth of a second too soon you would catch the flywheel when it still had speed enough to go up past center, and the boat would leap ahead, charging bull-fashion at the dock.

We had a good week at the camp. The bass were biting well 11 and the sun shone endlessly, day after day. We would be tired at night and lie down in the accumulated heat of the little bedrooms after the long hot day and the breeze would stir almost imperceptibly outside and the smell of the swamp drift in through the rusty screens. Sleep would come easily and in the morning the red squirrel would be on the roof, tapping out his gay routine. I kept remembering everything, lying in bed in the mornings—the small steamboat that had a long rounded stern like the lip of a Ubangi, and how quietly she ran on the moonlight sails, when the older boys played their mandolins and the girls sang and we ate doughnuts dipped in sugar, and how sweet the music was on the water in the shining night, and what it had felt like to think about girls then. After breakfast we would go up to the store and the things were in the same place—the minnows in a bottle, the plugs and spinners disarranged and pawed over by the youngsters from the boys' camp, the Fig Newtons and the Beeman's gum. Outside, the road was tarred and cars stood in front of the store. Inside, all was just as it had always been, except there was more Coca-Cola and not so much Moxie and root beer and birch beer and sarsaparilla. We would walk out with the bottle of pop apiece and sometimes the pop would backfire up our noses and hurt. We explored the streams, quietly, where the turtles slid off the sunny logs and dug their way into the soft bottom; and we lay on the town wharf and fed worms to the tame bass. Everywhere we went I had trouble making out which was I, the one walking at my side, the one walking in my pants.

One afternoon while we were at that lake a thunderstorm 12 came up. It was like the revival of an old melodrama that I had seen long ago with childish awe. The second-act climax of the drama of the electrical disturbance over a lake in America had not changed in any important respect. This was the big scene, still the big scene. The whole thing was so familiar, the first feeling of oppression and heat and a general air around camp of not wanting to go very far away. In midafternoon (it was all the same) a curious darkening of the sky, and a lull in everything that had made life tick; and then the way the boats suddenly swung the other way at their moorings with the coming of a breeze out of the new quarter, and the premonitory rumble. Then the kettle drum, then the snare, then the bass drum and cymbals, then crackling light against the dark, and the gods grinning and licking their chops in the hills. Afterward the calm, the rain steadily rustling in the calm lake, the return of light and hope and spirits, and the campers running out in joy and relief to go swimming in the rain, their bright cries perpetuating the deathless joke about how they were getting simply drenched, and the children screaming with delight at the new sensation of bathing in the rain, and the joke about getting drenched linking the generations in a strong indestructible chain. And the comedian who waded in carrying an umbrella.

13   When the others went swimming my son said he was going in, too. He pulled his dripping trunks from the line where they had hung all through the shower and wrung them out. Languidly, and with no thought of going in, I watched him, his hard little body, skinny and bare, saw him wince slightly as he pulled up around his vitals the small, soggy, icy garment. As he buckled the swollen belt, suddenly my groin felt the chill of death.

Reading Critically

1. Have you ever visited, many years later, a place you knew well? How had it changed? What feelings did you experience when you visited the place again? Discuss with your classmates the ways in which your feelings were similar to the feelings White describes in his essay.

2. Look up some newspapers and magazines (such as *Life, Look, Time,* and *Newsweek*) for August 1941. What was happening

in the world then? How does the tranquility of White's essay contrast with the events in the world at that time?

3. White describes a vacation where you get away from the world for a while. What kind of vacations do people take today? (Think of Disney World and similar self-contained vacation places before you answer this question.) What kinds of vacations do you like to take? If you could find the lake in Maine that White visits here, would you like to take a vacation like the one he describes? Why or why not?

4. In paragraph 7 White says that when he was a child the road to the farmhouse had three tracks but now it has only two. What changed? What other changes does White mention? What are the implications of those changes?

Responding Through Writing

1. Go through the essay and write down all the words, phrases, and sentences in which White describes his son. Using this information, write a paragraph in which you describe the boy in as much detail as you can, using only the information you copied from the essay. How complete is your description? What does it lack? What information about his son does White *not* give you in his essay? Can you provide any of that information?

2. Make a list of the changes you found in the essay in answer to item 4 in "Reading Critically" and compare your list with the lists your classmates have compiled. Using your list, write a paragraph in which you describe the kinds of changes White notes in his essay.

3. As White found out, things do not often go as we plan. Write the first draft of an essay in which you compare some event in your life with your expectations for that event. Did things work out the way you planned? What did you learn from that experience?

4. In the last sentence of the essay, White says that suddenly his "groin felt the chill of death." What is the relation of this conclusion to White's comment on "the fearful cold of the sea water" in the opening paragraph of the essay? If you are keeping a journal or notebook, write in it for at least five minutes about what the opening and closing paragraphs mean to you. Then compare your comments with your classmates' comments.

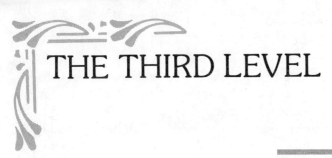

THE THIRD LEVEL

JACK FINNEY

Jack Finney (b. 1911) is the pen name of Walter Braden Finney, who began writing science fiction at age 35. Finney's writing is not limited to science fiction; his stories of mystery and intrigue have captivated audiences for decades. His best-known work is The Body Snatchers *(1955), which was made into the film* Invasion of the Body Snatchers *in 1956. The film, a parable of the anti-Communist hysteria sweeping the United States at that time, is considered a classic of science fiction. In 1978 the film was successfully remade, featuring Leonard Nimoy. Finney's other novels include* The Woodrow Wilson Dime *(1960) and* Time and Again *(1970). In 1983 he published the nonfiction* Forgotten News: The Crime of the Century and Other Lost Stories. *A collection of his most popular short stories,* About Time: 12 Short Stories by Jack Finney, *was published in 1986. The following story is included in that collection but was originally published in 1952.*

The presidents of the New York Central and the New York, New Haven and Hartford railroads will swear on a stack of time-tables that there are only two. But I say there are three, because I've *been* on the third level at Grand Central Station. Yes, I've taken the obvious step: I talked to a psychiatrist friend of mine, among others.

I told him about the third level at Grand Central Station, and he said it was a waking-dream wish fulfillment. He said I was unhappy. That made my wife kind of mad, but he explained that he meant the modern world is full of insecurity, fear, war, worry, and all the rest of it, and that I just want to escape. Well, hell, who doesn't? Everybody I know wants to escape, but they don't wander down into any third level at Grand Central Station.

2   But that's the reason, he said, and my friends all agreed. Everything points to it, they claimed. My stamp-collecting, for example—that's a "temporary refuge from reality." Well, maybe, but my grandfather didn't need any refuge from reality; things were pretty nice and peaceful in his day, from all I hear, and he started my collection. It's a nice collection, too, blocks of four of practically every U.S. issue, first-day covers, and so on. President Roosevelt collected stamps, too, you know.

3   Anyway, here's what happened at Grand Central. One night last summer I worked late at the office. I was in a hurry to get uptown to my apartment, so I decided to subway from Grand Central because it's faster than the bus.

4   Now, I don't know why this should have happened to me. I'm just an ordinary guy named Charley, thirty-one years old, and I was wearing a tan gabardine suit and a straw hat with a fancy band—I passed a dozen men who looked just like me. And I wasn't trying to escape from anything; I just wanted to get home to Louisa, my wife.

5   I turned into Grand Central from Vanderbilt Avenue and went down the steps to the first level, where you take trains like the Twentieth Century. Then I walked down another flight to the second level, where the suburban trains leave from, ducked into an arched doorway heading for the subway—and got lost. That's easy to do. I've been in and out of Grand Central hundreds of times, but I'm always bumping into new doorways and stairs and corridors. Once I got into a tunnel about a mile long and came out in the lobby of the Roosevelt Hotel. Another time I came up in an office building on Forty-sixth Street, three blocks away.

6   Sometimes I think Grand Central is growing like a tree, pushing out new corridors and staircases like roots. There's probably a long tunnel that nobody knows about feeling its way under the city right now, on its way to Times Square, and maybe another to Central Park. And maybe—because for so many people through the years Grand Central *has* been an exit, a way of escape—maybe that's

how the tunnel I got into . . . but I never told my psychiatrist friend about that idea.

The corridor I was in began angling left and slanting downward and I thought that was wrong, but I kept on walking. All I could hear was the empty sound of my own footsteps and I didn't pass a soul. Then I heard that sort of hollow roar ahead that means open space, and people talking. The tunnel turned sharp left; I went down a short flight of stairs and came out on the third level at Grand Central Station. For just a moment I thought I was back on the second level, but I saw the room was smaller, there were fewer ticket windows and train gates, and the information booth in the center was wood and old-looking. And the man in the booth wore a green eyeshade and long, black sleeve-protectors. The lights were dim and sort of flickering. Then I saw why; they were open-flame gaslights. 7

There were brass spittoons on the floor, and across the station a glint of light caught my eye; a man was pulling a gold watch from his vest pocket. He snapped open the cover, glanced at his watch, and frowned. He wore a dirty hat, a black four-button suit with tiny lapels, and he had a big, black, handle-bar mustache. Then I looked around and saw that everyone in the station was dressed like 1890 something; I never saw so many beards, sideburns and fancy mustaches in my life. A woman walked in through the train gate; she wore a dress with leg-of-mutton sleeves and skirts to the top of her high-buttoned shoes. Back of her, out on the tracks, I caught a glimpse of a locomotive, a very small Currier & Ives locomotive with a funnel-shaped stack. And then I knew. 8

To make sure, I walked over to a newsboy and glanced at the stack of papers at his feet. It was the *World;* and the *World* hasn't been published for years. The lead story said something about President Cleveland. I've found that front page since, in the Public Library files, and it was printed June 11, 1894. 9

I turned toward the ticket windows knowing that here—on the third level at Grand Central—I could buy tickets that would take Louisa and me anywhere in the United States we wanted to go. In the year 1894. And I wanted two tickets to Galesburg, Illinois. 10

Have you ever been there? It's a wonderful town still, with big old frame houses, huge lawns, and tremendous trees whose branches meet overhead and roof the streets. And in 1894, summer evenings were twice as long, and people sat out on their lawns, the men smoking cigars and talking quietly, the women waving palm-leaf fans, with the fireflies all around, in a peaceful world. To be 11

back there with the first World War still twenty years off, and
World War II over forty years in the future . . . I wanted two tickets
for that.

12   The clerk figured the fare—he glanced at my fancy hatband,
but he figured the fare—and I had enough for two coach tickets,
one way. But when I counted out the money and looked up, the
clerk was staring at me. He nodded at the bills. "That ain't money,
mister," he said, "and if you're trying to skin me you won't get very
far," and he glanced at the cash drawer beside him. Of course the
money was old-style bills, half again as big as the money we use
nowadays, and different-looking. I turned away and got out fast.
There's nothing nice about jail, even in 1894.

13   And that was that. I left the same way I came, I suppose. Next
day, during lunch hour, I drew $300 out of the bank, nearly all we
had, and bought old-style currency (that *really* worried my psychiatrist friend). You can buy old money at almost any coin dealer's,
but you have to pay a premium. My $300 bought less than $200
in old-style bills, but I didn't care; eggs were thirteen cents a dozen
in 1894.

14   But I've never again found the corridor that leads to the third
level at Grand Central Station, although I've tried often enough.

15   Louisa was pretty worried when I told her all this and didn't
want me to look for the third level any more, and after a while I
stopped; I went back to my stamps. But now we're *both* looking,
every week end, because now we have proof that the third level is
still there. My friend Sam Wiener disappeared! Nobody knew
where, but I sort of suspected because Sam's a city boy, and I used
to tell him about Galesburg—I went to school there—and he
always said he liked the sound of the place. And that's where he is,
all right. In 1894.

16   Because one night, fussing with my stamp collection, I
found—Well, do you know what a first-day cover is? When a new
stamp is issued, stamp collectors buy some and use them to mail
envelopes to themselves on the very first day of sale; and the
postmark proves the date. The envelope is called a first-day cover.
They're never opened; you just put blank paper in the envelope.

17   That night, among my oldest first-day covers, I found one that
shouldn't have been there. But there it was. It was there because
someone had mailed it to my grandfather at his home in Galesburg;
that's what the address on the envelope said. And it had been there
since July 18, 1894—the postmark showed that—yet I didn't remember it at all. The stamp was a six-cent, dull brown, with a
picture of President Garfield. Naturally, when the envelope came

to Granddad in the mail, it went right into his collection and stayed there—till I took it out and opened it.

The paper inside wasn't blank. It read: 18

> 941 Willard Street
> Galesburg, Illinois
> July 18, 1894
>
> Charley:
>
> I got to wishing that you were right. Then I got to *believing* you were right. And, Charley, it's true; I found the third level! I've been here two weeks, and right now, down the street at the Dalys', someone is playing a piano, and they're all out on the front porch singing *Seeing Nellie Home.* And I'm invited over for lemonade. Come on back, Charley and Louisa. Keep looking till you find the third level! It's worth it, believe me!

The note is signed Sam.

At the stamp and coin store I go to, I found out that Sam   19 bought $800 worth of old-style currency. That ought to set him up in a nice little hay, feed, and grain business; he always said that's what he really wished he could do, and he certainly can't go back to his old business. Not in Galesburg, Illinois, in 1894. His old business? Why, Sam was my psychiatrist.

Reading Critically

1. Do you wish that you could escape to the third level of Grand Central Station? Would you like to go there permanently? Why or why not? Discuss with your classmates.

2. If not the third level of Grand Central, is there any other place in the past that you would like to escape to? Discuss with your classmates.

3. Is there any place in the future that you would like to escape to?

4. Does this story seem to honestly reflect a need to rediscover a lost past, or is it basically one of those manipulative pieces of writing that rely on corny sentimentalism to drag the reader in? Discuss with your classmates.

Responding Through Writing

1. Do you have a "refuge" from reality like Charley's stamp collecting (paragraph 2)? Write the draft of an essay indicating why and how you use this refuge.

2. Do you know any buildings or groups of buildings like those described in paragraph 6, where it is likely you'll get lost in a maze of tunnels and corridors? Draw a map of the place in question and write an accompanying set of instructions about how not to get lost when taking a particular route through the place.

3. In paragraph 8, the author lists some of the features of an 1890s life-style. Pretend that you are a person from 100 years in the future and make a similar list for the 1990s.

4. For at least six more paragraphs, continue the letter that Sam sends to Charley.

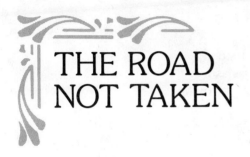

THE ROAD NOT TAKEN

ROBERT FROST

Although Robert Frost (1874–1963) is identified as the quintessential "New England" poet, he was born in San Francisco. After the death of his father when Frost was ten, his mother moved to Lawrence, Massachusetts. Frost attended Dartmouth College briefly, but he quit school and took a variety of jobs, including working as a bobbin boy in a clothing mill in Lawrence. He married in 1895. Two years later he enrolled at Harvard but dropped out after two years, and in 1900 he bought a farm in Derry, New Hampshire, where he lived for most of his life. Although he began to write poetry in 1894, he did not gain critical acclaim until he published A Boy's Will *in 1913, followed by* North of Boston *in 1914 while he was living in England. He received the Pulitzer Prize in 1924, 1931, 1937, and 1942, and the Poetry Society of America medal in 1941. In 1950 the U.S. Senate passed a unanimous resolution honoring him. Frost has been praised as the poet of the commonplace who sees more than most people do in ordinary things. Frost's poems "Stopping by Woods on a Snowy Evening" and "Mending Wall" are also included in this book. The following poem was originally published in* Mountain Interval *(1916).*

Two roads diverged in a yellow wood,
And sorry I could not travel both

And be one traveler, long I stood
And looked down one as far as I could
5   To where it bent in the undergrowth;

Then took the other, as just as fair,
And having perhaps the better claim,
Because it was grassy and wanted wear;
Though as for that, the passing there
10   Had worn them really about the same,

And both that morning equally lay
In leaves no step had trodden black.
Oh, I kept the first for another day!
Yet knowing how way leads on to way,
15   I doubted if I should ever come back.

I shall be telling this with a sigh
Somewhere ages and ages hence:
Two roads diverged in a wood, and I—
I took the one less traveled by,
20   And that has made all the difference.

Reading Critically

1. When Frost says that he is sorry that he cannot "travel both" roads, he is obviously talking about choices in life. Discuss with your classmates how you have had to choose one road over another and how you view the consequences of your choice.

2. Frost says that "knowing how way leads on to way, / I doubted if I should ever come back." Does he mean that choices in life are irrevocable? Are many of them in fact irrevocable? Discuss with your classmates.

3. Do the last two lines ("I took the one less traveled by, / And that has made all the difference") "make" the poem, or do they slightly detract from it? Why?

4. Frost says that he can see down the untaken road "to where it bent in the undergrowth." How does this line bring a sense of mystery (and of loss) to the poem? What do the bends in the road signify?

Responding Through Writing

1. Why do you think that the poem is entitled "The Road *Not* Taken," rather than the more positive "The Road Taken"? In your journal or notebook, write the first draft of a short essay about one road through life that you did *not* take, indicating what probably would have happened had you taken it.

2. This is a poem about the recognition that we cannot be all things in one lifetime. Is the metaphor of the two paths an apt one for this theme, or does it oversimplify the kinds of choices we have to make as we move through life? Write a response to this question that focuses on one or more junctures in your life where you were faced with a choice that was more than binary.

3. What choices regarding the major "roads" of your life are you likely to have to make in the next five years? Make a list of these choices, put the items in the list in chronological order, and write a few paragraphs discussing the relative importance of the choices you will likely have to make.

4. Are people likely to deceive themselves about their own capabilities when faced with major choices in life? Explore this topic in your journal or notebook for ten or fifteen minutes. Focus on two or more people you know.

CAUSE AND EFFECT

The cause-and-effect (causal analysis) essay is concerned with a special kind of relationship, the relationship between the agent or agency (cause) and the result or action (effect). Basically, cause-and-effect analysis seeks to answer one of two questions: "Why (or how) did something happen?" or "What were the results?" Both questions involve cause-and-effect analysis, but in different ways.

Cause-and-effect analysis is found not only in scientific writing but also in newspapers and magazines, as well as on television, in news broadcasts and other programs. After every election there are articles telling us the causes of the victory or defeat of various candidates, as well as stories discussing the effects of the election. Every day we read stories on why certain baseball teams cannot win the pennant this year, why the number of traffic accidents has increased, the causes of poor academic performance by high school students, and the causes of unemployment. Cause-and-effect writing abounds, even though the relationship between specific causes and effects may be highly debatable.

Organizing the Cause-and-Effect Essay

There are two basic ways to organize a cause-and-effect essay. First, you can proceed from a cause to an effect. In this method, you state the cause and then show the consequences. This is a common form of cause-and-effect writing.

A second method is to give an effect and then discuss the possible reasons or causes for that effect. This type of analysis, however, can be misleading. The connection between the effect and the cause may be speculative and beyond proof. Moreover, you have to be careful that you distinguish between the proximate cause and any intervening cause. For example, a car goes off the road, hitting a tree and killing the driver. Preliminary investigation reveals the driver had been drinking heavily just before the accident. Did the drinking cause the accident? Perhaps, but what if the driver suffered a heart attack just before the accident? What caused the accident? You must be careful not to ascribe a simple cause to an event that may result from complex causes and sometimes even hidden or unknown causes.

In organizing a cause-and-effect essay, you may begin with either the cause or the effect, depending on what you want to emphasize. If you are dealing with more than one cause or effect you may want to discuss first all the causes and then all the effects, or you may alternate them, discussing one set of cause-and-effect relationships, then a second set, and so on. However you organize your essay, be certain you make clear which cause is related to which effect, and why.

Use Careful Reasoning

When writing a cause-and-effect essay, you must use carefully stated reasoning. You should not give your audience any reason to question your logic. The following suggestions are designed to help you write logical cause-and-effect essays.

Before writing, list the causes and their effects next to each other. Examine each cause-and-effect relationship and label it *speculative* or *proved*. Note briefly how and in what order you will present each relationship. You might want to start with proved relationships and then proceed to speculative ones, or you may want to use only the speculative. Whatever you decide, be sure you know the basis for your decision, how each cause-and-effect relationship fits into the whole essay, and how each contributes to the purpose of the paper. You should determine also the probable effect each relationship will have on your intended audience.

Do not oversimplify cause-and-effect relationships. (Remember the example of the "drunk" driver.) Do not make the mistake of ascribing an effect to a simple cause; for example, that higher costs for electricity are the result of the greed of the utility companies, or that the increase in the number of automobile accidents is the result of more teenager drivers. You must fully explore all the possible causes and all the possible effects and avoid oversimplification.

Finally, do not mistake simple coincidence for a cause-and-effect relationship. This is really a case of jumping to conclusions. If you got dizzy once while drinking coffee, you should not jump to the conclusion that coffee makes you dizzy. There could be any number of reasons why you became dizzy. Simply because two incidents follow each other in time does not mean they have a cause-and-effect relationship. Firing the football coach at the end of the poor season does not mean he was the cause of the team's poor record, nor does hiring a new coach mean the team will have a good season, as many schools discover every year.

Effect to Cause

The question "Why (or how) did something happen?" seeks the cause when the effect is already known. So, for example, an essay that examines the possible causes of the government deficit is working from the known effect (large deficit) to possible causes (government spending on armaments, not enough revenues). Note that effect-to-cause essays discuss *possible* causes, because it is frequently difficult to be certain what causes many effects. Although there is evidence that being moderately overweight does not cause significant health problems, you should be careful in writing an essay in which you state without qualification that being overweight causes no health problems. So, too, in an essay about smoking, you would not want to overstate your case by asserting that all smokers will contract cancer. You will find great disagreement over the causes of teenage suicides, the widespread use of illegal drugs, high crime rates, government deficits, and high taxes; but that does not mean writers on these topics are not using cause-and-effect analysis. It does mean, however, that readers may not see the same cause-and-effect relationship as the writers.

Cause to Effect

The question "What were the results?" seeks the effect when the cause is already known. For example, an essay that examines the possible effect of legalizing all drugs is working from the known cause (legalizing drugs) to *possible* effects (decrease in crime, decrease in political corruption, increase in drug addiction). Again note that such an essay discusses the *possible* effects because it is difficult to be certain what effects will result from certain causes. You will, for example, find great disagreement over what would be the effect of removing all American troops from Europe, legalizing the use of all drugs, banning all nuclear weapons, or cutting the Pentagon budget by 50 percent, but that disagreement does not mean the writer is not using cause-and-effect analysis. It does mean that readers may not see the same cause-and-effect relationship that the writer sees.

The Purpose of the Cause-and-Effect Essay

A cause-and-effect essay may be written to persuade your audience to approve or disapprove of something. For example, you might argue that legalizing addictive drugs will reduce crime and political corruption, but increase the number of drug addicts. Or you may argue that lowering the drinking age to 18 will increase teenage alcoholism and deaths from drunk driving.

You may also use cause-and-effect analysis to inform your audience. This is a broad purpose, but a common one. Much of the cause-and-effect writing you read in newspapers and magazines is designed to inform you about a particular subject. For example, an article that discusses the effects of a recent change in the tax laws might inform you about certain changes you should make in how you compute your taxes, or more importantly, it might alert you to tax savings you can qualify for later if you make certain changes now in your spending habits. So, too, an essay about the effects of aerosol sprays on the ozone layer or of phosphates on the water supply might prompt you to stop using aerosol sprays and detergents with phosphates.

Finally, you may use cause-and-effect analysis to speculate

about what may be causing certain effects, or what effects might result from certain causes. A writer might speculate on the effects of space exploration on human civilization or on the causes of a sudden change in the legal philosophy behind the decisions of the Supreme Court. Such writing is hypothetical because the writer admits that there is no firm evidence relating the causes and effects about which he or she is writing.

Consider Your Audience

Once you have determined the purpose of your cause-and-effect essay, you need to consider your audience. If you are writing an essay to inform, you need to determine the general background information your audience possesses. You will need to explain any unfamiliar processes and terms that are part of the cause-and-effect relationship you are presenting. Also, while you may share some assumptions with your audience, do not assume that you share every assumption. Your audience may agree with your assumption that something must be done about the increase in violent crime, but your audience may not agree with your assumption that legalizing addictive drugs will solve the problem. Similarly, if you are using speculative cause-and-effect writing to persuade, do not pretend your cause-and-effect relationship is anything more than specula-tive. While you may believe that legalization of drugs will reduce crime, you should not present this cause-and-effect relationship as a fact. You should tell your audience that the relationship is specula-tive, and then you can discuss its merits—and its shortcomings.

As you read the items in this section, look for the elements of cause-and-effect writing. Read each selection as a writer and try to determine whether the author has used cause and effect intelligently. Locate each cause and each effect and determine whether the causal relationship is proved or speculative. What do you find particularly effective in the selection, and what do you find particularly weak? How would you change the selection to make it stronger?

LETTER FROM BIRMINGHAM JAIL[1]

MARTIN LUTHER KING, JR.

Martin Luther King, Jr. (1929–1968), was, more than anything, a man of action. He completed his undergraduate education, finished divinity school, and earned his Ph.D., all by the age of 26. In 1964, at the age of 35, King received the Nobel Peace Prize for his civil rights efforts. Combining his religious training with the nonviolent teachings of Mahatma Gandhi, King was one of the most prominent and eloquent leaders of the civil rights movement in America. Through powerful prose and moving oratory, he organized scores of peace marches and protests to advance his dream of racial equality. Sentenced to a jail term for holding one such rally, King composed the following letter in 1963 from his cell. Five years later, on April 14, 1968, Dr. King was assassinated in Memphis, Tennessee. "Letter from Birmingham Jail" was first published in Why We Can't Wait *(1963).*

1. AUTHOR'S NOTE: This response to a published statement by eight fellow clergy-men from Alabama (Bishop C. C. J. Carpenter, Bishop Joseph A. Durick, Rabbi Hilton L. Grafman, Bishop Paul Hardin, Bishop Holan B. Harmon, the Reverend George M. Murray, the Reverend Edward V. Ramage and the Reverend Earl Stallings) was composed under somewhat constricting circumstances. Begun on the margins of the newspaper in which the statement appeared while I was in jail, the letter was continued on scraps of writing paper supplied by a friendly Negro trusty, and concluded on a pad my attorneys were eventually permitted to leave me. Although the text remains in substance unaltered, I have indulged in the author's prerogative of polishing it for publication.

April 16, 1963

My Dear Fellow Clergymen:

While confined here in the Birmingham city jail, I came across   1
your recent statement calling my present activities "unwise and
untimely." Seldom do I pause to answer criticism of my work and
ideas. If I sought to answer all the criticisms that cross my desk, my
secretaries would have little time for anything other than such
correspondence in the course of the day, and I would have no time
for constructive work. But since I feel that you are men of genuine
good will and that your criticisms are sincerely set forth, I want to
try to answer your statement in what I hope will be patient and
reasonable terms.

I think I should indicate why I am here in Birmingham, since   2
you have been influenced by the view which argues against "outsiders coming in." I have the honor of serving as president of the
Southern Christian Leadership Conference, an organization operating in every southern state, with headquarters in Atlanta, Georgia.
We have some eighty-five affiliated organizations across the South,
and one of them is the Alabama Christian Movement for Human
Rights. Frequently we share staff, educational and financial resources with our affiliates. Several months ago the affiliate here in
Birmingham asked us to be on call to engage in a nonviolent
direct-action program if such were deemed necessary. We readily
consented, and when the hour came we lived up to our promise. So
I, along with several members of my staff, am here because I was
invited here. I am here because I have organizational ties here.

But more basically, I am in Birmingham because injustice is   3
here. Just as the prophets of the eighth century B.C. left their villages
and carried their "thus saith the Lord" far beyond the boundaries
of their home towns, and just as the Apostle Paul left his village of
Tarsus and carried the gospel of Jesus Christ to the far corners of
the Greco-Roman world, so am I compelled to carry the gospel of
freedom beyond my own home town. Like Paul, I must constantly
respond to the Macedonian call for aid.

Moreover, I am cognizant of the interrelatedness of all com-   4
munities and states. I cannot sit idly by in Atlanta and not be

concerned about what happens in Birmingham. Injustice anywhere is a threat to justice everywhere. We are caught in an inescapable network of mutuality, tied in a single garment of destiny. Whatever affects one directly, affects all indirectly. Never again can we afford to live with the narrow, provincial "outside agitator" idea. Anyone who lives inside the United States can never be considered an outsider anywhere within its bounds.

5   You deplore the demonstrations taking place in Birmingham. But your statement, I am sorry to say, fails to express a similar concern for the conditions that brought about the demonstrations. I am sure that none of you would want to rest content with the superficial kind of social analysis that deals merely with effects and does not grapple with underlying causes. It is unfortunate that demonstrations are taking place in Birmingham, but it is even more unfortunate that the city's white power structure left the Negro community with no alternative.

6   In any nonviolent campaign there are four basic steps: collection of the facts to determine whether injustices exist; negotiation; self-purification; and direct action. We have gone through all these steps in Birmingham. There can be no gainsaying the fact that racial injustice engulfs this community. Birmingham is probably the most thoroughly segregated city in the United States. Its ugly record of brutality is widely known. Negroes have experienced grossly unjust treatment in the courts. There have been more unsolved bombings of Negro homes and churches in Birmingham than in any other city in the nation. These are the hard brutal facts of the case. On the basis of these conditions, Negro leaders sought to negotiate with the city fathers. But the latter consistently refused to engage in good-faith negotiation.

7   Then, last September, came the opportunity to talk with leaders of Birmingham's economic community. In the course of the negotiations, certain promises were made by the merchants—for example, to remove the stores' humiliating racial signs. On the basis of these promises, the Reverend Fred Shuttlesworth and the leaders of the Alabama Christian Movement for Human Rights agreed to a moratorium on all demonstrations. As the weeks and months went by, we realized that we were the victims of a broken promise. A few signs, briefly removed, returned; the others remained.

8   As in so many past experiences, our hopes had been blasted, and the shadow of deep disappointment settled upon us. We had no alternative except to prepare for direct action, whereby we would

present our very bodies as a means of laying our case before the conscience of the local and the national community. Mindful of the difficulties involved, we decided to undertake a process of self-purification. We began a series of workshops on nonviolence, and we repeatedly asked ourselves: "Are you able to accept blows without retaliating?" "Are you able to endure the ordeal of jail?" We decided to schedule our direct-action program for the Easter season, realizing that except for Christmas, this is the main shopping period of the year. Knowing that a strong economic-withdrawal program would be the by-product of direct action, we felt that this would be the best time to bring pressure to bear on the merchants for the needed change.

Then it occurred to us that Birmingham's mayoralty election 9 was coming up in March, and we speedily decided to postpone action until after election day. When we discovered that the Commissioner of Public Safety, Eugene "Bull" Connor, had piled up enough votes to be in the run-off, we decided again to postpone action until the day after the run-off so that the demonstrations could not be used to cloud the issues. Like many others, we waited to see Mr. Connor defeated, and to this end we endured postponement after postponement. Having aided in this community need, we felt that our direct-action program could be delayed no longer.

You may well ask: "Why direct action? Why sit-ins, marches 10 and so forth? Isn't negotiation a better path?" You are quite right in calling for negotiation. Indeed, this is the very purpose of direct action. Nonviolent direct action seeks to create such a crisis and foster such a tension that a community which has constantly refused to negotiate is forced to confront the issue. It seeks so to dramatize the issue that it can no longer be ignored. My citing the creation of tension as part of the work of the nonviolent-resister may sound rather shocking. But I must confess that I am not afraid of the word "tension." I have earnestly opposed violent tension, but there is a type of constructive nonviolent tension which is necessary for growth. Just as Socrates felt that it was necessary to create a tension in the mind so that individuals could rise from the bondage of myths and half-truths to the unfettered realm of creative analysis and objective appraisal, so must we see the need for nonviolent gadflies to create the kind of tension in society that will help men rise from the dark depths of prejudice and racism to the majestic heights of understanding and brotherhood.

The purpose of our direct-action program is to create a situa- 11 tion so crisis-packed that it will inevitably open the door to negotiation. I therefore concur with you in your call for negotiation. Too long has our beloved Southland been bogged down in a tragic effort to live in monologue rather than dialogue.

12   One of the basic points in your statement is that the action that I and my associates have taken in Birmingham is untimely. Some have asked: "Why didn't you give the new city administration time to act?" The only answer that I can give to this query is that the new Birmingham administration must be prodded about as much as the outgoing one, before it will act. We are sadly mistaken if we feel that the election of Albert Boutwell as mayor will bring the millennium to Birmingham. While Mr. Boutwell is a much more gentle person than Mr. Connor, they are both segregationists, dedicated to maintenance of the status quo. I have hope that Mr. Boutwell will be reasonable enough to see the futility of massive resistance to desegregation. But he will not see this without pressure from devotees of civil rights. My friends, I must say to you that we have not made a single gain in civil rights without determined legal and nonviolent pressure. Lamentably, it is an historical fact that privileged groups seldom give up their privileges voluntarily. Individuals may see the moral light and voluntarily give up their unjust posture; but, as Reinhold Niebuhr has reminded us, groups tend to be more immoral than individuals.

13   We know through painful experience that freedom is never voluntarily given by the oppressor; it must be demanded by the oppressed. Frankly, I have yet to engage in a direct-action campaign that was "well timed" in the view of those who have not suffered unduly from the disease of segregation. For years now I have heard the word "Wait!" It rings in the ear of every Negro with piercing familiarity. This "Wait" has almost always meant "Never." We must come to see, with one of our distinguished jurists, that "justice too long delayed is justice denied."

14   We have waited for more than 340 years for our constitutional and God-given rights. The nations of Asia and Africa are moving with jetlike speed toward gaining political independence, but we still creep at horse-and-buggy pace toward gaining a cup of coffee at a lunch counter. Perhaps it is easy for those who have never felt the stinging darts of segregation to say, "Wait." But when you have seen vicious mobs lynch your mothers and fathers at will and drown your sisters and brothers at whim; when you have seen hate-filled policemen curse, kick and even kill your black brothers and sisters;

when you see the vast majority of your twenty million Negro brothers smothering in an airtight cage of poverty in the midst of an affluent society; when you suddenly find your tongue twisted and your speech stammering as you seek to explain to your six-year-old daughter why she can't go to the public amusement park that has just been advertised on television, and see tears welling up in her eyes when she is told that Funtown is closed to colored children, and see ominous clouds of inferiority beginning to form in her little mental sky, and see her beginning to distort her personality by developing an unconscious bitterness toward white people; when you have to concoct an answer for a five-year-old son who is asking: "Daddy, why do white people treat colored people so mean?"; when you take a cross-country drive and find it necessary to sleep night after night in the uncomfortable corners of your automobile because no motel will accept you; when you are humiliated day in and day out by nagging signs reading "white" and "colored"; when your first name becomes "nigger," your middle name becomes "boy" (however old you are) and your last name becomes "John," and your wife and mother are never given the respected title "Mrs."; when you are harried by day and haunted by night by the fact that you are a Negro, living constantly at tiptoe stance, never quite knowing what to expect next, and are plagued with inner fears and outer resentments; when you are forever fighting a degenerating sense of "nobodiness"—then you will understand why we find it difficult to wait. There comes a time when the cup of endurance runs over, and men are no longer willing to be plunged into the abyss of despair. I hope, sirs, you can understand our legitimate and unavoidable impatience.

You express a great deal of anxiety over our willingness to break laws. This is certainly a legitimate concern. Since we so diligently urge people to obey the Supreme Court's decision of 1954 outlawing segregation in the public schools, at first glance it may seem rather paradoxical for us consciously to break laws. One may well ask: "How can you advocate breaking some laws and obeying others?" The answer lies in the fact that there are two types of laws: just and unjust. I would be the first to advocate obeying just laws. One has not only a legal but a moral responsibility to obey just laws. Conversely, one has a moral responsibility to disobey unjust laws. I would agree with St. Augustine that "an unjust law is no law at all." 15

Now, what is the difference between the two? How does one 16 determine whether a law is just or unjust? A just law is a man-made code that squares with the moral law or the law of God. An unjust law is a code that is out of harmony with the moral law. To put it in the terms of St. Thomas Aquinas: An unjust law is a human law that is not rooted in eternal law and natural law. Any law that uplifts human personality is just. Any law that degrades human personality is unjust. All segregation statutes are unjust because segregation distorts the soul and damages the personality. It gives the segregator a false sense of superiority and the segregated a false sense of inferiority. Segregation, to use the terminology of the Jewish philosopher Martin Buber, substitutes an "I–it" relationship for an "I–thou" relationship and ends up relegating persons to the status of things. Hence segregation is not only politically, economically and sociologically unsound, it is morally wrong and sinful. Paul Tillich has said that sin is separation. Is not segregation an existential expression of man's tragic separation, his awful estrangement, his terrible sinfulness? Thus it is that I can urge men to obey the 1954 decision of the Supreme Court, for it is morally right; and I can urge them to disobey segregation ordinances, for they are morally wrong.

17   Let us consider a more concrete example of just and unjust laws. An unjust law is a code that a numerical or power majority group compels a minority group to obey but does not make binding on itself. This is *difference* made legal. By the same token, a just law is a code that a majority compels a minority to follow and that it is willing to follow itself. This is *sameness* made legal.

18   Let me give another explanation. A law is unjust if it is inflicted on a minority that, as a result of being denied the right to vote, had no part in enacting or devising the law. Who can say that the legislature of Alabama which set up that state's segregation laws was democratically elected? Throughout Alabama all sorts of devious methods are used to prevent Negroes from becoming registered voters, and there are some counties in which even though Negroes constitute a majority of the population, not a single Negro is registered. Can any law enacted under such circumstances be considered democratically structured?

19   Sometimes a law is just on its face and unjust in its application. For instance, I have been arrested on a charge of parading without a permit. Now, there is nothing wrong in having an ordinance which requires a permit for a parade. But such an ordinance becomes unjust when it is used to maintain segregation and to deny citizens the First-Amendment privilege of peaceful assembly and protest.

I hope you are able to see the distinction I am trying to point out. In no sense do I advocate evading or defying the law, as would the rabid segregationist. That would lead to anarchy. One who breaks an unjust law must do so openly, lovingly, and with a willingness to accept the penalty. I submit that an individual who breaks a law that conscience tells him is unjust, and who willingly accepts the penalty of imprisonment in order to arouse the conscience of the community over its injustice, is in reality expressing the highest respect for law. 20

Of course, there is nothing new about this kind of civil disobedience. It was evidenced sublimely in the refusal of Shadrach, Meshach and Abednego to obey the laws of Nebuchadnezzar, on the ground that a higher moral law was at stake. It was practiced superbly by the early Christians, who were willing to face hungry lions and the excruciating pain of chopping blocks rather than submit to certain unjust laws of the Roman Empire. To a degree, academic freedom is a reality today because Socrates practiced civil disobedience. In our own nation, the Boston Tea Party represented a massive act of civil disobedience. 21

We should never forget that everything Adolf Hitler did in Germany was "legal" and everything the Hungarian freedom fighters did in Hungary was "illegal." It was "illegal" to aid and comfort a Jew in Hitler's Germany. Even so, I am sure that, had I lived in Germany at the time, I would have aided and comforted my Jewish brothers. If today I lived in a Communist country where certain principles dear to the Christian faith are suppressed, I would openly advocate disobeying that country's anti-religious laws. 22

I must make two honest confessions to you, my Christian and Jewish brothers. First, I must confess that over the past few years I have been gravely disappointed with the white moderate. I have almost reached the regrettable conclusion that the Negro's great stumbling block in his stride toward freedom is not the White Citizen's Counciler or the Ku Klux Klanner, but the white moderate, who is more devoted to "order" than to justice; who prefers a negative peace which is the absence of tension to a positive peace which is the presence of justice; who constantly says: "I agree with you in the goal you seek, but I cannot agree with your methods of direct action"; who paternalistically believes he can set the timetable for another man's freedom; who lives by a mythical concept of time and who constantly advises the Negro to wait for a "more convenient season." Shallow understanding from people of good will is more frustrating than absolute misunderstanding from people of ill 23 will. Lukewarm acceptance is much more bewildering than outright rejection.

24   I had hoped that the white moderate would understand that law and order exist for the purpose of establishing justice and that when they fail in this purpose they become the dangerously structured dams that block the flow of social progress. I had hoped that the white moderate would understand that the present tension in the South is a necessary phase of the transition from an obnoxious negative peace, in which the Negro passively accepted his unjust plight, to a substantive and positive peace, in which all men will respect the dignity and worth of human personality. Actually, we who engage in nonviolent direct action are not the creators of tension. We merely bring to the surface the hidden tension that is already alive. We bring it out in the open, where it can be seen and dealt with. Like a boil that can never be cured so long as it is covered up but must be opened with all its ugliness to the natural medicines of air and light, injustice must be exposed, with all the tension its exposure creates, to the light of human conscience and the air of national opinion before it can be cured.

25   In your statement you assert that our actions, even though peaceful, must be condemned because they precipitate violence. But is this a logical assertion? Isn't this like condemning a robbed man because his possession of money precipitated the evil of robbery? Isn't this like condemning Socrates because his unswerving commitment to truth and his philosophical inquiries precipitated the act by the misguided populace in which they made him drink hemlock? Isn't this like condemning Jesus because his unique God-consciousness and never-ceasing devotion to God's will precipitated the evil act of crucifixion? We must come to see that, as the federal courts have consistently affirmed, it is wrong to urge an individual to cease his efforts to gain his basic constitutional rights because the quest may precipitate violence. Society must protect the robbed and punish the robber.

26   I had also hoped that the white moderate would reject the myth concerning time in relation to the struggle for freedom. I have just received a letter from a white brother in Texas. He writes: "All Christians know that the colored people will receive equal rights eventually, but is it possible that you are in too great a religious hurry. It has taken Christianity almost two thousand years to accomplish what it has. The teachings of Christ take time to come to earth." Such an attitude stems from a tragic misconception of time,

from the strangely irrational notion that there is something in the very flow of time that will inevitably cure all ills. Actually, time itself is neutral; it can be used either destructively or constructively. More and more I feel that the people of ill will have used time much more effectively than have the people of good will. We will have to repent in this generation not merely for the hateful words and actions of the bad people but for the appalling silence of the good people. Human progress never rolls in on wheels of inevitability; it comes through the tireless efforts of men willing to be co-workers with God, and without this hard work, time itself becomes an ally of the forces of social stagnation. We must use time creatively, in the knowledge that the time is always ripe to do right. Now is the time to make real the promise of democracy and transform our pending national elegy into a creative psalm of brotherhood. Now is the time to lift our national policy from the quicksand of racial injustice to the solid rock of human dignity.

You speak of our activity in Birmingham as extreme. At first   27
I was rather disappointed that fellow clergymen would see my nonviolent efforts as those of an extremist. I began thinking about the fact that I stand in the middle of two opposing forces in the Negro community. One is a force of complacency, made up in part of Negroes who, as a result of long years of oppression, are so drained of self-respect and a sense of "somebodiness" that they have adjusted to segregation; and in part of a few middle-class Negroes who, because of a degree of academic and economic security and because in some ways they profit by segregation, have become insensitive to the problems of the masses. The other force is one of bitterness and hatred, and it comes perilously close to advocating violence. It is expressed in the various black nationalist groups that are springing up across the nation, the largest and best-known being Elijah Muhammad's Muslim movement. Nourished by the Negro's frustration over the continued existence of racial discrimination, this movement is made up of people who have lost faith in America, who have absolutely repudiated Christianity, and who have concluded that the white man is an incorrigible "devil."

I have tried to stand between these two forces, saying that we   28
need emulate neither the "do-nothingism" of the complacent nor the hatred and despair of the black nationalist. For there is the more excellent way of love and nonviolent protest. I am grateful to God that, through the influence of the Negro church, the way of nonviolence became an integral part of our struggle.

29   If this philosophy had not emerged, by now many streets of the South would, I am convinced, be flowing with blood. And I am further convinced that if our white brothers dismiss as "rabble-rousers" and "outside agitators" those of us who employ nonviolent direct action, and if they refuse to support our nonviolent efforts, millions of Negroes will, out of frustration and despair, seek solace and security in black-nationalist ideologies—a development that would inevitably lead to a frightening racial nightmare.

30   Oppressed people cannot remain oppressed forever. The yearning for freedom eventually manifests itself, and that is what has happened to the American Negro. Something within has reminded him of his birthright of freedom, and something without has reminded him that it can be gained. Consciously or unconsciously, he has been caught up by the *Zeitgeist,* and with his black brothers of Africa and his brown and yellow brothers of Asia, South America and the Caribbean, the United States Negro is moving with a sense of great urgency toward the promised land of racial justice. If one recognizes this vital urge that has engulfed the Negro community, one should readily understand why public demonstrations are taking place. The Negro has many pent-up resentments and latent frustrations, and he must release them. So let him march; let him make prayer pilgrimages to the city hall; let him go on freedom rides— and try to understand why he must do so. If his repressed emotions are not released in nonviolent ways, they will seek expression through violence; this is not a threat but a fact of history. So I have not said to my people: "Get rid of your discontent." Rather, I have tried to say that this normal and healthy discontent can be channeled into the creative outlet of nonviolent direct action. And now this approach is being termed extremist.

31   But though I was initially disappointed at being categorized as an extremist, as I continued to think about the matter I gradually gained a measure of satisfaction from the label. Was not Jesus an extremist for love: "Love your enemies, bless them that curse you, do good to them that hate you, and pray for them which despitefully use you, and persecute you." Was not Amos an extremist for justice: "Let justice roll down like waters and righteousness like an ever-flowing stream." Was not Paul an extremist for the Christian gospel: "I bear in my body the marks of the Lord Jesus." Was not Martin Luther an extremist: "Here I stand; I cannot do otherwise, so help me God." And John Bunyan: "I will stay in jail to the end of my days before I make a butchery of my conscience." And

Abraham Lincoln: "This nation cannot survive half slave and half free." And Thomas Jefferson: "We hold these truths to be self-evident, that all men are created equal. . . ." So the question is not whether we will be extremists, but what kind of extremists we will be. Will we be extremists for hate or for love? Will we be extremists for the preservation of injustice or for the extension of justice? In that dramatic scene on Calvary's hill three men were crucified. We must never forget that all three were crucified for the same crime—the crime of extremism. Two were extremists for immorality, and thus fell below their environment. The other, Jesus Christ, was an extremist for love, truth and goodness, and thereby rose above his environment. Perhaps the South, the nation and the world are in dire need of creative extremists.

I had hoped that the white moderate would see this need. 32 Perhaps I was too optimistic; perhaps I expected too much. I suppose I should have realized that few members of the oppressor race can understand the deep groans and passionate yearnings of the oppressed race, and still fewer have the vision to see that injustice must be rooted out by strong, persistent and determined action. I am thankful, however, that some of our white brothers in the South have grasped the meaning of this social revolution and committed themselves to it. They are still all too few in quantity, but they are big in quality. Some—such as Ralph McGill, Lillian Smith, Harry Golden, James McBride Dabbs, Ann Braden and Sarah Patton Boyle—have written about our struggle in eloquent and prophetic terms. Others have marched with us down nameless streets of the South. They have languished in filthy, roach-infested jails, suffering the abuse and brutality of policemen who view them as "dirty nigger-lovers." Unlike so many of their modern brothers and sisters, they have recognized the urgency of the moment and sensed the need for powerful "action" antidotes to combat the disease of segregation.

Let me take note of my other major disappointment. I have 33 been so greatly disappointed with the white church and its leadership. Of course, there are some notable exceptions. I am not unmindful of the fact that each of you has taken some significant stands on this issue. I commend you, Reverend Stallings, for your Christian stand on this past Sunday, in welcoming Negroes to your worship service on a nonsegregated basis. I commend the Catholic leaders of this state for integrating Spring Hill College several years ago.

34   But despite these notable exceptions, I must honestly reiterate that I have been disappointed with the church. I do not say this as one of those negative critics who can always find something wrong with the church. I say this as a minister of the gospel, who loves the church; who was nurtured in its bosom; who has been sustained by its spiritual blessings and who will remain true to it as long as the cord of life shall lengthen.

35   When I was suddenly catapulted into the leadership of the bus protest in Montgomery, Alabama, a few years ago, I felt we would be supported by the white church. I felt that the white ministers, priests and rabbis of the South would be among our strongest allies. Instead, some have been outright opponents, refusing to understand the freedom movement and misrepresenting its leaders; all too many others have been more cautious than courageous and have remained silent behind the anesthetizing security of stained-glass windows.

36   In spite of my shattered dreams, I came to Birmingham with the hope that the white religious leadership of this community would see the justice of our cause and, with deep moral concern, would serve as the channel through which our just grievances could reach the power structure. I had hoped that each of you would understand. But again I have been disappointed.

37   I have heard numerous southern religious leaders admonish their worshipers to comply with a desegregation decision because it is the law, but I have longed to hear white ministers declare: "Follow this decree because integration is morally right and because the Negro is your brother." In the midst of blatant injustices inflicted upon the Negro, I have watched white churchmen stand on the sideline and mouth pious irrelevancies and sanctimonious trivialities. In the midst of a mighty struggle to rid our nation of racial and economic injustice, I have heard many ministers say: "Those are social issues, with which the gospel has no real concern." And I have watched many churches commit themselves to a completely other-worldly religion which makes a strange, un-Biblical distinction between body and soul, between the sacred and the secular.

38   I have traveled the length and breadth of Alabama, Mississippi and all the other southern states. On sweltering summer days and crisp autumn mornings I have looked at the South's beautiful churches with their lofty spires pointing heavenward. I have beheld the impressive outlines of her massive religious-education buildings. Over and over I have found myself asking: "What kind of people worship here? Who is their God? Where were their voices when

the lips of Governor Barnett dripped with words of interposition and nullification? Where were they when Governor Wallace gave a clarion call for defiance and hatred? Where were their voices of support when bruised and weary Negro men and women decided to rise from the dark dungeons of complacency to the bright hills of creative protest?"

Yes, these questions are still in my mind. In deep disappoint- 39 ment I have wept over the laxity of the church. But be assured that my tears have been tears of love. There can be no deep disappointment where there is not deep love. Yes, I love the church. How could I do otherwise? I am in the rather unique position of being the son, the grandson and the great-grandson of preachers. Yes, I see the church as the body of Christ. But, oh! How we have blemished and scarred that body through social neglect and through fear of being nonconformists.

There was a time when the church was very powerful—in the 40 time when the early Christians rejoiced at being deemed worthy to suffer for what they believed. In those days the church was not merely a thermometer that recorded the ideas and principles of popular opinion; it was a thermostat that transformed the mores of society. Whenever the early Christian entered a town, the people in power became disturbed and immediately sought to convict the Christians for being "disturbers of the peace" and "outside agitators." But the Christians pressed on, in the conviction that they were "a colony of heaven," called to obey God rather than man. Small in number, they were big in commitment. They were too God-intoxicated to be "astronomically intimidated." By their effort and example they brought an end to such ancient evils as infanticide and gladiatorial contests.

Things are different now. So often the contemporary church 41 is a weak, ineffectual voice with an uncertain sound. So often it is an archdefender of the status quo. Far from being disturbed by the presence of the church, the power structure of the average community is consoled by the church's silent—and often even vocal—sanction of things as they are.

But the judgment of God is upon the church as never before. 42 If today's church does not recapture the sacrificial spirit of the early church, it will lose its authenticity, forfeit the loyalty of millions, and be dismissed as an irrelevant social club with no meaning for the twentieth century. Every day I meet young people whose disappointment with the church has turned into outright disgust.

Perhaps I have once again been too optimistic. Is organized 43

religion too inextricably bound to the status quo to save our nation
and the world? Perhaps I must turn my faith to the inner spiritual
church, the church within the church, as the true *ekklesia* and the
hope of the world. But again I am thankful to God that some noble
souls from the ranks of organized religion have broken loose from
the paralyzing chains of conformity and joined us as active partners
in the struggle for freedom. They have left their secure congrega-
tions and walked the streets of Albany, Georgia, with us. They have
gone down the highways of the South on tortuous rides for freedom. Yes, they have gone to jail with us. Some have been dismissed
from their churches, have lost the support of their bishops and
fellow ministers. But they have acted in the faith that right defeated
is stronger than evil triumphant. Their witness has been the spiritual
salt that has preserved the true meaning of the gospel in these
troubled times. They have carved a tunnel of hope through the dark
mountain of disappointment.

44   I hope the church as a whole will meet the challenge of this
decisive hour. But even if the church does not come to the aid of
justice, I have no despair about the future. I have no fear about the
outcome of our struggle in Birmingham, even if our motives are
at present misunderstood. We will reach the goal of freedom in
Birmingham and all over the nation, because the goal of America
is freedom. Abused and scorned though we may be, our destiny is
tied up with America's destiny. Before the pilgrims landed at Plym-
outh, we were here. Before the pen of Jefferson etched the majestic
words of the Declaration of Independence across the pages of history, we were here. For more than two centuries our forebears
labored in this country without wages; they made cotton king; they
built the homes of their masters while suffering gross injustice and
shameful humiliation—and yet out of a bottomless vitality they
continued to thrive and develop. If the inexpressible cruelties of
slavery could not stop us, the opposition we now face will surely
fail. We will win our freedom because the sacred heritage of our
nation and the eternal will of God are embodied in our echoing
demands.

45   Before closing I feel impelled to mention one other point in
your statement that has troubled me profoundly. You warmly
commended the Birmingham police force for keeping "order" and
"preventing violence." I doubt that you would have so warmly
commended the police force if you had seen its dogs sinking their
teeth into unarmed, nonviolent Negroes. I doubt that you would
so quickly commend the policemen if you were to observe their
ugly and inhumane treatment of Negroes here in the city jail; if you

were to watch them push and curse old Negro women and young Negro girls; if you were to see them slap and kick old Negro men and young boys; if you were to observe them, as they did on two occasions, refuse to give us food because we wanted to sing our grace together. I cannot join you in your praise of the Birmingham police department.

It is true that the police have exercised a degree of discipline 46 in handling the demonstrators. In this sense they have conducted themselves rather "nonviolently" in public. But for what purpose? To preserve the evil system of segregation. Over the past few years I have consistently preached that nonviolence demands that the means we use must be as pure as the ends we seek. I have tried to make clear that it is wrong to use immoral means to attain moral ends. But now I must affirm that it is just as wrong, or perhaps even more so, to use moral means to preserve immoral ends. Perhaps Mr. Connor and his policemen have been rather nonviolent in public, as was Chief Pritchett in Albany, Georgia, but they have used the moral means of nonviolence to maintain the immoral end of racial injustice. As T. S. Eliot has said: "The last temptation is the greatest treason: To do the right deed for the wrong reason."

I wish you had commended the Negro sit-inners and demon- 47 strators of Birmingham for their sublime courage, their willingness to suffer and their amazing discipline in the midst of great provocation. One day the South will recognize its real heroes. They will be the James Merediths, with the noble sense of purpose that enables them to face jeering and hostile mobs, and with the agonizing loneliness that characterizes the life of the pioneer. They will be old, oppressed, battered Negro women, symbolized in a seventy-two-year-old woman in Montgomery, Alabama, who rose up with a sense of dignity and with her people decided not to ride segregated buses, and who responded with ungrammatical profundity to one who inquired about her weariness: "My feet is tired, but my soul is at rest." They will be the young high school and college students, the young ministers of the gospel and a host of their elders, courageously and nonviolently sitting in at lunch counters and willingly going to jail for conscience' sake. One day the South will know that when these disinherited children of God sat down at lunch counters, they were in reality standing up for what is best in the American dream and for the most sacred values in our Judaeo-Christian heritage, thereby bringing our nation back to those great wells of democracy which were dug deep by the founding fathers in their formulation of the Constitution and the Declaration of Independence.

48   Never before have I written so long a letter. I'm afraid it is much too long to take your precious time. I can assure you that it would have been much shorter if I had been writing from a comfortable desk, but what else can one do when he is alone in a narrow jail cell, other than write long letters, think long thoughts and pray long prayers?

49   If I have said anything in this letter that overstates the truth and indicates an unreasonable impatience, I beg you to forgive me. If I have said anything that understates the truth and indicates my having a patience that allows me to settle for anything less than brotherhood, I beg God to forgive me.

50   I hope this letter finds you strong in the faith. I also hope that circumstances will soon make it possible for me to meet each of you, not as an integrationist or a civil-rights leader but as a fellow clergyman and a Christian brother. Let us all hope that the dark clouds of racial prejudice will soon pass away and the deep fog of misunderstanding will be lifted from our fear-drenched communities, and in some not too distant tomorrow the radiant stars of love and brotherhood will shine over our great nation with all their scintillating beauty.

Yours for the cause of Peace and Brotherhood
Martin Luther King, Jr.

Reading Critically

1. Give a brief summary of the evidence King offers to justify his use of nonviolent direct action in Birmingham. (See, for example, paragraphs 6, 7, and 10.) Be sure to discuss how paragraph 14 helps support the specific reasons King offered previously.

2. This "letter" by King is considered one of the great statements on civil disobedience. Briefly summarize the long tradition of civil disobedience that King discusses. How does King place himself in this tradition? Discuss with your classmates why it is important that he place himself in this tradition.

3. Consult newspapers and magazines (*Time, Newsweek, U.S. News & World Report,* and *Life,* for example) for accounts of the events in Birmingham, Alabama, during March and April 1963. Prepare a brief report on events in the city at that time. Why was King in the Birmingham jail?

4. In an encyclopedia or biographical dictionary, look up St. Augustine, St. Thomas Aquinas, Martin Buber, and Paul Tillich. Prepare a brief report on what in their lives is relevant to King's discussion of civil disobedience. Make a list of the other people and events mentioned by King. What does the reference to each of them contribute to King's argument?

Responding Through Writing

1. What is "civil disobedience"? If you are keeping a journal or notebook in this course, write in it for five to ten minutes on what you think civil disobedience is. Then look up not just a definition of this term, but a discussion of it. Take notes on your research and compare your notes with your original notes in your journal. What did you learn about civil disobedience that you did not know or misunderstood before your research? Now write your own definition of civil disobedience and compare it to King's definition in his letter.

2. Although addressed to a group of clergymen, this letter was clearly written for a much wider audience. Who is that audience? What evidence in the letter indicates this wider audience? Write a paragraph in which you describe King's real audience for his letter. If King did intend his letter for a wider audience, why did he address it to the eight clergymen?

3. Write a list of the criteria King establishes for the use of nonviolent direct action. Now write without stopping for ten minutes, discussing whether you agree or disagree with these criteria. After discussing your notes with your classmates, write a paragraph

summarizing your attitude toward nonviolent direct action as proposed by King.

4. Write the first draft of an essay discussing whether you
think there are issues that justify nonviolent direct action today
according to King's principles. (You might consider such issues as
apartheid in South Africa, the proliferation of nuclear weapons,
abortion, and drug abuse.) After discussing your draft with your
classmates, rewrite your essay in final form.

BLACK CRIME, BLACK VICTIMS

LEE A. DANIELS

Lee Daniels is a reporter for the New York Times, *where he has worked on both the metropolitan and the business staff of the paper. His more recent articles in that newspaper have dealt mainly with the problems found in today's schools. Daniels has also contributed articles to the* New York Times Magazine, Essence, *and* Education Digest. *In his articles Daniels searches for and finds the unexpected aspect of the story, as he does in this article, where he points out: "Statistics show conclusively that blacks, not whites, proportionately are more often the victims of murder, rape, robbery, aggravated assault, burglary, larceny-theft, motor-vehicle theft and arson. . . ." The following story was published on May 16, 1982, in the* New York Times.

Jean Jones, a 37-year-old personnel specialist for an employ- 1
ment company, had just stepped off the bus one December evening
in her Brooklyn neighborhood and was walking home when, turning a corner, she saw a tall, thin man standing near an apparently
empty schoolyard a block ahead. Though preoccupied with other
thoughts, she instinctively crossed the well-lighted street, preferring
to walk past a row of brownstones that faced the schoolyard.

2   As she neared the end of the block, however, the man quickly crossed the street to confront her, pushing her backward with powerful jabs to her chest.

3   "I was terrified," recalls Miss Jones, speaking evenly but rapidly, her voice charged with emotion. "I said, 'What's wrong with you?' and tried to back away. I was going to run up the stairs of one of the houses, but I didn't notice there was a stairway behind me that went down. He could see it because he was much taller than I, and he pushed me into it.

4   "My head hit the cement, and I lost consciousness," she says, pausing to take a deep breath. "When I came to, he had come down the steps, straddled me and was beating me, punching me viciously on my head and face. I assume he was trying to kill me. I was pushing up, trying to hold him back and screaming, 'My God, help me.' While he was beating me, he was trying to pull up my clothes, but he couldn't because I had so many layers on."

5   According to the police report of the incident, a boy playing in the schoolyard heard Miss Jones's screams and ran for help, flagging down a police patrol car. The police found a man standing at the top of the stairwell with blood on his coat. He was arrested and charged with the attack.

6   The police officers, seeing Miss Jones's battered face, drove her immediately to the hospital. There, she underwent surgery for severe facial and oral injuries, but not before identifying the arrested man, whom the police brought to the hospital, as her assailant. She had also suffered a concussion and a severely sprained neck and left knee. Hospitalized for three weeks, she was out of work for four months afterward. Today, more than a year later, she remains under a doctor's care.

7   Her alleged assailant, charged with first-degree assault, was brought to trial in August 1981. Despite her emphatic and repeated identification of him as the man who had attacked her, the jury did not believe she had seen her attacker clearly enough to identify him, and the man was acquitted.

8   Both Miss Jones and the man who attacked her are black.

9   Within the last decade, changes within the black community, increased public concern about street crime and a depressed economy have made the disproportionate involvement of blacks in crime—as both predators and prey—a significant fact of urban and political life in the United States. Yet, because the issue includes the volatile and often-manipulated elements of race and class, blacks and whites

alike have avoided open, direct public discussion of the topic. That is, until recently. Today, a growing number of blacks, prompted by an epidemic of crime in their neighborhoods and by their fears that a national mood of racial reaction and social and fiscal retrenchment will provoke more street crime, are speaking out.

Although the disquiet among blacks is not new, the willingness 10 of prominent black individuals and groups to assume a higher public profile regarding the issue is. This surge of activity stems primarily from two considerations: Statistics show conclusively that blacks, not whites, proportionately are more often the victims of murder, rape, robbery, aggravated assault, burglary, larceny-theft, motor-vehicle theft and arson—what the F.B.I. defines as street crime. In addition, many blacks assert that society must be made to recognize that more rhetoric about "getting tough" is an ineffective response to street crime in view of abuses of plea-bargaining (a practice that invariably results in a lesser sentence for the offender), reductions in police forces and other economies the criminal-justice system has been forced to adopt. Instead, they say that the real answer lies in combining a hard-nosed approach to crime prevention and the prosecution of criminals *with* an equally determined effort to mitigate the social causes of crime—an effort in which the black community itself must play a major role.

The primary reason for "black on black" crime, as it is some- 11 times described, is that most street crimes are committed by poor people out of desperation, impulse and opportunity. According to Homer Broome, former director of the Law Enforcement Assistance Administration (now the Bureau of Justice Statistics), "These kinds of crimes have usually occurred within a one-mile radius of the perpetrator's and the victim's homes." Says Mr. Broome, now Los Angeles Public Works commissioner, "A very small percentage of the offenders are jumping in their cars and speeding to suburbia or traveling to white neighborhoods to commit their crimes. By and large, criminals operate in areas of opportunity and familiarity." Mr. Broome says that while the actual number of criminals in comparison with the general population is quite small, they are so active that their depredations have a devastating impact.

Such explanations, however, are unlikely to ease the physical 12 and emotional wounds of victims like George Lane, aged 70, who was attacked in the vestibule of a friend's building in the predominantly black neighborhood of Bedford-Stuyvesant in Brooklyn. His assailant struck Mr. Lane with a pistol, knocking out three front teeth and opening a gash on his face that required 12 stitches.

Although he has recovered his confidence and spirit, Mr. Lane says that after the attack he felt "a lot of distrust of black people in general."

13   These feelings of distrust and fear are typical, not only among crime victims but also among those who live with the steady anxiety that they may be next, according to a recent study conducted by New York's Victim Services Agency for the National Institute of Justice. Donald Cole, director of the agency's Bedford-Stuyvesant office, says, "I see people around here acting like nervous prey. Crime makes people bitter and afraid to trust each other, and we can't have a community without trust."

14   "The black community wasn't speaking to us about this before," says the director of the New York Police Department's Civilian Participations Programs division, Richard Shapiro. "But now, while the old issues like unemployment and decent housing remain, the 'new' issue of crime has risen to the forefront. People are just getting ripped off so much they're worrying about sheer survival." Mr. Shapiro says that about 150,000 civilians throughout the city are involved in some form of crime-prevention activity, and that "the black community is as active about this as the white community."

15   Some blacks blame black politicians for not being sufficiently forceful in addressing the issue. "Most of us have been speaking out for years about this," counters United States Representative Shirley Chisholm of Brooklyn. "But black politicians don't control law-enforcement budgets or how crime-fighting resources are used."

16   However, New York State Senator Leon Bogues, whose district includes part of Harlem, acknowledges that an intensive, organized campaign is needed. "There's a lot of activity, but it's splintered among individual groups," says Mr. Bogues, a former city probation officer. According to Mr. Bogues, one reason for the lack of concerted effort may be that "in the black community there are so many problems, sometimes it's difficult to single out one as a priority."

17   The lack of a concerted effort may also be a product of the ambivalence many black people feel toward the criminal-justice system—especially the police. The reasons are partly historical (during the era of Government-sanctioned segregation and discrimination, the criminal-justice system was used as a tool to directly oppress blacks), and partly due to continuing incidents of questionable force by police against blacks in many cities. On the one hand, the police are still accused of brutality in dealing with blacks; on

the other, they are charged with enforcing the law less vigorously in black neighborhoods than in white ones.

While noting that ambivalence, Thomas I. Atkins, general   18
counsel of the National Association for the Advancement of Colored People, declares, "We can't remain silent about this and still claim that our mission is to help people in our communities live better lives. Crime is extremely corrosive. It destroys our businesses and hinders our ability to organize politically because people won't come out at night. It drives down the value of property in our communities and undercuts the possibility of economic development because the area's unsafe. And it hurts our children by giving them negative role models and exposing them to unsafe situations. Any way you look at it, it just saps our life spirit."

The dimensions of black involvement in crime—as suspects,   19
convicts and victims—are startling. In 1980, according to the F.B.I.'s Uniform Crime Index, blacks, although they represent only 12 percent of the United States population, accounted for 44 percent of all arrests for violent crimes and nearly 30 percent of arrests for property crimes. The F.B.I. data indicated that, nationally, blacks are more than twice as likely as whites to be arrested.

Several Federal crime surveys, including one by the Bureau of   20
Justice Statistics, have shown that because the poor are more victimized by crime than others, blacks, who represent a disproportionate percentage of the poor, are more likely than whites to be the victims of violent crimes. According to information gathered by the National Center for Health Statistics, black males between the ages of 15 and 44 have an extremely high probability of being murdered compared to white males. Breaking this age cohort into two groups, 15 to 24 years and 25 to 44 years, the center found that homicide is the second leading cause of death for the former, and the leading cause of death for the latter. The murder rate for black males 15 to 24 years old is 66 of every 100,000; the rate for white males in this age group is 12.4 per 100,000. For the 25 to 44 age category, the murder rate for blacks is 106 per 100,000; for whites it is 14.8 per 100,000. New York City police officials recently reported that one finding of a study showed that black males were most often arrested for murder—and that black males were the most likely murder victims.

Introspective and articulate, his youthful-looking face framed   21
by a close-cut beard, he could be a graduate student. But at an age

when he could have been in college, he was "doing hard time," serving five years of a six- to 10-year sentence in a New York state prison for robbery and burglary. At age 32 and out of prison for eight years, As-Allah Gibson is now a counselor with the Fortune Society, a private agency seeking to help ex-offenders lead useful lives.

22   "When I was 13, my peer group was into car thefts, vandalism, truancy, muggings, store breaking and entering," says Mr. Gibson, who grew up in Brooklyn's Fort Greene neighborhood, the son of a Navy cook and a day worker, and the seventh of 10 children. "These weren't elaborately planned. It was just something you went out and did.

23   "There was a feeling on the street that you had to go to jail to be really accepted. It was a test you had to pass. I was arrested and detained for a while at 16. When I came home, it was clear to me that I was perceived as having passed a test. I could rap about it with the other guys who had been to jail, whereas before, when those sorts of things were discussed, I had been left out.

24   "My antisocial activities weren't antiwhite or antiblack, just anti anything. I just didn't care what color a person was. I did mug black people when I was in my teens. I don't think I thought anything of it at the time. They were simply people to be taken. I didn't feel any bond with them."

25   Asked what had spurred him to commit crimes, Mr. Gibson says that opportunity was only part of the reason.

26   "I was very angry," he explains. "There was a great deal of hostility between my father and me. And we were very poor. We lived in a small apartment. Often, we'd have no running water in the apartment, and we'd have to go to the basement to get water to flush the toilet with. I didn't have many clothes, and I felt ashamed of the ones I had. It made me very uncomfortable at school.

27   "I was very dissatisfied with my life, very angry about being poor. I felt we didn't deserve to be poor. Everybody around us was poor, too. But my perception then was that everybody was doing better, and it just increased my bitterness."

28   Referring to the current epidemic of crime involving black youths, Mr. Gibson says, "It's a very bleak situation. Unless black people take the situation in their own hands, we're going to lose a whole generation of children. I look on the streets and I see a lot of kids who are like I was—lost. They have no conception of themselves. They are more lost and better armed and harder to reach than I was."

Many blacks believe that the great percentage of black crime   29
stems primarily from "systemic racism"—manifested in high unemployment rates that provide an incentive to break the law; in poor
schools that fail to provide the necessary skills for upward mobility;
in police "hypervigilance" that often exposes blacks to random
arrests and violence, and in a double standard of justice that punishes
blacks for offenses that are dealt with in nonpunitive ways when the
offender is white. They contend that, despite society's clear reluctance, in economically troubled times, to support "massive solutions"—and its conviction that the ambitious programs of the 1960's
and 70's failed—the best way to reduce crime is to provide jobs,
educational opportunities and decent housing for the masses of poor
black people.

During the late 1800's and early 1900's, the urban lower classes   30
of white immigrants also had high crime rates (and suffered from
alcoholism, illiteracy and other attendants of poverty). The literature and newspaper editorials of the period were replete with comments about the "innate criminality" of certain groups. Yet the
crime rates of each group dropped as its economic status improved.

Yet, resolving the black crime problem is likely to be far more   31
difficult. Unlike the turn-of-century immigrants, who had to sur-
mount a hurdle that was primarily economic at a time when the
economy was expanding, the black lower classes face a deep reces-
sion complicated by a sharp decline in unskilled and blue-collar jobs.
In addition, racism has prevented blacks from amassing the political
and financial resources that the white ethnics could. The immediate
and long-term effects of the Reagan Administration's budget cuts
in domestic social programs—condemned by critics as being blunt
and mean-spirited in their approach to the proper task of paring
some Government social-welfare activities—also threaten to destroy the governmental framework for assistance needed for a serious, sustained attack on poverty in the United States, whether in
Appalachia or Watts. These cuts come at a time when the number
of black Americans trapped in poverty and dependent on Government services has grown.

Charles Silberman, in his 1978 book, "Criminal Justice, Crimi-   32
nal Violence," contended that more than simply poverty contributed to black street crime. Mr. Silberman argued that the disman-
tling of legal segregation and the resulting dispersion of middle- and
lower-middle-class blacks sundered the social controls and mores—
especially the influence of organized religion—that had previously
checked criminal behavior within the black community. The domi-
nance of middle-class values within the community, an unintended

effect of the segregation forced upon blacks as late as the 1960's, served to restrain the self-destructive tendency of the poor. At the same time, the middle and working classes provided the poor not only with role models but with skilled assistance for those seeking respectable ways to escape from poverty.

33   Mr. Silberman noted that although Puerto Ricans and American Indians as groups are generally poorer than blacks, their arrest and incarceration rates do not approach those of blacks. He conjectured that because these groups are more culturally homogenous and less assimilated, their communities have an internal cohesion poor black neighborhoods lack.

34   Racially engendered self-hatred and rage also play a significant role in black crime, says Dr. Alvin F. Poussaint, a psychiatrist on the staff of the Harvard Medical School. "Many lower-class blacks are continually primed for violent outbursts just by the problems of daily living," Dr. Poussaint says. They believe, he says, that they are dirt poor in a society that rewards everyone else with affluence. "They are black in a society that tells them black is bad."

35   Dr. Poussaint remarks that, unlike their middle-class brethren, the black poor generally lack the skills and resources to counteract feelings of inferiority and acts of discrimination. They lack positive directions in which to channel and discharge their anger. Consequently, the rage turns inward or is directed against other blacks. Many black street criminals, Dr. Poussaint says, manifest "a powerful subconscious drive toward self-destruction in that they ignore the obviously great probability of their being caught and caught immediately." According to Dr. Poussaint, studies of black-on-black murders have established evidence that some instances are " 'victim-precipitated'—that is, the victim subconsciously provokes his own murder by deliberately choosing to ignore the obvious consequences of an outburst."

36   Dr. Poussaint also mentions another crippling affliction of the black underclass: the extraordinarily high birth rate among poor black women, especially girls. Their birth rate, contrary to that of the rest of the American population, is sharply increasing. Because poverty, to a large extent, breeds crime; because unwed girls who become pregnant are often immediately abandoned by the fathers; because female-headed households are the poorest among all American households; because, in all ethnic groups, young people are those most susceptible to involvement in crime—the continued high birth rate among the black poor has explosive implications for the crime rate.

37   Since poverty plays a pivotal role in fostering crime, reducing

blacks' disproportionate participation in it must involve alleviating the festering problems of the black poor. Less sweeping measures targeted specifically at crime can also help, including putting more blacks on police forces and in the criminal-justice system, increasing police efforts to reduce the drug trafficking that occurs in many poor black communities and encouraging police support of community anticrime efforts. For example, the New York City Police Department, by adopting in 1977 a strict regulation governing the use of deadly force—subsequently reducing its "most controversial shootings" by 75 percent without jeopardizing officers or hampering police work—and by seeking to involve community groups in crime prevention, has demonstrated that police officials can breach the barrier of distrust between them and the black community.

Finally, many blacks believe that they themselves must act to   38 reduce crime within their neighborhoods. They endorse a strategy of insisting that their elected representatives and city officials speak out against crime and take steps to reduce it; becoming actively involved in the public schools and youth-employment programs and in the operation of their local police precincts, and mounting local anticrime efforts, such as escort services for the elderly, civilian volunteer patrols and building- and block-watch groups. Successful examples of such efforts, though scattered, are numerous.

Vacant lots, abandoned buildings and decrepit occupied struc-   39 tures characterize much of the neighborhood surrounding Miller Avenue in Brooklyn's East New York. Here and there, groups of idle young men stand idly. Many of them, according to residents and police, are drug dealers and small-time hoodlums. But, along a four-block stretch of Miller Avenue between Blake and Riverdale Streets, there is a startling difference. The street and sidewalks are free of litter. The brick, one- and two-family houses, most of the residences, have the look of assiduous maintenance. This section belongs to the Miller Avenue Block Association. Here, the residents, primarily blue-collar and lower-middle class, watch over one another's children at play outdoors. Ernest Johnson, a 12-year resident and father of four children, says, "We don't allow our children to curse or be rowdy on the street. My neighbors have the right to discipline my kids if they're misbehaving."

James Saunders, the block-association president, says residents   40 organized in the early 1970's to try to reverse the decline precipitated by a massive urban renewal program of the 1950's that destroyed large numbers of homes before it was itself abandoned. An immediate priority was crime prevention. Residents watched over their neighbors' homes, sought and got new, high-intensity street lights and painted the trunks of curbside trees white so that would-be muggers could not hide so easily against them in the darkness. The block association has also formed an escort service for elderly residents, persuaded the Parks Department to undertake a $360,000 renovation of the area's block-square Martin Luther King Jr. Park and is converting an abandoned building into a youth center. "We've stuck together, and it's really made a difference," says Louise Long, a 15-year resident.

41   Mr. Saunders praised police officers from the nearby 75th Precinct for their cooperation. "We call, and they come right away. They know what we're trying to do here, and I think they appreciate it." One night patrol team routinely drives by Mr. Saunder's house at the beginning of its shift and discreetly toots the car horn to announce that it is on duty.

42   The Miller Avenue area isn't free of crime. Muggings occasionally occur, and residents say they remain concerned about the drug trafficking on the fringes of the neighborhood. But this part of Miller Avenue is far different from what it might have been had its residents given up hope. Explaining the neighborhood's motivation, Mr. Saunders says, "We live here. We're trying to raise our families here. If we don't look out for our homes and our children, who will?"

43   Reducing black street crime, however, must involve more than scattered, individual efforts. Robert L. Woodson, a resident fellow at the American Enterprise Institute in Washington, has examined several groups in different cities—among them, the House of Umoja in Philadelphia, I-CRY in New York City, the South Arsenal Neighborhood Development Corporation in Hartford, and La Playa de Ponce in Ponce, P.R. Mr. Woodson says that these neighborhood organizations, which he calls "mediating structures," have achieved striking success in deterring poor youths from criminal activities. All of these groups inculcate lower-class youths with a value system that gives them a sense of self-worth and responsibility to their community.

44   The black lower class, living in neighborhoods where there is little incentive to be law abiding, has shown its longing for order and meaning by its historical attraction to such fundamentalist religious and political movements as Marcus Garvey's University Negro Improvement Association of the 1920's and the Black Muslims and the civil-rights movement of the 1960's, all of which depended heavily on the cultural influence of religion within the black community. Mr. Woodson contends that today's black na-

tional and local institutions, particularly churches and fraternal organizations, must undertake a large-scale effort to provide a moral
framework if poor black neighborhoods are to be rescued from
crime and disorder.

Obviously, the effort necessary to transform small crime-pre-   45
vention efforts into a mass movement will be enormous. And it is
unclear whether such an approach could succeed in the current
economically straitened environment. But the problem is so serious
and the stakes so high that many blacks feel they have no alternative
but to try.

Charles Payton Jr., a 27-year-old musician, was stabbed   46
through the heart and died shortly after midnight on Father's Day,
June 17, 1979, as he tried to retrieve his stolen guitar from the owner
of a small grocery store in his Brooklyn neighborhood. His killer
eventually was sentenced to one to three years in prison. Yet, though
convicted of second-degree manslaughter, the man is out on bail,
appealing his sentence.

Charles and Emma Payton (their names and that of their son   47
have been changed) find the death of the second oldest of their five
children overwhelming. And so, with grief etched like wrinkles into
their faces, they sit in the wood-paneled den of their home, where
they have lived for nearly 30 years. They describe the anguish,
frustration, anger and bewilderment that have haunted them for
nearly three years. "Our family has tried to live properly," says Mr.
Payton, a mid-level white-collar worker for a large corporation, "to
abide by the law, to be charitable to those less privileged. Then this
happens.

"You're left in a state of confusion. I've had some terrible   48
thoughts. I've had to beat my fists against the wall to control my
emotions. But you think of your responsibilities to the rest of the
family. You go on, but there are moments when you seem to have
lost the light."

"I did want to move from here," says Mrs. Payton.   49

"There's too much to remind me of him when I walk out into   50
the street."

"I thought about it, too," says Mr. Payton. "I'm not overly   51
happy we're here, but it's bad all over. It doesn't matter where you
are. The system doesn't change. The issue is whether you can control
crime and exact punishment."

His voice hardens as he considers the sentence given his son's   52
killer. "The verdict was guilty, but by the time they sentenced him,
it seemed like we were the losers."

Reading Critically

1. To what extent does your reaction to this essay depend on your own experiences with violent crime? If you feel comfortable doing so, discuss with your classmates any such experiences you may have had. How did those experiences color your (and your classmates') reaction to this essay?

2. What kind of picture does Daniels indirectly paint of the police? How closely does this picture match the ways in which you and your classmates view the police?

3. From reading this essay, do you conclude that crime is caused primarily by poverty, or by the evil intentions of criminals? Cite evidence, drawn from both this essay and other sources (such as newspapers, magazines, books, and other courses you have taken) to support your opinion.

4. Why do youth gang members see going to jail as proof of "manhood" (paragraph 23)? If you have ever engaged in "manly" behavior that was against the law, why did you do it? Do you think that women sometimes encourage such "manly" behavior?

Responding Through Writing

1. Write for five minutes without stopping about how you would react to an attack like that experienced by Ms. Jones (paragraphs 1 to 4). Discuss your reactions with your classmates.

2. Write the first drafts of the introductions for two essays on black crime: one for a black audience, the other for a mixed audience of whites and blacks.

3. How do you define "getting tough" on crime? List at least three measures you think would help to fight crime. Write the first draft of a short paper in which you argue how your proposed measures would work.

4. If you are keeping a journal or notebook in this course, note in it ways in which you are sometimes tempted to "take the law into your own hands." From your journal entries, write an essay in which you discuss what might happen if people took the law into their own hands.

ANSWER IN
THE AFFIRMATIVE

M.F.K. FISHER

Mary Francis Kennedy Fisher (b. 1908) writes about food, but her way of discussing the rewards and responsibilities of preparing it and eating it have made her a unique stylist in American letters. Born in Albion, Michigan, and a graduate of Illinois College, Occidental College, and UCLA, Fisher also spent three years in France, where she attended the University of Dijon. In her many books—among them are Consider the Oyster *(1941),* The Gastronomical Me *(1943), and* How to Cook a Wolf *(1942)—she expounds on how food can be used to enhance life. She says she is "concerned with man's fundamental need to celebrate the high points of his life by eating and drinking." The following story was first published in* The New Yorker *on December 6, 1982.*

1   Yesterday I thought about Mr. Ardamanian and the time I let him make love to me.

2   I say "make love," but it was not that, exactly. It was quite beyond maleness and femaleness. It was a strange thing, one I seldom think of, not because I am ashamed but because it never bothers me. When I do think back upon it, I am filled with a kind of passive

wonder that I should have let it happen and that it never bothered me, for I am not the kind of woman who stands still under the hands of an unloved man, nor am I in any way the kind who willy-nilly invites such treatment.

There is a novel by Somerset Maugham in which an actress lets   3 a stranger sleep with her for one night in a train. As I recall it, she never manages to call up any native shame about this queer adventure but instead comes to recollect it with a certain smugness, pleased with her own wild daring. I do not feel smug about Mr. Ardamanian's caresses; until yesterday, I believed myself merely puzzled by their happening, or at least their happening to *me*.

Yesterday, I had to make a long drive alone in the car. It was   4 a hundred miles or so. I was tired before I started, and filled with a bleak solitariness that gradually became self-conscious, so that before I had passed through the first big town and got out into the vineyards again I was, in spite of myself, thinking of my large bones, my greying hair, my occasional deep weariness at being forty years old and harassed as most forty-year-old women are by overwork, too many bills, outmoded clothes. I thought of ordering something extravagant for myself, like a new suit—black, or perhaps even dark red. Then I thought that I had gained some pounds lately, as always when I am a little miserable, and I began to reproach myself: I was turning slothful, I was slumping, I was neglecting my fine femaleness in a martyr-like and indulgent mood of hyperwifeliness, supermotherliness. I was a fool, I said bitterly, despondently, as I sped with caution through another town.

I began to think about myself younger, slimmer, less harried,   5 and less warped by the world's weight. I thought with a kind of tolerant amusement that when I was in my twenties I never noticed my poundage, taking for granted that it was right. Now, I reminded myself as I shot doggedly through the vineyards and then a little town and then the peach orchards near Ontario—now I shuddered, no matter how gluttonously, from every pat of butter, and winced away from every encouraging Martini as if it held snake venom. Still I was fat, and I was tired and old, and when had it happened? Just those few years ago, I had been slender, eager, untwisted by fatigue.

I had been a good woman, too. I had never lusted for any man   6 but the one I loved. That was why it was so strange, the time Mr. Ardamanian came to the house with my rug.

We were living near a college where my husband taught, in   7 a beautiful shack held together by layers of paint. I was alone much of the time, and I buzzed like a happy bee through the three rooms, straightening and polishing them. I was never ill at ease or wistful for company, being young, healthy, and well-loved.

8   We were very poor, and my mother said, "Jane, why don't you have Mr. Ardamanian take a few of these old rugs of mine and make them into one of his nice hash-rugs for your living room? It wouldn't cost much, and anything he can do for our family he will love to do."

9   I thought of Mr. Ardamanian, and of the twenty years or so of seeing him come, with great dignity, to roll up this rug and that rug in our house—for my mother had a great many—and then walk down to his car lightly under the balanced load. He knew us all, first me and my little sister, then the two younger siblings, and my grandmother and the various cooks we had, and even Father. He came in and out of the house, and watched us grow, year after year, while he cleaned and mended rugs for us. Mother told us his name was that of a great family in Armenia, and, true enough, every time since then when I have seen it in books or on shopfronts, mostly for rugs, I have known it to be part of his pride.

10   He was small, very old and grey, it seemed, when I was a little girl. He had a high but quiet voice, deep flashing eyes, and strong, white, even teeth. He called my mother Lady. That always pleased me. He did not say Missus, or even Madam, or Lady So-and-So. He said *Lady*. He dressed in good grey suits, and although he rolled up big rugs and carried them lightly to his car, he was never dusty.

11   Mother went ahead with her generous plan, and Mr. Ardamanian did come to the little house near the college, bearing upon his old shoulders a fairly handsome hash-rug made of scraps. He stood at the door under the small pink roses that climbed everywhere, and he looked as he had always looked to me over those twenty years.

12   He bowed, said, "Your lady mother has sent me," and came in.

13   I felt warm and friendly toward him, this strange familiar from my earliest days, and as the two of us silently laid the good solid rug upon the painted floor, under my sparse furniture, I was pleased to be with him. We finished the moving, and the rug looked fine, very rich and thick, if not what I was used to at home—the big, worn Baluchistans, the glowing Bokharas.

14   Then—I do not quite remember, but I think it started by his saying, in his rather high, courteous voice, the one I knew over so many years, "You are married now. You look very happy. You

look like a woman at last, and you have grown a little here
. . . not yet enough here . . ." and he began very delicately, very
surely, to touch me on my waist, my shoulder, my small young
breasts.

It was, and I know it even now, a wonderful feeling. It was   15
as if he were a sculptor. He had the most fastidiously intelligent
hands I had ever met with, and he used them with the instinct of
an artist moving over something he understood creatively, something alive, deathless, pulsating with beauty but beyond desire.

I stood, silent and entranced, for I do not know how long,   16
while Mr. Ardamanian seemed to mold my outlines into classical
loveliness. I looked with a kind of adoration at his remote, aged face,
and felt his mysteriously knowing hands move, calm as God's, over
my body. I was, for those moments of complete easy-breathing
silence, as beautiful as any statue ever carved in stone or wood or
jade. I was beyond reproach.

I heard my husband come up the path through the mimosa   17
trees. The old man's hands dropped away. I went to the door,
unruffled, and I introduced the two men. Then Mr. Ardamanian
went gracefully away, and it was not until an hour or so later that
I began to remember the strange scene and to wonder what would
have happened if he had led me gently to the wide couch and made
love to me in the way I, because of my youngness, most easily
understood. I felt a vague shame, perhaps, because of my upbringing
and my limited spiritual vocabulary, and the whole thing puzzled
me in a very minor and peripheral way. There had been no faintest
spark of lust between us, no fast urgent breath, no need. . . .

So I found myself thinking of all this yesterday, alone in the   18
car. I felt bitter, seeing myself, toward the end of the tiring trip,
as a thickening exhausted lump without desire or desirability. I
thought fleetingly of the tall, slim, ripe woman who had stood
under those ancient hands.

When I got to my mother's house, I needed quiet and a glass   19
of sherry and reassuring family talk to jolt me out of a voluptuous
depression. Mind you, it was not being forty that really puzzled and
hurt me; it was simply that I had got that far along without realizing
that I could indeed grow thicker and careless, and let myself eat and
drink too much, and wear white gloves with a hole in them, and
in general become slovenly.

Almost the first thing my mother said was that she was waiting   20
for Mr. Ardamanian. I jerked in my chair. It seemed too strange,
to have thought about him that morning for the first time in many

years. Suddenly I was very upset, for of all things in the world I did not want that old man who had once found me worth touching to see me tired, mopish, middle-aged. I felt cruelly cheated at this twist and I cried out, "But he can't be alive still! Mother, he must be a hundred years old."

21   She looked at me with some surprise at my loud protest and said, "Almost. But he is still a good rug man."

22   I was stunned. It seemed a proof to me of all my dour thoughts during the long ride. Oh, the hell with it, I thought; what can it matter to an old ghost that I'm no longer young and beautiful, if once I was, to his peculiar vision? "That hideous hash-rug fell apart," I said ungraciously, and paid no heed to my mother's enigmatic gaze.

23   When he came, he did look somewhat older—or, rather, drier—but certainly not fifteen or eighteen years so. His temples had sunk a little, and his bright, even teeth were too big for his mouth, but his dark eyes flashed politely, and he insisted on moving furniture and carrying in the clean rolls of Oriental carpet without any help. He performed neatly, a graceful old body indeed.

24   "Do not move, Lady," he said to my mother, and he whisked a small rug under her footstool without seeming to lift it. I stood about aimlessly, watching him and thinking about him and myself, in a kind of misery.

25   At the end, when he had carried the dirty rugs out to his car and had told my mother when he would come back, he looked at me, and then stepped quite close.

26   "Which one are you?" he asked.

27   "I'm the oldest," I said, wondering what he would remember of me.

28   And immediately I saw that it was everything, everything—not of me as a little growing child but of me his creation. His eyes blazed, and fell in an indescribable pattern from my cheeks to my shoulders to my breasts to the hidden cave of my navel, and then up over the bones of my ribs and down again to the softened hollows of my waist. We were back in the silent little house near the college, and I was filled with a sense of complete relaxation, to have this old man still recognize me, and to have him do with his eyes what once he had so strangely and purely done with his hands. I knew that it was something that would never happen again. What is more, I knew that when I was an old woman it would strengthen me, as it strengthened me that very minute when I was tired and forty and thick, that once Mr. Ardamanian had made me into a statue.

The question about seduction still remains, of course, in an 29
academic way. Would he have done any more to me than what he
did, and, indeed, would anything more have been possible—not
from the standpoint of his indubitable virility, no matter what his
age, but from that of our spiritual capacity to pile nectar into the
brimming cup? I can never know, nor do I care.

I was filled with relief, standing passively there before my 30
mother in the familiar room. I felt strong and fresh.

He smiled his gleaming smile, bowed to my mother, and then 31
said directly to me, "Lady, it is good that I met you again. Goodbye."

When he had gone, as poised as a praying mantis under his last 32
roll of rugs, my mother said, pretending to be cross, "I thought *I*
was his Lady, not you!" She smiled remotely.

Mother and I talked together through the afternoon, about 33
children and bills and such, but not about Mr. Ardamanian. There
seemed no need to, then or ever.

Reading Critically

1. What do you think of the opening line of the story ("Yesterday I thought about Mr. Ardamanian and the time I let him make
love to me")? Does it make you want to read on, or does it put you
off? Is your real reaction to that line different from the reaction you
would tell to other people? Discuss with your classmates. Does the
second sentence of the story ("I say 'make love,' but it was not that,
exactly") make you want to read on? When you read that line, were
you relieved or disappointed? Why?

2. What do you think Mr. Ardamanian wanted from Fisher?
What did she want from him? What did they get from each other?

3. Fisher says at the end of paragraph 17, "There had been no
faintest spark of lust between us, no fast urgent breath, no need.
. . ." and then breaks off. No "need" for what?

4. Why do Fisher and her mother *not* talk about Mr. Ardamanian?

Responding Through Writing

1. In paragraph 20 Fisher becomes very upset about the prospect of meeting Mr. Ardamanian again. She is afraid that he will notice that she has gained weight and is perhaps in other ways not as attractive as she once was. What makes her feel this way? Have you had similar feelings about the way old friends see you? Write a few paragraphs in your private notebook reacting to those feelings.

2. In paragraph 19, Fisher speaks of being in a "voluptuous depression." What do you think she means by this term? Have you ever luxuriated in depression? Again in a private notebook, write about how you have sometimes dealt with depression.

3. Why does the *memory* of her experience with Mr. Ardamanian become important for Fisher later on in her life? Do you have memories of odd incidents that have surprisingly grown important for you over the years? Write a short essay indicating how some less-than-major experience became very important to you over time as a memory.

4. Evaluate the first sentence in paragraph 7: "We were living near a college where my husband taught, in a beautiful shack held together by layers of paint." What does this sentence *indirectly* say about Fisher's life with her husband? Write a few paragraphs and see whether you can describe relationships *indirectly* as Fisher does.

THE WOMAN WARRIOR

MAXINE HONG KINGSTON

Maxine Hong Kingston was born in 1940 in Stockton, California, of Chinese emigrant parents. From 1965 to the present, Kingston has devoted her life to teaching while continuing her writing. She began teaching high school in California, moved to Hawaii for several years, and is presently a professor at Eastern Michigan University. Her vivid prose and exotic style excited critics and readers with her first book, The Woman Warrior: Memoirs of a Girlhood Among Ghosts *(1975). Subsequent books, including* China Men *(1980),* Hawaii One Summer *(1987), and* Tripmaster Monkey *(1988), have also received great praise from critics. The following is an excerpt from* The Woman Warrior.

When we Chinese girls listened to the adults talking-story, we   1
learned that we failed if we grew up to be but wives or slaves. We
could be heroines, swordswomen. Even if she had to rage across all
China, a swordswoman got even with anybody who hurt her family. Perhaps women were once so dangerous that they had to have
their feet bound. It was a woman who invented white crane boxing
only two hundred years ago. She was already an expert pole fighter,
daughter of a teacher trained at the Shao-lin temple, where there

lived an order of fighting monks. She was combing her hair one morning when a white crane alighted outside her window. She teased it with her pole, which it pushed aside with a soft brush of its wing. Amazed, she dashed outside and tried to knock the crane off its perch. It snapped her pole in two. Recognizing the presence of great power, she asked the spirit of the white crane if it would teach her to fight. It answered with a cry that white crane boxers imitate today. Later the bird returned as an old man, and he guided her boxing for many years. Thus she gave the world a new martial art.

2   This was one of the tamer, more modern stories, mere introduction. My mother told others that followed swordswomen through woods and palaces for years. Night after night my mother would talk-story until we fell asleep. I couldn't tell where the stories left off and the dreams began, her voice the voice of the heroines in my sleep. And on Sundays, from noon to midnight, we went to the movies at the Confucius Church. We saw swordswomen jump over houses from a standstill; they didn't even need a running start.

3   At last I saw that I too had been in the presence of great power, my mother talking-story. After I grew up, I heard the chant of Fa Mu Lan, the girl who took her father's place in battle. Instantly I remembered that as a child I had followed my mother about the house, the two of us singing about how Fa Mu Lan fought gloriously and returned alive from war to settle in the village. I had forgotten this chant that was once mine, given me by my mother, who may not have known its power to remind. She said I would grow up a wife and a slave, but she taught me the song of the warrior woman, Fa Mu Lan. I would have to grow up a warrior woman. . . .

4   My American life has been such a disappointment.

5   "I got straight A's, Mama."

6   "Let me tell you a true story about a girl who saved her village."

7   I could not figure out what was my village. And it was important that I do something big and fine, or else my parents would sell me when we made our way back to China. In China there were solutions for what to do with little girls who ate up food and threw tantrums. You can't eat straight A's.

8   When one of my parents or the emigrant villagers said, "Feeding girls is feeding cowbirds," I would thrash on the floor and scream so hard I couldn't talk. I couldn't stop.

9   "What's the matter with her?"

10   "I don't know. Bad, I guess. You know how girls are. 'There's no profit in raising girls. Better to raise geese than girls.' "

"I would hit her if she were mine. But then there's no use   11
wasting all that discipline on a girl. 'When you raise girls, you're
raising children for strangers.' "

"Stop that crying!" my mother would yell. "I'm going to hit   12
you if you don't stop. Bad girl! Stop!" I'm going to remember
never to hit or to scold my children for crying, I thought, because
then they will only cry more.

"I'm not a bad girl," I would scream. "I'm not a bad girl. I'm   13
not a bad girl." I might as well have said, "I'm not a girl."

"When you were little, all you had to say was 'I'm not a bad   14
girl,' and you could make yourself cry," my mother says, talking-
story about my childhood.

I minded that the emigrant villagers shook their heads at my   15
sister and me. "One girl—and another girl," they said, and made
our parents ashamed to take us out together. The good part about
my brothers being born was that people stopped saying, "All girls,"
but I learned new grievances. "Did you roll an egg on *my* face like
that when *I* was born?" Did you have a full-month party for *me?*"
"Did you turn on all the lights?" "Did you send *my* picture to
Grandmother?" "Why not? Because I'm a girl? Is that why not?"
"Why didn't you teach me English?" "You like having me beaten
up at school, don't you?"

"She is very mean, isn't she?" the emigrant villagers would say.   16

"Come, children. Hurry. Hurry. Who wants to go out with   17
Great-Uncle?" On Saturday mornings my great-uncle, the ex-river
pirate, did the shopping. "Get your coats, whoever's coming."

"I'm coming. I'm coming. Wait for me."   18

When he heard girls' voices, he turned on us and roared, "No   19
girls!" and left my sisters and me hanging our coats back up, not
looking at one another. The boys came back with candy and new
toys. When they walked through Chinatown, the people must have
said, "A boy—and another boy—and another boy!" At my great-
uncle's funeral I secretly tested out feeling glad that he was dead—
the six-foot bearish masculinity of him.

I went away to college—Berkeley in the sixties—and I stud-   20
ied, and I marched to change the world, but I did not turn into a
boy. I would have liked to bring myself back as a boy for my parents
to welcome with chickens and pigs. That was for my brother, who
returned alive from Vietnam.

If I went to Vietnam, I would not come back; females desert   21
families. It was said, "There is an outward tendency in females,"
which meant that I was getting straight A's for the good of my
future husband's family, not my own. I did not plan ever to have
a husband. I would show my mother and father and the nosey

emigrant villagers that girls have no outward tendency. I stopped getting straight A's.

22   And all the time I was having to turn myself American-feminine, or no dates.

23   There is a Chinese words for the female *I*—which is "slave." Break the women with their own tongues!

24   I refused to cook. When I had to wash dishes, I would crack one or two. "Bad girl," my mother yelled, and sometimes that made me gloat rather than cry. Isn't a bad girl almost a boy?

25   "What do you want to be when you grow up, little girl?"

26   "A lumberjack in Oregon."

27   Even now, unless I'm happy, I burn the food when I cook. I do not feed people. I let dirty dishes rot. I eat at other people's tables but won't invite them to mine, where the dishes are rotting.

28   If I could not eat, perhaps I could make myself a warrior like the swordswoman who drives me. I will—I must—rise and plow the fields as soon as the baby comes out.

Reading Critically

1. Most parents would be pleased and proud if their daughter received straight A's in school. Why is Kingston's family (at least in her eyes) hostile to her straight A's? Why does she stop getting A's? If faced with a similar situation, what would you do?

2. What does Kingston mean when she says that her mother would "talk-story" until they fell asleep? What are some of the "talk-stories" her mother relates? What is the purpose of these stories? In what ways are these stories similar to and yet different from the fairy tales you heard as a child? How is the story of Molly Pitcher in the American Revolution similar to the story of Fa Mu Lan? (If you don't know the story of Molly Pitcher, look up an account of the Battle of Monmouth.) Discuss with your classmates what these two stories suggest about the roles of women in their respective societies.

3. Look up a discussion of the Chinese practice of foot bind-ing to which Kingston refers in paragraph 1. Prepare a report for discussion with your classmates. What was the purpose of this practice? What does Kingston suggest was the purpose of this prac-tice? When was it outlawed in China? What does this practice suggest about the status of women in China and Chinese culture?

4. Why does Kingston say in paragraph 3 that she "would have to grow up a warrior woman"? What kind of warrior does she mean? What lessons was her mother teaching her through the stories she told her? Given the conclusion of the essay, in what ways was her mother successful?

Responding Through Writing

1. Why does Kingston begin her essay by summarizing the tale of the girl who invented white crane boxing? Write a paragraph in which you discuss the purpose of this story. Now discuss with your classmates how the image of the white crane suggests a theme for Kingston's essay.

2. Write an introductory paragraph that would come before the first paragraph of this essay. Discuss your paragraph with your classmates, and compare your paragraph with theirs. How does adding such a paragraph affect the essay?

3. Kingston conveys vivid pictures with just a few words and phrases, as, for example, in paragraph 17 where she describes her great uncle as "the ex-river pirate." List other examples of such vivid words and phrases.

4. How effective is Kingston's conclusion? Discuss with your classmates whether this conclusion is exaggerated or compellingly honest. Write your own conclusion for the essay, and discuss your conclusion with your classmates. How does this change in conclu-sion affect the essay?

THIN MAY BE IN, BUT FASHION ISN'T HEALTH

WILLIAM IRA BENNETT and JOEL GURIN

William Ira Bennett (b. 1941) received an A.B. from Harvard in 1962 and an M.D. from Harvard Medical School in 1969. He has been the science and medicine editor for Harvard University Press and the director of the writing program at the Massachusetts Institute of Technology. Bennett has written articles on science and health for Atlantic, Vogue, *and the* Columbia Journalism Review. *He is associate editor of the* Harvard Medical School Health Letter.

Joel Gurin (b. 1953) was born in Ann Arbor, Michigan, and received an A.B. from Harvard in 1982. He is coeditor of The Horizons of Health *(1977), and contributes to* Atlantic, The Nation, Harvard, *and* Smithsonian.

Bennett and Gurin are coauthors of The Dieter's Dilemma: Eating Less and Weighing More *(1982). The book lays the blame for the excess weight of Americans to our sedentary life-style rather than on food intake and suggests that increased exercise, rather than dieting, is the key to permanent weight loss. The following essay was first published in the May issue of* Science 1982.

Go into a typical doctor's office, and you will find posted on   1
the wall, near the scales, the venerable "height–weight chart." It says
that, for example, a six-foot man with a light frame should weigh
between 152 and 162 pounds. Anything above that "desirable
weight" is *overweight,* and, as generations of people have been led
to believe, overweight is bad for you.

The truth is, there is nothing terribly scientific about the charts.   2
They are not based on any real medical evidence, and there is no
good reason to believe that most people who are heavier than the
charts' "desirable" range are any less healthy for it. The key phrase
here is "most people."

This does not include truly obese people, a category compris-   3
ing those who are more than 25 percent over their chart weight.
Such people *are* at greater risk of developing high blood pressure,
diabetes, and heart disease. Also at greater risk are those who have
a family history of these diseases. Medical research shows that such
people, as well as those who already have these diseases, can and
should improve their health by losing excess weight. However,
many of the millions of Americans trying to lose weight do not fall
in any of these categories and, therefore, have no medical reason to
slim down. These people may not look as trim as a fashion model,
but that's fashion, not health.

The height–weight charts grew out of the life insurance indus-   4
try's desire to find a convenient way of identifying high risk customers. It began in 1901 when Oscar H. Rogers of the New York
Life Insurance Company refined the practice of looking for risk
factors that would predict a higher death rate in applicants. He
found that fat policyholders died younger than those of average
weight. The insurance industry didn't care whether fatness *caused*
disease and death. It was enough for them to see an association.

It was not long, however, before insurance companies began   5
to think of this marker as a cause of early death. They reasoned that
if they could get overweight people to reduce, customers might live
longer (and pay more premiums). A pioneer in this effort was Louis
I. Dublin, a young biologist who went to work in 1909 for the
Metropolitan Life Insurance Company. For the next 43 years Dublin, who was passionately committed to public health education,
served Metropolitan not only as chief statistician but as house intel-

lectual and publicist. Dublin coined the phrase "America's No. 1 Health Problem" and applied it to obesity in a campaign to get so-called overweight people to slim down.

6   In the 1940s, Dublin produced his table of "Ideal Weights," as it was first called. In addition to actuarial figures, it used three somewhat faulty premises. One was Dublin's belief that people should not gain weight after the age of 25. The second assumption was that people could be assigned to one of three "frame" sizes. To this day there is no objective way to measure frames. The third and most critical assumption was that buyers of life insurance were representative of the population at large. It is known now that they are not.

7   While Dublin's tables were gaining acceptance, medical researchers were beginning one of the most far-reaching studies of health ever undertaken, a study that would prove Dublin wrong.

8   In 1948 about half the population of Framingham, Massachusetts, between the ages of 30 and 62, some 5,200 men and women, were enrolled in a study that continues to this day. They were examined every two years, and when they died, the cause of death was carefully determined. Although the sample was smaller than Dublin's, it was more representative of Americans at large.

9   In 1980 the Framingham doctors concluded that, among men, life expectancy was worst for the lightest weight group. Above this level, weight did not have much effect on life expectancy unless it was more than 25 percent above average. Among women, death rates were highest for the lightest and the heaviest, but between the extremes, weight had little correlation with mortality. If the data hint at a "best" weight, it is at or somewhat above the national average for men and women.

Reading Critically

1. In an encyclopedia or art history textbook, locate paintings by Titian or Rubens featuring the female form. Compare those paintings with ads for women's clothes in *Vogue, Cosmopolitan,* or some similar magazine. What do the paintings and pictures tell you

regarding the relationship between beauty and weight? How have ideas about that relationship changed? Are those changes "fair"? Discuss with your classmates.

2. Bennett and Gurin begin this essay by referring to a chart in a doctor's office. Do you think that people place too much confidence in doctors? If your own doctor ordered you to lose or gain weight or to otherwise substantially alter your life-style, would you take his or her orders at face value or would you question them? Why? Discuss with your classmates.

3. What is your reaction to the methods of the "Framingham Study" mentioned at the end of the essay? How did that study differ from Dublin's study? In which study do you place the most credence? If you have some knowledge of statistical methodology, comment on this question for the benefit of the rest of your class.

4. Discuss with your classmates the meaning of "average" in terms of weight, height, athletic prowess, reading ability, and so forth. Do most people fall close to the average in most areas? Do you feel average in most areas of your life? In which areas do you feel apart from the average? In what ways is *average* a difficult term to define?

Responding Through Writing

1. Does society have instinctive prejudices against overweight people? If so, what are those prejudices? Do you share them? Are those prejudices "bad," or do they help keep people healthy? React to these questions for ten minutes in your journal or notebook.

2. Assume that you have received a letter from your doctor saying that unless you give up the foods you like most and lose 35 pounds, you are in for serious trouble and are at risk for a heart attack or stroke. Write an answer to that letter telling your doctor what you think of his or her advice and what you plan to do.

3. Write the short draft of an essay in which you compare the advantages and disadvantages of being either significantly over-weight or underweight. Make this a serious essay in which you discuss issues of health and social interaction. Use specific examples to illustrate your generalizations.

4. Do the same as asked in item 3, but this time make your comparison amusing, possibly sarcastic, tongue-in-cheek. Choose some new examples.

POLITICS AND THE ENGLISH LANGUAGE

GEORGE ORWELL

George Orwell, the pen name of Eric Blair (1903–1950), is best known for his novels Nineteen Eighty-Four *(1949) and* Animal Farm *(1945) and his essays on language and politics in publications including* London Observer *and the London* Times. *Orwell was born in Bengal, India, and educated at Eton. A great traveler throughout his life, he worked as a dishwasher, private tutor, teacher, and part-time bookstore assistant, among other jobs during his travels, and he fought for the Loyalist forces in the Spanish Civil War. He spent the years 1922 to 1927 serving in the British Colonial Police in Burma. Among Orwell's novels are* Down and Out in Paris and London *(1933),* Burmese Days *(1934), and* Keep the Aspidistra Flying *(1936); his nonfiction works include* Homage to Catalonia *(1938) and* The Road to Wigan Pier *(1937). Orwell once wrote that "when I sit down to write a book, I do not say to myself, 'I am going to produce a work of art.' I write it because there is some lie that I want to expose." Orwell died of tuberculosis at the age of 46 after living in seclusion on the island of Jura off the coast of Scotland. Orwell also wrote the essays "Shooting an Elephant" and "A Hanging," which are included in this book. The following selection was originally published in* Horizon *magazine in April 1946.*

1   Most people who bother with the matter at all would admit that the English language is in a bad way, but it is generally assumed that we cannot by conscious action do anything about it. Our civilization is decadent and our language—so the argument runs— must inevitably share in the general collapse. It follows that any struggle against the abuse of language is a sentimental archaism, like preferring candles to electric light or hansom cabs to aeroplanes. Underneath this lies the half-conscious belief that language is a natural growth and not an instrument which we shape for our own purposes.

2   Now, it is clear that the decline of a language must ultimately have political and economic causes: it is not due simply to the bad influence of this or that individual writer. But an effect can become a cause, reinforcing the original cause and producing the same effect in an intensified form, and so on indefinitely. A man may take to drink because he feels himself to be a failure, and then fail all the more completely because he drinks. It is rather the same thing that is happening to the English language. It becomes ugly and inaccurate because our thoughts are foolish, but the slovenliness of our language makes it easier for us to have foolish thoughts. The point is that the process is reversible. Modern English, especially written English, is full of bad habits which spread by imitation and which can be avoided if one is willing to take the necessary trouble. If one gets rid of these habits one can think more clearly, and to think clearly is a necessary first step towards political regeneration so that the fight against bad English is not frivolous and is not the exclusive concern of professional writers. I will come back to this presently, and I hope that by that time the meaning of what I have said here will have become clearer. Meanwhile, here are five specimens of the English language as it is now habitually written.

3   These five passages have not been picked out because they are especially bad—I could have quoted far worse if I had chosen—but because they illustrate various of the mental vices from which we now suffer. They are a little below the average, but are fairly representative samples. I number them so that I can refer back to them when necessary:

(1) I am not, indeed, sure whether it is not true to say that the Milton who once seemed not unlike a seventeenth-century Shelley had not become, out of an experience ever more bitter in each year, more alien [*sic*] to the founder of that Jesuit sect which nothing could induce him to tolerate.

Professor Harold Laski
(Essay in *Freedom of Expression*).

(2) Above all, we cannot play ducks and drakes with a native battery of idioms which prescribes such egregious collocations of vocables as the basic *put up with* for *tolerate* or *put at a loss* for *bewilder*.

Professor Lancelot Hogben *(Interglossa)*.

(3) On the one side we have the free personality: by definition it is not neurotic, for it has neither conflict nor dream. Its desires, such as they are, are transparent, for they are just what institutional approval keeps in the forefront of consciousness; another institutional pattern would alter their number and intensity; there is little in them that is natural, irreducible, or culturally dangerous. But *on the other side,* the social bond itself is nothing but the mutual reflection of these self-secure integrities. Recall the definition of love. Is not this the very picture of a small academic? Where is there a place in this hall of mirrors for either personality or fraternity?

Essay on Psychology in *Politics* (New York)

(4) All the "best people" from the gentlemen's clubs, and all the frantic fascist captains, united in common hatred of Socialism and bestial horror of the rising tide of the mass revolutionary movement, have turned to acts of provocation, to foul incendiarism, to medieval legends of poisoned wells, to legalize their own destruction of proletarian organizations, and rouse the agitated petty-bourgeoisie to chauvinistic fervor on behalf of the fight against the revolutionary way out of the crisis.

Communist Pamphlet.

(5) If a new spirit *is* to be infused into this old country, there is one thorny and contentious reform which must be tackled, and that is the humanization and galvanization of the B.B.C. Timidity here will bespeak canker and atrophy of the soul. The heart of Britain may be sound and of strong beat, for instance, but the British lion's roar at present is like that of Bottom in Shakespeare's *Midsummer Night's Dream*—as gentle as any sucking dove. A virile new Britain cannot continue indefinitely to be traduced in the eyes or rather ears, of the world by the effete languors of Langham Place, brazenly masquerading as "standard English." When the voice of Britain is heard at nine o'clock, better far and infinitely less ludicrous to hear aitches honestly dropped than the present priggish, inflated, inhibited, school-ma'amish arch braying of blameless bashful mewing maidens!

Letter in Tribune.

4   Each of these passages has faults of its own, but, quite apart from avoidable ugliness, two qualities are common to all of them. The first is staleness of imagery: the other is lack of precision. The writer either has a meaning and cannot express it, or he inadvertently says something else, or he is almost indifferent as to whether his words mean anything or not. This mixture of vagueness and sheer incompetence is the most marked characteristic of modern English prose, and especially of any kind of political writing. As soon as certain topics are raised, the concrete melts into the abstract and no one seems able to think of turns of speech that are not hackneyed: prose consists less and less of *words* chosen for the sake of their meaning, and more and more of *phrases* tacked together like the sections of a prefabricated henhouse. I list below, with notes and examples, various of the tricks by means of which the work of prose-construction is habitually dodged:

Dying Metaphors

5   A newly invented metaphor assists thought by evoking a visual image, while on the other hand a metaphor which is technically "dead" (e.g. *iron resolution*) has in effect reverted to being an ordinary word and can generally be used without loss of vividness. But in between these two classes there is a huge dump of worn-out

metaphors which have lost all evocative power and are merely used because they save people the trouble of inventing phrases for themselves. Examples are: *Ring the changes on, take up the cudgels for, toe the line, ride roughshod over, stand shoulder to shoulder with, play into the hands of, no axe to grind, grist to the mill, fishing in troubled waters, rift within the lute, on the order of the day, Achilles' heel, swan song, hotbed.* Many of these are used without knowledge of their meaning (what is a "rift," for instance?), and incompatible metaphors are frequently mixed, a sure sign that the writer is not interested in what he is saying. Some metaphors now current have been twisted out of their original meaning without those who use them even being aware of the fact. For example, *toe the line* is sometimes written *tow the line.* Another example is *the hammer and the anvil,* now always used with the implication that the anvil gets the worst of it. In real life it is always the anvil that breaks the hammer, never the other way about; a writer who stopped to think what he was saying would be aware of this, and would avoid perverting the original phrase.

Operators or Verbal False Limbs

These save the trouble of picking out appropriate verbs and nouns, and at the same time pad each sentence with extra syllables which give it an appearance of symmetry. Characteristic phrases are *render inoperative, militate against, make contact with, be subjected to, give rise to, give grounds for, have the effect of, play a leading part (role) in, make itself felt, take effect, exhibit a tendency to, serve the purpose of, etc., etc.* The keynote is the elimination of simple verbs. Instead of being a single word, such as *break, stop, spoil, mend, kill,* a verb becomes a *phrase,* made up of a noun or adjective tacked on to some general-purpose verb such as *prove, serve, form, play, render.* In addition, the passive voice is wherever possible used in preference to the active, and noun constructions are used instead of gerunds *(by examination of* instead of *by examining).* The range of verbs is further cut down by means of the *-ize* and *de-* formations, and the banal statements are given an appearance of profundity by means of the *not un-* formation. Simple conjunctions and prepositions are replaced by such phrases as *with respect to, having regard to, the fact that, by dint of, in view of, in the interests of, on the hypothesis that;* and the ends of sentences are saved from anticlimax by such resounding common-places as *greatly to be desired, cannot be left out of account, a development to be expected in the near future, deserving of serious consideration, brought to a satisfactory conclusion,* and so on and so forth.

Pretentious Diction

7   Words like *phenomenon, element, individual* (as noun), *objective, categorical, effective, virtual, basic, primary, promote, constitute, exhibit, exploit, utilize, eliminate, liquidate,* are used to dress up simple statements and give an air of scientific impartiality to biased judgments. Adjectives like *epoch-making, epic, historic, unforgettable, triumphant, age-old, inevitable, inexorable, veritable,* are used to dignify the sordid processes of international politics, while writing that aims at glorifying war usually takes on an archaic color, its characteristic words being: *realm, throne, chariot, mailed fist, trident, sword, shield, buckler, banner, jackboot, clarion.* Foreign words and expressions such as *cul de sac, ancien régime, deus ex machina, mutatis mutandis, status quo, gleichschaltung, weltanschauung,* are used to give an air of culture and elegance. Except for the useful abbreviations *i.e., e.g.,* and *etc.,* there is no real need for any of the hundreds of foreign phrases now current in English. Bad writers, and especially scientific, political and sociological writers, are nearly always haunted by the notion that Latin or Greek words are grander than Saxon ones, and unnecessary words like *expedite, ameliorate, predict, extraneous, deracinated, clandestine, subaqueous* and hundreds of others constantly gain ground from their Anglo-Saxon opposite numbers.[1] The jargon peculiar to Marxist writing (*hyena, hangman, cannibal, petty bourgeois, these gentry, lacquey, flunkey, mad dog, White Guard,* etc.) consists largely of words and phrases translated from Russian, German or French; but the normal way of coining a new word is to use a Latin or Greek root with the appropriate affix and, where necessary, the *-ize* formation. It is often easier to make up words of this kind (*deregionalize, impermissible, extramarital, nonfragmentary* and so forth) than to think up the English words that will cover one's meaning. The result, in general, is an increase in slovenliness and vagueness.

Meaningless Words

8   In certain kinds of writing, particularly in art criticism and literary criticism, it is normal to come across long passages which

---

1. An interesting illustration of this is the way in which the English flower names which were in use till very recently are being ousted by Greek ones, *snapdragon* becoming *antirrhinum, forget-me-not* becoming *myosotis,* etc. It is hard to see any practical reason for this change of fashion: it is probably due to an instinctive turning-away from the more homely word and a vague feeling that the Greek word is scientific.

are almost completely lacking in meaning.[2] Words like *romantic, plastic, values, human, dead, sentimental, natural, vitality,* as used in art criticism, are strictly meaningless, in the sense that they not only do not point to any discoverable object, but are hardly ever expected to do so by the reader. When one critic writes, "The outstanding feature of Mr. X's work is its living quality," while another writes, "The immediately striking thing about Mr. X's work is its peculiar deadness," the reader accepts this as a simple difference of opinion. If words like *black* and *white* were involved, instead of the jargon words *dead* and *living,* he would see at once that language was being used in an improper way. Many political words are similarly abused. The word *Fascism* has now no meaning except in so far as it signifies "something not desirable." The words *democracy, socialism, freedom, patriotic, realistic, justice,* have each of them several different meanings which cannot be reconciled with one another. In the case of a word like *democracy,* not only is there no agreed definition, but the attempt to make one is resisted from all sides. It is almost universally felt that when we call a country democratic we are praising it: consequently the defenders of every kind of régime claim that it is a democracy, and fear that they might have to stop using the word if it were tied down to any one meaning. Words of this kind are often used in a consciously dishonest way. That is, the person who uses them has his own private definition, but allows his hearer to think he means something quite different. Statements like *Marshal Pétain was a true patriot, The Soviet Press is the freest in the world, The Catholic Church is opposed to persecution,* are almost always made with intent to deceive. Other words used in variable meanings, in most cases more or less dishonestly, are: *class, totalitarian, science, progressive, reactionary, bourgeois, equality.*

Now that I have made this catalogue of swindles and perversions, let me give another example of the kind of writing that they lead to. This time it must of its nature be an imaginary one. I am going to translate a passage of good English into modern English of the worst sort. Here is a well-known verse from *Ecclesiastes:* 9

"I returned and saw under the sun, that the race is not to the swift, nor the battle to the strong, neither yet bread to the wise, nor 10

---

2. Example: "Comfort's catholicity of perception and image, strangely Whitmanesque in range, almost the exact opposite in aesthetic compulsion, continues to evoke that trembling atmospheric accumulative hinting at a cruel, an inexorably serene timelessness. . . . Wrey Gardiner scores by aiming at simple bull's-eyes with precision. Only they are not so simple, and through this contented sadness runs more than the surface bittersweet of resignation." *(Poetry Quarterly.)*

yet riches to men of understanding, nor yet favour to men of skill; but time and chance happeneth to them all."

11   Here it is in modern English:

12   "Objective consideration of contemporary phenomena compels the conclusion that success or failure in competitive activities exhibits no tendency to be commensurate with innate capacity, but that a considerable element of the unpredictable must invariably be taken into account."

13   This is a parody, but not a very gross one. Exhibit (3), above, for instance, contains several patches of the same kind of English. It will be seen that I have not made full translation. The beginning and ending of the sentence follow the original meaning fairly closely, but in the middle the concrete illustrations—race, battle, bread—dissolve into the vague phrase "success or failure in competitive activities." This had to be so, because no modern writer of the kind I am discussing—no one capable of using phrases like "objective consideration of contemporary phenomena"—would ever tabulate his thoughts in that precise and detailed way. The whole tendency of modern prose is away from concreteness. Now analyse these two sentences a little more closely. The first contains forty-nine words but only sixty syllables, and all its words are those of everyday life. The second contains thirty-eight words of ninety syllables: eighteen of its words are from Latin roots, and one from Greek. The first sentence contains six vivid images, and only one phrase ("time and chance") that could be called vague. The second contains not a single fresh, arresting phrase, and in spite of its ninety syllables it gives only a shortened version of the meaning contained in the first. Yet without a doubt it is the second kind of sentence that is gaining ground in modern English. I do not want to exaggerate. This kind of writing is not yet universal, and outcrops of simplicity will occur here and there in the worst-written page. Still, if you or I were told to write a few lines on the uncertainty of human fortunes, we should probably come much nearer to my imaginary sentence than to the one from *Ecclesiastes*.

14   As I have tried to show, modern writing at its worst does not consist in picking out words for the sake of their meaning and inventing images in order to make the meaning clearer. It consists in gumming together long strips of words which have already been set in order by someone else, and making the results presentable by sheer humbug. The attraction of this way of writing is that it is easy. It is easier—even quicker, once you have the habit—to say *In my opinion it is not an unjustifiable assumption that* than to say *I think*.

If you use ready-made phrases, you not only don't have to hunt about for words; you also don't have to bother with the rhythms of your sentences, since these phrases are generally so arranged as to be more or less euphonious. When you are composing in a hurry—when you are dictating to a stenographer, for instance, or making a public speech—it is natural to fall into a pretentious, Latinized style. Tags like *a consideration which we should do well to bear in mind* or *a conclusion to which all of us would readily assent* will save many a sentence from coming down with a bump. By using stale metaphors, similes and idioms, you save much mental effort, at the cost of leaving your meaning vague, not only for your reader but for yourself. This is the significance of mixed metaphors. The sole aim of a metaphor is to call up a visual image. When these images clash—as in *The Fascist octopus has sung its swan song, the jackboot is thrown into the melting pot*—it can be taken as certain that the writer is not seeing a mental image of the objects he is naming: in other words he is not really thinking. Look again at the examples I gave at the beginning of this essay. Professor Laski (1) uses five negatives in fifty-three words. One of these is superfluous, making nonsense of the whole passage, and in addition there is the slip *alien* for *akin,* making further nonsense, and several avoidable pieces of clumsiness which increase the general vagueness. Professor Hogben (2) plays ducks and drakes with a battery which is able to write prescriptions, and, while disapproving of the everyday phrase *put up with,* is unwilling to look *egregious* up in the dictionary and see what it means; (3) if one takes an uncharitable attitude towards it, is simply meaningless; probably one could work out its intended meaning by reading the whole of the article in which it occurs. In (4), the writer knows more or less what he wants to say, but an accumulation of stale phrases chokes him like tea leaves blocking a sink. In (5), words and meaning have almost parted company. People who write in this manner usually have a general emotional meaning—they dislike one thing and want to express solidarity with another—but they are not interested in the detail of what they are saying. A scrupulous writer, in every sentence that he writes, will ask himself at least four questions, thus: What am I trying to say? What words will express it? What image or idiom will make it clearer? Is this image fresh enough to have an effect? And he will probably ask himself two more: Could I put it more shortly? Have I said anything that is avoidably ugly? But you are not obliged to go to all this trouble. You can shirk it by simply throwing your mind open and letting the ready-made phrases come crowding in. They will construct your sentences for you—even think your thoughts for you, to a certain extent—and at need they will perform the important service of partially concealing your meaning even from yourself. It is at this point that the special connection between politics and the debasement of language becomes clear.

15   In our time it is broadly true that political writing is bad writing. Where it is not true, it will generally be found that the writer is some kind of rebel, expressing his private opinions and not a "party line." Orthodoxy, of whatever color, seems to demand a lifeless, imitative style. The political dialects to be found in pamphlets, leading articles, manifestos, White Papers and the speeches of under-secretaries do, of course, vary from party to party, but they are all alike in that one almost never finds in them a fresh, vivid, home-made turn of speech. When one watches some tired hack on the platform mechanically repeating the familiar phrases—*bestial atrocities, iron heel, bloodstained tyranny, free peoples of the world, stand shoulder to shoulder*—one often has a curious feeling that one is not watching a live human being but some kind of dummy: a feeling which suddenly becomes stronger at moments when the light catches the speaker's spectacles and turns them into black discs which seem to have no eyes behind them. And this is not altogether fanciful. A speaker who uses that kind of phraseology has gone some distance towards turning himself into a machine. The appropriate noises are coming out of his larynx, but his brain is not involved as it would be if he were choosing his words for himself. If the speech he is making is one that he is accustomed to make over and over again, he may be almost unconscious of what he is saying, as one is when one utters the responses in church. And this reduced state of consciousness, if not indispensable, is at any rate favorable to political conformity.

16   In our time, political speech and writing are largely the defence of the indefensible. Things like the continuance of British rule in India, the Russian purges and deportations, the dropping of the atom bombs on Japan, can indeed be defended, but only by arguments which are too brutal for most people to face, and which do not square with the professed aims of political parties. Thus political language has to consist largely of euphemism, question-begging and sheer cloudy vagueness. Defenceless villages are bombarded from the air, the inhabitants driven out into the countryside, the cattle machine-gunned, the huts set on fire with incendiary bullets: this is called *pacification*. Millions of peasants are robbed of their farms and sent trudging along the roads with no more than they can carry: this

is called *transfer of population* or *rectification of frontiers*. People are imprisoned for years without trial, or shot in the back of the neck or sent to die of scurvy in Arctic lumber camps: this is called *elimination of unreliable elements*. Such phraseology is needed if one wants to name things without calling up mental pictures of them. Consider for instance some comfortable English professor defending Russian totalitarianism. He cannot say outright, "I believe in killing off your opponents when you can get good results by doing so." Probably, therefore, he will say something like this:

"While freely conceding that the Soviet régime exhibits certain features which the humanitarian may be inclined to deplore, we must, I think, agree that a certain curtailment of the right to political opposition is an unavoidable concomitant of transitional periods, and that the rigors which the Russian people have been called upon to undergo have been amply justified in the sphere of concrete achievement."   17

The inflated style is itself a kind of euphemism. A mass of Latin   18
words falls upon the facts like soft snow, blurring the outlines and covering up all the details. The great enemy of clear language is insincerity. When there is a gap between one's real and one's declared aims, one turns as it were instinctively to long words and exhausted idioms, like a cuttlefish squirting out ink. In our age there is no such thing as "keeping out of politics." All issues are political issues, and politics itself is a mass of lies, evasions, folly, hatred and schizophrenia. When the general atmosphere is bad, language must suffer. I should expect to find—this is a guess which I have not sufficient knowledge to verify—that the German, Russian and Italian languages have all deteriorated in the last ten or fifteen years, as a result of dictatorship.

But if thought corrupts language, language can also corrupt   19
thought. A bad usage can spread by tradition and imitation, even among people who should and do know better. The debased language that I have been discussing is in some ways very convenient. Phrases like *a not unjustifiable assumption, leaves much to be desired, would serve no good purpose, a consideration which we should do well to bear in mind,* are a continuous temptation, a packet of aspirins always at one's elbow. Look back through this essay, and for certain you will find that I have again and again committed the very faults I am protesting against. By this morning's post I have received a pamphlet dealing with conditions in Germany. The author tells me that he "felt impelled" to write it. I open it at random, and here is almost the first sentence that I see: "[The Allies] have an opportu-

nity not only of achieving a radical transformation of Germany's social and political structure in such a way as to avoid a nationalistic reaction in Germany itself, but at the same time of laying the foundations of a cooperative and unified Europe." You see, he "feels impelled" to write—feels, presumably, that he has something new to say—and yet his words, like cavalry horses answering the bugle, group themselves automatically into the familiar dreary pattern. This invasion of one's mind by ready-made phrases *(lay the foundations, achieve a radical transformation)* can only be prevented if one is constantly on guard against them, and every such phrase anesthetizes a portion of one's brain.

20   I said earlier that the decadence of our language is probably curable. Those who deny this would argue, if they produced an argument at all, that language merely reflects existing social conditions, and that we cannot influence its development by any direct tinkering with words and constructions. So far as the general tone or spirit of a language goes, this may be true, but it is not true in detail. Silly words and expressions have often disappeared, not through any evolutionary process but owing to the conscious action of a minority. Two recent examples were *explore every avenue* and *leave no stone unturned,* which were killed by the jeers of a few journalists. There is a long list of flyblown metaphors which could similarly be got rid of if enough people would interest themselves in the job; and it should also be possible to laugh the *not un-* formation out of existence,[3] to reduce the amount of Latin and Greek in the average sentence, to drive out foreign phrases and strayed scientific words, and, in general, to make pretentiousness unfashionable. But all these are minor points. The defence of the English language implies more than this, and perhaps it is best to start by saying what it does *not* imply.

21   To begin with it has nothing to do with archaism, with the salvaging of obsolete words and turns of speech, or with the setting up of a "standard English" which must never be departed from. On the contrary, it is especially concerned with the scrapping of every word or idiom which has outworn its usefulness. It has nothing to do with correct grammar and syntax, which are of no importance so long as one makes one's meaning clear, or with the avoidance of Americanisms, or with having what is called a "good prose style." On the other hand it is not concerned with fake simplicity and the attempt to make written English colloquial. Nor does it even imply

3. One can cure oneself of the *not un-* formation by memorizing this sentence: A not unblack dog was chasing a not unsmall rabbit across a not ungreen field.

in every case preferring the Saxon word to the Latin one, though it does imply using the fewest and shortest words that will cover one's meaning. What is above all needed is to let the meaning choose the word, and not the other way about. In prose, the worst thing one can do with words is to surrender to them. When you think of a concrete object, you think wordlessly, and then, if you want to describe the thing you have been visualizing you probably hunt about till you find the exact words that seem to fit it. When you think of something abstract you are more inclined to use words from the start, and unless you make a conscious effort to prevent it, the existing dialect will come rushing in and do the job for you, at the expense of blurring or even changing your meaning. Probably it is better to put off using words as long as possible and get one's meaning as clear as one can through pictures or sensations. Afterwards one can choose—not simply *accept*— the phrases that will best cover the meaning, and then switch round and decide what impression one's words are likely to make on another person. This last effort of the mind cuts out all stale or mixed images, all prefabricated phrases, needless repetitions, and humbug and vagueness generally. But one can often be in doubt about the effect of a word or a phrase, and one needs rules that one can rely on when instinct fails. I think the following rules will cover most cases:

  i. Never use a metaphor, simile or other figure of speech which you are used to seeing in print.
  ii. Never use a long word where a short one will do.
  iii. If it is possible to cut a word out, always cut it out.
  iv. Never use the passive where you can use the active.
  v. Never use a foreign phrase, a scientific word or a jargon word if you can think of an everyday English equivalent.
  vi. Break any of these rules sooner than say anything outright barbarous.

These rules sound elementary, and so they are, but they demand a deep change of attitude in anyone who has grown used to writing in the style now fashionable. One could keep all of them and still write bad English, but one could not write the kind of stuff that I quoted in those five specimens at the beginning of this article.

I have not here been considering the literary use of language, 22 but merely language as an instrument for expressing and not for concealing or preventing thought. Stuart Chase and others have come near to claiming that all abstract words are meaningless, and have used this as a pretext for advocating a kind of political quietism. Since you don't know what Fascism is, how can you struggle against Fascism? One need not swallow such absurdities as this, but one ought to recognize that the present political chaos is connected with the decay of language, and that one can probably bring about some improvement by starting at the verbal end. If you simplify your English, you are freed from the worst follies of orthodoxy. You cannot speak any of the necessary dialects, and when you make a stupid remark its stupidity will be obvious, even to yourself. Political language—and with variations this is true of all political parties, from Conservatives to Anarchists—is designed to make lies sound truthful and murder respectable, and to give an appearance of solidity to pure wind. One cannot change this all in a moment, but one can at least change one's own habits, and from time to time one can even, if one jeers loudly enough, send some worn-out and useless phrase—some *jackboot, Achilles' heel, hotbed, melting pot, acid test, veritable inferno* or other lump of verbal refuse—into the dustbin where it belongs.

Reading Critically

1. "What is above all needed," writes Orwell in paragraph 21, "is to let the meaning choose the word, and not the other way about." Give at least one example of how you can let words choose the meaning when you are writing. Orwell goes on to write in this same paragraph that "Probably it is better to put off using words as long as possible and get one's meaning as clear as one can through pictures or sensations." Given the influence of television and television images on our lives (especially our political lives), is Orwell's advice still sound? How would you change this advice to reflect our television-image environment? How do images on television "choose their meanings"?

2. What audience do you think Orwell had in mind for his essay? What does Orwell assume about his audience? If Orwell were to publish his essay for the first time today, what publications do you think would publish it? Discuss with your classmates how

Orwell would have to change his essay to reflect the influence of modern media.

3. Throughout his essay, Orwell gives many examples of bad writing. Why do you think he concentrates on bad examples rather than good ones? Find at least two examples of contemporary writing (from magazines, newspapers, or other sources) that Orwell would consider bad and explain to your classmates why the writing is bad.

4. Although this essay by Orwell is considered a "classic," this is probably the first time you have read it. Why do you think it continues to be reprinted and read? What parts of the essay seem out of date to you? What parts of the essay still offer sound advice for today? Discuss with your classmates what you think Orwell would say about the language of politicians today.

Responding Through Writing

1. "Look back through this essay," writes Orwell in paragraph 19, "and for certain you will find that I have again and again committed the very faults I am protesting against." List some of the faults Orwell claims he has committed in his essay. Compare your list with the lists drawn up by your classmates. How do your lists agree and disagree?

2. If you are keeping a journal or notebook in this course, write in it for five to ten minutes on the kind of language (the language used in advertising, the language used by politicians, etc.) that concerns you the most. What exactly is it that concerns you, and what do you think you can do about it? Compare your comments with those of your classmates.

3. Collect at least one example of bad writing for each of Orwell's four categories: "dying metaphors, operators or verbal false limbs, pretentious diction, and meaningless words." Write a

paragraph on each example, explaining how it can be rewritten into clear prose. Discuss your examples and revisions with your classmates, and as a group compile a list of the ten worst examples.

4. In paragraphs 10 through 12 Orwell rewrites a famous passage from the Bible. Take a similarly well-known piece of short prose and rewrite it the way Orwell did. Did you have any trouble rewriting the passage? Why is it easy or difficult to do such a rewriting? Compare your rewritten passage with those of your classmates.

THE WEAPON

FREDRIC BROWN

Fredric Brown (b. 1906) attended both Hanover College in Indiana and The University of Cincinnati, where he majored in classical literature. After college, Brown worked as a proofreader and wrote detective stories on the side. His first published story, "The Moon for a Nickel" (1938), gained him popular acclaim, and encouraged by this, Brown began to write regularly. Today, he is perhaps best known for his detective stories, collections of which include Mostly Murder *(1953) and* The Shaggy Dog and Other Murders *(1963), but his works of science fiction have also gained him much praise. Brown's science fiction novels include* What Mad Universe *(1949),* Martians, Go Home *(1955), and* The Mind Thing *(1961). The following story first appeared in* Astounding Science Fiction *magazine in April 1951.*

The room was quiet in the dimness of early evening. Dr. James 1
Graham, key scientist of a very important project, sat in his favorite
chair, thinking. It was so still that he could hear the turning of pages
in the next room as his son leafed through a picture book.

Often Graham did his best work, his most creative thinking, 2
under these circumstances, sitting alone in an unlighted room in his
own apartment after the day's regular work. But tonight his mind
would not work constructively. Mostly he thought about his men-

tally arrested son—his only son—in the next room. The thoughts were loving thoughts, not the bitter anguish he had felt years ago when he had first learned of the boy's condition. The boy was happy; wasn't that the main thing? And to how many men is given a child who will always be a child, who will not grow up to leave him? Certainly that was rationalization, but what is wrong with rationalization when— The doorbell rang.

3   Graham rose and turned on lights in the almost-dark room before he went through the hallway to the door. He was not annoyed; tonight, at this moment, almost any interruption to his thoughts was welcome.

4   He opened the door. A stranger stood there; he said, "Dr. Graham? My name is Niemand; I'd like to talk to you. May I come in a moment?"

5   Graham looked at him. He was a small man, nondescript, obviously harmless—possibly a reporter or an insurance agent.

6   But it didn't matter what he was. Graham found himself saying, "Of course. Come in, Mr. Niemand." A few minutes of conversation, he justified himself by thinking, might divert his thoughts and clear his mind.

7   "Sit down," he said, in the living room. "Care for a drink?"

8   Niemand said, "No, thank you." He sat in the chair; Graham sat on the sofa.

9   The small man interlocked his fingers; he leaned forward. He said, "Dr. Graham, you are the man whose scientific work is more likely than that of any other man to end the human race's chance for survival."

10   A crackpot, Graham thought. Too late now he realized that he should have asked the man's business before admitting him. It would be an embarrassing interview—he disliked being rude, yet only rudeness was effective.

11   "Dr. Graham, the weapon on which you are working—"

12   The visitor stopped and turned his head as the door that led to a bedroom opened and a boy of fifteen came in. The boy didn't notice Niemand; he ran to Graham.

13   "Daddy, will you read to me now?" The boy of fifteen laughed the sweet laughter of a child of four.

14   Graham put an arm around the boy. He looked at his visitor, wondering whether he had known about the boy. From the lack of surprise on Niemand's face, Graham felt sure he had known.

15   "Harry"—Graham's voice was warm with affection—"Daddy's busy. Just for a little while. Go back to your room; I'll come and read to you soon."

"Chicken Little? You'll read me *Chicken Little?"*   16

"If you wish. Now run along. Wait. Harry, this is Mr. Nie-   17
mand."

The boy smiled bashfully at the visitor. Niemand said, "Hi,   18
Harry," and smiled back at him, holding out his hand. Graham,
watching, was sure now that Niemand had known: the smile and
the gesture were for the boy's mental age, not his physical one.

The boy took Niemand's hand. For a moment it seemed that   19
he was going to climb into Niemand's lap, and Graham pulled him
back gently. He said, "Go to your room now, Harry."

The boy skipped back into his bedroom, not closing the door.   20

Niemand's eyes met Graham's and he said, "I like him," with   21
obvious sincerity. He added, "I hope that what you're going to read
to him will always be true."

Graham didn't understand. Niemand said, *"Chicken Little,* I   22
mean. It's a fine story—but may *Chicken Little* always be wrong
about the sky falling down."

Graham suddenly had liked Niemand when Niemand had   23
shown liking for the boy. Now he remembered that he must close
the interview quickly. He rose, in dismissal.

He said, "I fear you're wasting your time and mine, Mr.   24
Niemand. I know all the arguments, everything you can say I've
heard a thousand times. Possibly there is truth in what you believe,
but it does not concern me. I'm a scientist, and only a scientist. Yes,
it is public knowledge that I am working on a weapon, a rather
ultimate one. But, for me personally, that is only a by-product of
the fact that I am advancing science. I have thought it through, and
I have found that that is my only concern."

"But, Dr. Graham, is humanity *ready* for an ultimate   25
weapon?"

Graham frowned. "I have told you my point of view, Mr.   26
Niemand."

Niemand rose slowly from the chair. He said, "Very well, if   27
you do not choose to discuss it, I'll say no more." He passed a
hand across his forehead. "I'll leave, Dr. Graham. I wonder,
though . . . may I change my mind about the drink you offered
me?"

Graham's irritation faded. He said, "Certainly. Will whisky   28
and water do?"

"Admirably."   29

Graham excused himself and went into the kitchen. He got the   30
decanter of whisky, another of water, ice cubes, glasses.

When he returned to the living room, Niemand was just   31

leaving the boy's bedroom. He heard Niemand's "Good night, Harry," and Harry's happy " 'Night, Mr. Niemand."

32   Graham made drinks. A little later, Niemand declined a second one and started to leave.

33   Niemand said, "I took the liberty of bringing a small gift to your son, doctor. I gave it to him while you were getting the drinks for us. I hope you'll forgive me."

34   "Of course. Thank you. Good night."

35   Graham closed the door; he walked through the living room into Harry's room. He said, "All right, Harry. Now I'll read to—"

36   There was sudden sweat on his forehead, but he forced his face and his voice to be calm as he stepped to the side of the bed. "May I see that, Harry?" When he had it safely, his hands shook as he examined it.

37   He thought, *only a madman would give a loaded revolver to an idiot.*

Reading Critically

1. What do you think of the "rationalization" in paragraph 2? Are there people who might like to have "permanent" children? Have you ever wanted to permanently remain at one stage of your life? Which stage? Why?

2. Would you or your classmates like to have someone else remain permanently at a specific age, a boyfriend or girlfriend, for example, even if you had to continue to grow older? What would be the advantages and the disadvantages?

3. Why does Mr. Niemand give Harry the loaded revolver? Is his action dangerous, symbolic, or both?

4. Is this story successful because of its simplicity, or does that simplicity mask important complexities about the story's theme?

Responding Through Writing

1. Why does Brown make Mr. Niemand a very polite character? Is the politeness analogous in some way to Graham's belief in himself as a rational scientist? Write a short "rational" response to the story. Assume that your audience is a group of atomic scientists.

2. Take the opposite tack from item 1 and write a reaction to the story for an audience of nuclear protesters.

3. Write a few paragraphs discussing the relevance of *Chicken Little* to the story.

4. Discuss in a short essay the significance of the word *madman* in the final line of the story.

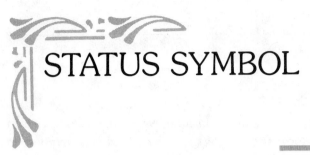

STATUS SYMBOL

MARI EVANS

Mari Evans published her first book of poetry Where Is All the Music?
*in 1968, and with that collection established herself as a contemporary
American poet. During the following decade, Evans taught Black Studies
at Purdue University, Washington University, and Cornell University,
among others. Evans has produced, directed, and written for television's*
The Black Experience *and published numerous essays, poems, and short
stories in such publications as* Black Scholar *and* Black Books Bulletin.
Her books of poetry include I Am a Black Woman *(1970) and* Night-
star *(1981). The following poem was first published in* I Am a Black
Woman.

   i
Have Arrived
   i
  am the
5 New Negro

   i
am the result of
President Lincoln
World War I

and Paris   10
the
Red Ball Express
white drinking fountains
sitdowns and
sit-ins   15
Federal Troops
Marches on Washington
    and
prayer meetings . . .

today   20
They hired me
it
is a status
job . . .

along   25
with my papers
They
gave me my
Status Symbol
the   30
key
to the
White . . . Locked . . .
John

Reading Critically

1. Where has Evans "Arrived"? Is she speaking only about herself or about minorities in general? Have you ever felt that you had "arrived"? What words might substitute for *arrived?* Discuss with your classmates.

2. Do you think that efforts by business to recruit minorities are really sincere attempts to help eliminate racism, or are they

cynical efforts that cover up racism with window dressing? Discuss with your classmates.

3. Why is Evans's position a "status" job? What do you think the job might entail? Try with your classmates to imagine Evans in a variety of employment contexts, and discuss the kinds of jobs she might be offered.

4. Does the thin column in which the poem visually appears add anything to its meaning? Why, in more than one sense, is the John "White"?

Responding Through Writing

1. Is this poem an accurate reflection of contemporary life, or are the ideas and reactions expressed by Evans out-of-date? Write a few paragraphs in your journal or notebook applying the concerns of the poem to contemporary conditions.

2. Check the historical references in the poem. Why, for example, does Evans mention Paris? How were blacks treated in Paris (as compared to in America) in the 1920s and 1930s? What was the "Red Ball Express" of World War II? Make a list of these references and write a few sentences discussing each in terms of the poem's themes.

3. Do you sense overstatement in the poem? Do the images adequately develop Evans's point? Does she overstate her case in any particular passage? Write two or three paragraphs in response to these questions.

4. Why does Evans use a lowercase *i?* In what other ways does she alternate between capital and small letters to get her point across? Rewrite the poem in the form of a prose paragraph, according to conventional grammar and usage rules. What is lost? What is gained?

PART VII

DEFINITION

For most people, the word *definition* immediately brings to mind the dictionary. If we don't know what a word means, it's nice to think that we can look up the meaning in a book. Actually, dictionary definitions are very limited. While a good dictionary might give you a fair idea of what a Scottish kilt looks like or how a penguin moves around, it simply cannot adequately define how the Federal Reserve System works or what justice is. To define abstract ideas or to explain the functions of complex systems, we have to go beyond the dictionary.

Why, as writers, do we need to make definitions? One writing teacher we know thinks the need for definition so important that at the beginning of each semester he gives his students this assignment:

> In a 500-word essay, discuss the relationship between socialism and the American way of life.

In response to this assignment, students invariably begin their essays with sentences like these:

> Socialism is completely alien to the American way of life.
> Socialism is compatible with the American way of life.

The point of view expressed in these sentences is not important for our discussion. What is important is that both writers have failed to define what they mean by the vague term *socialism* and that nebulous phrase *the American way of life*. The word *socialism* could refer to widely differing social systems, from those of the democratic societies of Scandinavia and France to those of the restrictive regimes of the Soviet Union and Eastern Europe. There are so many "ways of life" in America that the phrase *American way of life* defies definition. To respond adequately to the assignment, writers would have to specify exactly the sense in which they use the term *socialism,* and they would have to specify as well which aspects of life in America they wished to discuss.

To write intelligent essays on this topic, writers would have to define their terms. For example:

> Socialism, as reflected in the state-run economies of Eastern Europe, is alien to the American tradition of individual economic initiative.

or

> Socialism, defined in a broad sense as government intervention in the economy to help the poor, is an extension of a long-standing tradition of mutual assistance among Americans.

In recent American elections, the terms *conservative* and *liberal* were used both to praise some candidates and to discredit others. In some instances, the people using these words defined them in concrete ways; in many instances, however, these words were purposely left undefined so that they could be used in vague and misleading ways. "Conservatives" were sometimes painted as being inhumane, of not caring about the poor and homeless, while "liberals" were sometimes painted as being soft on crime and national defense. While it is perfectly possible that some "conservatives" are in fact unsympathetic to the poor, and while it is equally possible that some "liberals" feel sorrier for criminals than for victims of crime, it is equally possible (and in all probability more likely) that the majority of "conservatives" do care about their poorer neighbors and that the majority of "liberals" want to defend their country and to stop crime. The floating of undefined terms like *conservative, liberal, reactionary, radical,* and so forth obscures the real positions on which a candidate should stand or fall.

Types of Definition

Most definitions by their nature are imperfect, so writers use them in a *provisional* way. The definitions of *socialism* mentioned above are not meant to be the last word on the subject, but only to signal that a potentially ambiguous term is being used in a specific way. Thus, while your definitions should be thoughtful and accurate, they do not have to be exhaustive. Definitions are really road signs to tell your readers what you mean. Good road signs are never cluttered, and they should point the way clearly.

There are a variety of ways to approach writing clear definitions:

1. *Logical definition* distinguishes an item from others like it. A beret is a cap that is flat, round, and usually made of felt. Plague is a disease that is a persistent epidemic. A friend is a person to whom we feel close.

2. *Definition by negation* says what something is not. FM radio is the opposite of AM. Chinese is not at all like English. A friend won't let you down.

3. *Operational definition* tells how something works or what it is used for. A rolling pin is for flattening dough. A Dutch door lets the outside air in but keeps animals out. A friend will be there when you need her.

4. *Definition by description* mentions some of the observable attributes of an item. A penguin is a bird with short wings and webbed feet. A clarinet is a long, black woodwind instrument with a flare at the end. A friend is someone who really talks to you.

5. *Definition by metaphor* compares one thing to another. War is hell. The Midwest is America's breadbasket. A friend is one's greatest treasure.

6. *Definition by quotation* uses the well-put words of others to define:
   "Old men are children for a second time."—Aristophanes
   "Ambition, the soldier's virtue."—Shakespeare
   "A fool at forty is a fool indeed."—Edward Young

Definition and Your Audience

An apparently minor point that writers often overlook is the requirement to suit definitions to particular audiences. An English person, for example, would want to stop and define what he or she meant by "tea" when writing for Americans, but would certainly not to do so for an English audience. An audience of foreigners unfamiliar with American laws and traditions would expect an American writer to define the words *unconstitutional, Republican, midwesterner,* and so forth. Most Americans, on the other hand, would become bored and possibly annoyed if a writer continually stopped to define or explain such generally well-known terms. The expression *prime number* would have to be defined for a nonspecialist audience, but certainly not for an audience of mathematicians. The expression *acceptable level of radiation,* on the other hand, might be used in a general sense without a special definition for a lay audience, but could require a definition for an audience of scientists who might want to know in exact scientific terms what the writer meant by the word. From point to point in almost any piece of writing, decisions have be made about whether to define a term specifically. The most important factor in such decisions is audience. Respect your readers. Do not confuse them with undefined terms, but do not patronize—and alienate—them by defining terms they are likely to know.

The essays in this section are all examples of extended definition; that is, each uses one or more methods of definition, at length, to define its subject. Read and discuss these essays to help you learn, first, how to write extended definitions and, second, how to use the various methods of definition mentioned above.

WHAT IS HAPPINESS?

JOHN CIARDI

John Ciardi (1916–1986), poet, critic, essayist, translator, and teacher, has been copiously praised by other critics for his perception, wit, and writing skill. After receiving degrees from Tufts College and the University of Michigan and serving in the Air Force during the World War II, Ciardi taught at the University of Kansas, Harvard, and Rutgers. He published voluminously and won wide regard for his verse translation of Dante's Divine Comedy. *His book about poetry,* How Does a Poem Mean? *became a standard college text. Apart from his many honors and important professional positions (poetry editor of* Saturday Review, *director of the* Bread Loaf Writers' Conference), *Ciardi perhaps reached his widest audience during the last years of his life with his weekly lecture about the history of words on* Morning Edition *of National Public Radio. The following essay originally appeared in* Saturday Review *in 1964.*

The right to pursue happiness is issued to Americans with their
birth certificates, but no one seems quite sure which way it ran. It
may be we are issued a hunting license but offered no game. Jona-
than Swift seemed to think so when he attacked the idea of happiness
as "the possession of being well-deceived," the felicity of being "a
fool among knaves." For Swift saw society as Vanity Fair, the land
of false goals.

1

2   It is, of course, un-American to think in terms of fools and knaves. We do, however, seem to be dedicated to the idea of buying our way to happiness. We shall all have made it to Heaven when we possess enough.

3   And at the same time the forces of American commercialism are hugely dedicated to making us deliberately unhappy. Advertising is one of our major industries, and advertising exists not to satisfy desires but to create them—and to create them faster than any man's budget can satisfy them. For that matter, our whole economy is based on a dedicated insatiability. We are taught that to possess is to be happy, and then we are made to want. We are even told it is our duty to want. It was only a few years ago, to cite a single example, that car dealers across the country were flying banners that read "You Auto Buy Now." They were calling upon Americans, as an act approaching patriotism, to buy at once, with money they did not have, automobiles they did not really need, and which they would be required to grow tired of by the time the next year's models were released.

4   Or look at any of the women's magazines. There, as Bernard DeVoto once pointed out, advertising begins as poetry in the front pages and ends as pharmacopoeia and therapy in the back pages. The poetry of the front matter is the dream of perfect beauty. This is the baby skin that must be hers. These, the flawless teeth. This, the perfumed breath she must exhale. This, the sixteen-year-old figure she must display at forty, at fifty, at sixty, and forever.

5   Once past the vaguely uplifting fiction and feature articles, the reader finds the other face of the dream in the back matter. This is the harness into which Mother must strap herself in order to display that perfect figure. These, the chin straps she must sleep in. This is the salve that restores all, this is her laxative, these are the tablets that melt away fat, these are the hormones of perpetual youth, these are the stockings that hide varicose veins.

6   Obviously no half-sane person can be completely persuaded either by such poetry or by such pharmacopoeia and orthopedics. Yet someone is obviously trying to buy the dream as offered and spending billions every year in the attempt. Clearly the happiness-market is not running out of customers, but what is it trying to buy?

7   The idea "happiness," to be sure, will not sit still for easy definition: the best one can do is to try to set some extremes to the idea and then work in toward the middle. To think of happiness as acquisitive and competitive will do to set the materialistic extreme. To think of it as the idea one senses in, say, a holy man of India will do to set the spiritual extreme. That holy man's idea of

happiness is in needing nothing from outside himself. In wanting nothing, he lacks nothing. He sits immobile, rapt in contemplation, free even of his own body. Or nearly free of it. If devout admirers bring him food he eats it; if not, he starves indifferently. Why be concerned? What is physical is an illusion to him. Contemplation is his joy and he achieves it through a fantastically demanding discipline, the accomplishment of which is itself a joy within him.

Is he a happy man? Perhaps his happiness is only another sort   8 of illusion. But who can take it from him? And who will dare say it is more illusory than happiness on the installment plan?

But, perhaps because I am Western, I doubt such catatonic   9 happiness, as I doubt the dreams of the happiness-market. What is certain is that his way of happiness would be torture to almost any Western man. Yet these extremes will still serve to frame the area within which all of us must find some sort of balance. Thoreau—a creature of both Eastern and Western thought—had his own firm sense of that balance. His aim was to save on the low levels in order to spend on the high.

Possession for its own sake or in competition with the rest of   10 the neighborhood would have been Thoreau's idea of the low levels. The active discipline of heightening one's perception of what is enduring in nature would have been his idea of the high. What he saved from the low was time and effort he could spend on the high. Thoreau certainly disapproved of starvation, but he would put into feeding himself only as much effort as would keep him functioning for more important efforts.

Effort is the gist of it. There is no happiness except as we take   11 on life-engaging difficulties. Short of the impossible, as Yeats put it, the satisfactions we get from a lifetime depend on how high we choose our difficulties. Robert Frost was thinking in something like the same terms when he spoke of "The pleasure of taking pains." The mortal flaw in the advertised version of happiness is in the fact that it purports to be effortless.

We demand difficulty even in our games. We demand it   12 because without difficulty there can be no game. A game is a way of making something hard for the fun of it. The rules of the game are an arbitrary imposition of difficulty. When the spoil-sport ruins the fun, he always does so by refusing to play by the rules. It is easier to win at chess if you are free, at your pleasure, to change the wholly arbitrary rules, but the fun is in winning within the rules. No difficulty, no fun.

The buyers and sellers at the happiness-market seem too often   13 to have lost their sense of the pleasure of difficulty. Heaven knows what they are playing, but it seems a dull game. And the Indian holy man seems dull to us, I suppose, because he seems to be refusing to play anything at all. The Western weakness may be in the illusion that happiness can be bought. Perhaps the Eastern weakness is in the idea that there is such a thing as perfect (and therefore static) happiness.

14   Happiness is never more than partial. There are no pure states of mankind. Whatever else happiness may be, it is neither in having nor in being, but in becoming. What the Founding Fathers declared for us as an inherent right, we should do well to remember, was not happiness but the *pursuit* of happiness. What they might have under-lined, could they have foreseen the happiness-market, is the cardinal fact that happiness is in the pursuit itself, in the meaningful pursuit of what is life-engaging and life-revealing, which is to say, in the idea of *becoming*. A nation is not measured by what it possesses or wants to possess, but by what it wants to become.

15   By all means let the happiness-market sell us minor satisfactions and even minor follies so long as we keep them in scale and buy them out of spiritual change. I am no customer for either puritanism or asceticism. But drop any real spiritual capital at those bazaars, and what you come home to will be your own poorhouse.

Reading Critically

1. Do you agree with Ciardi's maxim (paragraph 12): "No difficulty, no fun," a variation on "No pain, no gain"? Must some pain and difficulty always precede real happiness? Discuss with your classmates.

2. Is happiness, as Ciardi says (paragraph 14), "never more than partial"? What then of lovers' statements like "You make me completely happy"? Have you or any of your classmates ever been "completely happy?" When? Why?

3. Be honest. Which ads in magazines and on television actu-ally appeal to you? Do you think you are being taken in, in the sense

explained by Ciardi in paragraphs 3 and 4? Bring some of the ads in question to class and discuss them with your classmates.

4. Ciardi ends by making a distinction between *being* and *becoming.* In what sense is this distinction at the heart of the essay? How is it implicitly present in the examples Ciardi has already presented?

Responding Through Writing

1. What is the difference between *happiness* and the *pursuit of happiness?* Why can the first never be a human right? Discuss these questions for five or six paragraphs in your notebook or journal.

2. St. Theresa of Avila is reputed to have said that there is more weeping over answered prayers than over unanswered ones. How is her statement a comment on the nature of happiness and its relation to human perception? Write a brief essay indicating how you think Ciardi would react to her statement.

3. Note Ciardi's use of the rules of games as a metaphor for the relation between difficulty and happiness. What other metaphors could he have used (cooking, studying?) and how well would they work? Use one such metaphor to structure the first draft of an essay of your own on the subject of happiness.

4. Ciardi criticizes advertising as a promoter of false happiness. What other aspects of society promote false happiness? Choose one and write the first draft of an essay in the same vein as Ciardi's.

ON SELF-RESPECT

JOAN DIDION

Essayist, novelist, journalist, playwright, and screenwriter, Joan Didion (b. 1934) has been praised for her "surgical prose." A graduate of the University of California at Berkeley, Didion has become famous for her interior monologues and observations of society. Her most famous collections of essays are Slouching Towards Bethlehem *(1968) and* The White Album *(1979). The author of several novels, Didion has also written two nonfiction books,* Salvador *(1983) and* Miami *(1987), that detail the social conditions in their respective locales. With her husband, John Gregory Dunne, Didion has also cowritten four screenplays, the most famous of which is* A Star Is Born *(1976). Didion also wrote "On Keeping a Notebook," which appears elsewhere in this book. The following essay was first published in 1961 in* Vogue *magazine.*

1   Once, in a dry season, I wrote in large letters across two pages of a notebook that innocence ends when one is stripped of the delusion that one likes oneself. Although now, some years later, I marvel that a mind on the outs with itself should have nonetheless made painstaking record of its every tremor, I recall with embarrassing clarity the flavor of those particular ashes. It was a matter of misplaced self-respect.

I had not been elected to Phi Beta Kappa. This failure could   2
scarcely have been more predictable or less ambiguous (I simply did
not have the grades), but I was unnerved by it; I had somehow
thought myself a kind of academic Raskolnikov, curiously exempt
from the cause–effect relationships which hampered others. Although even the humorless nineteen-year-old that I was must have
recognized that the situation lacked real tragic stature, the day that
I did not make Phi Beta Kappa nonetheless marked the end of
something, and innocence may well be the word for it. I lost the
conviction that lights would always turn green for me, the pleasant
certainty that those rather passive virtues which had won me approval as a child automatically guaranteed me not only Phi Beta
Kappa keys but happiness, honor, and the love of a good man; lost
a certain touching faith in the totem power of good manners, clean
hair, and proven competence on the Stanford-Binet scale. To such
doubtful amulets had my self-respect been pinned, and I faced
myself that day with the nonplused apprehension of someone who
has come across a vampire and has no crucifix at hand.

Although to be driven back upon oneself is an uneasy affair   3
at best, rather like trying to cross a border with borrowed creden-
tials, it seems to me now the one condition necessary to the begin-
nings of real self-respect. Most of our platitudes notwithstanding,
self-deception remains the most difficult deception. The tricks that
work on others count for nothing in that very well-lit back alley
where one keeps assignations with oneself: no winning smiles will
do here, no prettily drawn lists of good intentions. One shuffles
flashily but in vain through one's marked cards—the kindness done
for the wrong reason, the apparent triumph which involved no real
effort, the seemingly heroic act into which one had been shamed.
The dismal fact is that self-respect has nothing to do with the
approval of others—who are, after all, deceived easily enough; has
nothing to do with reputation, which, as Rhett Butler told Scarlett
O'Hara, is something people with courage can do without.

To do without self-respect, on the other hand, is to be an   4
unwilling audience of one to an interminable documentary that
details one's failings, both real and imagined, with fresh footage
spliced in for every screening. *There's the glass you broke in anger,
there's the hurt on X's face; watch now, this next scene, the night Y came
back from Houston, see how you muff this one.* To live without self-
respect is to lie awake some night, beyond the reach of warm milk,
phenobarbital, and the sleeping hand on the coverlet, counting up
the sins of commission and omission, the trusts betrayed, the promises subtly broken, the gifts irrevocably wasted through sloth or

cowardice or carelessness. However long we postpone it, we eventually lie down alone in that notoriously uncomfortable bed, the one we make ourselves. Whether or not we sleep in it depends, of course, on whether or not we respect ourselves.

5   To protest that some fairly improbable people, some people who *could not possibly respect themselves,* seem to sleep easily enough is to miss the point entirely, as surely as those people miss it who think that self-respect has necessarily to do with not having safety pins in one's underwear. There is a common superstition that "self-respect" is a kind of charm against snakes, something that keeps those who have it locked in some unblighted Eden, out of strange beds, ambivalent conversations, and trouble in general. It does not at all. It has nothing to do with the face of things, but concerns instead a separate peace, a private reconciliation. Although the careless, suicidal Julian English in *Appointment in Samarra* and the careless, incurably dishonest Jordan Baker in *The Great Gatsby* seem equally improbable candidates for self-respect, Jordan Baker had it, Julian English did not. With that genius for accommodation more often seen in women than in men, Jordan took her own measure, made her own peace, avoided threats to that peace: "I hate careless people," she told Nick Carraway. "It takes two to make an accident."

6   Like Jordan Baker, people with self-respect have the courage of their mistakes. They know the price of things. If they choose to commit adultery, they do not then go running, in an access of bad conscience, to receive absolution from the wronged parties; nor do they complain unduly of the unfairness, the undeserved embarrassment, of being named co-respondent. In brief, people with self-respect exhibit a certain toughness, a kind of moral nerve; they display what was once called *character,* a quality which, although approved in the abstract, sometimes loses ground to other, more instantly negotiable virtues. The measure of its slipping prestige is that one tends to think of it only in connection with homely children and United States senators who have been defeated, preferably in the primary, for reelection. Nonetheless, character—the willingness to accept responsibility for one's own life—is the source from which self-respect springs.

7   Self-respect is something that our grandparents, whether or not they had it, knew all about. They had instilled in them, young, a certain discipline, the sense that one lives by doing things one does not particularly want to do, by putting fears and doubts to one side, by weighing immediate comforts against the possibility of larger, even intangible, comforts. It seemed to the nineteenth century admirable, but not remarkable, that Chinese Gordon put on a clean white

suit and held Khartoum against the Mahdi; it did not seem unjust that the way to free land in California involved death and difficulty and dirt. In a diary kept during the winter of 1846, an emigrating twelve-year-old named Narcissa Cornwall noted coolly: "Father was busy reading and did not notice that the house was being filled with strange Indians until Mother spoke about it." Even lacking any clue as to what Mother said, one can scarcely fail to be impressed by the entire incident: the father reading, the Indians filing in, the mother choosing the words that would not alarm, the child duly recording the event and noting further that those particular Indians were not, "fortunately for us," hostile. Indians were simply part of the *donnée*.

In one guise or another, Indians always are. Again, it is a 8 question of recognizing that anything worth having has its price. People who respect themselves are willing to accept the risk that the Indians will be hostile, that the venture will go bankrupt, that the liaison may not turn out to be one in which *every day is a holiday because you're married to me*. They are willing to invest something of themselves; they may not play at all, but when they do play, they know the odds.

That kind of self-respect is a discipline, a habit of mind that 9 can never be faked but can be developed, trained, coaxed forth. It was once suggested to me that, as an antidote to crying, I put my head in a paper bag. As it happens, there is a sound physiological reason, something to do with oxygen, for doing exactly that, but the psychological effect alone is incalculable: it is difficult in extreme to continue fancying oneself Cathy in *Wuthering Heights* with one's head in a Food Fair bag. There is a similar case for all the small disciplines, unimportant in themselves; imagine maintaining any kind of swoon, commiserative or carnal, in a cold shower.

But those small disciplines are valuable only insofar as they 10 represent larger ones. To say that Waterloo was won on the playing fields of Eton is not to say that Napoleon might have been saved by a crash program in cricket; to give formal dinners in the rain forest would be pointless did not the candlelight flickering on the liana call forth deeper, stronger disciplines, values instilled long before. It is a kind of ritual, helping us to remember who and what we are. In order to remember it, one must have known it.

To have that sense of one's intrinsic worth which constitutes 11 self-respect is potentially to have everything: the ability to discriminate, to love and to remain indifferent. To lack it is to be locked within oneself, paradoxically incapable of either love or indifference. If we do not respect ourselves, we are on the one hand forced to despise those who have so few resources as to consort with us, so little perception as to remain blind to our fatal weaknesses. On the other, we are peculiarly in thrall to everyone we see, curiously determined to live out—since our self-image is untenable—their false notions of us. We flatter ourselves by thinking this compulsion to please others an attractive trait: a gist for imaginative empathy, evidence of our willingness to give. *Of course* I will play Francesca to your Paolo, Helen Keller to anyone's Annie Sullivan: no expectation is too misplaced, no role too ludicrous. At the mercy of those we cannot but hold in contempt, we play roles doomed to failure before they are begun, each defeat generating fresh despair at the urgency of divining and meeting the next demand made upon us.

12   It is the phenomenon sometimes called "alienation from self." In its advanced stages, we no longer answer the telephone, because someone might want something; that we could say *no* without drowning in self-reproach is an idea alien to this game. Every encounter demands too much, tears the nerves, drains the will, and the specter of something as small as an unanswered letter arouses such disproportionate guilt that answering it becomes out of the question. To assign unanswered letters their proper weight, to free us from the expectations of others, to give us back to ourselves— there lies the great, the singular power of self-respect. Without it, one eventually discovers the final turn of the screw: one runs away to find oneself, and finds no one at home.

Reading Critically

1. State your own definition of *self-respect.* What is Didion's definition of *self-respect?* (See paragraph 6.) In what way is your definition similar to Didion's, and in what way does it differ? Why does Didion say that self-respect is necessary? Why do you think self-respect is or isn't necessary?

2. How does Didion define *character* in paragraph 6? Given her definition of *character,* what distinction does she make between character and self-respect? What connections does she see between

the two? Discuss with your classmates whether character or something else is the source self-respect.

3. Is Didion writing for an audience other than herself, or is this an essay of self-exploration? What specifically in the essay can you cite to support your answer? If Didion is writing this essay for an audience other than herself, what kind of audience is it? What do her frequent allusions to works of literature and history reveal about her intended audience?

4. Throughout her essay Didion makes frequent allusions to various works of literature such as *Crime and Punishment, The Great Gatsby, Appointment in Samarra,* and *Wuthering Heights.* Explain the meaning of each of these allusions. Discuss with your classmates how these allusions help you better understand her discussion.

Responding Through Writing

1. If, as Didion says, self-respect has nothing to do with the approval of others, what is the relation of one's self-respect to others? What does Didion mean in paragraph 6 when she says that "people with self-respect have the courage of their mistakes. They know the price of things"? If you are keeping a journal or notebook in this course, write in it for five to ten minutes about a time you accepted responsibility for a mistake you made, and what you gained from that experience.

2. Before she begins to discuss what self-respect is in paragraph 5, Didion discusses the effects of a lack of self-respect. Why is this negative approach actually a good approach to defining an abstract term like *self-respect?* Write a paragraph developing a negative definition for *self-respect,* and a paragraph developing a positive definition.

3. In a few sentences describe the tone that Didion establishes in the first paragraph. What does the opening word "once" contribute to the tone? What do the phrases "in a dry season" and "the

flavor of those particular ashes" contribute to the tone of the essay? Write a list of similar phrases in the essay that contribute to the tone.

4. Write a sentence in which you state the main idea of this essay. After discussing your sentence with your classmates, write the first draft of an essay in which you give your own definition of self-respect, using illustrations from your own life, literature, history, and other sources.

THE INVISIBLE MAN

RALPH ELLISON

Ralph Waldo Ellison (b. 1914) was born in Oklahoma City and educated at Tuskegee Institute. After graduation he moved to New York City, where, with the prompting of novelist Richard Wright, he became a writer. His one novel, Invisible Man *(1940), won Ellison the National Book Award, and has been placed by many critics among the most important American works of literature of this century. Although Ellison did not publish a second novel, he wrote many stories, essays, and articles. Next to* Invisible Man, *his most widely read work is a collection of essays entitled* Shadow and Act *(1964). He also recently published a collection of essays, lectures, personal reminiscences, and interviews entitled* Going to the Territory *(1986). The following selection is an excerpt from* Invisible Man.

 I am an invisible man. No, I am not a spook like those who haunted Edgar Allan Poe; nor am I one of your Hollywood-movie ectoplasms. I am a man of substance, of flesh and bone, fiber and liquids—and I might even be said to possess a mind. I am invisible, understand, simply because people refuse to see me. Like the bodiless heads you see sometimes in circus sideshows, it is as though I have been surrounded by mirrors of hard, distorting glass. When they approach me they see only my surroundings, themselves, or figments of their imagination—indeed, everything and anything except me.

2   Nor is my invisibility exactly a matter of a bio-chemical accident to my epidermis. That invisibility to which I refer occurs because of a peculiar disposition of the eyes of those with whom I come in contact. A matter of the construction of their *inner* eyes, those eyes with which they look through their physical eyes upon reality. I am not complaining, nor am I protesting either. It is sometimes advantageous to be unseen, although it is most often rather wearing on the nerves. Then too, you're constantly being bumped against by those of poor vision. Or again, you often doubt if you really exist. You wonder whether you aren't simply a phantom in other people's minds. Say, a figure in a nightmare which the sleeper tries with all his strength to destroy. It's when you feel like this that, out of resentment, you begin to bump people back. And, let me confess, you feel that way most of the time. You ache with the need to convince yourself that you do exist in the real world, that you're a part of all the sound and anguish, and you strike out with your fists, you curse and you swear to make them recognize you. And, alas, it's seldom successful.

3   One night I accidentally bumped into a man, and perhaps because of the near darkness he saw me and called me an insulting name. I sprang at him, seized his coat lapels and demanded that he apologize. He was a tall blond man, and as my face came close to his he looked insolently out of his blue eyes and cursed me, his breath hot in my face as he struggled. I pulled his chin down sharp upon the crown of my head, butting him as I had seen the West Indians do, and I felt his flesh tear and the blood gush out, and I yelled, "Apologize! Apologize!" But he continued to curse and struggle, and I butted him again and again until he went down heavily, on his knees, profusely bleeding. I kicked him repeatedly, in a frenzy because he still uttered insults though his lips were frothy with blood. Oh yes, I kicked him! And in my outrage I got out my knife and prepared to slit his throat, right there beneath the lamplight in the deserted street, holding him by the collar with one hand, and opening the knife with my teeth—when it occurred to me that the man had not *seen* me, actually; that he, as far as he knew, was in the midst of a walking nightmare! And I stopped the blade, slicing the air as I pushed him away, letting him fall back to the street. I stared at him hard as the lights of a car stabbed through the darkness. He lay there, moaning on the asphalt; a man almost killed by a phantom. It unnerved me. I was both disgusted and ashamed. I was like a drunken man myself, wavering about on weakened legs. Then I was amused. Something in this man's thick head had sprung

out and beaten him within an inch of his life. I began to laugh at
this crazy discovery. Would he have awakened at the point of
death? Would Death himself have freed him for wakeful living?
But I didn't linger. I ran away into the dark, laughing so hard I
feared I might rupture myself. The next day I saw his picture in the
Daily News, beneath a caption stating that he had been "mugged."
Poor fool, poor blind fool, I thought with sincere compassion,
mugged by an invisible man!

Reading Critically

1. Supposedly, we live in an age of instant access to information through television, radio, newspapers, magazines, and other
sources. How is it possible for anyone to remain "invisible" in a
society so thoroughly covered by television and other media? What
people or groups of people are invisible in our society today? How
"visible" are the poor, the homeless, the handicapped? Why do
people turn their heads and not "see" the street people? What other
people or groups of people are "invisible" in our society? Discuss
at least one group of people that is "invisible" to you.

2. Why does Ellison attack the man? Is it simply because the
man insulted him? What does Ellison mean when he says that
"something in this man's thick head had sprung out and beaten
him"?

3. How do you respond to Ellison's attack on the man who
insulted him? Do you think Ellison overreacted? What do you
think Ellison should have done?

4. Ellison, of course, is a black man who is invisible in a white
world. What information does Ellison give you that tells you he
is black? Why doesn't he just say he is black and the man he attacks
is white?

Responding Through Writing

1. How does the first sentence of this essay get your attention? Write a paragraph in which you discuss how the first sentence of the essay sets the tone and structure of the rest of the essay.

2. How is Ellison defining a new meaning for the word *invisible* as it applies to minority groups? Write a paragraph that gives that definition. Discuss with your classmates what else Ellison is defining in this essay. Based upon this discussion, write a short essay in which you discuss all the definitions Ellison is giving in his essay.

3. After discussing his invisibility in abstract terms in the first two paragraphs, how does Ellison use the specific example in paragraph 3 to give concrete illustration to that abstract discussion? Write a paragraph in which you discuss what the incident in paragraph 3 contributes to Ellison's definition.

4. Write the first draft of an essay in which you propose ways in which an invisible group can become visible. Discuss your draft with your classmates. Based upon this discussion, rewrite your draft in final form.

TO NOBLE COMPANIONS

Gail Godwin (b. 1937) began her postcollege career as a reporter for the Miami Herald *and then worked for the U.S. Travel Service at the American Embassy in London. In the early 1970s she returned to academia at the University of Iowa and published her first novel,* The Perfectionists *(1970). Since then she has published a collection of short stories, written numerous free-lance articles, and recently published her seventh novel,* A Southern Family *(1987). Her writing for the most part pivots on classical feminist issues and on perceptions of the self and the physical world. Her interest in writing, she says, is precipitated by the need "to expand awareness of the possibilities of experience." She currently lives in Woodstock, New York. The following essay first appeared in* Harper's *magazine in August 1973.*

The dutiful first answer seems programmed into us by our 1 meager expectations: "A friend is one who will be there in times of trouble." But I believe this is a skin-deep answer to describe skin-deep friends. There is something irresistible about misfortune to human nature, and standbys for setbacks and sicknesses (as long as they are not too lengthy, or contagious) can usually be found.

They can be *hired*. What I value is not the "friend" who, looming sympathetically above me when I have been dashed to the ground, appears gigantically generous in the hour of my reversal; more and more I desire friends who will endure my ecstasies with me, who possess wings of their own and who will fly with me. I don't mean this as arrogance (I am too superstitious to indulge long in that trait), and I don't fly all that often. What I mean is that I seek (and occasionally find) friends with whom it is possible to drag out all those beautiful, old, outrageously *aspiring* costumes and rehearse together for the Great Roles; persons whose qualities groom me and train me up for love. It is for these people that I reserve the glowing hours, too good not to share. It is the existence of these people that reminds me that the words "friend" and "free" grew out of each other. (OE *freo,* not in bondage, noble, glad; OE *freon,* to love; OE *freond,* friend.)

2   When I was in the eighth grade, I had a friend. We were shy and "too serious" about our studies when it was becoming fashionable with our classmates to acquire the social graces. We said little at school, but she would come to my house and we would sit down with pencils and paper, and one of us would say: "Let's start with a train whistle today." We would sit quietly together and write separate poems or stories that grew out of a train whistle. Then we would read them aloud. At the end of that school year, we, too, were transformed into social creatures and the stories and poems stopped.

3   When I lived for a time in London, I had a friend. He was in despair and I was in despair, but our friendship was based on the small flicker of foresight in each of us that told us we would be sorry later if we did not explore this great city because we had felt bad at the time. We met every Sunday for five weeks and found many marvelous things. We walked until our despairs resolved themselves and then we parted. We gave London to each other.

4   For almost four years I have had a remarkable friend whose imagination illumines mine. We write long letters in which we often discover our strangest selves. Each of us appears, sometimes prophetically, sometimes comically, in the other's dreams. She and I agree that, at certain times, we seem to be parts of the same mind. In my most sacred and interesting moments, I often think: "Yes, I must tell _____." We have never met.

5   It is such exceptional (in a sense divine) companions I wish to salute. I have seen the glories of the world reflected briefly through our encounters. One bright hour with their kind is worth more to

me than a lifetime guarantee of the services of a Job's comforter whose "helpful" lamentations will only clutter the healing silence necessary to those darkest moments in which I would rather be my own best friend.

Reading Critically

1. Since Godwin discusses the etymology of the words *free* and *friend* only briefly, look up these words in the *Oxford English Dictionary* and prepare more detailed etymologies of them. Discuss with your classmates these etymologies and what they contribute to a better understanding of the word *friend.*

2. In paragraph 5 Godwin refers to a "Job's comforter." Prepare a summary of the Book of Job in the Bible. Who are Job's comforters? What do they do? In what ways are such comforters not really friends? According to Godwin, what does a real friend do for you during your time of trouble? Discuss with your classmates your definition of a real friend.

3. What does Godwin mean when she says in the last sentence of paragraph 3, "we gave London to each other"? How is this the work of a good friend? How does this friend fit the definition of *friend* Godwin gives in the first paragraph of the essay? What do real friends give each other?

4. Why does Godwin say that the really valuable friend is not the one who is there in time of trouble but who is there to share the good times? How might this reversal of the common understanding of a friendship bother you? Would you want friends just to share the good times and not help you through the bad times?

Responding Through Writing

1. How would Godwin's essay change if she had begun it with either the last paragraph or with the etymology of *friend* and *free?* Write a different paragraph with which she could have opened her essay. Discuss with your classmates how your opening paragraph would affect the rest of the essay.

2. Write a paragraph in which you describe the audience of this essay. Cite specific evidence in the essay that tells you something about the intended audience. (See for example the last sentence of paragraph 1.) Discuss your paragraph with your classmates and decide whether you and they can be considered part of this intended audience.

3. Godwin's purpose in this essay is not simply to define the word *friend.* After reading paragraph 5 again, write a paragraph in which you discuss her larger purpose. What does the title of the essay reveal about Godwin's purpose?

4. In the first two sentences of her essay, Godwin gives and rejects a common definition of a friend. Then she provides a description of what she means by a friend. Write some notes on how her descriptive definition differs from the definition she has rejected. What is the emphasis of each definition? How do the definitions differ? Discuss with your classmates which definition you prefer and why.

NEW SUPERSTITIONS
FOR OLD

MARGARET MEAD

Margaret Mead (1902–1978) received her doctoral degree in anthropology from Columbia University in 1926 and immediately left New York for the islands of the Pacific Ocean. Fluent in several languages and cultures, she conducted research on those islands and published the results of her research in several books, the most famous of which is Coming of Age in Samoa *(1928), a book that revolutionized the field of anthropology. Although Mead's views about sexual openness among Pacific islanders have been challenged, she is still regarded as an important figure in comparative studies of social structures. A prolific and diverse author, Mead brought her knowledge of Pacific communities to modern Western problems of education, mental health, and ecology, as well as growth, change, and structure of culture. She received many awards and honors in her profession but continued until her death to explain her findings in a prose style accessible to the lay reader. Among her books are* The Study of Culture at a Distance, The Golden Age of American Anthropology, *and* Continuities in Culture Evolution. *The following selection is from* A Way of Seeing *(1966).*

1   Once in a while there is a day when everything seems to run smoothly and even the riskiest venture comes out exactly right. You exclaim, "This is my lucky day!" Then as an afterthought you say, "Knock on wood!" Of course, you do not really believe that knocking on wood will ward off danger. Still, boasting about your own good luck gives you a slightly uneasy feeling—and you carry out the little protective ritual. If someone challenged you at that moment, you would probably say, "Oh, that's nothing. Just an old superstition."

2   But when you come to think about it, what is a superstition?

3   In the contemporary world most people treat old folk beliefs as superstitions—the belief, for instance, that there are lucky and unlucky days or numbers, that future events can be read from omens, that there are protective charms or that what happens can be influenced by casting spells. We have excluded magic from our current world view, for we know that natural events have natural causes.

4   In a religious context, where truths cannot be demonstrated, we accept them as a matter of faith. Superstitions, however, belong to the category of beliefs, practices and ways of thinking that have been discarded because they are inconsistent with scientific knowledge. It is easy to say that other people are superstitious because they believe what we regard to be untrue. "Superstition" used in that sense is a derogatory term for the beliefs of other people that we do not share. But there is more to it than that. For superstitions lead a kind of half life in a twilight world where, sometimes, we partly suspend our disbelief and act as if magic worked.

5   Actually, almost every day, even in the most sophisticated home, something is likely to happen that evokes the memory of some old folk belief. The salt spills. A knife falls to the floor. Your nose tickles. Then perhaps, with a slightly embarrassed smile, the person who spilled the salt tosses a pinch over his left shoulder. Or someone recites the old rhyme, "Knife falls, gentleman calls." Or as you rub your nose you think, That means a letter. I wonder who's writing? No one takes these small responses very seriously or gives them more than a passing thought. Sometimes people will preface one of these ritual acts—walking around instead of under a ladder or hastily closing an umbrella that has been opened inside a house—

with such a remark as "I remember my great-aunt used to . . ." or "Germans used to say you ought not. . . ." And then, having placed the belief at some distance away in time or space, they carry out the ritual.

Everyone also remembers a few of the observances of child-hood—wishing on the first star; looking at the new moon over the right shoulder; avoiding the cracks in the sidewalk on the way to school while chanting, "Step on a crack, break your mother's back"; wishing on white horses, on loads of hay, on covered bridges, on red cars; saying quickly, "Bread-and-butter" when a post or a tree separated you from the friend you were walking with. The adult may not actually recite the formula "Star light, star bright . . ." and may not quite turn to look at the new moon, but his mood is tempered by a little of the old thrill that came when the observance was still freighted with magic.

Superstition can also be used with another meaning. When I discuss the religious beliefs of other peoples, especially primitive peoples, I am often asked, "Do they really have a religion, or is it all just superstition?" The point of contrast here is not between a scientific and a magical view of the world but between the clear, theologically defensible religious beliefs of members of civilized societies and what we regard as the false and childish views of the heathen who "bow down to wood and stone." Within the civilized religions, however, where membership includes believers who are educated and urbane and others who are ignorant and simple, one always finds traditions and practices that the more sophisticated will dismiss offhand as "just superstition" but that guide steps of those who live by older ways. Mostly these are very ancient beliefs, some handed on from one religion to another and carried from country to country around the world.

Very commonly, people associate superstition with the past, with very old ways of thinking that have been supplanted by modern knowledge. But new superstitions are continually coming into being and flourishing in our society. Listening to mothers in the park in the 1930's, one heard them say, "Now, don't you run out into the sun, or Polio will get you." In the 1940's elderly people explained to one another in tones of resignation, "It was the Virus that got him down." And every year the cosmetics industry offers us new magic—cures for baldness, lotions that will give every woman radiant skin, hair coloring that will restore to the middle-aged the charm and romance of youth—results that are promised if we will just follow the simple directions. Families and individuals also have their cherished, private superstitions. You must leave by the back door when you are going on a journey, or you must wear a green dress when you are taking an examination. It is a kind of joke, of course, but it makes you feel safe.

9   These old half-beliefs and new half-beliefs reflect the keenness of our wish to have something come true or to prevent something bad from happening. We do not always recognize new superstitions for what they are, and we still follow the old ones because someone's faith long ago matches our contemporary hopes and fears. In the past people "knew" that a black cat crossing one's path was a bad omen, and they turned back home. Today we are fearful of taking a journey and would give anything to turn back—and then we notice a black cat running across the road in front of us.

10   Child psychologists recognize the value of the toy a child holds in his hand at bedtime. It is different from his thumb, with which he can close himself in from the rest of the world, and it is different from the real world, to which he is learning to relate himself. Psychologists call these toys—these furry animals and old, cozy baby blankets—"transitional objects"; that is, objects that help the child move back and forth between the exactions of everyday life and the world of wish and dream.

11   Superstitions have some of the qualities of these transitional objects. They help people pass between the areas of life where what happens has to be accepted without proof and the areas where sequences of events are explicable in terms of cause and effect, based on knowledge. Bacteria and viruses that cause sickness have been identified; the cause of symptoms can be diagnosed and a rational course of treatment prescribed. Magical charms no longer are needed to treat the sick; modern medicine has brought the whole sequence of events into the secular world. But people often act as if this change had not taken place. Laymen still treat germs as if they were invisible, malign spirits, and physicians sometimes prescribe antibiotics as if they were magic substances.

12   Over time, more and more of life has become subject to the controls of knowledge. However, this is never a one-way process. Scientific investigation is continually increasing our knowledge. But if we are to make good use of this knowledge, we must not only rid our minds of old, superseded beliefs and fragments of magical practice, but also recognize new superstitions for what they are. Both are generated by our wishes, our fears and our feelings of helplessness in difficult situations.

13   Civilized peoples are not alone in having grasped the idea of superstitions—beliefs and practices that are superseded but that still may evoke compliance. The idea is one that is familiar to every

people, however primitive, that I have ever known. Every society has a core of transcendent beliefs—beliefs about the nature of the universe, the world and man—that no one doubts or questions. Every society also has a fund of knowledge related to practical life—about the succession of day and night and of the seasons; about correct ways of planting seeds so that they will germinate and grow; about the processes involved in making dyes or the steps necessary to remove the deadly poison from manioc roots so they become edible. Island peoples know how the winds shift and they know the star toward which they must point the prow of the canoe exactly so that as the sun rises they will see the first fringing palms on the shore toward which they are sailing.

This knowledge, based on repeated observations of reliable   14
sequences, leads to ideas and hypotheses of the kind that underlie scientific thinking. And gradually as scientific knowledge, once developed without conscious plan, has become a great self-corrective system and the foundation for rational planning and action, old magical beliefs and observances have had to be discarded.

But it takes time for new ways of thinking to take hold, and   15
often the transition is only partial. Older, more direct beliefs live on in the hearts and minds of elderly people. And they are learned by children who, generation after generation, start out life as hopefully and fearfully as their forebears did. Taking their first steps away from home, children use the old rituals and invent new ones to protect themselves against the strangeness of the world into which they are venturing.

So whatever has been rejected as no longer true, as limited,   16
provincial and idolatrous, still leads a half life. People may say, "It's just a superstition," but they continue to invoke the ritual's protection or potency. In this transitional, twilight state such beliefs come to resemble dreaming. In the dream world a thing can be either good or bad; a cause can be an effect and an effect can be a cause. Do warts come from touching toads, or does touching a toad cure the wart? Is sneezing a good omen or a bad omen? You can have it either way—or both ways at once. In the same sense, the half-acceptance and half-denial accorded superstitions give us the best of both worlds.

Superstitions are sometimes smiled at and sometimes frowned   17
upon as observances characteristic of the old-fashioned, the unenlightened, children, peasants, servants, immigrants, foreigners or backwoods people. Nevertheless, they give all of us ways of moving back and forth among the different worlds in which we live—the sacred, the secular and the scientific. They allow us to keep a private

world also, where, smiling a little, we can banish danger with a gesture and summon luck with a rhyme, make the sun shine in spite of storm clouds, force the stranger to do our bidding, keep an enemy at bay and straighten the paths of those we love.

Reading Critically

1. Make a list of several "superstitious" practices and exchange your list with your classmates. Which practices do you find most surprising? Discuss with your classmates the cultural or family origins of the items on your lists.

2. What "new" superstitions do you find in today's advertising and news stories with regard to the maintenance of health and the spread of disease? How do you react to them?

3. Is there a relation between superstition and science, as suggested by Mead in paragraphs 12 and 13? Are some of our scientific "discoveries" rooted in superstition? Which ones?

4. To what extent does religion encourage superstition? To what extent does religion run counter to superstitious beliefs? Does Mead avoid the relation between religion and superstition? Why?

Responding Through Writing

1. If you could expand or update Mead's essay, how would you go about doing so? Make a list of examples of "new" superstitious behavior.

2. Choose three or four of the superstitions listed in response to item 1 and write a short essay indicating what they have in common.

3. Mead writes in a familiar, congenial tone. Is this appropriate for the discussion of a scientific subject? If you are taking a course
in the sciences or social sciences, rewrite a passage in one of your
textbooks to make it sound more "human."

4. Is the conclusion ("straighten the paths of those we love")
an effective one? Does it in any way sum up the essay, or does it
seem to go off on a tangent? Can you write a more adequate
conclusion in a few paragraphs?

WHERE IS
THE MIDWEST?

SUSAN WINTSCH

Susan Wintsch (b. 1950) is a free-lance science writer and editor whose writing has appeared in such publications as Geology Today, Geographical Magazine, New Scientist, Garden Magazine, *and the* Christian Science Monitor. *After graduating from the University of Rochester (1972) with a degree in Geology and English, Wintsch attended the University of Illinois, where she earned a master's degree in Geology (1974), and Indiana University, where she earned a master's degree in Journalism (1977). Wintsch has been an editor for the U.S. Office of Technology Assessment and UNESCO, as well as an environmental reporter for* The Bloomington (*Indiana*) Herald, *a science writer at the University of Leeds in Yorkshire, England, and office manager for the Clay Minerals Society in Washington, D.C. Wintsch calls Bloomington, Indiana, home, a town that, by some definitions, is in the Midwest. In much of her writing, Wintsch attempts to make concrete and specific what is often abstract. In this essay, she goes beyond a simple definition of the Midwest as a geographical location and attempts to define the area and the word as representing all that is considered typically "American." For Wintsch, "the Midwest—long synonymous with the American self-image . . . seems to be 'somewheres' deeply rooted in American experience and thought." The following essay first appeared in the March 1988 issue of* TWA Ambassador *magazine, the in-flight magazine of Trans World Airlines.*

A sizable chunk of the North American continent belongs to 1
the fabled Midwest. Just how sizable depends on whom you talk to.
Twenty-two years ago Roy Meyer, in a study of American farm
novels, defined the American Midwest as "that great central area of
the nation including the 12 states of Ohio, Indiana, Illinois, Michigan, Wisconsin, Minnesota, Iowa, Missouri, Kansas, Nebraska,
South Dakota, and North Dakota." This view of the Midwest as
everything from Ohio westward through Kansas and northward to
the Canadian border may be convenient for some purposes—like
writing textbooks—but is not without its challengers. Today, as in
the past, the Midwest is a term loosely used and rarely defined with
precision.

In fact, Americans have grappled with the question of the 2
Midwest's regional boundaries since before the turn of the century,
when popular writers began to use the term "Middle West" without
really agreeing on what it was they were describing.

The situation had not much changed by 1973, prompting one 3
scholar to complain, "Everyone within or outside the Middle West
knows of its existence, but no one seems sure where it begins or
ends." Going even further in his 1981 book *The Nine Nations of
North America, Washington Post* writer Joel Garreau suggested that
those who would lump Ohio with Nebraska, and Cleveland with
Omaha don't understand how America really works. Garreau called
the "midwest" a myth, an outmoded geographical concept.

Nevertheless, when University of Kansas geographer James 4
Shortridge recently surveyed some 2,000 university students across
the nation, he found the concept of a Midwest alive and well.
Shortridge was intrigued that the Midwest the students defined was
centered somewhat west of the classic 12-state "textbook" model.
And he has some interesting ideas about why this is so.

As a geographer, Shortridge had already begun thinking about 5
how regional terms like "Appalachia," the "Great Plains," and the
"Corn Belt" evolve. He found himself dwelling more and more on
the problem of the Midwest, to his mind the vaguest and most
profound of American regional concepts.

The name "Middle West" (later shortened to Midwest) seems 6
to have come into use about 100 years ago. In 1898, Kansas journalist
Charles Moreau Harger used the term casually, as if it had at least

some precedence in the popular literature. His Middle West described the plains area of Kansas and Nebraska as distinct from the newer states of Minnesota and the Dakotas to the north, and from Texas and the Indian territories to the south. He used "Middle West" in a latitudinal sense.

7   Not until about 1912, according to Shortridge, did "Middle West" come into its own as a major regional term, one denoting an east–west rather than a north–south division. Yet as the term gained familiarity, its exact meaning remained elusive. During the first decade of this century two conflicting schools of thought emerged. Harger and several other authors continued using "Middle West" to describe the central plains areas of Kansas and Nebraska, a gradually maturing agricultural society still occasionally referred to as part of the West. Other commentators used "Midwest" in a much broader sense to include Minnesota and the Dakotas, Ohio, and Indiana as well. Harger himself vacillated, at one point putting the term "Middle West" in quotes and admitting it could be only vaguely defined.

8   In 1916, Rollin Lynde Hartt, writing in *The Century* magazine, playfully illustrated just how shaky the geographical identity of this hugely sprawling Midwest actually remained:

9   Although the prairies begin at Batavia, New York, Buffalonians resent being termed Middle-Westerners. Omaha, I should describe as unquestionably Middle-Western, yet there are Middle-Westerners who repudiate Nebraska, and only tepidly accept Kansas. . . . A dear soul in Montana remarked to me: "How jolly to hear that you came from the East! I'm an Easterner myself.
10   I lived in Iowa."
    Where then is the Middle West? In the words of the immortal Artemus, I answer, "Nowheres—nor anywheres else."

11   Although a broader definition of the Midwest gradually became the preferred one, 20th-century geographers have been as inconsistent as turn-of-the-century writers in their use of the term "Midwest"—so complained scholar Joseph W. Brownell in 1960 when he made what was apparently the first attempt to define the "vernacular" Midwest—the Midwest as the American population,

not just professional geographers, was then defining it. Brownell surveyed 536 postmasters within a several-hundred-mile radius of Chicago with a single question: "In your opinion, does your community lie in the Midwest?"

Almost 90 percent of the individuals surveyed responded, and   12 nearly 55 percent answered yes. They described a core region spread across all or almost all of Ohio, Indiana, Illinois, Wisconsin, Minnesota, Iowa, Missouri, the Dakotas, Kansas, and Nebraska. More than half of Michigan and the western half of Oklahoma also defined the core which, all told, covered 20 percent of the continental United States and accounted for 28 percent of the nation's population.

The boundaries of this region were sharp in the northwest   13 along the western borders of the Dakotas and in the southeast along the southern borders of Illinois and Missouri. Peripheral zones, where neighboring communities disagreed about their designation, spilled across broad areas of Oklahoma and Colorado.

Many of the postmasters west of the Mississippi considered that   14 river to be the eastern border of the region. As one explained, "We resent persons from Ohio and Indiana referring to themselves as 'midwesterners' as actually they are 'mideasterners.'"

Shortridge thinks that a great deal more lies behind the term   15 "Midwest" in the minds of Americans than any fixed set of boundaries, and he believes he has evidence of this in his survey results. In his survey, students were given a map of the United States and asked to draw a line around the Midwest. They were also asked to list the characteristics they associated with the Midwest and its peoples.

The resulting summary map contained some surprises. Over 50   16 percent of the students excluded Chicago—traditionally hailed as the "capital" of the Midwest. Wyoming was midwestern to as many students as was Ohio, and, in general, the Midwest that emerged from the survey was more westerly than the 12-state "textbook" Midwest. Students from the Northeast, Southwest, and West centered the Midwest in Kansas and Nebraska, as did students from those two states, creating the dominant pattern on the composite map. Students from Illinois, Iowa, Missouri, North Dakota, South Dakota, and Wisconsin tended to put their own states at the core of the Midwest, a tendency that was not widely shared outside their state borders. Students from Michigan, Indiana, and Ohio included themselves as marginally midwestern, placing the region's core far to the west. These three states were not included in the Midwest by the majority of students living outside their borders.

17   Shortridge proposes that as urbanization and industrialization profoundly changed the Great Lakes and Ohio Valley states in this century, two choices emerged: "modify the rural image of the Middle West to conform to the new reality in these states . . . or shift the regional core westward to the Great Plains where rural society still prevailed." His survey indicates that Americans may have elected the latter course.

18   What intrigued Shortridge most were not the differing geographic definitions revealed in the survey, but the overwhelmingly similar responses to the question about midwestern characteristics. These strongly parallel images of rural independence and pastoral democracy that first emerged in the popular literature about the Midwest in the early years of this century. Shortridge wonders whether the Midwest isn't as much an actual place as an idea—an idea that is now more compatible with life on the plains than the modern reality of the more industrialized and urban "midwestern" states like Indiana and Ohio.

19   As early as 1910 the vision of the Midwest as rural America, as the most American and friendliest part of America, held a firm place in the national psyche. As one traveler from "back East" exclaimed, "There are Midwesterners who slap you on the back after an hour's acquaintance." Shortridge has found in many turn-of-the-century descriptions of the Midwest (wherever authors located the region geographically) a life-cycle analogy—one still employed, though somewhat differently, in the 1980s. In contrast with the older, more aristocratic and tradition-bound eastern states (where, one Iowan observed in 1912, the children are so listless "they have to be incited to play"); and unlike the very young, energetic, and somewhat raw West, the Midwest was seen as the region of balance and maturity, the seat of a near-perfect democracy.

20   An economic depression affecting the central plains in the 1880s and 1890s, Shortridge believes, was a watershed event. According to commentators of the time, the region emerged from hard times confident and optimistic, having "outgrown the undesirable traits of youth such as thriftlessness, impatience, radicalism, and boomer philosophy." The first generation of midwesterners had already buried their parents, and in cases, children, in midwestern sod, establishing roots that gradually replaced those tugging at them from the east.

21   As the 20th century opened, the Midwest began to be extolled as a "fat land" of rural abundance. A professor of economics at Harvard University, traveling through Kansas in the early 1900s, dubbed the corn belt "the most considerable area in the world where

agriculture is uniformly prosperous." As for the corn growers, they were "an independent progressive class, drawing their sustenance from the soil and not from other people."

It was not until about 1915 that hints of excessive conserva- 22 tism, of "fished out" communities north of the Ohio valley, of industrial squalor here and there, contradicted some of the over-whelmingly flattering portrayals in turn-of-the-century reports. Al-most invariably, criticisms were overshadowed by new and stronger praise for the region.

Shortridge's survey illustrates that much of the positive imag- 23 ery that persists in association with the Midwest is rural in emphasis. Only students from Indiana and Ohio associated industry with the Midwest, and even they saw the Midwest primarily as a place of fields and farms.

Many students used terms related to a life cycle in describing 24 the region, but the images that emerged were more those of increas-ing age than young maturity. Terms like "traditional" overshad-owed "progressive" and "liberal." Synonyms for intolerance were offered about five times more frequently than phrases from the past like "open-mindedness." On the other hand, Shortridge notes, no respondent described the Midwest as smug or self-satisfied, nor were adjectives such as corrupt or nonegalitarian used to describe this region of the country.

If geographers follow Shortridge's lead, the Midwest—long 25 synonymous with the American self-image—will come to be viewed more in terms of this symbolism than as any fixed place.

Where, then, is the Middle West? It may indeed be "no- 26 wheres—nor anywheres else." But, in concept, at least, it seems to be "somewheres" deeply rooted in American experience and thought.

Reading Critically

1. Does your city or town have its own delimited subregions? What are they? Where are they? Do you and your classmates agree?

2. Is there any real need, in your opinion, to define accurately the Midwest or any other area of the United States? Discuss with

your classmates to see whether you can come up with at least five such needs.

3. Do you and your classmates differ on where the Midwest or other areas of the country "really" are? Does it surprise you the the Midwest was originally a latitudinal concept? Why do you think it changed to a longitudinal concept?

4. What role do rivers play in American boundaries? Do you and your classmates tend to think of people according to where they live in relation to various rivers?

Responding Through Writing

1. In addition to Appalachia, the Great Plains, and the Corn Belt, what other areas of the country can you name? What gave rise to these regional concepts? Make a list of the various areas of the country as you see them and write a short paragraph defining the essential characteristics of each region.

2. On a map of the United States, mark off five (and only five) regions. In a short essay discuss the reasons (social, economic, historical, and other) for creating the regions the way you did.

3. Wintsch places considerable reliance on geographical source materials. How well does she use those materials? Consult the geographical reference materials available in your library and write a short report on the accuracy of Wintsch's research.

4. In what sense is this essay more about ideas than about geography? Write at least the first draft of an essay about how notions of regional identification (e.g., "I'm proud that I'm a New Englander") operate for better or for worse in American life.

LIGHT OF
OTHER DAYS

BOB SHAW

*Bob Shaw was born in 1931 in Belfast, Northern Ireland. After comple-
ting technical high school, Shaw began working as a public relations
officer for a local aircraft manufacturer. Giving up this career for journalism, in 1966 he went to work for Belfast Telegraph Newspapers. After
four years of staff and free-lance writing, Shaw returned to public relations
work, though he never stopped writing science fiction. Nearly two dozen
science fiction novels later, including* One Million Tomorrows *(1970),*
Orbitsville *(1974), and* The Ragged Astronaut *(1986), Shaw now
lives with his family in England and is still writing novels and contributing short stories to American and British science fiction magazines. The
following story was originally published in* Analog Science Fiction/
Science Fact *in 1966.*

Leaving the village behind, we followed the heady sweeps of   1
the road up into a land of slow glass.
    I had never seen one of the farms before and at first found them   2
slightly eerie—an effect heightened by imagination and circum-
stance. The car's turbine was pulling smoothly and quietly in the
damp air so that we seemed to be carried over the convolutions of

the road in a kind of supernatural silence. On our right the mountain sifted down into an incredibly perfect valley of timeless pine, and everywhere stood the great frames of slow glass, drinking light. An occasional flash of afternoon sunlight on their wind bracing created an illusion of movement, but in fact the frames were deserted. The rows of windows had been standing on the hillside for years, staring into the valley, and men only cleaned them in the middle of the night when their human presence would not matter to the thirsty glass.

3   They were fascinating, but Selina and I didn't mention the windows. I think we hated each other so much we both were reluctant to sully anything new by drawing it into the nexus of our emotions. The holiday, I had begun to realize, was a stupid idea in the first place. I had thought it would cure everything, but, of course, it didn't stop Selina being pregnant and, worse still, it didn't even stop her being angry about being pregnant.

4   Rationalizing our dismay over her condition, we had circulated the usual statements to the effect that we would have *liked* having children—but later on, at the proper time. Selina's pregnancy had cost us her well-paid job and with it the new house we had been negotiating and which was far beyond the reach of my income from poetry. But the real source of our annoyance was that we were face to face with the realization that people who say they want children later always mean they want children never. Our nerves were thrumming with the knowledge that we, who had thought ourselves so unique, had fallen into the same biological trap as every mindless rutting creature which ever existed.

5   The road took us along the southern slopes of Ben Cruachan until we began to catch glimpses of the gray Atlantic far ahead. I had just cut our speed to absorb the view better when I noticed the sign spiked to a gatepost. It said: "SLOW GLASS—Quality High, Prices Low—J. R. Hagan." On an impulse I stopped the car on the verge, wincing slightly as tough grasses whipped noisily at the body-work.

6   "Why have we stopped?" Selina's neat, smoke-silver head turned in surprise.

7   "Look at that sign. Let's go up and see what there is. The stuff might be reasonably priced out here."

8   Selina's voice was pitched high with scorn as she refused, but I was too taken with my idea to listen. I had an illogical conviction that doing something extravagant and crazy would set us right again.

9   "Come on," I said, "the exercise might do us some good. We've been driving too long anyway."

She shrugged in a way that hurt me and got out of the car.   10
We walked up a path made of irregular, packed clay steps nosed
with short lengths of sapling. The path curved through trees which
clothed the edge of the hill and at its end we found a low farmhouse.
Beyond the little stone building tall frames of slow glass gazed out
towards the voice-stilling sight of Cruachan's ponderous descent
towards the waters of Loch Linnhe. Most of the panes were perfectly
transparent but a few were dark, like panels of polished ebony.

As we approached the house through a neat cobbled yard a tall   11
middle-aged man in ash-colored tweeds arose and waved to us. He
had been sitting on the low rubble wall which bounded the yard,
smoking a pipe and staring towards the house. At the front window
of the cottage a young woman in a tangerine dress stood with a
small boy in her arms, but she turned disinterestedly and moved out
of sight as we drew near.

"Mr. Hagan?" I guessed.   12

"Correct. Come to see some glass, have you? Well, you've   13
come to the right place." Hagan spoke crisply, with traces of the
pure highland which sounds so much like Irish to the unaccustomed
ear. He had one of those calmly dismayed faces one finds on elderly
road-menders and philosophers.

"Yes," I said. "We're on holiday. We saw your sign."   14

Selina, who usually has a natural fluency with strangers, said
nothing. She was looking towards the now empty window with
what I thought was a slightly puzzled expression.

"Up from London, are you? Well, as I said, you've come to   15
the right place—and at the right time, too. My wife and I don't see
many people this early in the season."

I laughed. "Does that mean we might be able to buy a little   16
glass without mortgaging our home?"

"Look at that now," Hagan said, smiling helplessly. "I've   17
thrown away any advantage I might have had in the transaction.
Rose, that's my wife, says I never learn. Still, let's sit down and talk
it over." He pointed at the rubble wall then glanced doubtfully at
Selina's immaculate blue skirt. "Wait till I fetch a rug from the
house." Hagan limped quickly into the cottage, closing the door
behind him.

"Perhaps it wasn't such a marvelous idea to come up here," I   18
whispered to Selina, "but you might at least be pleasant to the man.
I think I can smell a bargain."

"Some hope," she said with deliberate coarseness. "Surely even   19
you must have noticed that ancient dress his wife is wearing? He
won't give much away to strangers."

20   "Was that his wife?"

21   "Of course that was his wife."

22   "Well, well," I said, surprised. "Anyway, try to be civil with him. I don't want to be embarrassed."

23   Selina snorted, but she smiled whitely when Hagan reappeared and I relaxed a little. Strange how a man can love a woman and yet at the same time pray for her to fall under a train.

24   Hagan spread a tartan blanket on the wall and we sat down, feeling slightly self-conscious at having been translated from our city-oriented lives into a rural tableau. On the distant slate of the loch, beyond the watchful frames of slow glass, a slow-moving steamer drew a white line towards the south. The boisterous mountain air seemed almost to invade our lungs, giving us more oxygen than we required.

25   "Some of the glass farmers around here," Hagan began, "give strangers, such as yourselves, a sales talk about how beautiful the autumn is in this part of Argyll. Or it might be spring, or the winter. I don't do that—any fool knows that a place which doesn't look right in summer never looks right. What do you say?"

26   I nodded compliantly.

27   "I want you just to take a good look out towards Mull, Mr. . . ."

28   "Garland."

29   ". . . Garland. That's what you're buying if you buy my glass, and it never looks better than it does at this minute. The glass is in perfect phase, none of it is less than ten years thick—and a four-foot window will cost you two hundred pounds."

30   *"Two hundred!"* Selina was shocked. "That's as much as they charge at the Scenedow shop in Bond Street."

31   Hagan smiled patiently, then looked closely at me to see if I knew enough about slow glass to appreciate what he had been saying. His price had been much higher than I had hoped—but *ten years thick!* The cheap glass one found in places like the Vistaplex and Paneorama stores usually consisted of a quarter of an inch of ordinary glass faced with a veneer of slow glass perhaps only ten or twelve months thick.

32   "You don't understand, darling," I said, already determined to buy. "This glass will last ten years and it's in phase."

33   "Doesn't that only mean it keeps time?"

34   Hagan smiled at her again, realizing he had no further necessity to bother with me. "Only, you say! Pardon me, Mrs. Garland, but you don't seem to appreciate the miracle, the genuine honest-to-goodness miracle, of engineering precision needed to produce a piece of glass in phase. When I say the glass is ten years thick it

means it takes light ten years to pass through it. In effect, each one of those panes is ten light-years thick—more than twice the distance to the nearest star—so a variation in actual thickness of only a millionth of an inch would . . ."

He stopped talking for a moment and sat quietly looking   35
towards the house. I turned my head from the view of the loch and saw the young woman standing at the window again. Hagan's eyes were filled with a kind of greedy reverence which made me feel uncomfortable and at the same time convinced me Selina had been wrong. In my experience husbands never looked at wives that way, at least, not at their own.

The girl remained in view for a few seconds, dress glowing   36
warmly, then moved back into the room. Suddenly I received a distinct, though inexplicable, impression she was blind. My feeling was that Selina and I were perhaps blundering through an emotional interplay as violent as our own.

"I'm sorry," Hagan continued, "I thought Rose was going to   37
call me for something. Now, where was I, Mrs. Garland? Ten light-years compressed into a quarter of an inch means . . ."

I ceased to listen, partly because I was already sold, partly   38
because I had heard the story of slow glass many times before and had never yet understood the principles involved. An acquaintance with scientific training had once tried to be helpful by telling me to visualize a pane of slow glass as a hologram which did not need coherent light from a laser for the reconstitution of its visual information, and in which every photon of ordinary light passed through a spiral tunnel coiled outside the radius of capture of each atom in the glass. This gem of, to me, incomprehensibility not only told me nothing, it convinced me once again that a mind as nontechnical as mine should concern itself less with causes than effects.

The most important effect, in the eyes of the average individ-   39
ual, was that light took a long time to pass through a sheet of slow glass. A new piece was always jet black because nothing had yet come through, but one could stand the glass beside, say, a woodland lake until the scene emerged, perhaps a year later. If the glass was then removed and installed in a dismal city flat, the flat would—for that year—appear to overlook the woodland lake. During the year it wouldn't be merely a very realistic but still picture—the water would ripple in sunlight, silent animals would come to drink, birds would cross the sky, night would follow day, season would follow season. Until one day, a year later, the beauty held in the subatomic pipelines would be exhausted and the familiar gray cityscape would reappear.

Apart from its stupendous novelty value, the commercial suc-   40 cess of slow glass was founded on the fact that having a scenedow was the exact emotional equivalent of owning land. The meanest cave dweller could look out on misty parks—and who was to say they weren't his? A man who really owns tailored gardens and estates doesn't spend his time proving his ownership by crawling on his ground, feeling, smelling, tasting it. All he receives from the land are light patterns, and with scenedows those patterns could be taken into coal mines, submarines, prison cells.

41   On several occasions I have tried to write short pieces about the enchanted crystal but, to me, the theme is so ineffably poetic as to be, paradoxically, beyond the reach of poetry—mine at any rate. Besides, the best songs and verse had already been written, with prescient inspiration, by men who had died long before slow glass was discovered. I had no hope of equaling, for example, Moore with his:

Oft in the stilly night,
Ere slumber's chain has bound me,
Fond Memory brings the light,
Of other days around me . . .

42   It took only a few years of slow glass to develop from a scientific curiosity to a sizable industry. And much to the astonishment of us poets—those of us who remain convinced that beauty lives though lilies die—the trappings of that industry were no different from those of any other. There were good scenedows which cost a lot of money, and there were inferior scenedows which cost rather less. The thickness, measured in years, was an important factor in the cost but there was also the question of *actual* thickness, or phase.

43   Even with the most sophisticated engineering techniques available thickness control was something of a hit-and-miss affair. A coarse discrepancy could mean that a pane intended to be five years thick might be five and a half, so that light which entered in summer emerged in winter; a fine discrepancy could mean that noon sunshine emerged at midnight. These incompatibilities had their peculiar charm—many night workers, for example, liked having their own private time zones—but, in general, it cost more to buy scenedows which kept closely in step with real time.

44   Selina still looked unconvinced when Hagan had finished speaking. She shook her head almost imperceptibly and I knew he

had been using the wrong approach. Quite suddenly the pewter helmet of her hair was disturbed by a cool gust of wind, and huge clean tumbling drops of rain began to spang round us from an almost cloudless sky.

"I'll give you a check now," I said abruptly, and saw Selina's green eyes triangulate angrily on my face. "You can arrange delivery?"   45

"Aye, delivery's no problem," Hagan said, getting to his feet. "But wouldn't you rather take the glass with you?"   46

"Well, yes—if you don't mind." I was shamed by his readiness to trust my scrip.   47

"I'll unclip a pane for you. Wait here. It won't take long to slip it into a carrying frame." Hagan limped down the slope towards the seriate windows, through some of which the view towards Linnhe was sunny, while others were cloudy and a few pure black.   48

Selina drew the collar of her blouse closed at her throat. "The least he could have done was invite us inside. There can't be so many fools passing through that he can afford to neglect them."   49

I tried to ignore the insult and concentrated on writing the check. One of the outsize drops broke across my knuckles, splattering the pink paper.   50

"All right," I said, "let's move in under the eaves till he gets back." You worm, I thought as I felt the whole thing go completely wrong. I just had to be a fool to marry you. A prize fool, a fool's fool—and now that you've trapped part of me inside you I'll never ever, never ever, *never ever* get away.   51

Feeling my stomach clench itself painfully, I ran behind Selina to the side of the cottage. Beyond the window the neat living room, with its coal fire, was empty but the child's toys were scattered on the floor. Alphabet blocks and a wheelbarrow the exact color of freshly pared carrots. As I stared in, the boy came running from the other room and began kicking the blocks. He didn't notice me. A few moments later the young woman entered the room and lifted him, laughing easily and wholeheartedly as she swung the boy under her arm. She came to the window as she had done earlier. I smiled self-consciously, but neither she nor the child responded.   52

My forehead prickled icily. *Could they both be blind?* I sidled away.   53

Selina gave a little scream and I spun towards her.   54

"The rug!" she said. "It's getting soaked."   55

She ran across the yard in the rain, snatched the reddish square from the dappling wall and ran back, towards the cottage door. Something heaved convulsively in my subconscious.   56

"Selina," I shouted. "Don't open it!"   57

58   But I was too late. She had pushed open the latched wooden door and was standing, hand over mouth, looking into the cottage. I moved close to her and took the rug from her unresisting fingers.

59   As I was closing the door I let my eyes traverse the cottage's interior. The neat living room in which I had just seen the woman and child was, in reality, a sickening clutter of shabby furniture, old newspapers, cast-off clothing and smeared dishes. It was damp, stinking and utterly deserted. The only object I recognized from my view through the window was the little wheelbarrow, paintless and broken.

60   I latched the door firmly and ordered myself to forget what I had seen. Some men who live alone are good housekeepers; others just don't know how.

61   Selina's face was white. "I don't understand. I don't understand it."

62   "Slow glass works both ways," I said gently. "Light passes out of a house as well as in."

63   "You mean . . . ?"

64   "I don't know. It isn't our business. Now steady up—Hagan's coming back with our glass." The churning in my stomach was beginning to subside.

65   Hagan came into the yard carrying an oblong, plastic-covered frame. I held the check out to him, but he was staring at Selina's face. He seemed to know immediately that our uncomprehending fingers had rummaged through his soul. Selina avoided his gaze. She was old and ill-looking, and her eyes stared determinedly towards the nearing horizon.

66   "I'll take the rug from you, Mr. Garland," Hagan finally said. "You shouldn't have troubled yourself over it."

67   "No trouble. Here's the check."

68   "Thank you." He was still looking at Selina with a strange kind of supplication. "It's been a pleasure to do business with you."

69   "The pleasure was mine," I said with equal, senseless formality. I picked up the heavy frame and guided Selina towards the path which led to the road. Just as we reached the head of the now slippery steps Hagan spoke again.

70   "Mr. Garland!"

71   I turned unwillingly.

72   "It wasn't my fault," he said steadily. "A hit-and-run driver got them both, down on the Oban road six years ago. My boy was only seven when it happened. I'm entitled to keep something."

73   I nodded wordlessly and moved down the path, holding my

wife close to me, treasuring the feel of her arms locked around me. At the bend I looked back through the rain and saw Hagan sitting with squared shoulders on the wall where we had first seen him.

He was looking at the house, but I was unable to tell if there   74 was anyone at the window.

Reading Critically

1. What problems (for individuals and for society as a whole) do you think slow glass would cause if it were real? What benefits would it provide? Discuss with your classmates whether you would want slow glass to be available if it were possible.

2. What does Garland mean when he says that "having a scenedow was the exact emotional equivalent of owning land"? What emotional needs does slow glass fulfill? What technological devices do we use to fulfill emotional needs? (Think about television, automobiles, videotape players, record players, and other devices.) Discuss with your classmates one technological device you couldn't live without, and why you couldn't live without it. Make a list of all the devices mentioned in your discussion with your classmates. What devices are mentioned most?

3. While slow glass has obviously had a great effect on society, this story concentrates on the effects of slow glass on individuals. How is the life of each character in the story affected by slow glass?

4. Look up the word *window* in a dictionary. What does it mean? How does the meaning of *window* help you understand the meaning of *scenedow?* Where in the story does Shaw define what the word *scenedow* means? What do you need to understand about slow glass in order to understand the word *scenedow?*

Responding Through Writing

1. Slow glass, of course, doesn't exist. How does Shaw present slow glass so you accept its reality? What tone does he use when he discusses the technical aspects of slow glass? Write a short description of how slow glass works.

2. Read paragraphs 11, 19, 35, 36, and 52, and make notes on what information in these paragraphs prepares you for the ending of the story. Using your notes, write a paragraph in which you explain how the ending of the story is not a surprise.

3. Shaw got the title of his story from the lines of the poem quoted in paragraph 41. What are the implications of that poem for the story? Write one sentence in which you state the theme of the story. Using this sentence, write the first draft a short essay in which you explain the relation of the title of the story to the theme of the story. Revise your draft after discussing it with your classmates.

4. Which character in this story is most vivid for you? What kind of person is this character? Write a short description of this character, concentrating on the character's personality.

THE UNKNOWN CITIZEN

W. H. AUDEN

Wystan Hugh Auden (1907–1973), English poet, playwright, librettist, and essayist, enjoyed great fame as a poet. Even before Auden graduated from Christ Church College of Oxford University in the late 1920s, he was recognized for his talent. In 1948, he won the Pulitzer Prize for The Age of Anxiety *(1947). Auden's other collections of poetry include* Another Time *(1940) and* The Shield of Achilles *(1955). The following poem was written in March 1939 and originally published in* Collected Poems *(1945).*

(To JS/07/M/378
This Marble Monument
Is Erected by the State)

He was found by the Bureau of Statistics to be
One against whom there was no official complaint,
And all the reports on his conduct agree

That, in the modern sense of an old-fashioned word, he was a saint,
5 For in everything he did he served the Greater Community.
Except for the War till the day he retired
He worked in a factory and never got fired,
But satisfied his employers, Fudge Motors Inc.
Yet he wasn't a scab or odd in his views,
10 For his Union reports that he paid his dues,
(Our report on his Union shows it was sound)
And our Social Psychology workers found
That he was popular with his mates and liked a drink.
The Press are convinced that he bought a paper every day
And that his reactions to advertisements were normal in every
15   way.
Policies taken out in his name prove that he was fully insured,
And his Health-card shows he was once in hospital but left it cured.
Both Producers Research and High-Grade Living declare
He was fully sensible to the advantages of the Installment Plan
20 And had everything necessary to the Modern Man,
A phonograph, radio, a car and a frigidaire.
Our researchers into Public Opinion are content
That he held the proper opinions for the time of year;
When there was peace, he was for peace; when there was war, he
    went.
25 He was married and added five children to the population,
Which our Eugenist says was the right number for a parent of his
    generation,
And our teachers report that he never interfered with their educa-
tion.
Was he free? Was he happy? The question is absurd:
Had anything been wrong, we should certainly have heard.

Reading Critically

1. The Unknown Citizen seems to have all the things a modern person would want. What, then, is lacking in his life? Discuss
with your classmates. What would you offer the Unknown Citizen
to make his life more worthwhile?

2. Can the Unknown Citizen's lot be improved without making radical changes in the nature of society? In what specific ways is Auden's description of the Unknown Citizen an indictment of society as a whole?

3. Why do you think that Auden ironically says that asking about freedom and happiness is absurd? How do you and your classmates define these terms? What questions tend to emerge as you try to work toward those definitions?

4. Do the issues addressed by Auden become more serious as the poem moves along? Which issues are trivial, which serious? Is there any single matter you find at the poem's heart?

Responding Through Writing

1. Do you see yourself or your classmates in the picture of the Unknown Citizen? Explore this question for at least two pages in your private journal or notebook.

2. What contemporary examples might you add to the poem to make it true to our times? Draw up a list.

3. Write a draft of a prose version of Auden's poem. In that draft, use the contemporary references developed in item 2 to describe a typical "unknown citizen" of today.

4. Why is this poem an indictment of statistical methodology? In a page or two in your journal or notebook, discuss some of the ways in which statistics can be used to distort reality. Use specific examples to illustrate your major points.

PART VIII

ARGUMENT

Many people associate the word *argument* with loud words and fights. Actually, the word *argument* technically refers to the process one goes through in stating and defending a position on a particular issue. What are the essential components of a good argument? What must you do to convince your readers that they ought to agree with your position?

First, clearly state your *thesis.* Let's say that your general topic is gun control. Here are two sample theses:

A. Handguns should be outlawed because they are a leading cause of murders, suicides, and accidental deaths.

B. Even though they may be used to commit crimes, handguns should *not* be outlawed for two reasons:

(1) criminals would have guns even if guns were outlawed;

(2) handguns are a major means of self-defense for law-abiding citizens.

These two theses are different in several respects. Not only is one *for* handgun control and the other *against* it, but one is short, the other elaborate. Both theses, however, are complete sentences that say something concrete about the subject of handgun control, and both, moreover, spell out for the reader the ways in which the writer is going to illustrate and support the major contentions of the argument. A good thesis is always presented in a complete sentence, and is written in such a way as to predict how you intend to develop your essay.

State Your Thesis Early

The thesis sentence of an argument usually appears in the first paragraph. That sentence should not only indicate the substance of the argument but should give readers some indication of the organizational pattern of the entire essay. Thesis A, for example, implicitly suggests an essay that will discuss in some detail, and with examples for illustration, how handguns figure in murders, suicides, and accidental deaths. If the writer has taken care early in the essay to state a thesis clearly, then by sticking to that thesis, he or she should be able to organize the body of the essay without difficulty. The outline for the essay developing thesis A would probably look something like this:

Paragraph 1. Introductory remarks (perhaps a vivid example) and statement of thesis.

Paragraph 2. Examples (and perhaps some statistics) to show that handguns are consistently used in murders.

Paragraph 3. Examples (and perhaps statistics) to show that handguns are the leading instrument of suicide.

Paragraph 4. Examples (and perhaps statistics) to show that handguns are a leading instrument of accidental deaths.

Paragraph 5. Conclusion: summary of statistics and major examples to reinforce thesis.

Thesis B suggests an essay that will present evidence to show (1) that if guns were outlawed criminals would still have them, and (2) that handguns are needed for self-defense. In organizing the argument to develop this thesis, the writer of the essay would naturally come up with a pattern of organization that looked much like this:

Paragraph 1. Introductory remarks (perhaps a vivid example) and statement of thesis.

Paragraph 2. Examples (and perhaps statistics) to show the existence of an illegal gun market used by criminals.

Paragraph 3. Discussion concerning the difficulties of eliminating this illegal market.

Paragraph 4.   Examples (and perhaps statistics) supporting use of handguns for self-defense.

Paragraph 5.   Conclusion: summary of statistics, examples, and discussions that support the thesis.

Of course, these organizational patterns would vary somewhat from writer to writer, and as should be obvious, neither of these essays needs to be limited to five paragraphs. Both essays, whatever their length, however, will follow the standard pattern for most argumentative writing:

1. State and briefly illustrate the thesis (paragraph 1).
2. Support the thesis with examples (middle paragraphs).
3. Restate the thesis in light of the middle paragraph illustrations (concluding paragraph).

Deductive Versus Inductive Arguments

The method of argumentative organization illustrated above is often called *deductive*. The deductive method is the most common method of argument because it usually is the clearest. That is, the reader knows from the beginning what the main point of the argument is going to be. The opposite method is called *inductive*. Using the inductive method, you essentially turn the order of the deductive method around. That is, you would present your major examples and let them suggest the thesis. You might, for the sake of clarity, explicitly state your thesis near the end of your essay, or you might simply allow it to be implied by the force of your examples.

All good arguments are neatly organized. The writers of good arguments, after they have discovered in the stages of prewriting how they want to treat their topic, begin their first drafts with a clear plan in mind. In successive drafts, you may want to vary your initial organizational plan. Remember, however, that in order to vary a plan you must have a plan in the first place. So, in the first drafts of an argument it is almost always a good idea to be as explicit and as clearly organized as possible, for the sake of clarifying your ideas to your readers—and to yourself.

Dealing with Objections

After you have practiced developing arguments as suggested above, you will probably find it useful to begin varying the pattern of your argumentative essays so as to anticipate objections that will likely be raised against your thesis. Remember that even "friendly" readers are likely to note objections to any argument as they read through it. By meeting those objections you show your readers that you are in control of your subject matter. Here is one way to deal with anticipated objections to an argument. To incorporate a discussion of objections into your argument, all you have to do is present those objections and respond to them prior to your conclusion. The best writers do not try to defeat every objection, for they know that almost any good argument will naturally have a flaw or two. Better to acknowledge that your position has its shortcomings—but also to indicate that they are less serious than the shortcomings of opposing arguments.

How to Present Both Sides of an Argument

Some argumentative essays do not firmly espouse a single position, but examine two or more sides of a particular issue with a view to determining which is strongest. Here is an outline for such an argument. The writer, for purposes of this example, is discussing the pros and cons of a computer company's entrance to the college market. In this case the essay's format is spelled out in a "sentence outline."

Outline

Section 1.

Statement of the problem: There is a large market for computers in colleges. Ideally we should enter this market, but our resources are limited and we may not be able to service what we sell.

Section 2.

Argument for one side: The college market is so large that our competitors can't possibly meet demand. Our latest software is especially useful for college humanities courses.

Section 3.

Argument for the other side: After initial gains, our entry into the college market would be a disaster. We have virtually no service staff to back up the sales force. To service this new market, we would have to divert resources from present markets. Soon we would be stretched very thin and would not likely be able to service even our regular customers.

Section 4.

Conclusion: Show superiority of either argument 1 or 2, or argue a synthesis of the two sides: Do not enter into the college market unless a way can be found to expand our service departments.

Whatever the organizational plan for an argument, there are two argumentative processes to which every writer should continually pay attention:

1. Define your terms.
2. Read and revise your argument to eliminate fallacies.

Define Your Terms

First, define your terms. This simply means you should clearly indicate to the reader the precise sense in which you use the key words in your argument. Let's say that in an economics course you've been asked to argue for or against the establishment of an economic community in Latin America. To argue effectively either way, you first have to define *economic community*. Does it require the elimination of all tariffs and trade barriers or just selected ones? You also have to define the word *establishment*. Does it mean putting something into practice immediately or doing so gradually, over a course of years or even decades? Finally, what is meant by *Latin*

America? Do you want to include both South and Central America? What about the Caribbean nations? As you can probably see, it's wise to get these terms pinned down *before* you start to develop your argument. Failure to do so in your introductory paragraph means that your argument is left open to question.

Eliminate Fallacies

Second, revise your early drafts to eliminate fallacies from your argument. Some of the common fallacies are these:

1. *AFTER THIS, THEREFORE BECAUSE OF THIS (POST HOC, ERGO PROPTER HOC)*

   > Susan gets a cold and happens to have a lot of cheese in the refrigerator. She nibbles on the cheese constantly for five days and suddenly feels well again. She now tells her friends that eating cheese cures colds.

The fallacy is easy to see in the example of Susan and the cheese. In the following example, the fallacy may be harder to spot.

> There is a change of government in France and the French economy collapses a month later. A newspaper concludes that the new government ruined the economy.

Such a conclusion would be unwarranted unless compelling evidence were presented to support it. Any number of factors could have caused the collapse of the economy.

2. *THE MISSING PROPOSITION*
   This is another common fallacy:

   > All chickens have wings. All ducks have wings. Therefore, all chickens are ducks.

But sometimes absurdity is not so easy to spot:

> Many hoodlums have punk haircuts. Susan has a punk haircut. Therefore, Susan is a hoodlum.

And even harder to spot:

> Communists favor better relations with Cuba. My senator favors better relations with Cuba. Therefore, my senator is a Communist.

3. *BEGGING THE QUESTION*
This fallacy involves the assumption that a case has already been made when in fact it has not:

> A great university such as ours cannot afford to ignore the recent advances in teaching methods.

This statement begs the question in at least two ways. It assumes that the university in question is "great," whatever that ambiguous term may mean, and it assumes that there really have been "advances" in teaching methods. The writer had better be prepared to show that the changes in teaching methods that will be discussed really are "advances."

A short introduction to a selection of essays such as this cannot hope to cover the wide array of fallacies likely to be commonly found in arguments, nor can it cover in detail the kinds of arguments germane to particular disciplines or the varieties of developmental patterns for arguments. The following essays, however, should give you some indication of the wide variety and scope of thoughtful argumentation.

WHY DON'T WE COMPLAIN?

WILLIAM F. BUCKLEY, JR.

A Yale graduate, William F. Buckley, Jr. (b. 1925), began infuriating liberals in the early 1950s with books, articles, and essays espousing his conservative political values. In 1965, Buckley ran for mayor of New York City as the Conservative Party candidate. An eloquent, persuasive, and sometimes even charming lecturer and writer, Buckley is the founder and editor of the conservative magazine The National Review *and the host of television's* Firing Line. *A prolific writer, he is the author of almost two dozen books, including several spy novels, the most recent of which is* Mongoose, R.I.P. *(1988). The following selection was originally published in* Esquire *magazine in January 1961.*

1   It was the very last coach and the only empty seat on the entire train, so there was no turning back. The problem was to breathe. Outside, the temperature was below freezing. Inside the railroad car the temperature must have been about 85 degrees. I took off my overcoat, and a few minutes later my jacket, and noticed that the car was flecked with the white shirts of the passengers. I soon found my hand moving to loosen my tie. From one end of the car to the

other, as we rattled through Westchester County, we sweated; but we did not moan.

I watched the train conductor appear at the head of the car.   2
"Tickets, all tickets, please!" In a more virile age, I thought, the passengers would seize the conductor and strap him down on a seat over the radiator to share the fate of his patrons. He shuffled down the aisle, picking up tickets, punching commutation cards. *No one addressed a word to him.* He approached my seat, and I drew a deep breath of resolution. "Conductor," I began with a considerable edge to my voice. . . . Instantly the doleful eyes of my seatmate turned tiredly from his newspaper to fix me with a resentful stare: what question could be so important as to justify my sibilant intrusion into his stupor? I was shaken by those eyes. I am incapable of making a discreet fuss, so I mumbled a question about what time were we due in Stamford (I didn't even ask whether it would be before or after dehydration could be expected to set in), got my reply, and went back to my newspaper and to wiping my brow.

The conductor had nonchalantly walked down the gauntlet of   3
eighty sweating American freemen, and not one of them had asked him to explain why the passengers in that car had consigned to suffer. There is nothing to be done when the temperature *outdoors* is 85 degrees, and indoors the air conditioner has broken down; obviously when that happens there is nothing to do, except perhaps curse the day that one was born. But when the temperature outdoors is below freezing, it takes a positive act of will on somebody's part to set the temperature *indoors* at 85. Somewhere a valve was turned too far, a furnace overstocked, a thermostat maladjusted: something that could easily be remedied by turning off the heat and allowing the great outdoors to come indoors. All this is so obvious. What is not obvious is what has happened to the American people.

It isn't just the commuters, whom we have come to visualize   4
as a supine breed who have got on to the trick of suspending their sensory faculties twice a day while they submit to the creeping dissolution of the railroad industry. It isn't just they who have given up trying to rectify irrational vexations. It is the American people everywhere.

A few weeks ago at a large movie theatre I turned to my wife   5
and said, "The picture is out of focus." "Be quiet," she answered. I obeyed. But a few minutes later I raised the point again, with mounting impatience. "It will be all right in a minute," she said apprehensively. (She would rather lose her eyesight than be around when I make one of my infrequent scenes.) I waited. It was *just* out

of focus—not glaringly out, but out. My vision is 20–20, and I assume that is the vision, adjusted, of most people in the movie house. So, after hectoring my wife throughout the first reel, I finally prevailed upon her to admit that it *was* off, and very annoying. We then settled down, coming to rest on the presumption that: a) someone connected with the management of the theatre must soon notice the blur and make the correction; or b) that someone seated near the rear of the house would make the complaint in behalf of those of us up front; or c) that—any minute now—the entire house would explode into catcalls and foot stamping, calling dramatic attention to the irksome distortion.

6   What happened was nothing. The movie ended, as it had begun *just* out of focus, and as we trooped out, we stretched our faces in a variety of contortions to accustom the eye to the shock of normal focus.

7   I think it is safe to say that everybody suffered on that occasion. And I think it is safe to assume that everyone was expecting someone else to take the initiative in going back to speak to the manager. And it is probably true even that if we had supposed the movie would run right through the blurred image, someone surely would have summoned up the purposive indignation to get up out of his seat and file his complaint.

8   But notice that no one did. And the reason no one did is because we are all increasingly anxious in America to be unobtrusive, we are reluctant to make our voices heard, hesitant about claiming our rights; we are afraid that our cause is unjust, or that if it is not unjust, that it is ambiguous; or if not even that, that it is too trivial to justify the horrors of a confrontation with Authority; we will sit in an oven or endure a racking headache before undertaking a head-on, I'm-here-to-tell-you complaint. That tendency to passive compliance, to a heedless endurance, is something to keep one's eyes on—in sharp focus.

9   I myself can occasionally summon the courage to complain, but I cannot, as I have intimated, complain softly. My own instinct is so strong to let the thing ride, to forget about it—to expect that someone will take the matter up, when the grievance is collective, in my behalf—that it is only when the provocation is at a very special key, whose vibrations touch simultaneously a complexus of nerves, allergies, and passions, that I catch fire and find the reserves of courage and assertiveness to speak up. When that happens, I get quite carried away. My blood gets hot, my brow wet, I become unbearably and unconscionably sarcastic and bellicose; I am girded for a total showdown.

Why should that be? Why could not I (or anyone else) on that   10
railroad coach have said simply to the conductor, "Sir"—I take that
back: that sounds sarcastic—"Conductor, would you be good
enough to turn down the heat? I am extremely hot. In fact, I tend
to get hot every time the temperature reaches 85 degr—" Strike that
last sentence. Just end it with the simple statement that you are
extremely hot, and let the conductor infer the cause.

Every New Year's Eve I resolve to do something about the   11
Milquetoast in me and vow to speak up, calmly, for my rights, and
for the betterment of our society, on every appropriate occasion.
Entering last New Year's Eve I was fortified in my resolve because
that morning at breakfast I had had to ask the waitress three times
for a glass of milk. She finally brought it—after I had finished my
eggs, which is when I don't want it any more. I did not have the
manliness to order her to take the milk back, but settled instead for
a cowardly sulk, and ostentatiously refused to drink the milk—
though I later paid for it—rather than state plainly to the hostess,
as I should have, why I had not drunk it, and would not pay for
it.

So by the time the New Year ushered out the Old, riding in   12
on my morning's indignation and stimulated by the gastric juices
of resolution that flow so faithfully on New Year's Eve, I rendered
my vow. Henceforward I would conquer my shyness, my despicable
disposition to supineness. I would speak out like a man against the
unnecessary annoyances of our time.

Forty-eight hours later, I was standing in line at the ski repair   13
store in Pico Peak, Vermont. All I needed, to get on with my skiing,
was the loan, for one minute, of a small screwdriver, to tighten a
loose binding. Behind the counter in the workshop were two men.
One was industriously engaged in servicing the complicated requirements of a young lady at the head of the line, and obviously
he would be tied up for quite a while. The other—"Jiggs," his
workmate called him—was a middle-aged man, who sat in a chair
puffing a pipe, exchanging small talk with his working partner. My
pulse began its telltale acceleration. The minutes ticked on. I stared
at the idle shopkeeper, hoping to shame him into action, but he was
impervious to my telepathic reproof and continued his small talk
with his friend, brazenly insensitive to the nervous demands of six
good men who were raring to ski.

Suddenly my New Year's Eve resolution struck me. It was   14
now or never. I broke from my place in line and marched to the
counter. I was going to control myself. I dug my nails into my
palms. My effort was only partially successful.

15   "If you are not too busy," I said icily, "would you mind handing me a screwdriver?"

16   Work stopped and everyone turned his eyes on me, and I experienced that mortification I always feel when I am the center of centripetal shafts of curiosity, resentment, perplexity.

17   But the worst was yet to come. "I am sorry, sir," said Jiggs deferentially, moving the pipe from his mouth. "I am not supposed to move. I have just had a heart attack." That was the signal for a great whirring noise that descended from heaven. We looked, stricken, out the window, and it appeared as though a cyclone had suddenly focused on the snowy courtyard between the shop and the ski lift. Suddenly a gigantic army helicopter materialized, and hovered down to a landing. Two men jumped out of the plane carrying a stretcher, tore into the ski shop, and lifted the shopkeeper onto the stretcher. Jiggs bade his companion goodby, was whisked out the door, into the plane, up to the heavens, down—we learned—to a near-by army hospital. I looked up manfully—into a score of man-eating eyes. I put the experience down as a reversal.

18   As I write this, on an airplane, I have run out of paper and need to reach into my briefcase under my legs for more. I cannot do this until my empty lunch tray is removed from my lap. I arrested the stewardess as she passed empty-handed down the aisle on the way to the kitchen to fetch the lunch trays for the passengers up forward who haven't been served yet. "Would you please take my tray?" "Just a *moment, sir!*" she said, and marched on sternly. Shall I tell her that since she is headed for the kitchen *anyway,* it could not delay the feeding of the other passengers by more than two seconds necessary to stash away my empty tray? Or remind her that not fifteen minutes ago she spoke unctuously into the loudspeaker the words undoubtedly devised by the airline's highly paid public relations counselor: "If there is anything I or Miss French can do for you to make your trip more enjoyable, *please* let us—" I have run out of paper.

19   I think the observable reluctance of the majority of Americans to assert themselves in minor matters is related to our increased sense of helplessness in an age of technology and centralized political and economic power. For generations, Americans who were too hot, or too cold, got up and did something about it. Now we call the plumber, or the electrician, or the furnace man. The habit of looking after our own needs obviously had something to do with the assertiveness that characterized the American family familiar to readers of American literature. With

the technification of life goes our direct responsibility for our
material environment, and we are conditioned to adopt a position
of helplessness not only as regards the broken air conditioner, but
as regards the overheated train. It takes an expert to fix the former, but not the latter; yet these distinctions, as we withdraw into
helplessness, tend to fade away.

Reading Critically

1. Why in paragraph 2 does Buckley hesitate to complain?
What stated and unstated circumstances lead him to back off from
the train conductor? Describe a time you were in a similar situation
(though not necessarily on a train) yourself. Discuss with your
classmates what made you complain or remain silent.

2. Do you tend to complain constantly about everyday annoyances, such as rude or inattentive clerks or waiters, people who
talk in movie theaters, people who play their radios loudly in public,
bad bus service, or products that don't work properly? Discuss with
your classmates what you think of people who "complain all the
time."

3. A complaint against a perceived injustice can be more than
just a complaint about bad train service. A complaint can alter
society. Choose one example from history (such as the civil rights
movement, the women's movement, the complaints of the Southern
states against the federal government in 1861, the complaints of the
American colonists against the British government, or the complaints of the handicapped against government authorities because
of the physical and economic barriers they face) where a complaint
has lead to positive or negative consequences. What does your
example say about the role of complaints in our society and in
history?

4. Discuss how technology has made us less independent. Pick one technological "advance" that you think you could do without, and explain to your classmates how life would be better without it.

Responding Through Writing

1. If you are keeping a journal or notebook in this course, write in it for five to ten minutes on a specific time you really wanted to complain but didn't. In addition to describing the incident that made you want to complain, give your reasons for not complaining. Now compare your account with the accounts written by your classmates. How similar are the reasons given by everyone? How similar are these reasons to Buckley's reasons for not complaining? Using the information from this discussion, write the first draft of an essay on ways to make people feel more free to complain.

2. Write a brief list of all the examples Buckley uses in his essay. Choose the example you find most effective and in a short paragraph explain why you think it is persuasive. Now choose the example you find least effective and explain why it is unconvincing. Divide your list of examples into two categories: those that you think are "typical" examples and those that you think are "unusual" examples. Which examples do you think are more effective? Why are they effective? What does Buckley's choice of examples tell you about the audience for whom he was writing?

3. Write one sentence in which you state Buckley's central idea. (See paragraph 8.) Why does Buckley wait until he is almost midway through his essay to state his main idea? Rewrite paragraph 8 so that it can be the first paragraph in the essay. How does opening with such a paragraph change the essay?

4. Buckley says that while technological developments like the computer and the telephone may have improved our living standards, they have also narrowed our lives. What is the relation between technology and helplessness that Buckley draws in para-

graph 19? Make a list of some of the technological advances that you think have narrowed our lives. You may want to start with television replacing reading, the automobile replacing walking, the telephone replacing letter writing, and the computer starting to replace typewriters and other things. Write the draft of an essay using items in your list as examples.

IS THE EARTH ROUND OR FLAT?

ALAN LIGHTMAN

Alan Lightman (b. 1948) grew up in Memphis, Tennessee. A Phi Beta Kappa graduate of Princeton and a National Science Foundation Fellow of the California Institute of Technology, Lightman currently teaches astronomy and physics at Harvard University. Since 1979 Lightman has been a staff member of the Smithsonian Astrophysical Observatory in Cambridge, and he contributes to numerous periodicals, including Smithsonian, *the* Boston Globe, Harper's, *and* The New Yorker. *Also a poet, Lightman's pieces have been anthologized in the* Yearbook of American Poetry *and have earned him the Rhysling Award for 1983. His books include* Revealing the Universe *(1982),* Time Travel and Papa Joe's Pipe *(1984), and* A Modern Day Yankee in a Connecticut Court *(1986). The following essay is contained in* Time Travel and Papa Joe's Pipe *and was originally published in the March issue of* Science 82.

1   I propose that there are few of us who have personally verified that the Earth is round. The suggestive globe in the den or the Apollo photographs don't count. These are secondhand pieces of

evidence that might be thrown out entirely in court. When you think about it, most of us simply believe what we hear. Round or flat, whatever. It's not a life-or-death matter, unless you happen to live near the edge.

A few years ago I suddenly realized, to my dismay, that I 2 didn't know with certainty if the Earth were round or flat. I have scientific colleagues, geodesists they are called, whose sole business is determining the detailed shape of the Earth by fitting mathematical formulae to someone else's measurements of the precise locations of test stations on the Earth's surface. And I don't think those people really know either.

Aristotle is the first person in recorded history to have given 3 proof that the Earth is round. He used several different arguments, most likely because he wanted to convince others as well as himself. A lot of people believed everything Aristotle said for 19 centuries.

His first proof was that the shadow of the Earth during a lunar 4 eclipse is always curved, a segment of a circle. If the Earth were any shape but spherical, the shadow it casts, in some orientations, would not be circular. (That the normal phases of the moon are crescent-shaped reveals the moon is round.) I find this argument wonderfully appealing. It is simple and direct. What's more, an inquisitive and untrusting person can knock off the experiment alone, without special equipment. From any given spot on the Earth, a lunar eclipse can be seen about once a year. You simply have to look up on the right night and carefully observe what's happening. I've never done it.

Aristotle's second proof was that stars rise and set sooner for 5 people in the East than in the West. If the Earth were flat from east to west, stars would rise as soon for Occidentals as for Orientals. With a little scribbling on a piece of paper, you can see that these observations imply a round Earth, regardless of whether it is the Earth that spins around or the stars that revolve around the Earth. Finally, northbound travelers observe previously invisible stars appearing above the northern horizon, showing the Earth is curved from north to south. Of course, you do have to accept the reports of a number of friends in different places or be willing to do some traveling.

Aristotle's last argument was purely theoretical and even phil- 6 osophical. If the Earth had been formed from smaller pieces at some time in the past (or *could* have been so formed), its pieces would fall toward a common center, thus making a sphere. Furthermore, a sphere is clearly the most perfect solid shape. Interestingly, Aristotle placed as much emphasis on this last argument as on the first two. Those days, before the modern "scientific method," observational check wasn't required for investigating reality.

7   Assuming for the moment that the Earth is round, the first person who measured its circumference accurately was another Greek, Eratosthenes (276–195 B.C.). Eratosthenes noted that on the first day of summer, sunlight struck the bottom of a vertical well in Syene, Egypt, indicating the sun was directly overhead. At the same time in Alexandria, 5,000 stadia distant, the sun made an angle with the vertical equal to ¹⁄₅₀ of a circle. (A stadium equaled about a tenth of a mile.) Since the sun is so far away, its rays arrive almost in parallel. If you draw a circle with two radii extending from the center outward through the perimeter (where they become local verticals), you'll see that a sun ray coming in parallel to one of the radii (at Syene) makes an angle with the other (at Alexandria) equal to the angle between the two radii. Therefore Eratosthenes concluded that the full circumference of the Earth is 50 × 5,000 stadia, or about 25,000 miles. This calculation is within one percent of the best modern value.

8   For at least 600 years educated people have believed the Earth is round. At nearly any medieval university, the quadrivium was standard fare, consisting of arithmetic, geometry, music, and astronomy. The astronomy portion was based on the *Tractatus de Sphaera,* a popular textbook first published at Ferrara, Italy, in 1472 and written by a 13th-century, Oxford-educated astronomer and mathematician, Johannes de Sacrobosco. The *Sphaera* proves its astronomical assertions, in part, by a set of diagrams with movable parts, a graphical demonstration of Aristotle's second method of proof. The round Earth, being the obvious center of the universe, provides a fixed pivot for the assembly. The cutout figures of the sun, the moon, and the stars revolve about the Earth.

9   By the year 1500, 24 editions of the *Sphaera* had appeared. There is no question that many people *believed* the Earth was round. I wonder how many *knew* this. You would think that Columbus and Magellan might have wanted to ascertain the facts for themselves before waving good-bye.

10   To protect my honor as a scientist, someone who is supposed to take nothing for granted, I set out with my wife on a sailing voyage in the Greek islands. I reasoned that at sea I would be able to calmly observe landmasses disappear over the curve of the Earth and thus convince myself, firsthand, that the Earth is round.

11   Greece seemed a particularly satisfying place to conduct my experiment. I could sense those great ancient thinkers looking on approvingly, and the layout of the place is perfect. Hydra rises about

2,000 feet above sea level. If the Earth has a radius of 4,000 miles, as they say, then Hydra should sink down to the horizon at a distance of about 50 miles, somewhat less than the distance we were to sail from Hydra to Kea. The theory was sound and comfortable. At the very least, I thought, we would have a pleasant vacation.

As it turned out, that was all we got. Every single day was 12 hazy. Islands faded from view at a distance of only eight miles, when the land was still a couple of degrees above the horizon. I learned how much water vapor was in the air but nothing about the curvature of the Earth.

I suspect that there are quite a few items we take on faith, even 13 important things, even things we could verify without much trouble. Is the gas we exhale the same as the gas we inhale? (Do we indeed burn oxygen in our metabolism, as they say?) What is our blood made of? (Does it indeed have red and white "cells"?) These questions could be answered with a balloon, a candle, and a microscope.

When we finally do the experiment, we relish the knowledge. 14 At one time or another, we have all learned something for ourselves, from the ground floor up, taking no one's word for it. There is a special satisfaction and joy in being able to tell somebody something you have pieced together from scratch, something you really know. I think that exhilaration is a big reason why people do science.

Someday soon, I'm going to catch the Earth's shadow in a 15 lunar eclipse, or go to sea in clear air, and find out for sure if the Earth is round or flat. Actually, the Earth is reported to flatten at the poles, because it rotates. But that's another story.

Reading Critically

1. How would you go about verifying that the earth is indeed round? Is there any way to do this without relying on "secondhand" evidence, such as photographs from space? Does it really matter what shape the earth is? Sherlock Holmes, in *A Study in Scarlet,* says to Dr. Watson that it makes no difference at all to him whether the earth travels around the sun, or vice versa. Does it make a difference to you? Discuss these questions with your classmates.

2. Apart from religious belief, are there things besides the roundness of the earth that we take on faith? Would it be possible to operate in our daily lives without taking things on faith? Give some examples to support your position and ask your classmates to provide examples of their own.

3. How were many of the great discoverers of the past treated by society? What of Galileo and Columbus? Bring to class for discussion a brief account of one such person.

4. We may indeed "know" that the earth is round, but are there other scientific things about which we remain profoundly ignorant: the structure of the atom, the force that unifies nature, the nature of time, the causes of drug addiction, the natures of pain and of pleasure? Is human ignorance greater than we usually think? Discuss with your classmates.

Responding Through Writing

1. What does this essay tell you about the usefulness of personal observations in constructing a good argument? See especially the example of the disappearing islands in paragraphs 11 and 12. In a few paragraphs suggest some additional examples from personal observation that would help to further develop Lightman's essay.

2. Lightman uses several examples from the history of science and philosophy in order to bolster his case. Are some of these examples more effective than others? Are any of them too technical for an informal essay? Pick your favorite example from this essay and use it to develop an essay of your own on a related topic.

3. Is this essay mainly about the nature of the earth or about the nature of scientific investigation and argument? If the latter, what other kinds of examples could Lightman have used to make his point? List those examples.

4. Lightman seems to be saying that it is better to learn things for yourself than to learn them from others or from books. Is experience the best teacher? In what sense is this question a central theme of the essay? In your journal or notebook explore some instance in your life where your own personal experience was at odds with advice you received from books, parents, or friends.

COFFEE, TOAST AND CALIPERS

RUSSELL BAKER

Russell Baker (b. 1925) is the Pulitzer Prize–winning columnist of the New York Times *and perhaps the best known and most popular current political satirist. A 1947 graduate of Johns Hopkins University, Baker began his career in journalism in 1947 with the* Baltimore Sun. *In 1954 he began covering the White House, Congress, and national politics for the* New York Times, *and in 1980 he published a collection of his columns in* So This Is Depravity. *A fiercely comical writer, Baker won both the George Polk Award for Commentary and the Pulitzer Prize for Distinguished Commentary in 1979. His article "How to Hypnotize Yourself into Forgetting the Vietnam War" was dramatized and filmed for Public Television. He won the Pulitzer again in 1983. R. Z. Sheppard praised Baker for "writing to preserve his sanity for at least one more day." His other books include* Poor Russell's Almanac *(1972),* The Upside Down Man *(1977), and* The Rescue of Miss Yaskell and Other Pipe Dreams *(1983). The following essay first appeared in the* New York Times *in 1979.*

1   One of the morning papers said that some hard facts were beginning to emerge.

"Have you heard about the facts?" I asked my breakfast companion.   2

"What about them?" she said.   3

"They are hard," I said.   4

"That's ridiculous," she said. "Facts have no molecular structure and can, therefore, be neither hard nor soft. An artifact, on the other hand, is an object, having mass and texture, and is, hence, capable of possessing the quality loosely defined as hardness, or such other qualities as softness, sponginess, sliminess, scratchiness or oiliness, to name but a few. The hardness you ascribe to the facts indicates quite clearly that they are not facts, but artifacts."   5

"It says right here in the paper," said I, "that some hard facts are beginning to emerge."   6

"I doubt it," she said.   7

"Doubt what?"   8

"That the facts are emergent. When did the revolutions of the planets around the sun emerge?"   9

"At the creation," I said.   10

"Exactly," she said. "The planets revolved around the sun for eternities. That is a fact. It was a fact before there was anybody on earth sensible enough to realize it was a fact. The fact did not emerge when somebody pointed a telescope at the sky and deduced the nature of planetary relationships to the sun. The fact was merely discovered. It had been a fact all along and would still be a fact today if nobody had ever discovered it."   11

"Keeping that in mind, consider your newspaper report that some hard facts are beginning to emerge. I have already disposed of the absurd possibility that these facts can be hard, soft, scratchy, oily, etcetera, and have shown that facts exist independently of their discovery—"   12

She paused out of respect for the glaze seeping over my eyeballs. "Are you bored?" she asked.   13

"Give it to me right from the shoulder," I begged. "Are some facts beginning to emerge or is this newspaper giving me false facts?"   14

"As briefly as possible," she said, "your newspaper is merely stating that some facts, possibly long existent, have now come to its attention. These facts are, of course, not hard. They may, however, be interesting, dull, amusing, important or trivial to you, depending upon your interests. We may conclude that they are interesting and important to the editor of your newspaper since he gives them space he knows to be valuable. It is quite likely that he wishes these facts to seem interesting and important to you, rather   15 than dull and trivial, since he has allowed his writer to prefix the word 'facts' with the idiotic but attention-getting word 'hard'."

16   "I wish I hadn't brought it up," I said.

17   "To answer your second question," she continued, "it is impossible for your newspaper to give you false facts."

18   "How about some more coffee?"

19   "Your newspaper," she said, "might very well report that the planets do not revolve around the sun but that the sun revolves around the earth. Misinformation of this sort appears frequently in the press, but it is not a false fact, since it is not a fact at all. It is merely an error or, if published with intent to deceive, a lie or, if published with intent to hoodwink, a hoax. A fact cannot be false. Failure to grasp this childish truth led Senator Joseph McCarthy to expose the muddle of his own mind when he said he had 'facts, which if true,' would reveal Communist conspiracy in government."

20   "Not Joe McCarthy—not at this hour of the morning," I gasped.

21   "It took scarcely an iota of brain," she went on, "to see that Mr. McCarthy did not have facts, but only assertions which might be untrue."

22   "Are you sure you've got your facts straight?" I asked.

23   "Facts," she said, "approach infinity in number and are not subject to arrangement in linear sequence in either two or three dimensions, except for the purposes of systematic reasoning, which process requires us to ignore the inconvenient random existence of numberless facts apparently irrelevant to our line of thought, despite a large body of evidence that random facts discarded during the attempt to establish a pure line of reasoning often come back to wreck it."

24   "Is that so?" I asked.

25   "That's a fact," she said, "and it isn't hard either. It's just a fact."

Reading Critically

1. Look up at least one article on Senator Joseph McCarthy, who is mentioned in paragraph 19. According to your research, what was McCarthy's argument concerning Communists in the State Department? What were his "facts"? Where did McCarthy get his "facts"?

2. How does Baker explain the difference between fact and assertion? (See paragraphs 19 to 21.) What is the difference between fact and assertion for you? How do you and Baker agree or disagree on what is fact and what is assertion? With reference to a recent news story, discuss how you and your classmates agree or disagree on what is fact and what is assertion.

3. How should facts be used in argument? (See paragraph 23.) Baker writes that to construct an argument you (1) select the appropriate facts, and (2) arrange them to prove a point. How do you construct an argument? Discuss with your classmates how they go about constructing an argument.

4. According to Baker, what are inconvenient facts? (See paragraph 23.) What do you do about inconvenient facts when you construct an argument? If you must not ignore those facts that don't help your argument because they will "come back to wreck" your argument, what can you do about such facts?

Responding Through Writing

1. Write a short definition of *irony*. Using your definition, find at least two instances of irony in Baker's essay, then write a paragraph in which you show how these instances fit your definition.

2. If Baker's purpose is to teach a serious lesson about argument, why does he start his essay in such an ironic and humorous way? Write a serious, nonhumorous opening for this essay that still achieves Baker's purpose. How does your new opening affect the rest of the essay? What other changes would you have to make in the essay because of your new opening?

3. Examine the setting in this essay. Why does Baker choose the breakfast table to discuss "hard" facts? What does this setting contribute to the essay? Rewrite Baker's essay using a cocktail party, fraternity party, or similar social function as the setting.

4. Figuratively speaking, to what extent are facts "hard"? Select an article from a weekly news magazine such as *Time, Newsweek,* or *U.S. News & World Report* and write a short report in which you separate fact from opinion in the article, and in which you state how you know which parts of the article are facts and which opinion. Discuss your report with your classmates, explaining the basis for your distinction between fact and opinion.

THE CIVIL RIGHTS MOVEMENT: WHAT GOOD WAS IT?

ALICE WALKER

Alice Walker (b. 1944) graduated from Sarah Lawrence College in 1965. She is best known for The Color Purple *(1982), a novel exploring the perceptions of a young black woman. Her short story collection,* In Love and Trouble: Stories of Black Women *(1973), explores the lives and thoughts of 13 black women of various backgrounds. Most critics agree that her depiction of black women is extremely sympathetic and that her view of men, black or white, is not very positive. The following essay was first published in* American Scholar *magazine in the autumn of 1967.*

Someone said recently to an old black lady from Mississippi, whose legs had been badly mangled by local police who arrested her for "disturbing the peace," that the civil rights movement was dead, and asked, since it was dead, what she thought about it. The old lady replied, hobbling out of his presence on her cane, that the civil rights movement was like herself, "if it's dead, it shore ain't ready to lay down!"

This old lady is a legendary freedom fighter in her small town in the Delta. She has been severely mistreated for insisting on her rights as an American citizen. She has been beaten for singing movement songs, placed in solitary confinement in prisons for talking about freedom, and placed on bread and water for praying aloud to God for her jailers' deliverance. For such a woman the civil rights movement will never be over as long as her skin is black. It also will never be over for twenty million others with the same "affliction," for whom the movement can never "lay down," no matter how it is killed by the press and made dead and buried by the white American public. As long as one black American survives, the struggle for equality with other Americans must also survive. This is a debt we owe to those blameless hostages we leave to the future, our children.

3   Still, white liberals and deserting civil rights sponsors are quick to justify their disaffection from the movement by claiming that it is all over. "And since it is over," they will ask, "would someone kindly tell me what has been gained by it?" They then list statistics supposedly showing how much more advanced segregation is now than ten years ago—in schools, housing, jobs. They point to a gain in conservative politicians during the last few years. They speak of ghetto riots and of the recent survey that shows that most policemen are admittedly too anti-Negro to do their jobs in ghetto areas fairly and effectively. They speak of every area that has been touched by the civil rights movement as somehow or other going to pieces.

4   They rarely talk, however, about human attitudes among Negroes that have undergone terrific changes just during the past seven to ten years (not to mention all those years when there was a movement and only the Negroes knew about it). They seldom speak of changes in personal lives because of the influence of people in the movement. They see general failure and few, if any, individual gains.

5   They do not understand what it is that keeps the movement from "laying down" and Negroes from reverting to their former *silent* second-class status. They have apparently never stopped to wonder why it is always the white man—on his radio and in his newspaper and on his television—who says that the movement is dead. If a Negro were audacious enough to make such a claim, his fellows might hanker to see him shot. The movement is dead to the white man because it no longer interests him. And it no longer interests him because he can afford to be uninterested: he does not have to live by it, with it, or for it, as Negroes must. He can take a rest from the news of beatings, killings and arrests that reach him from North and South—if his skin is white. Negroes cannot now

and will never be able to take a rest from the injustices that plague them for they—not the white man—are the target.

Perhaps it is naïve to be thankful that the movement "saved" a large number of individuals and gave them something to live for, even if it did not provide them with everything they wanted. (Materially, it provided them with precious little that they wanted.) When a movement awakens people to the possibilities of life, it seems unfair to frustrate them by then denying what they had thought was offered. But what was offered? What was promised? What was it all about? What good did it do? Would it have been better, as some have suggested, to leave the Negro people as they were, unawakened, unallied with one another, unhopeful about what to expect for their children in some future world?

I do not think so. If knowledge of my condition is all the freedom I get from a "freedom movement," it is better than unawareness, forgottenness and hopelessness, the existence that is like the existence of a beast. Man only truly lives by knowing, otherwise he simply performs, copying the daily habits of others, but conceiving nothing of his creative possibilities as a man, and accepting someone else's superiority and his own misery.

When we are children, growing up in our parents' care, we await the spark from the outside world. Sometimes our parents provide it—if we are lucky—sometimes it comes from another source far from home. We sit, paralyzed, surrounded by our anxiety and dread, hoping we will not have to grow up into the narrow world and ways we see about us. We are hungry for a life that turns us on; we yearn for a knowledge of living that will save us from our innocuous lives that resemble death. We look for signs in every strange event; we search for heroes in every unknown face.

It was just six years ago that I began to be alive. I had, of course, been living before—for I am now twenty-three—but I did not really know it. And I did not know it because nobody told me that I—a pensive, yearning, typical high-school senior, but Negro—existed in the minds of others as I existed in my own. Until that time my mind was locked apart from the outer contours and complexion of my body as if it and the body were strangers. The mind possessed both thought and spirit—I wanted to be an author or a scientist—which the color of the body denied. I had never seen myself and existed as a statistic exists, or as a phantom. In the white world I walked, less real to them than a shadow; and being young and well-hidden among the slums, among people who also did not exist—either in books or in films or in the government of their own lives—I waited to be called to life. And, by a miracle, I was called.

10   There was a commotion in our house that night in 1960. We had managed to buy our first television set. It was battered and overpriced, but my mother had gotten used to watching the afternoon soap operas at the house where she worked as maid, and nothing could satisfy her on days when she did not work but a continuation of her "stories." So she pinched pennies and bought a set.

11   I remained listless through her "stories," tales of pregnancy, abortion, hypocrisy, infidelity and alcoholism. All these men and women were white and lived in houses with servants, long staircases that they floated down, patios where liquor was served four times a day to "relax" them. But my mother, with her swollen feet eased out of her shoes, her heavy body relaxed in our only comfortable chair, watched each movement of the smartly coiffed women, heard each word, pounced upon each innuendo and inflection, and for the duration of these "stories" she saw herself as one of them. She placed herself in every scene she saw, with her braided hair turned blonde, her two hundred pounds compressed into a sleek size seven dress, her rough dark skin smooth and *white*. Her husband became dark and handsome, talented, witty, urbane, charming. And when she turned to look at my father sitting near her in his sweat shirt with his smelly feet raised on the bed to "air," there was always a tragic look of surprise on her face. Then she would sigh and go out to the kitchen looking lost and unsure of herself. My mother, a truly great woman—who raised eight children of her own and half a dozen of the neighbors' without a single complaint—was convinced that she did not exist compared to "them." She subordinated her soul to theirs and became a faithful and timid supporter of the "Beautiful White People." Once she asked me, in a moment of vicarious pride and despair, if I didn't think that "they" were "jest naturally smarter, prettier, better." My mother asked this; a woman who never got rid of any of her children, never cheated on my father, was never a hypocrite if she could help it, and never even tasted liquor. She could not even bring herself to blame "them" for making her believe what they wanted her to believe: that if she did not look like them, think like them, be sophisticated and corrupt-for-comfort's-sake like them, she was a nobody. Black was not a color on my mother, it was a shield that made her invisible. The heart that beat out its life in the great shadow cast by the American white people never knew that it was really "good."

12   Of course, the people who wrote the soap opera scripts always made the Negro maids in them steadfast, trusty and wise in a home-remedial sort of way; but my mother, a maid for nearly forty

years, never once identified herself with the scarcely glimpsed black servant's face beneath the ruffled cap. Like everyone else, in her daydreams at least, she thought she was free.

Six years ago, after half-heartedly watching my mother's soap operas and wondering whether there wasn't something more to be asked of life, the civil rights movement came into my life. Like a good omen for the future, the face of Dr. Martin Luther King, Jr., was the first black face I saw on our new television screen. And, as in a fairy tale, my soul was stirred by the meaning for me of his mission—at the time he was being rather ignominiously dumped into a police van for having led a protest march in Alabama—and I fell in love with the sober and determined face of the movement. The singing of "We Shall Overcome"—that song betrayed by nonbelievers in it—rang for the first time in my ears. The influence that my mother's soap operas might have had on me became impossible. The life of Dr. King, seeming bigger and more miraculous than the man himself, because of all he had done and suffered, offered a pattern of strength and sincerity I felt I could trust. He had suffered much because of his simple belief in nonviolence, love and brotherhood. Perhaps the majority of men could not be reached through these beliefs, but because Dr. King kept trying to reach them in spite of danger to himself and his family, I saw in him the hero for whom I had waited so long.

What Dr. King promised was not a ranch-style house and an acre of manicured lawn for every black man, but jail and finally freedom. He did not promise two cars for every family, but the courage one day for all families everywhere to walk without shame and unafraid on their own feet. He did not say that one day it will be us chasing prospective buyers out of our prosperous well-kept neighborhoods, or in other ways exhibiting our snobbery and ignorance as all other ethnic groups before us have done; what he said was that we had a right to live anywhere in this country we chose, and a right to a meaningful well-paying job to provide us with the upkeep of our homes. He did not say we had to become carbon copies of the white American middle-class; but he did say we had the right to become whatever we wanted to become.

Because of the movement, because of an awakened faith in the newness and imagination of the human spirit, because of "black and white together"—for the first time in our history in some human relationship on and off TV—because of the beatings, the arrests, the hell of battle during the past years, I have fought harder for my life and for a chance to be myself, to be something more than a shadow or a number, than I have ever done before in my life. Before there had seemed to be no real reason for struggling beyond the effort for daily bread. Now there was a chance at that other that Jesus meant when He said we could not live by bread alone.

16   I have fought and kicked and fasted and prayed and cursed and cried myself to the point of existing. It has been like being born again, literally. Just "knowing" has meant everything to me. Knowing has pushed me out into the world, into college, into places, into people.

17   Part of what existence means to me is knowing the difference between what I am now and what I was then. It is being capable of looking after myself intellectually as well as financially. It is being able to tell when I am being wronged and by whom. It means being awake to protect myself and the ones I love. It means being a part of the world community, and being *alert* to which part it is that I have joined, and knowing how to change to another part if that part does not suit me. To know is to exist; to exist is to be involved, to move about, to see the world with my own eyes. This, at least, the movement has given me.

18   The hippies and other nihilists would have me believe that it is all the same whether the people in Mississippi have a movement behind them or not. Once they have their rights, they say, they will run all over themselves trying to be just like everybody else. They will be well-fed, complacent about things of the spirit, emotionless, and without that marvelous humanity and "soul" that the movement has seen them practice time and time again. What has the movement done, they ask, with the few people it has supposedly helped? Got them white-collar jobs, moved them into standardized ranch houses in white neighborhoods, given them intellectual accents to go with their nondescript gray flannel suits? "What are these people now?" they ask. And then they answer themselves, "Nothings!"

19   I would find this reasoning—which I have heard many, many times, from hippies and nonhippies alike—amusing, if I did not also consider it serious. For I think it is a delusion, a copout, an excuse to disassociate themselves from a world in which they feel too little has been changed or gained. The real question, however, it appears to me, is not whether poor people will adopt the middle-class mentality once they are well-fed, rather, it is whether they will ever be well-fed enough to be able to choose whatever mentality they think will suit them. The lack of a movement did not keep my mother from *wishing* herself bourgeois in her daydreams.

20   There is widespread starvation in Mississippi. In my own state of Georgia there are more hungry families than Lester Maddox

would like to admit—or even see fed. I went to school with children who ate red dirt. The movement has prodded and pushed some liberal senators into pressuring the government for food so that the hungry may eat. Food stamps that were two dollars and out of the reach of many families not long ago have been reduced to fifty cents. The price is still out of the reach of some families, and the government, it seems to a lot of people, could spare enough free food to feed its own people. It angers people in the movement that it does not; they point to the billions in wheat we send free each year to countries abroad. Their government's slowness while people are hungry, its unwillingness to believe that there are Americans starving, its stingy cutting of the price of food stamps, make many civil rights workers throw up their hands in disgust. But they do not give up. They do not withdraw into the world of psychedelia. They apply what pressure they can to make the government give away food to hungry people. They do not plan so far ahead in their disillusionment with society that they can see these starving families buying identical ranch-style houses and sending their snobbish children to Bryn Mawr and Yale. They take first things first and try to get them fed.

They do not consider it their business, in any case, to say what 21 kind of life the people they help must lead. How one lives is, after all, one of the rights left to the individual—when and if he has opportunity to choose. It is not the prerogative of the middle-class to determine what is worthy of aspiration.

There is also every possibility that the middle-class people of 22 tomorrow will turn out ever so much better than those of today. I even know some middle-class people of today who are not *all* bad. Often, thank God, what monkey sees, monkey *avoids* doing at all costs. So it may be, concerning what is deepest in him, with the Negro.

I think there are so few Negro hippies today because middle- 23 class Negroes, although well-fed, are not careless. They are required by the treacherous world they live in to be clearly aware of whoever or whatever might be trying to do them in. They are middle-class in money and position, but they cannot afford to be middle-class in complacency. They distrust the hippie movement because they know that it can do nothing for Negroes as a group but "love" them, which is what all paternalists claim to do. And since the only way Negroes can survive (which they cannot do, unfortunately, on love alone) is with the support of the group, they are wisely wary and stay away.

A white writer tried recently to explain that the reason for the 24 relatively few Negro hippies is that Negroes have built up a "super-cool" that cracks under LSD and makes them have a "bad trip." What this writer doesn't guess at is that Negroes are needing drugs less than ever these days for any kind of trip. While the hippies are "tripping," Negroes are going after power, which is so much more important to their survival and their children's survival than LSD and pot.

25   Everyone would be surprised if the Israelis ignored the Arabs and took up "tripping" and pot smoking. In this country we are the Israelis. Everybody who can do so would like to forget this, of course. But for us to forget it for a minute would be fatal. "We Shall Overcome" is just a song to most Americans, *but we must do it.* Or die.

26   What good was the civil rights movement? If it had just given this country Dr. King, a leader of conscience for once in our lifetime, it would have been enough. If it had just taken black eyes off white television stories, it would have been enough. If it had fed one starving child, it would have been enough.

27   If the civil rights movement is "dead," and if it gave us nothing else, it gave us each other forever. It gave some of us bread, some of us shelter, some of us knowledge and pride, all of us comfort. It gave us our children, our husbands, our brothers, our fathers, as men reborn and with a purpose for living. It broke the pattern of black servitude in this country. It shattered the phony "promise" of white soap operas that sucked away so many pitiful lives. It gave us history and men far greater than Presidents. It gave us heroes, selfless men of courage and strength, for our little boys to follow. It gave us hope for tomorrow. It called us to life.

28   Because we live, it can never die.

Reading Critically

1. Is there, as Walker suggests, a fundamental difference between how blacks and whites view civil rights? Is the difference a basic one or just a matter of degree? Discuss with your classmates.

2. What words, phrases, and references date this essay? Do you think that Walker's ideas are as true now as they were in the years

just after the high points of the civil rights movement? Have conditions for minorities gotten better, worse, or have they stayed about the same? Is the civil rights movement dead, or has it become transformed into something else? Discuss with your classmates and comment. What facts can you cite to support your position?

3. Discuss Walker's mother's reaction to soap operas (paragraph 11). Have you experienced some of the same tendencies? Do you tend to identify with fictional people who live luxurious life-styles? Why or why not? Discuss with your classmates.

4. Walker interprets Martin Luther King as having said that blacks "had the right to become whatever we wanted to become." Can you become whatever you want to become? What are your limitations? What should society do to help people meet their personal goals? What are society's limitations in helping people? Discuss with your classmates.

Responding Through Writing

1. Walker implies that reformers should do more than argue for gradual economic change. They should try to transform the basis of society itself. Write two essay introductions, one for and one against her position. Develop one of these essays with examples.

2. As early as the second paragraph, Walker's rhetoric exhibits an aggressive tone. Do you find this positive or negative? Where else in the essay does Walker's tone become especially noticeable? Rewrite those sections of the essay. Are the results better or worse than the originals? In which ways?

3. Does Walker strike a good balance between personal examples and wider generalizations, or does she lean too heavily in one of those directions? Make two lists, one of examples, the other of generalizations that you think would help to extend and strengthen Walker's essay.

4. In what sense does Martin Luther King become a symbolic center for the essay? Note how Walker uses his words as touchstones to which she comes back again and again, weaving those words together with her own examples. Were you impressed at any particular point by this writing strategy? If so, write a short essay of your own using King or some other prominent historical figure as a "base" to touch several times.

THE END OF PLAY

MARIE WINN

Marie Winn was born in 1936 in Prague, Czechoslovakia, and came to the United States with her parents in 1939. She graduated from Radcliffe College in 1956 and Columbia University in 1959. Winn divides her writing between children's and adult literature, but even her adult books deal with the problems facing youth. In 1977 she published The Plug-In Drug: Television, Children and the Family *and recently followed up with* Unplugging the Plug-In Drug *(1987). Her other adult books include* Children Without Childhood *(1983) and* The Baby Reader *(1973). Winn also contributes articles to the* New York Times Magazine, *the* New York Times Book Review, *and* Parade. *The following essay was originally published in* Children Without Childhood.

Of all the changes that have altered the topography of childhood, the most dramatic has been the disappearance of childhood play. Whereas a decade or two ago children were easily distinguished from the adult world by the very nature of their play, today children's occupations do not differ greatly from adult diversions.

Infants and toddlers, to be sure, continue to follow certain timeless patterns of manipulation and exploration; adolescents, too, have not changed their free-time habits so very much, turning as they ever have towards adult pastimes and amusements in their drive for autonomy, self-mastery, and sexual discovery. It is among the

1

ranks of school-age children, those six-to-twelve-year-olds who once avidly filled their free moments with childhood play, that the greatest change is evident. In the place of traditional, sometimes ancient childhood games that were still popular a generation ago, in the place of fantasy and make-believe play—"You be the mommy and I'll be the daddy"—doll play or toy-soldier play, jump-rope play, ball-bouncing play, today's children have substituted television viewing and, most recently, video games.

2   Many parents have misgivings about the influence of television. They sense that a steady and time-consuming exposure to passive entertainment might damage the ability to play imaginatively and resourcefully, or prevent this ability from developing in the first place. A mother of two school-age children recalls: "When I was growing up, we used to go out into the vacant lots and make up week-long dramas and sagas. This was during third, fourth, fifth grades. But my own kids have never done that sort of thing, and somehow it bothers me. I wish we had cut down on the TV years ago, and maybe the kids would have learned how to play."

3   The testimony of parents who eliminate television for periods of time strengthens the connection between children's television watching and changed play patterns. Many parents discover that when their children don't have television to fill their free time, they resort to the old kinds of imaginative, traditional "children's play." Moreover, these parents often observe that under such circumstances "they begin to seem more like children" or "they act more childlike." Clearly, a part of the definition of childhood, in adults' minds, resides in the nature of children's play.

4   Children themselves sometimes recognize the link between play and their own special definition as children. In an interview about children's books with four ten-year-old girls, one of them said: "I read this story about a girl my age growing up twenty years ago—you know, in 1960 or so—and she seemed so much younger than me in her behavior. Like she might be playing with dolls, or playing all sorts of children's games, or jump-roping or something." The other girls all agreed that they had noticed a similar discrepancy between themselves and fictional children in books of the past: those children seemed more like children. "So what do *you* do in your spare time, if you don't play with dolls or play make-believe games or jump rope or do things kids did twenty years ago?" they were asked. They laughed and answered, "We watch TV."

5   But perhaps other societal factors have caused children to give up play. Children's greater exposure to adult realities, their knowledge of adult sexuality, for instance, might make them more sophisticated, less likely to play like children. Evidence from the counter-

culture communes of the sixties and seventies adds weight to the argument that it is television above all that has eliminated children's play. Studies of children raised in a variety of such communes, all television-free, showed the little communards continuing to fill their time with those forms of play that have all but vanished from the lives of conventionally reared American children. And yet these counterculture kids were casually exposed to all sorts of adult matters—drug taking, sexual intercourse. Indeed, they sometimes incorporated these matters into their play: "We're mating," a pair of six-year-olds told a reporter to explain their curious bumps and grinds. Nevertheless, to all observers the commune children preserved a distinctly childlike and even innocent demeanor, an impression that was produced mainly by the fact that they spent most of their time playing. Their play defined them as belonging to a special world of childhood.

6   Not all children have lost the desire to engage in the old-style childhood play. But so long as the most popular, most dominant members of the peer group, who are often the most socially precocious, are "beyond" playing, then a common desire to conform makes it harder for those children who still have the drive to play to go ahead and do so. Parents often report that their children seem ashamed of previously common forms of play and hide their involvement with such play from their peers. "My fifth-grader still plays with dolls," a mother tells, "but she keeps them hidden in the basement where nobody will see them." This social check on the play instinct serves to hasten the end of childhood for even the least advanced children.

7   What seems to have replaced play in the lives of great numbers of preadolescents these days, starting as early as fourth grade, is a burgeoning interest in boy–girl interactions—"going out" or "going together." These activities do not necessarily involve going anywhere or doing anything sexual, but nevertheless are the first stage of a sexual process that used to commence at puberty or even later. Those more sophisticated children who are already involved in such manifestly unchildlike interests make plain their low opinion of their peers who still *play*. "Some of the kids in the class are real weird," a fifth-grade boy states. "They're not interested in going out, just in trucks and stuff, or games pretending they're monsters. Some of them don't even *try* to be cool."

Video Games Versus Marbles

8   Is there really any great difference, one might ask, between that gang of kids playing video games by the hour at their local candy

store these days and those small fry who used to hang around together spending equal amounts of time playing marbles? It is easy to see a similarity between the two activities: each requires a certain amount of manual dexterity, each is almost as much fun to watch as to play, each is simple and yet challenging enough for that middle-childhood age group for whom time can be so oppressive if unfilled.

9   One significant difference between the modern pre-teen fad of video games and the once popular but now almost extinct pastime of marbles is economic: playing video games costs twenty-five cents for approximately three minutes of play; playing marbles, after a small initial investment, is free. The children who frequent video-game machines require a considerable outlay of quarters to subsidize their fun; two, three, or four dollars is not an unusual expenditure for an eight- or nine-year-old spending an hour or two with his friends playing Asteroids or Pac-Man or Space Invaders. For most of the children the money comes from their weekly allowance. Some augment this amount by enterprising commercial ventures— trading and selling comic books, or doing chores around the house for extra money.

10   But what difference does it make *where* the money comes from? Why should that make video games any less satisfactory as an amusement for children? In fact, having to pay for the entertainment, whatever the source of the money, and having its duration limited by one's financial resources changes the nature of the game, in a subtle way diminishing the satisfactions it offers. Money and time become intertwined, as they so often are in the adult world and as, in the past, they almost never were in the child's world. For the child playing marbles, meanwhile, time has a far more carefree quality, bounded only by the requirements to be home by supper-time or by dark.

11   But the video-game-playing child has an additional burden—a burden of choice, of knowing that the money used for playing Pac-Man could have been saved for Christmas, could have been used to buy something tangible, perhaps something "worthwhile," as his parents might say, rather than being "wasted" on video games. There is a certain sense of adultness that spending money imparts, a feeling of being a consumer, which distinguishes a game with a price from its counterparts among the traditional childhood games children once played at no cost.

12   There are other differences as well. Unlike child-initiated and child-organized games such as marbles, video games are adult-created mechanisms not entirely within the child's control, and thus less

likely to impart a sense of mastery and fulfillment: the coin may get jammed, the machine may go haywire, the little blobs may stop eating the funny little dots. Then the child must go to the store-keeper to complain, to get his money back. He may be "ripped off" and simply lose his quarter, much as his parents are when they buy a faulty appliance. This possibility of disaster gives the child's play a certain weight that marbles never imposed on its light-hearted players.

Even if a child has a video game at home requiring no coin   13 outlay, the play it provides is less than optimal. The noise level of the machine is high—too high, usually, for the child to conduct a conversation easily with another child. And yet, according to its enthusiasts, this very noisiness is a part of the game's attraction. The loud whizzes, crashes, and whirrs of the video-game machine "blow the mind" and create an excitement that is quite apart from the excitement generated simply by trying to win a game. A traditional childhood game such as marbles, on the other hand, has little built-in stimulation; the excitement of playing is generated entirely by the players' own actions. And while the pace of a game of marbles is close to the child's natural physiological rhythms, the frenzied activities of video games serve to "rev up" the child in an artificial way, almost in the way a stimulant or an amphetamine might. Meanwhile the perceptual impact of a video game is similar to that of watching television—the action, after all, takes place on a television screen—causing the eye to defocus slightly and creating a certain alteration in the child's natural state of consciousness.

Parents' instinctive reaction to their children's involvement   14 with video games provides another clue to the difference between this contemporary form of play and the more traditional pastimes such as marbles. While parents, indeed most adults, derive open pleasure from watching children at play, most parents today are not delighted to watch their kids flicking away at the Pac-Man machine. This does not seem to them to be real play. As a mother of two school-age children anxiously explains, "We used to do real child-hood sorts of things when I was a kid. We'd build forts and put on crazy plays and make up new languages, and just generally we *played*. But today my kids don't play that way at all. They like video games and of course they still go in for sports outdoors. They go roller skating and ice skating and skiing and all. But they don't seem to really *play*."

Some of this feeling may represent a certain nostalgia for the   15 past and the old generation's resistance to the different ways of the new. But it is more likely that most adults have an instinctive understanding of the importance of play in their own childhood. This feeling stokes their fears that their children are being deprived of something irreplaceable when they flip the levers on the video machines to manipulate the electronic images rather than flick their fingers to send a marble shooting towards another marble.

Play Deprivation

16   In addition to television's influence, some parents and teachers ascribe children's diminished drive to play to recent changes in the school curriculum, especially in the early grades.

17   "Kindergarten, traditionally a playful port of entry into formal school, is becoming more academic, with children being taught specific skills, taking tests, and occasionally even having homework," begins a report on new directions in early childhood education. Since 1970, according to the United States census, the proportion of three- and four-year-olds enrolled in school has risen dramatically, from 20.5 percent to 36.7 percent in 1980, and these nursery schools have largely joined the push towards academic acceleration in the early grades. Moreover, middle-class nursery schools in recent years have introduced substantial doses of academic material into their daily programs, often using those particular devices originally intended to help culturally deprived preschoolers in compensatory programs such as Headstart to catch up with their middle-class peers. Indeed, some of the increased focus on academic skills in nursery schools and kindergartens is related to the widespread popularity among young children and their parents of *Sesame Street,* a program originally intended to help deprived children attain academic skills, but universally watched by middle-class toddlers as well.

18   Parents of the *Sesame Street* generation often demand a "serious," skill-centered program for their preschoolers in school, afraid that the old-fashioned, play-centered curriculum will bore their alphabet-spouting, number-chanting four- and five-year-olds. A few parents, especially those whose children have not attended television classes or nursery school, complain of the high-powered pace of kindergarten these days. A father whose five-year-old daughter attends a public kindergarten declares: "There's a lot more pressure put on little kids these days than when we were kids, that's for sure. My daughter never went to nursery school and never watched *Sesame,* and she had a lot of trouble when she entered kindergarten this fall. By October, just a month and a half into the program, she was already flunking. The teacher told us

our daughter couldn't keep up with the other kids. And believe me, she's a bright kid! All the other kids were getting gold stars and smiley faces for their work, and every day Emily would come home in tears because she didn't get a gold star. Remember when we were in kindergarten? We were *children* then. We were allowed just to play!"

A kindergarten teacher confirms the trend towards early academic pressure. "We're expected by the dictates of the school system to push a lot of curriculum," she explains. "Kids in our kindergarten can't sit around playing with blocks any more. We've just managed to squeeze in one hour of free play a week, on Fridays."   19

The diminished emphasis on fantasy and play and imaginative activities in early childhood education and the increased focus on early academic-skill acquisition have helped to change childhood from a play-centered time of life to one more closely resembling the style of adulthood: purposeful, success-centered, competitive. The likelihood is that these preschool "workers" will not metamorphose back into players when they move on to grade school. This decline in play is surely one of the reasons why so many teachers today comment that their third- or fourth-graders act like tired businessmen instead of like children.   20

What might be the consequences of this change in children's play? Children's propensity to engage in that extraordinary series of behaviors characterized as "play" is perhaps the single great dividing line between childhood and adulthood, and has probably been so throughout history. The make-believe games anthropologists have recorded of children in primitive societies around the world attest to the universality of play and to the uniqueness of this activity to the immature members of each society. But in those societies, and probably in Western society before the middle or late eighteenth century, there was always a certain similarity between children's play and adult work. The child's imaginative play took the form of imitation of various aspects of adult life, culminating in the gradual transformation of the child's play from make-believe work to *real* work. At this point, in primitive societies or in our own society of the past, the child took her or his place in the adult work world and the distinctions between adulthood and childhood virtually vanished. But in today's technologically advanced society there is no place for the child in the adult work world. There are not enough jobs, even of the most menial kind, to go around for adults, much less for children. The child must continue to be dependent on adults for many years while gaining the knowledge and skills necessary to become a working member of society.   21

22   This is not a new situation for children. For centuries children have endured a prolonged period of dependence long after the helplessness of early childhood is over. But until recent years children remained childlike and playful far longer than they do today. Kept isolated from the adult world as a result of deliberate secrecy and protectiveness, they continued to find pleasure in socially sanctioned childish activities until the imperatives of adolescence led them to strike out for independence and self-sufficiency.

23   Today, however, with children's inclusion in the adult world both through the instrument of television and as a result of a deliberately preparatory, integrative style of child rearing, the old forms of play no longer seem to provide children with enough excitement and stimulation. What then are these so-called children to do for fulfillment if their desire to play has been vitiated and yet their entry into the working world of adulthood must be delayed for many years? The answer is precisely to get involved in those areas that cause contemporary parents so much distress: addictive television viewing during the school years followed, in adolescence or even before, by a search for similar oblivion via alcohol and drugs; exploration of the world of sensuality and sexuality before achieving the emotional maturity necessary for altruistic relationships.

24   Psychiatrists have observed among children in recent years a marked increase in the occurrence of depression, a state long considered antithetical to the nature of childhood. Perhaps this phenomenon is at least somewhat connected with the current sense of uselessness and alienation that children feel, a sense that play may once upon a time have kept in abeyance.

Reading Critically

1. Winn writes that academic pressure is largely responsible for "play deprivation" (paragraph 16 ff.). Discuss with your classmates the relationship between play and academic work in your own childhood, in high school, and in college. How has that relationship changed over the years?

2. Discuss Winn's comparison between video games and marbles (paragraphs 8 to 15). Does spending money on electronic games necessarily make today's children feel more "adult" than generations of other children felt when they bought baseball or ballet equipment? Is the experience of being "ripped off" when the machine eats your quarter really more intense than when the bully steals your marbles? Was marbles really the lighthearted game Winn makes it out to be? (Ask your parents and grandparents.) In short, in what ways might Winn's argument be based on false comparisons?

3. At the end of paragraph 13, Winn talks about the "child's natural state of consciousness." Is there any such thing as a "natural" state of consciousness? If not, then what are the main elements that help to construct the ways in which we perceive and think? If you or any of your classmates have taken philosophy courses, especially any that touched upon the writings of Jean-Jacques Rousseau, bring what you have learned to the discussion of this question.

4. Do Winn's conclusions (paragraphs 23 and 24) logically grow out of the evidence she presents in the body of her essay, or do those conclusions exceed the evidence? Does she, in short, *show* that TV viewing leads to oblivion like that produced by alcohol and drugs? Discuss with your classmates some examples to further support or to argue against her conclusion.

Responding Through Writing

1. Do you and your classmates see causes other than TV that are responsible for a "loss of play"? What of the rising divorce rate, the change in women's roles, the availability of travel at early ages, the candor of the tabloid press, etc.? In short, does Winn's argument flow from a grand oversimplification that blames TV? If so, reformulate an argument about the "loss of play" and write the introduction to an essay in which that argument would be developed.

2. To what extent was your parents' play as children conditioned by TV? Interview them about how the programs they

watched influenced them. Ask the same questions of your grandparents regarding radio programs. Do your parents and grandparents seem to have suffered from their exposure to TV and radio? Use the highlights of the interviews to sketch the draft of an argumentative essay dealing with the effects of TV and radio on personality development.

3. Can you imagine having been raised in a hippie commune in the 1960s (paragraph 5)? What do you speculate your childhood would have been like? Make a list of what you would have done during a typical day. Write a short essay in your notebook or journal contrasting your present life with the life you might now lead had you been raised as a hippie.

4. Winn clearly and directly states her argument's thesis in the first paragraph. What is that thesis? How does paragraph 2 develop the argumentative thesis stated in paragraph 1? After discussing the seven questions above, make whatever changes you think necessary in that thesis and sketch the draft of an essay that develops the new thesis.

THE CASE
FOR TORTURE

MICHAEL E. LEVIN

Michael E. Levin (b. 1943) graduated from Michigan State University and Columbia University and was a member of the Department of Philosophy at Columbia University from 1968 to 1980. He is the author of many articles dealing with philosophy, ethics, and intellectual pursuits. The author of The Socratic Method *(1987) and* Metaphysics and the Mind–Body Problem *(1979), Levin also contributes to numerous publications such as* National Review, American Scholar, Variety, *and various science magazines. His most recent book is* Feminism and Freedom *(1988). He is currently a professor of philosophy at The City College of New York. The following essay first appeared in* Newsweek *in June of 1982.*

It is generally assumed that torture is impermissible, a throw-back to a more brutal age. Enlightened societies reject it outright, and regimes suspected of using it risk the wrath of the United States. 1

I believe this attitude is unwise. There are situations in which torture is not merely permissible but morally mandatory. More-over, these situations are moving from the realm of imagination to fact. 2

3   **Death:** Suppose a terrorist has hidden an atomic bomb on
Manhattan Island which will detonate at noon on July 4 unless
. . . (here follow the usual demands for money and release of his
friends from jail). Suppose, further, that he is caught at 10 A.M. of
the fateful day, but—preferring death to failure—won't disclose
where the bomb is. What do we do? If we follow due process—wait
for his lawyer, arraign him—millions of people will die. If the only
way to save those lives is to subject the terrorist to the most
excruciating possible pain, what grounds can there be for not doing
so? I suggest there are none. In any case, I ask you to face the
question with an open mind.

4   Torturing the terrorist is unconstitutional? Probably. But millions of lives surely outweigh constitutionality. Torture is barbaric?
Mass murder is far more barbaric. Indeed, letting millions of innocents die in deference to one who flaunts his guilt is moral cowardice, an unwillingness to dirty one's hands. If *you* caught the terrorist,
could you sleep nights knowing that millions died because you
couldn't bring yourself to apply the electrodes?

5   Once you concede that torture is justified in extreme cases, you
have admitted that the decision to use torture is a matter of balanc-
ing innocent lives against the means needed to save them. You must
now face more realistic cases involving more modest numbers.
Someone plants a bomb on a jumbo jet. He alone can disarm it, and
his demands cannot be met (or if they can, we refuse to set a
precedent by yielding to his threats). Surely we can, we must, do
anything to the extortionist to save the passengers. How can we tell
300, or 100, or 10 people who never asked to be put in danger, "I'm
sorry, you'll have to die in agony, we just couldn't bring ourselves
to . . ."

6   Here are the results of an informal poll about a third, hypothetical, case. Suppose a terrorist group kidnapped a newborn baby
from a hospital. I asked four mothers if they would approve of
torturing kidnappers if that were necessary to get their own new-
borns back. All said yes, the most "liberal" adding that she would
like to administer it herself.

7   I am not advocating torture as punishment. Punishment is
addressed to deeds irrevocably past. Rather, I am advocating torture
as an acceptable measure for preventing future evils. So understood,
it is far less objectionable than many extant punishments. Opponents
of the death penalty, for example, are forever insisting that execut-
ing a murderer will not bring back his victim (as if the purpose of
capital punishment were supposed to be resurrection, not deterrence

or retribution). But torture, in the cases described, is intended not to bring anyone back but to keep innocents from being dispatched. The most powerful argument against using torture as a punishment or to secure confessions is that such practices disregard the rights of the individual. Well, if the individual is all that important—and he is—it is correspondingly important to protect the rights of individuals threatened by terrorists. If life is so valuable that it must never be taken, the lives of the innocents must be saved even at the price of hurting the one who endangers them.

Better precedents for torture are assassination and pre-emptive   8 attack. No Allied leader would have flinched at assassinating Hitler, had that been possible. (The Allies did assassinate Heydrich.) Americans would be angered to learn that Roosevelt could have had Hitler killed in 1943—thereby shortening the war and saving millions of lives—but refused on moral grounds. Similarly, if nation A learns that nation B is about to launch an unprovoked attack, A has a right to save itself by destroying B's military capability first. In the same way, if the police can by torture save those who would otherwise die at the hands of kidnappers or terrorists, they must.

Idealism: There is an important difference between terrorists   9 and their victims that should mute talk of the terrorists' "rights." The terrorist's victims are at risk unintentionally, not having asked to be endangered. But the terrorist knowingly initiated his actions. Unlike his victims, he volunteered for the risks of his deed. By threatening to kill for profit or idealism, he renounces civilized standards, and he can have no complaint if civilization tries to thwart him by whatever means necessary.

Just as torture is justified only to save lives (not extort confes-   10 sions or recantations), it is justifiably administered only to those *known* to hold innocent lives in their hands. Ah, but how can the authorities ever be sure they have the right malefactor? Isn't there a danger of error and abuse? Won't We turn into Them?

Questions like these are disingenuous in a world in which   11 terrorists proclaim themselves and perform for television. The name of their game is public recognition. After all, you can't very well intimidate a government into releasing your freedom fighters unless you announce that it is your group that has seized its embassy. "Clear guilt" is difficult to define, but when 40 million people see a group of masked gunmen seize an airplane on the evening news, there is not much question about who the perpetrators are. There will be hard cases where the situation is murkier. Nonetheless, a line demarcating the legitimate use of torture can be drawn. Torture only the obviously guilty, and only for the sake of saving innocents, and the line between Us and Them will remain clear.

12   There is little danger that the Western democracies will lose their way if they choose to inflict pain as one way of preserving order. Paralysis in the face of evil is the greater danger. Some day soon a terrorist will threaten tens of thousands of lives, and torture will be the only way to save them. We had better start thinking about this.

Reading Critically

1. What does Levin mean by "the line between Us and Them" (paragraph 11)? Who is "Us"? Who is "Them"? Apply this question to various contemporary contexts: Northern Ireland, Israel, Lebanon, Libya, South Africa, Angola, Central America, China. How do you deal with the fact that one person's "terrorist" is often another person's "freedom fighter"? Discuss with your classmates.

2. Does Levin avoid an important argument against torture: that once you allow torture in any context you implicitly condone it in other contexts? If you admit the use of torture at all, where do you draw the line to prevent its use?

3. Evaluate Levin's statement in paragraph 11 that we should "torture only the obviously guilty." Who decides who is "obviously" guilty: the police, the newspapers, "public opinion"? Discuss with your classmates.

4. Do some research on the effectiveness of "truth" drugs. Have such drugs made torture obsolete as a means of obtaining information? If so, does torture still have other uses, among them the creation of fear and intimidation? What do your findings bring to your evaluation of Levin's argument? Discuss with your classmates.

Responding Through Writing

1. Do you find any flaw in Levin's definition of the term *terrorist?* Write for a page or two in your journal or notebook exploring what the word *terrorist* means, or ought to mean.

2. Would you, like the mother in paragraph 6, like to torture anyone yourself? Who? What kinds of torture? You may want to write in your private notebook on this topic. Then again, you may want to ignore this question.

3. Levin makes good use of hypothetical quotations. Finish the quotation at the end of paragraph 5: "I'm sorry, you'll have to die in agony, we just couldn't bring ourselves to . . ."

4. Write a letter to Amnesty International (322 Eighth Avenue, New York, NY 10001) asking for information on the use of torture in today's world. Write a response to the information you receive.

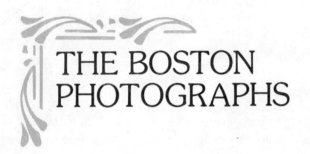

THE BOSTON PHOTOGRAPHS

NORA EPHRON

Nora Ephron was born in 1941 in New York City and spent the early part of her career working as a reporter for the New York Post. *Her writing has also appeared in* Esquire, New York *magazine,* Oui, McCall's, *and* Cosmopolitan. *She is the author of a number of provocative books on the culture of our times, including* Wallflower at the Orgy *(1970),* Crazy Salad: Some Things About Women *(1975), and* Scribble, Scribble: Notes on the Media *(1979). Her controversial novel* Heartburn *(1983) indirectly chronicles the final six weeks of her marriage to the journalist Carl Bernstein, which ended in divorce. She is also responsible, with Alice Arden, for the screenplay of the motion picture* Silkwood. *The following selection was first published in* Esquire *magazine in November 1975. (Note that three of the photos discussed in this selection have been reproduced on pages 505–506.)*

1   "I made all kinds of pictures because I thought it would be a good rescue shot over the ladder . . . never dreamed it would be anything else. . . . I kept having to move around because of the light set. The sky was bright and they were in deep shadow. I was making pictures with a motor drive and he, the fire fighter, was reaching up and, I don't know, everything started falling. I followed the girl

down taking pictures . . . I made three or four frames. I realized what was going on and I completely turned around, because I didn't want to see her hit."

You probably saw the photographs. In most newspapers, there   2
were three of them. The first showed some people on a fire escape—a fireman, a woman and a child. The fireman had a nice strong jaw and looked very brave. The woman was holding the child. Smoke was pouring from the building behind them. A rescue ladder was approaching, just a few feet away, and the fireman had one arm around the woman and one arm reaching out toward the ladder. The second picture showed the fire escape slipping off the building. The child had fallen on the escape and seemed about to slide off the edge. The woman was grasping desperately at the legs of the fireman, who had managed to grab the ladder. The third picture showed the woman and child in midair, falling to the ground. Their arms and legs were outstretched, horribly distended. A potted plant was falling too. The caption said that the woman, Diana Bryant, nineteen, died in the fall. The child landed on the woman's body and lived.

The pictures were taken by Stanley Forman, thirty, of the   3
Boston Herald American. He used a motor-driven Nikon F set at 1/250, f5.6-S. Because of the motor, the camera can click off three frames a second. More than four hundred newspapers in the United States alone carried the photographs: the tear sheets from overseas are still coming in. The *New York Times* ran them on the first page of its second section; a paper in south Georgia gave them nineteen columns; the *Chicago Tribune,* the *Washington Post* and the *Washington Star* filled almost half their front pages, the *Star* under a somewhat redundant headline that read: SENSATIONAL PHOTOS OF RESCUE ATTEMPT THAT FAILED.

The photographs are indeed sensational. They are pictures of   4
death in action, of that split second when luck runs out, and it is impossible to look at them without feeling their extraordinary impact and remembering, in an almost subconscious way, the morbid fantasy of falling, falling off a building, falling to one's death. Beyond that, the pictures are classics, old-fashioned but perfect examples of photojournalism at its most spectacular. They're throwbacks, really, fire pictures, 1930s tabloid shots; at the same time they're technically superb and thoroughly modern—the sequence could not have been taken at all until the development of the motor-driven camera some sixteen years ago.

Most newspaper editors anticipate some reader reaction to   5
photographs like Forman's; even so, the response around the country was enormous, and almost all of it was negative. I have read hun-

dreds of the letters that were printed in letters-to-the-editor sections, and they repeat the same points. "Invading the privacy of death." "Cheap sensationalism." "I thought I was reading the *National Enquirer.*" "Assigning the agony of a human being in terror of imminent death to the status of a side-show act." "A tawdry way to sell newspapers." The *Seattle Times* received sixty letters and calls; its managing editor even got a couple of them at home. A reader wrote the *Philadelphia Inquirer:* "*Jaws* and *Towering Inferno* are playing downtown; don't take business away from people who pay good money to advertise in your own paper." Another reader wrote the *Chicago Sun-Times:* "I shall try to hide my disappointment that Miss Bryant wasn't wearing a skirt when she fell to her death. You could have had some award-winning photographs of her underpants as her skirt billowed over her head, you voyeurs." Several newspaper editors wrote columns defending the pictures: Thomas Keevil of the *Costa Mesa* (California) *Daily Pilot* printed a ballot for readers to vote on whether they would have printed the pictures; Marshall L. Stone of Maine's *Bangor Daily News,* which refused to print the famous assassination picture of the Vietcong prisoner in Saigon, claimed that the Boston pictures showed the dangers of fire escapes and raised questions about slumlords. (The burning building was a five-story brick apartment house on Marlborough Street in the Back Bay section of Boston.)

6   For the last five years, the *Washington Post* has employed various journalists as ombudsmen, whose job is to monitor the paper on behalf of the public. The *Post*'s current ombudsman is Charles Seib, former managing editor of the *Washington Star;* the day the Boston photographs appeared, the paper received over seventy calls in protest. As Seib later wrote in a column about the pictures, it was "the largest reaction to a published item that I have experienced in eight months as the *Post*'s ombudsman. . . .

7   "In the *Post*'s newsroom, on the other hand, I found no doubts, no second thoughts . . . the question was not whether they should be printed but how they should be displayed. When I talked to editors . . . they used words like 'interesting' and 'riveting' and 'gripping' to describe them. The pictures told of something about life in the ghetto, they said (although the neighborhood where the tragedy occurred is not a ghetto, I am told). They dramatized the need to check on the safety of fire escapes. They dramatically conveyed something that had happened, and that is the business we're in. They were news. . . .

8   "Was publication of that [third] picture a bow to the same taste for the morbidly sensational that makes gold mines of disaster

movies? Most papers will not print the picture of a dead body except in the most unusual circumstances. Does the fact that the final picture was taken a millisecond before the young woman died make a difference? Most papers will not print a picture of a bare female breast. Is that a more inappropriate subject for display than the picture of a human being's last agonized instant of life?" Seib offered no answers to the questions he raised, but he went on to say that although as an editor he would probably have run the pictures, as a reader he was revolted by them.

In conclusion, Seib wrote: "Any editor who decided to print 9 those pictures without giving at least a moment's thought to what purpose they served and what their effect was likely to be on the reader should ask another question: Have I become so preoccupied with manufacturing a product according to professional traditions and standards that I have forgotten about the consumer, the reader?"

It should be clear that the phone calls and letters and Seib's own 10 reaction were occasioned by one factor alone: the death of the woman. Obviously, had she survived the fall, no one would have protested; the pictures would have had a completely different impact. Equally obviously, had the child died as well—or instead—Seib would undoubtedly have received ten times the phone calls he did. In each case, the pictures would have been exactly the same—only the captions, and thus the responses, would have been different.

But the questions Seib raises are worth discussing—though not 11 exactly for the reasons he mentions. For it may be that the real lesson of the Boston photographs is not the danger that editors will be forgetful of reader reaction, but that they will continue to censor pictures of death precisely because of that reaction. The protests Seib fielded were really a variation on an old theme—and we saw plenty of it during the Nixon–Agnew years—the "Why doesn't the press print the good news?" argument. In this case, of course, the objections were all dressed up and cleverly disguised as righteous indignation about the privacy of death. This is a form of puritanism that is often justifiable; just as often it is merely puritanical.

Seib takes it for granted that the widespread though fairly 12 recent newspaper policy against printing pictures of dead bodies is a sound one; I don't know that it makes any sense at all. I recognize that printing pictures of corpses raises all sorts of problems about taste and titillation and sensationalism; the fact is, however, that people die. Death happens to be one of life's main events. And it is irresponsible—and more than that, inaccurate—for newspapers to fail to show it, or to show it only when an astonishing set of photos comes in over the Associated Press wire. Most papers covering fatal automobile accidents will print pictures of mangled cars. But the significance of fatal automobile accidents is not that a great deal of steel is twisted but that people die. Why not show it? That's what accidents are about. Throughout the Vietnam war, editors were reluctant to print atrocity pictures. Why *not* print them? That's what that war was about. Murder victims are almost never photographed; they are granted their privacy. But their relatives are relentlessly pictured on their way in and out of hospitals and morgues and funerals.

13   I'm not advocating that newspapers print these things in order to teach their readers a lesson. The *Post* editors justified their printing of the Boston pictures with several arguments in that direction; every one of them is irrelevant. The pictures don't show anything about slum life; the incident could have happened anywhere, and it did. It is extremely unlikely that anyone who saw them rushed out and had his fire escape strengthened. And the pictures were not news—at least they were not national news. It is not news in Washington, or New York, or Los Angeles that a woman was killed in a Boston fire. The only newsworthy thing about the pictures is that they were taken. They deserve to be printed because they are great pictures, breathtaking pictures of something that happened. That they disturb readers is exactly as it should be: that's why photojournalism is often more powerful than written journalism.

Thinking Critically

1. What are your thoughts on the appropriateness of printing these photographs in a newspaper and of reprinting them here (see pages 505–506)? Do you strongly agree or strongly disagree with any of the newspaper readers' comments in paragraph 5? Discuss with your classmates.

2. The *Washington Post* reporters (paragraph 7) justified the printing of the photographs on the grounds that they were "news." The masthead of the *New York Times* reads "All the News That's Fit to Print." Discuss the contradictions in and between these two quotations.

(1)

(2)

(3)

3. As an exercise, arrange with your classmates to gather newspaper photographs that are of questionable taste. Bring these photographs to class and discuss their appeal.

4. Are newspapers and TV stations more sensitive to displaying sexuality than they are to depicting death and brutality? Are you more likely to see a naked person or a dead person on the evening news? What accounts for public attitudes in this regard?

Responding Through Writing

1. Is photojournalism, as Ephron says in paragraph 13, "often more powerful than written journalism"? Substantiate your answer

in a short essay using at least two examples of photojournalism and two parallel examples of written journalism. In the essay, comment on why the pictures are or are not more powerful than the written accounts.

2. Should the news be controlled by reader (or viewer) reaction? Write two short responses, one indicating whether this should be done, the other indicating how it might be done.

3. Why is the headline, "SENSATIONAL PHOTOS OF RESCUE ATTEMPT THAT FAILED," called "somewhat redundant" by the author (paragraph 3)? Gather some examples of redundancy from journalism and advertising and discuss them in a short essay.

4. Does Ephron adequately argue to her conclusion that the pictures "deserve to be printed because they are great pictures"? Respond to that conclusion with a short written statement of support or rebuttal.

NUCLEAR AUTUMN

BEN BOVA

Benjamin William Bova (b. 1932) graduated from Temple University in 1954 with a degree in journalism. At one time a professor of physics at the Massachusetts Institute of Technology, Bova is currently the editing director of Omni *magazine and has published over two dozen science fiction novels and several short stories. His best-known short stories are in the "Chet Kinsman" series, which includes "Test in Orbit" (1965) and "Zero Gee" (1972). Bova's novels include* Millennium *(1976),* The Starcrossed *(1975), and* The Multiple Man *(1976). More recently, Bova published* Prometheus *(1986) and* Voyager Two: The Alien Within *(1986). The following short story was published as part of an anthology,* Nuclear War *(1988), edited by Gregory Benfort and Martin Harry Greenberg.*

1   "They're bluffing" said the President of the United States.

2   "Of course they're bluffing," agreed her science advisor. "They have to be."

3   The Chairman of the Joint Chiefs of Staff, a grizzled old infantry general, looked grimly skeptical.

4   For a long, silent moment they faced each other in the cool, quiet confines of the Oval Office. The science advisor looked young

and handsome enough to be a television personality, and indeed had been one for a while before he allied himself with the politician who sat behind the desk. The President looked younger than she actually was, thanks to modern cosmetics and a ruthless self-discipline. Only the general seemed to be old, a man of an earlier generation, gray-haired and wrinkled, with light brown eyes that seemed sad and weary.

"I don't believe they're bluffing," he said. "I think they mean   5 exactly what they say—either we cave in to them or they launch their missiles."

The science advisor gave him his most patronizing smile.   6 "General, they *have* to be bluffing. The numbers prove it."

"The only numbers that count," said the general, "are that we   7 have cut our strategic ballistic missile force by half since this Administration came into office."

"And made the world that much safer," said the President. Her   8 voice was firm, with a sharp edge to it.

The general shook his head. "Ma'am, the only reason I have   9 not tendered my resignation is that I know full well the nincompoop you intend to appoint in my place."

The science advisor laughed. Even the President smiled at the   10 old man.

"The Soviets are not bluffing," the general repeated. "They   11 mean exactly what they say."

With a patient sigh, the science advisor explained, "General,   12 they cannot—repeat, can *not*—launch a nuclear strike at us or anyone else. They know the numbers as well as we do. A large nuclear strike, in the 3000-megaton range, will so damage the environment that the world will be plunged into a Nuclear Winter. Crops and animal life will be wiped out by months of subfreezing temperatures. The sky will be dark with soot and grains of pulverized soil. The sun will be blotted out. All life on Earth will die."

The general waved an impatient hand. "I know your story.   13 I've seen your presentations."

"Then how can the Russians attack us, when they know they'll   14 be killing themselves even if we don't retaliate?"

"Maybe they haven't seen your television specials. Maybe they   15 don't believe in Nuclear Winter."

"But they have to!" said the science advisor. "The numbers are   16 the same for them as they are for us."

"Numbers," grumbled the general.   17

"Those numbers describe reality," the science advisor insisted.   18 "And the men in the Kremlin are realists. They understand what

Nuclear Winter means. Their own scientists have told them exactly what I've told you."

19   "Then why did they insist on this Hot Line call?"

20   Spreading his hands in the gesture millions had come to know from his television series, the science advisor replied, "They're reasonable men. Now that they know nuclear weapons are unusable, they are undoubtedly trying to begin negotiations to resolve our differences without threatening nuclear war."

21   "You think so?" muttered the general.

22   The President leaned back in her swivel chair. "We'll find out what they want soon enough," she said. "Kolgoroff will be on the Hot Line in another minute or so."

23   The science advisor smiled at her. "I imagine he'll suggest a summit meeting to negotiate a new disarmament treaty."

24   The general said nothing.

25   The President touched a green square on the keypad built into the desk's surface. A door opened and three more people—a man and two women—entered the Oval Office: the Secretary of State, the Secretary of Defense, and the National Security Advisor.

26   Exactly when the digital clock on the President's desk read 12:00:00, the large display screen that took up much of the wall opposite her desk lit up to reveal the face of Yuri Kolgoroff, General Secretary of the Communist Party and President of the Soviet Union. He was much younger than his predecessors had been, barely in his mid-fifties, and rather handsome in a Slavic way. If his hair had been a few shades darker and his chin just a little rounder, he would have looked strikingly like the President's science advisor.

27   "Madam President," said Kolgoroff, in flawless American-accented English, "it is good of you to accept my invitation to discuss the differences between our two nations."

28   "I am always eager to resolve differences," said the President.

29   "I believe we can accomplish much." Kolgoroff smiled, revealing large white teeth.

30   "I have before me," said the President, glancing at the computer screen on her desk, "the agenda that our ministers worked out. . . ."

31   "There is no need for that," said the Soviet leader. "Why encumber ourselves with such formalities?"

32   The President smiled. "Very well. What do you have in mind?"

33   "It is very simple. We want the United States to withdraw all its troops from Europe and to dismantle NATO. Also, your military and naval bases in Japan, Taiwan, and the Philippines must be

disbanded. Finally, your injunctions against the Soviet Union concerning trade in high-technology items must be ended."

The President's face went white. It took her a moment to   34
gather the wits to say, "And what do you propose to offer in
exchange for these . . . concessions?"

"In exchange?" Kolgoroff laughed. "Why, we will allow you   35
to live. We will refrain from bombing your cities."

"You're insane!" snapped the President.   36

Still grinning, Kolgoroff replied, "We will see who is sane and   37
who is mad. One minute before this conversation began, I ordered
a limited nuclear attack against every NATO base in Europe, and
a counterforce attack against the ballistic missiles still remaining in
your silos in the American midwest."

The red panic light on the President's communications console   38
began flashing frantically.

"But that's impossible!" burst the science advisor. He leaped   39
from his chair and pointed at Kolgoroff's image in the big display
screen. "An attack of that size will bring on Nuclear Winter! You'll
be killing yourselves as well as us!"

Kolgoroff smiled pityingly at the scientist. "We have comput-   40
ers also, professor. We know how to count. The attack we have
launched is just below the threshold for Nuclear Winter. It will not
blot out the sun everywhere on Earth. Believe me, we are not such
fools as you think."

"But . . ."   41

"But," the Soviet leader went on, smile vanished and voice   42
iron hard, "should you be foolish enough to launch a counterstrike
with your remaining missiles or bombers, that *will* break the camel's
back, so to speak. The additional explosions of your counterstrike
will bring on Nuclear Winter."

"You can't be serious!"   43

"I am deadly serious," Kolgoroff replied. Then a faint hint of   44
his smile returned. "But do not be afraid. We have not targeted
Washington. Or any of your cities, for that matter. You will
live—under Soviet governance."

The President turned to the science advisor. "What should I   45
do?"

The science advisor shook his head.   46

"What should I do?" she asked the others seated around her.   47

They said nothing. Not a word.   48

She turned to the general. "What should I do?"   49

He got to his feet and headed for the door. Over his shoulder   50
he answered, "Learn Russian."

Reading Critically

1. Along with your classmates, take the parts of the various characters in the story. Begin your own dialogue with the sequence that starts with the words "They're bluffing."

2. Along with your classmates, do some research on the possibilities for a nuclear winter. What precisely is a nuclear winter? What are the possibilities that a nuclear winter may come to pass?

3. Does the fact that the president in the story is a woman color the story's action one way or another? Discuss with your classmates.

4. Is Bova's main point in the story a literal one concerning nuclear winter, or is his aim to discuss the larger issues about how important government decisions affecting the lives of millions of people are made? Apart from its potential destructiveness, what major point is he making about science? Discuss with your classmates.

Responding Through Writing

1. What makes the ending of the story so surprising? Rewrite the ending to make it even more surprising.

2. If your college has a film resource center, arrange to view some film dealing with atomic war. Do you think that this film accurately portrays the ineptness likely to lead us into nuclear war? What evidence can you marshal to support your position? In your notebook or journal, write the draft of an essay discussing your reactions to the film.

3. Read some of Ben Bova's other works dealing with futuristic defense strategies. Have his views in any way been prophetic? Summarize and comment upon one of Bova's other short stories or novels.

4. Write a reply from the President of the United States to General Secretary Kolgoroff.

TO HIS COY MISTRESS

ANDREW MARVELL

Andrew Marvell (1621–1678) is known for a poetry in which very serious themes are handled with a playful wit and irony. Marvell traveled widely in Europe after graduating from Cambridge University in 1638 and later became assistant to John Milton, whom he probably saved from imprisonment or worse after the monarchy was restored in England in 1660. Marvell led the life of a Yorkshire country gentleman and represented the city of Hull in Parliament. While Marvell's poetry gained little serious attention during his life and immediately following his death, modern critics have come to appreciate Marvell's talent for verse. In his last years, Marvell devoted most of his poems to the subject of politics. While other poems speak to such topics as love and religious toleration, critics have recognized a "passion for freedom" that seems to run through all of his poems. Marvell is today recognized as perhaps chief among the "minor" poets of the English language. The following poem was published posthumously in 1681 in a collection entitled Miscellaneous Poems.

    Had we but world enough, and time,
This coyness, Lady, were no crime.
We would sit down, and think which way

To walk, and pass our long love's day.
Thou by the Indian Ganges' side   5
Shouldst rubies find; I by the tide
Of Humber would complain. I would
Love you ten years before the Flood,
And you should, if you please, refuse
Till the conversion of the Jews.   10
My vegetable love should grow
Vaster than empires and more slow;
An hundred years should go to praise
Thine eyes, and on thy forehead gaze;
Two hundred to adore each breast,   15
But thirty thousand to the rest;
An age at least to every part,
And the last age should show your heart.
For, Lady, you deserve this state,
Nor would I love at lower rate.   20
    But at my back I always hear
Time's winged chariot hurrying near;
And yonder all before us lie
Deserts of vast eternity.
Thy beauty shall no more be found,
Nor, in thy marble vault, shall sound   25
My echoing song; then worms shall try
That long-preserved virginity,
And your quaint honor turn to dust,
And into ashes all my lust:
The grave's a fine and private place,   30
But none, I think, do there embrace.
    Now therefore, while the youthful hue
Sits on thy skin like morning lew,
And while thy willing soul transpires
At every pore with instant fires,   35
Now let us sport us while we may,
And now, like amorous birds of prey,
Rather at once our time devour
Than languish in his slow-chapped power.
Let us roll all our strength and all   40
Our sweetness up into one ball,
And tear our pleasures with rough strife
Through the iron gates of life;
Thus, though we cannot make our sun
Stand still, yet we will make him run.   45

Reading Critically

1. On first reading, the poem seems to have seduction as its central theme. On closer reading, however, we see that Marvell's purpose also deals with the brevity of life and the necessity to "seize the day." Can "seize the day" (Latin, *carpe diem*) work effectively as a guiding principle for life? Have you ever won or lost something important in life simply because you did or did not "seize the day"? Discuss with your classmates.

2. For the women in the class: If this poem were addressed to you, how would you react? Discuss among yourselves, and then discuss with the men. Do the women in your class have, by and large, different reactions to this poem than those of the men, or are reactions much the same for both genders?

3. Discuss the balance between seriousness and humor in the poem. Marvell uses astoundingly funny lines ("two hundred to adore each breast") to build up to a serious theme that includes the contemplation of death. In what ways do you think humor and seriousness interact in the poem in a positive way? In a negative way? Discuss with your classmates.

4. Do the final lines of the poem make sense? How can Marvell make the sun run? Discuss with your classmates.

Responding Through Writing

1. Write a modern prose version of Marvell's poem. Do it in the form of a letter. If you are a woman, write it to a man. Make copies of what you have written, *leaving off your name,* and share these with the class. It should be fun.

2. Pick one of the letters written in response to item 1 and answer it. Sign your name only if you wish to.

3. Discuss the imagery of the poem with your classmates. What, for example, is "Time's winged chariot"? Why is it "hurrying near"? Make a list of your favorite images in the poem and write a corresponding list, with parallel but contemporary images.

4. What do you make of the tomb metaphor (lines 25 to 31)? Is Marvell necessarily talking about a literal tomb, or might he be talking about a life without joy and spontaneity, a kind of walking death? In your private journal or notebook, write a draft of a short essay on "walking death."

ACKNOWLEDGMENTS

ANGELOU, MAYA: "Sister Flowers," from *I Know Why the Caged Bird Sings* by Maya Angelou. Copyright © 1969 by Maya Angelou. Reprinted by permission of Random House, Inc.

AUDEN W.H.: "The Unknown Citizen." Reprinted by permission of Faber and Faber Ltd. from *Collected Poems* by W. H. Auden. Copyright 1940 and renewed 1968.

AUSTIN, JAMES A.: "Four Kinds of Chance." Copyright © 1974 by Saturday Review Magazine Co. Reprinted by permission of Omni Publications International Ltd.

BAKER, RUSSELL: "Coffee, Toast and Calipers." Copyright © 1973 by The New York Times Company. Reprinted by permission.

BALDWIN, JAMES: From *Notes of a Native Son* by James Baldwin. Copyright © 1955, renewed 1983 by James Baldwin. Reprinted by permission of Beacon Press.

BENNETT, WILLIAM, AND GURIN, JOEL: "Thin May Be In, but Fashion Isn't Health." Copyright 1982 by the AAAS. With the permission of the authors.

BOVA, BEN: "Nuclear Autumn," Copyright © 1985 by Baen Enterprises.

BROWN, FREDERIC: "The Weapon." Copyright © 1951 by Davis Publications. Reprinted by permission of the author and the author's agents, Scott Meredith Literary Agency, Inc., 845 Third Avenue, New York, NY 10022.

BUCKLEY, WILLIAM F., JR.: "Why Don't We Complain?" Reprinted by permission of the Wallace Literary Agency, Inc. Copyright © 1961 by William F. Buckley, Jr.

CATTON, BRUCE: "Grant and Lee: A Study in Contrasts," from *The American Story.* Copyright © 1956 U.S. Capitol Historical Society. Reprinted by permission.

CHEEVER, JOHN: "A Miscellany of Characters That Will Not Appear." Copyright © 1960 by John Cheever. Reprinted from *The Stories of John Cheever,* by permission of Alfred A. Knopf, Inc.

CIARDI, JOHN: "What Is Happiness?" Copyright © 1964 by Saturday Review Magazine Co. Reprinted by permission of Omni Publications International Ltd.

CLINES, FRANCIS X.: "The Morning After, in the Morgue." Copyright © 1977 by The New York Times Company. Reprinted by permission.

DANIELS, LEE A.: "Black Crime, Black Victims." Copyright © 1982 by The New York Times Company. Reprinted by permission.

DIDION, JOAN: "On Keeping a Notebook" from *Slouching Towards Bethlehem* by Joan Didion. Copyright © 1966, 1967, 1968 by Joan Didion. Reprinted by permission of Farrar, Straus and Giroux, Inc. "On Self-Respect" from *Slouching Towards Bethlehem* by Joan Didion. Copyright © 1961, 1968 by Joan Didion. Reprinted by permission of Farrar, Straus and Giroux, Inc.

ELLISON, RALPH: From *Invisible Man* by Ralph Ellison. Prologue copyright 1952 by Ralph Ellison. Reprinted by permission of Random House, Inc.

EPHRON, NORA: "The Boston Photographs." From *Scribble, Scribble: Notes on the Media* by Nora Ephron. Copyright © 1978 by Nora Ephron. Photographs accompanying this article by Stanley J. Forman, Pulitzer Prize 1976. Reprinted by permission of Alfred A. Knopf, Inc.

EVANS, MARI: "Status Symbol," in *I Am a Black Woman,* published by William Morrow and Co. Copyright © 1970 by Mari Evans Phemster. Reprinted by permission of the author.

FINKLE, DAVID: "Sticky Fingers." Copyright © 1987 by New York Woman.

FINNEY, JACK: "The Third Level." From *About Time: Twelve Short Stories.* Copyright © 1976 by Jack Finney.

FISHER, M. F. K.: "Answer in the Affirmative." From *Sister Age* by M. F. K. Fisher. Copyright © 1983 by M. F. K. Fisher. Reprinted by permission of Alfred A. Knopf, Inc. Originally published in *The New Yorker,* Dec. 6, 1982.

FLEMING, ANNE TAYLOR: "Losing People." Copyright © 1980 by the New York Times Company. Reprinted by permission.

FROST, ROBERT: "Stopping by Woods on a Snowy Evening," "The Mending Wall," "The Road Not Taken." From *The Poetry of Robert Frost,* edited by Edward Connery Lathem. Copyright © 1969 by Holt, Rinehart and Winston, Inc. Copyright © 1962 by Robert Frost. Copyright © 1975 by Lesley Frost Ballantine. Reprinted by permission of Henry Holt and Co., Inc.

GESS, DENISE: "Catalina Court." Copyright © 1985 by Denise Gess. Reprinted by permission of the author.

GODWIN, GAIL: "To Noble Companions." Copyright © 1973 by *Harper's Magazine.* All rights reserved. Reprinted from the August issue by special permission.

GOPNIK, ADAM: "I Was a Slave to Art." Copyright © 1983 by *Harper's Magazine.* All rights reserved. Reprinted from the July issue by special permission.

GREGORY, DICK: "Not Poor, Jut Broke." From *Nigger: An Autobiography* by Dick Gregory with Robert Lipsyte. Copyright © 1964 by Dick Gregory Enterprises, Inc. Reprinted by permission of the publisher, E. P. Dutton, a division of Penguin Books USA Inc.

HARRIS, SYDNEY J.: "One Person's Facts Are Another's Fiction." Copyright © 1977 by Field Newspaper Syndicate. Reprinted with special permission of NAS, Inc.

HUGHES, LANGSTON: "Salvation," from *The Big Sea* by Langston Hughes. Copyright © 1940 by Langston Hughes. Copyright renewed © 1968 by Arna Bontemps and George Houston Bass. Reprinted by permission of Hill and Wang, a division of Farrar, Straus and Giroux, Inc.

JACKSON, SHIRLEY: "One Ordinary Day with Peanuts" by Shirley Jackson. Copyright © 1955 by Shirley Jackson. Copyright renewed 1983 by Lawrence Hyman, Barry Hyman, Sarah Elias. Reprinted by permission of Brandt & Brandt Literary Agents, Inc.

KELLER, GEORGEANNE: "An Enormous Maze with No Ready Exit." Copyright © 1981 by The New York Times Company. Reprinted by permission.

KING, MARTIN LUTHER, JR.: "Letter from a Birmingham Jail" from *Why We Can't Wait* by Martin Luther King, Jr. Copyright © 1963, 1964 by Martin Luther King, Jr. Reprinted by permission of Harper & Row Publishers, Inc.

KINGSTON, MAXINE HONG: "The Woman Warrior." From *The Woman Warrior: Memoirs of a Girlhood Among Ghosts.* Copyright © 1975, 1976 by Maxine Hong Kingston. Reprinted by permission of Alfred A. Knopf, Inc.

LEVIN, MICHAEL: "The Case for Torture." Copyright © 1982 by Michael Levin.

LIGHTMAN, ALAN: "Is the Earth Round or Flat?" From *Time Travel and Papa Joe's Pipe* by Alan Lightman (New York: Penguin). Copyright © 1982 by the American Association for the Advancement of Science. Originally appeared in *Science,* March 1982, pp. 24, 26.

MEAD, MARGARET: "New Superstitions for Old." From *A Way of Seeing* by Margaret Mead. Text copyright © 1961, 1962, 1963, 1964, 1965, 1966, 1967, 1968, 1969, and 1970 by Margaret Mead. By permission of William Morrow and Co., Inc.

MEBANE, MARY: "Black Wasn't Beautiful," from *Mary.* Copyright © 1981 by Viking Penguin, Inc.

MOON, WILLIAM LEAST HEAT: "Nameless, Tennessee," from *Blue Highways: A Journey into America.* Copyright © 1982 by Little, Brown and Co.

MORRIS, DESMOND: From *Manwatching,* Harry N. Abrams, Inc., 1987. Text © 1977 Desmond Morris. All rights reserved. Reprinted by permission of the publisher.

OATES, JOYCE CAROL: "The Lady with the Pet Dog," from *Marriages and Infidelities* by Joyce Carol Oates. Copyright © 1968, 1969, 1970, 1971, 1972 by Joyce Carol Oates. Reprinted by permission of Vanguard Press, a Division of Random House, Inc.

OPPENHEIM, IRENE: "On Waitressing," from *The Threepenny Review,* Summer 1986.

ORWELL, GEORGE: "A Hanging," "Shooting an Elephant," from *Shooting an Elephant and Other Essays* by George Orwell, copyright 1950 by Sonia Brownell Orwell, renewed 1978 by Sonia Pitt-Rivers, reprinted by permission of Harcourt Brace Jovanovich, Inc. "Politics and the English Language" by George Orwell, renewed 1974 by Sonia Orwell, reprinted from *Shooting an Elephant and Other Essays* by George Orwell by permission of Harcourt Brace Jovanovich, Inc.

OUCHI, WILLIAM: *Theory Z,* © 1981, Addison-Wesley Publishing Co., Inc., Reading, Mass. Excerpts from pages 155–156. Reprinted by permission.

ROBINSON, EDWIN ARLINGTON: "Richard Cory." Originally published by Charles Scribner's Sons.

RODRIGUEZ, RICHARD: "Aria." From *Hunger of Memory* by Richard Rodriguez. Copyright © 1981 by Richard Rodriguez. Reprinted by permission of David R. Godine, Publisher.

ROSS, DAVID: "Welcome to the War, Boys," from *Everything We Had,* edited by Al Santoli. Copyright © 1981 by Random House, Inc.

SHAW, BOB: "Light of Other Days." Copyright © 1966 by Bob Shaw. Reprinted by permission of the author.

SHEEHY, GAIL: From *Passages: Predictable Crises of Adult Life* by Gail Sheehy. Copyright © 1974, 1976 by Gail Sheehy. Reprinted by permission of the publisher, E. P. Dutton, a division of Penguin Books USA Inc.

TALESE, GAY: "New York," copyright © 1960 by Gay Talese, reprinted by permission.

TUAN, YI-FU: "American Space, Chinese Place." Copyright © 1974 by *Harper's Magazine.* All rights reserved. Reprinted from the July issue by special permission.

WALKER, ALICE: "The Civil Rights Movement: What Good Was It?" From *In Search of Our Mothers' Gardens,* copyright © 1967 by Alice Walker, reprinted by permission of Harcourt Brace Jovanovich, Inc.

WHITE, E. B.: "Once More to the Lake" from *Essays of E. B. White.* Copyright 1941 by E. B. White. Reprinted by permission of Harper & Row, Publishers, Inc.

WINN, MARIE: "The End of Play." From *Children Without Childhood* by Marie Winn. Copyright © 1981, 1983 by Marie Winn. Reprinted by permission of Pantheon Books, a Division of Random House, Inc.

WINTSCH, SUSAN: "Where Is the Midwest?" Reprinted courtesy *TWA Ambassador,* carried aboard TWA, © 1988. East/West Network, publisher.

WOOLF, VIRGINIA: "The Death of the Moth" from *The Death of the Moth and Other Essays,* copyright 1942 by Harcourt Brace Jovanovich, Inc., renewed 1970 by Marjorie T. Parsons, Executrix, reprinted by permission of the publisher.

INDEX OF AUTHORS
AND TITLES